At His Feet

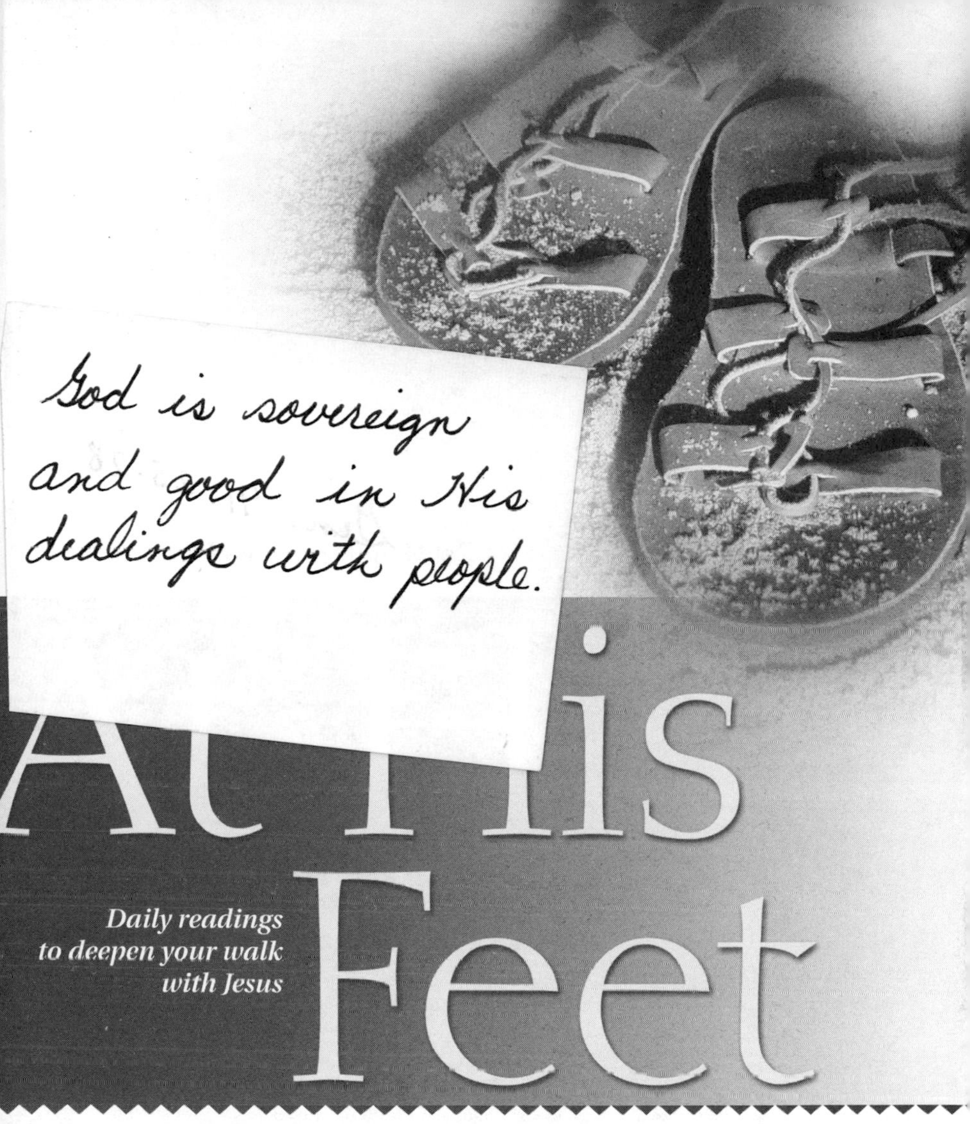
God is sovereign
and good in His
dealings with people.
At His
Feet
Daily readings
to deepen your walk
with Jesus

At His Feet

Daily readings to deepen your walk with Jesus

Chris Tiegreen

TYNDALE HOUSE PUBLISHERS, INC., Wheaton, Illinois

Visit Tyndale's exciting Web site at www.tyndale.com

Edited by Paula Kirk

Cover designed by Zandrah Maguigad

Interior pages designed by Lon Foster

Library of Congress Cataloging-in-Publication Data

Tiegreen, Chris.
At His feet: daily readings to deepen your walk with Jesus / Chris Tiegreen.
p. cm.
ISBN 0-8423-8125-2
1. Devotional calendars. I. Title.

BV4811.T54 2003
242'.2—dc21 2003050747

Printed in the United States of America

10 09 08 07 06 05 04 03
10 9 8 7 6 5 4 3 2 1

Dedication

In Memoriam

John Hoover
Whose devotional writing, devotional living,
and visionary teaching influenced
Christians around the world for the
Glory of God.

Acknowledgments

Walk Thru the Bible thanks the following people for their part in the creation and publication of this book: Jim Gabrielsen, Paula Kirk, Robyn Holmes, Lon Foster, Alan Phillips, and all the members of the publishing team who supported and prayed for this project.

We greatly appreciate the encouragement and assistance of our Tyndale partners, especially John Van Diest, Janis Long Harris, and Barbara Kois.

Walk Thru the Bible

Walk Thru the Bible is an international Christian educational organization that contributes to spiritual growth worldwide through innovative Bible teaching in publications, seminars, and videos. Walk Thru the Bible has taught more people the life-changing truths than any other Bible seminar organization, hosting millions of participants in its live Bible seminars since 1976. Presenting biblical content in an easy-to-understand and memorable format, Walk Thru the Bible's video curriculum, devotional publications, and seminars equip millions each year to read and study the Bible.

What started as a vision to teach the Bible in a new way, fostering retention and understanding, has expanded into a worldwide movement. In the early 1970s Bruce Wilkinson developed *Walk Thru the Old Testament* and *Walk Thru the New Testament* seminars as an innovative way to teach an overview or survey of the Bible. By enabling people to actively participate in the learning process through memorable hand signs, the Word of God came alive and lives were changed. Bruce trained several friends to present the seminar in churches and the demand for this teaching grew quickly, leading to the formation of the organization that today has thousands of instructors around the world.

Walk Thru the Bible is a not-for-profit organization which is governed by a board of directors and is a member of the Evangelical Council for Financial Accountability. The President and CEO is Chip Ingram who is also the teaching pastor on the widely distributed daily radio broadcast Living on the Edge.

Walk Thru the Bible has four major outreaches including: Seminars, Publications, LifeChange Video, and International. The seminars today include the original Bible surveys and many additional series including: *A Biblical Portrait of Marriage, Understanding the Love of Your Life, Solving the People Puzzle, The Seven Laws of the Learner, Teaching with Style, The Prayer of Jabez, The Secrets of the Vine*, and many others.

The printing of the first *Daily Walk* in 1978 launched Walk Thru the Bible's publishing ministry. *Daily Walk* is a monthly publication that helps people understand their Bible while reading it through in one year. *Daily Walk* is one of several devotional magazines published by the organization including: *Closer Walk, Family Walk, YouthWalk, Quiet Walk, Tapestry*, and *indeed.*

The vision of Walk Thru the Bible's international program is to train, equip, and sustain one qualified Bible teacher for every population group of 50,000 in the world. This bold program has expanded into country after country as Christian leaders of each region are trained for this teaching ministry. As a result, millions of people receive Bible training each year throughout the world.

LifeChange Video distributes innovative Bible instruction from several major teachers including: Bruce Wilkinson, Howard Hendricks, Chip Ingram, and Ronald Blue. Titles include: *The Seven Laws of the Teacher, Experiencing Spiritual Breakthroughs, Holy Ambition, The Vision of the Leader, Mastering Your Money, A Biblical Portrait of Marriage,* and *Personal Holiness in Times of Temptation.* Each video series is designed for group use with leader's guides and student workbooks to guide the discussion.

By focusing on the central themes of Scripture and their practical application to life, Walk Thru the Bible enjoys wide acceptance in denominations and fellowships around the world. In addition, it has carefully initiated strategic ministry alliances with many Christian organizations and missions of wide diversity and backgrounds.

From the first seminar to the latest product, the goal of Walk Thru the Bible is always to teach the Word to the world for lasting lifechange, in this generation, for the glory of God.

For more information visit our Web site at www.walkthru.org or contact:

Walk Thru the Bible®
4201 North Peachtree Road
Atlanta GA 30341-1207
770-458-9300

Daily Readings

"Let the word of Christ dwell in you richly as you teach and admonish one another with all wisdom...."

Colossians 3:16

Ultimate Authority

"I am the Alpha and the Omega, the First and the Last, the Beginning and the End."

(Revelation 22:13)

In Word There is no greater claim to authority than this. Those who would take the words of Jesus as good suggestions, spiritual advice, recommendations for a moral and happy life, or any other such expression of human wisdom must consider this verse—He is the Alpha and Omega. Those who believe that the Bible does not claim that Jesus is God incarnate must also account for this, for in Revelation 1:8 and 21:6 it is God the Father who says He is the Alpha and Omega. There cannot be two Alphas and Omegas, Firsts and Lasts, Beginnings and Ends—the Father and the Son are one.

When this truth grips us, discipleship takes off. There can be no casual reading of the Gospels when we understand that the words of Jesus are the words not only of a great teacher but of God Himself, the Creator of the universe, the author of all wisdom and the knower of all mysteries. There is nothing truer or more complete in this world—no more accurate prophecy, no better psychology, no sager advice—than the teaching that comes straight from mouth of the living God; in fact, there is no other opinion worth heeding. His words are the owner's manual for our hearts.

"If you accept the authority of Jesus in your life, then you accept the authority of His words."

—Colin Urquhart

In Deed Ask yourself these probing questions: Do you hear His words casually, as though they are mere suggestions? Or do you voraciously consume His teaching as the key to life, dependent on it for your very existence? Are His words like a fragrant aroma—pleasing, but not entirely necessary? Or are they like oxygen—a matter of life and death? They were true before the foundation of the world and they will be true for all eternity. Savor them well.

God in the Flesh

"I and the Father are one." (John 10:30)

In Word "Jesus never claimed to be God." So goes a common mantra among those who reject Christian claims. But it is an argument from ignorance of the Scriptures. Jesus *often* claimed to be God. True, He never said "I am God," but He might as well have. This verse is the clearest statement, though cults will water it down and deny that He was claiming deity. "He was only claiming to be one in purpose, not in essence," they commonly argue. But Jesus' listeners certainly understood what He meant as they picked up stones to throw at Him. "You, a mere man, claim to be God," they charged (v. 33). Jesus often made extravagant claims, and His enemies always knew the implications.

Every time Jesus forgave sins, every time people worshiped Him without rebuke, every time He said "I am," He was claiming to be God. It is unmistakable, if one knows the context of the Gospels. No one familiar with the Hebrew Scriptures would dare to forgive sin unless He was claiming deity. But Jesus did (Mark 2:7; Matthew 9:2-3; Luke 5:21). No one allows people to fall down and worship Him, or to cry out, "My Lord and My God," unless He is making divine claims. But Jesus frequently did (Matthew 14:33; 28:9, 17; Luke 24:52; John 9:38; 20:28). No one would dare use the holy name of God for Himself as a casual mistake. But Jesus spelled it out (Exodus 3:14; John 8:58). The attempts to stone Him for blasphemy were frequent. His opponents clearly knew what He was saying.

"No founder of any religion has dared to claim for himself one fraction of the assertions made by Jesus Christ."
—Henry Heydt

In Deed The next time someone tells you Jesus never claimed to be God, ignore him. Better yet, correct him. And the next time you read His words casually, as though they were simply advice from a good teacher, remind yourself of this truth. Jesus is not just a good teacher; He is the eternal God, once clothed in human flesh and now inviting Himself into your day. With reverence, let Him in.

Extravagant Mercy

"I have not come to call the righteous, but sinners."
(Mark 2:17)

In Word What was in the mind of God when He came up with this plan? We will never know the fullness of His thoughts. But consider the oddity of a righteous and holy God who bypasses those who have tried to clean themselves up in order to demonstrate grace to those who haven't. Consider the mystery of a God who creates a race that He fully knows will collapse into rebellion and depravity, simply so He can redeem that race. Ponder the wisdom behind a creation so thoroughly lost that only those who know their lostness are eligible to be found. Who may know the mind of this God?

We can't completely understand the reason behind this strange creation. For centuries, perplexed philosophers have contemplated the mystery of evil, and few answers, if any, have satisfied. But imagine the counsel within the holy Trinity before the foundation of the world. We know God created us that He might be known. But known how? In a perfect world, He could have demonstrated His power, His purity, His wisdom, His creativity—all of His attributes. Except one. Mercy. How can a merciful God be known in a perfect world? He can't. The imperfect had to come.

"Amazing love! How can it be that Thou, my God, should die for me."
—Charles Wesley

In Deed God desires to be known in His mercy. Not just mercy, in fact, but *extravagant* mercy. Incomprehensibly extravagant mercy. Mind-boggling mercy. The kind of mercy that bridges such a vast expanse that those who see it are compelled to fall on their faces in gratitude and worship. Do you know this mercy? Let's sit with the tax-collectors and sinners at this table and drink it in. Let the Pharisees grumble. We are learning the mind of God.

Shedding the Old

"Take off the grave clothes and let him go."

(John 11:44)

In Word Is this an afterthought reported by John or a statement laden with meaning? Perhaps we should not make too much of the fact that Jesus is specific in His instructions after Lazarus exits the tomb. But in the framework of inspired Scripture, words are included for a purpose.

Bound by strips of linen around his hands and feet, with a cloth over his face, Lazarus hears this explicit command first after he is called out of the grave: "Take off the grave clothes and let him go." The stunned onlookers surely needed some instruction, and Lazarus, disoriented and still confined, surely needed assistance. At first he sees nothing. He has only heard the voice of Jesus. The visual illustration is good theology. When Jesus raises us out of our sinful state of death, there is something left to do before we run free. The grave clothes must go.

"We should always regard communion with other believers as an eminent means of grace."
—J. C. Ryle

In Deed What grave clothes have had us bound? Habitual sins? Guilt? The philosophies of this age? We must be free of them, and we are helpless to shed them on our own. Jesus tells our loved ones to help. He raises us to new life, but we in the church must be in the business of "taking off grave clothes and letting people go." In bearing one another's burdens, in being priests unto each other, in our fellowship with one another, we, the walking resurrected, are assisting one another in removing the remnants of death.

Consider two questions: 1) How do you need the assistance of others in shedding your burial garments? 2) How can you help others shed theirs? This—freedom from the trappings and legacy of death—is the work of the fellowship of believers.

True Greatness

"Whoever wants to become great among you must be your servant." (Matthew 20:26)

In Word It doesn't take us long as Christians to realize that the world's value system is in direct contrast to God's. In fact, to arrive at the world's measuring stick, we could almost simply turn God's measuring stick upside down. Those things He values most rate low on the world's scale; and those things the world greatly values rarely place very high on God's scale of importance. The world values achievement, reputation, wealth, self-assurance, prestige, and the like. Not so with God. Jesus says that greatness can be found in servanthood. This runs so counter to our human nature that few Christians have experienced this truth.

What is true servanthood? Many mistake it for slavery—being on call for the whims and pleasures of another. Biblical servanthood is different. It actively seeks the true well-being of others. Just as Jesus served His disciples and us in a completely unexpected way—dying for sins rather than overthrowing our earthly enemies—we are called to do what's best for others, even if they don't know how to define that. It deepens their relationship with God and further establishes them in the kingdom. It demonstrates grace.

"He who stays not in his littleness, loses his greatness."

—Francis de Sales

In Deed Do we spend our days looking for those whom we might serve? Probably not. Our own agendas—godly though they may be—become so large and consuming that we rarely depart from them, at least not without feeling inconvenienced. Yet servanthood is integral to the Gospel. Nowhere else does Jesus give us a path to greatness. Our desire to accomplish great things for God's kingdom can only be fulfilled on this principle. Need an illustration? Think of a life that began in a lowly stable and ended in human sacrifice for the sins of the world. It was servanthood from beginning to end. And no greater life was ever lived.

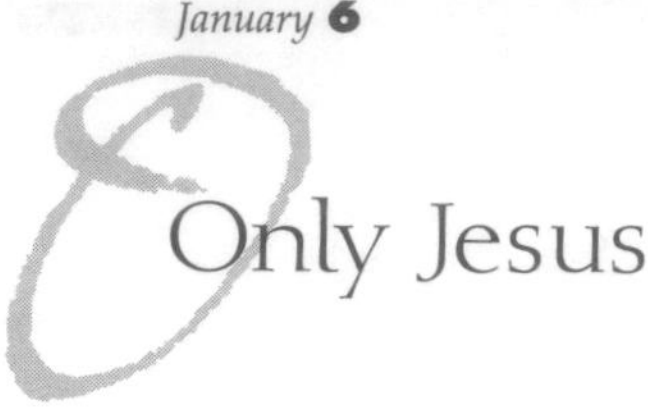

Only Jesus

"I am the way and the truth and the life. No one comes to the Father except through me." (John 14:6)

In Word This is the scandalous claim of Jesus. No one would have complained if He had simply taught about God. No one would have been upset if He had simply presented His take on the Scriptures. But He went much further. He presented Himself. He did not propose simply a way to God, He proposed Himself as the unique entrance into knowing who God is. That is the scandal of the Gospel, and that's what got Jesus crucified by a broad coalition of Jewish leaders, Roman authorities, and a mob mentality.

It's also a huge stumbling block to non-believers. The exclusiveness of Jesus' claims is good evangelistic material and a necessary part of any gospel presentation, but it contradicts the spirit of our age. People want an adviser, not a Lord. They want a mentor, not a Master. The prevailing mood of our culture is to accept some of the truth of Jesus without accepting His unique claims of divinity. People appreciate Jesus the philosopher but avoid Jesus the King of all creation at all costs. It's simply too demanding to follow one Lord to the exclusion of all others.

"Of all the great sages and prophets throughout world history, Jesus alone claimed to be God-become-man."
—Luis Palau

In Deed Doesn't this mindset seep into the Christian's perspective as well? Most of us know, theologically, to reject such a compromising view of the Savior. But in practice, what do we really think? How many lords do we really have? Most of us could probably identify rivals to Jesus to whom we sometimes bow. A career field? A political perspective? A relationship? A lifestyle? A philosophy? We daily consume information from a variety of sources, many of which tell us another way, another truth, another life. We try to ignore them, but sometimes we accommodate them. We let many sources direct us, when in reality there is only one revelation—Jesus Himself. His claim is exclusive and we hesitate to narrow ourselves to Him alone. But that's what He insists on. He's the only way.

The Daily Bread Principle

"Give us each day our daily bread." (Luke 11:3)

In Word More than a million people had been led straight into the desert. It was clearly a deliverance, but to what? There was no food. But God had a solution. He always does. Manna, a mysterious bread from heaven, would fall to them daily. They could gather only enough for one day, no more (except on the day before Sabbath). If they gathered more, it would rot. It could not be hoarded. They would just have to trust, at the end of each day, that the manna would come again on the next day. They would just have to believe God for tomorrow. "In this way I will test them and see whether they will follow my instructions," God said (Exodus 16:4). Saving up was not an option.

Saving up is not an option for us, either. Yes, we can buy a week's worth of groceries at a time, but that's not what Jesus is talking about. True bread, heavenly bread, is given on a day-by-day basis. We cannot pray or worship enough for the whole week on Sunday. The directions we got yesterday won't apply today. We cannot tithe the first portion of our paychecks and think that our sacrifice is done for the month. The daily bread principle is unalterable. You can't store up the things you need from God. You have to keep coming back for them, keep trusting Him for them, day after day after day.

"You will never need more than God can supply."
—J. I. Packer

In Deed Why is this so? Because God insists—absolutely insists—that we have a relationship with Him. Relationships must be maintained. He knows well that if He gives us our supplies for a week or a month we will only seek Him once a week or once a month. The temptation is great to gather in all that we can today —physically, psychologically, emotionally, and spiritually. But the daily bread principle is always at work, in all areas. There is no loving trust when there's a full storeroom.

Just as our loved ones are not content with one "I love you" for the year, God is not content with a periodic appearance before Him. Manna doesn't work that way, and neither do relationships. Ask for daily bread in every area of life. And come back again tomorrow.

Unattached to Self

"Do not resist an evil person." (Matthew 5:39)

In Word There is perhaps no more difficult point for the flesh to wrestle with than this one. Non-resistance is not our natural inclination when we're confronted with evil. And, in fact, there are surely qualifications that need to be applied to this verse. Are despots to be given passive permission to pillage and destroy? Are serious moral issues to be forfeited to a secular culture? Are we to express no opinion at all?

Surely Jesus means for us to resist evil. We are encouraged—even commanded—at several points in Scripture to stand firm against the evil one. So what does He mean by this? He means that when people confront us, we are to counter evil with good (Romans 12:21). Mercy triumphs over judgment (James 2:13). Evil aggression is never defeated by an evil response.

"True charity means returning good for evil—always."
—Mary Mazzarello

Watchman Nee tells a story of a Chinese Christian who used to go to great pains to pump water from an irrigation stream into his rice field. Every night, his neighbor, whose fields were lower, would make a breach in the dividing wall and drain the Christian's water into his own fields. The theft was repeated frequently. The Christian asked his friends for advice about the right thing to do. A fellow believer advised that Christians ought to do something more than what is right. The next few days, the Christian filled the neighbor's fields first before filling his own. The neighbor knew his acts were evil, but he was amazed at the Christian's non-resistance. Good won out over evil. The neighbor soon became a Christian. He had observed a higher way.*

In Deed What is your reaction to evil and offensive people? No, God does not tell you to be a doormat. He does, however, tell you to demonstrate a goodness that surpasses anything this world has known. Give evil people a glimpse of heaven. Do not fall to their level; we were born from a much higher source. Let them see it and be amazed.

*Watchman Nee, *Sit, Walk, Stand,* Tyndale/Christian Literature Crusade, 1988, pp. 32-33.

Unattached to Dignity

"If someone strikes you on the right cheek, turn to him the other also." (Matthew 5:39)

In Word In Jesus' code of ethics, there is no room for an inflated sense of dignity. That isn't to say that we have no dignity; created in the image of God, we could have no less. What Jesus prohibits is our instinct to defend our "approval rating" in others' eyes. We are not to guard our image as though our self-esteem depends on people. We are children of God, a kingdom of priests, and one with Christ. Why would we be zealous for the opinions of a sinfully competitive culture? We can be content with what's truly valuable.

"Revenge is the most worthless weapon in the world."
—David Augsburger

Why are we so concerned about the impression we make on others? And why are we so convinced that a vigorous defense of our rights makes a better impression than our humility? Jesus articulates what ought to be clear to us: Honor comes to those who do not strive for it. The most admired are the most humble. The kingdom of God is well-represented not by the strident and the over-assertive, but by those who know their heavenly citizenship and are entirely content with it. That's how we can become unattached to our reputation; we already know who we are.

Jesus doesn't tell His people to be doormats. He tells us to be reasonable. We don't need to assert ourselves to be valued. We don't need to respond to evil with evil. The best resistance against aggression is to give it no ground for continuing. We are to defy it by showing its holy alternative. Evil is exposed in the face of humility. It does not know how to disturb a truly peaceful heart.

In Deed How do you respond when people offend you? Even when the offense is real, the response should be a display of the character of God rather than the impulses of men. The world expects eye for eye and tooth for tooth. But no one who plays by those rules stands out from the crowd. There is no witness to the kingdom of God—this kingdom of grace—when we miss occasions to show it. We must decide which is more important to us: a defense of our dignity before others, or a demonstration of the holy kingdom.

Unattached to Things

"If someone wants to sue you and take your tunic, let him have your cloak as well." (Matthew 5:40)

In Word In Jesus' code of ethics, there is no room for a desperate attachment to possessions. He never says we can't have them, but by example and by His teaching we learn that they are never to get in the way of our discipleship. Just as a demonstration of the kingdom of God is more important than a defense of our reputation in the opinions that don't really matter, so is it more important than the things we own. No material possession is worth sacrificing the display of God's kind of grace. When given the opportunity to show what is really important to us, we must take it.

"God made man to be somebody, not just to have things."
—Anonymous

What is it about our possessions that makes us so attached to them? Is it the way they make us feel? We have complete validation and security before God in our relationship with Jesus. What piece of property can add to that? But we hang on to our things as though they define us. What a misappropriation of God's mercies! He has defined us already, and our position in Him is high above the things of this world. Yet we cling to them with misplaced passions. What must God think when the heart He gave us is so earthly directed, even when offered such heavenly joys?

Things are temporary. We can be unattached to them because they offer us nothing we don't already have. We can't take them with us when we go, and we wouldn't want to. They will pale in comparison to the treasures that have already been laid up for us in Christ. Our hold on them—or their hold on us—reveals how much or how little we believe that.

In Deed When a situation compels you to choose between demonstrating grace to another or maintaining your grip on your things, which do you choose? We must decide which is more important to us: a defense of our physical possessions on earth, or a demonstration of the kingdom of God.

Unattached to Time

"If someone forces you to go one mile, go with him two miles." (Matthew 5:41)

In Word In Jesus' code of ethics, there is no room for a zealous protection of our time and our energy. They are to be spent for kingdom purposes. Often, that means that they are to be spent for others.

What is it that makes us guard our time so protectively? Most of us balance families, jobs, church, rest and recreation, and any other interests we might have. Time is scarce. No one gets more than 24 hours a day. We must figure out how to balance all of our many responsibilities, and the relentless clock will not slow down for us. Time is perhaps the most valued commodity in our culture, often even more than money.

"Time is given us to use in view of eternity."
—Anonymous

In all of our juggling, do we leave time for service? God gets the firstfruits of our paychecks. Does He get the firstfruits of our time and of our effort? Think of what we are saying when He does not. Perhaps we are overestimating the importance of our own agenda. Is our schedule really that sacred? Perhaps we are not flexible enough to respond to God's Spirit. Are we just focused on getting things done, or are we wanting to help build an eternal kingdom? How we spend our time and our effort will show us, the world, and God what our priorities are.

Of all the sacrifices we are asked to make, this is one of our most challenging. How can we become unattached to our time? Consider the eternity that lies before us. Who has more time to do good than the children of the eternal God?

In Deed When our time is unfairly demanded of us, how do we respond? Again, Jesus does not ask us to be doormats. He asks us to be witnesses. We are the display of His kingdom's truths. If tasks are a greater priority to us than relationships, how will this world see His values? God asks us to take a stand in the face of evil for kingdom principles. We must decide which is more important to us: protecting our precious time, or demonstrating the kingdom of God.

Our Love

"Do you love me?" (John 21:17)

In Word "Do you love me?" Jesus' question to Peter is more than a sentimental inquiry. It goes to the heart of the purpose of man. Many have observed that if the greatest commandment is to love God with all of one's heart, soul, mind, and strength, then the greatest sin of all is to fail this commandment. And how Peter had failed! A three-fold denial of Jesus is graciously forgiven here in John's gospel with a three-fold opportunity to affirm his love for the risen Christ. But how contrary to the greatest commandment his denial was, and how deep the shame of such a failure. No wonder Peter wept bitterly.

What about us? Who among us has kept the great commandment for even a few minutes? We may not consider ourselves grossly sinful. Yet the one thing we were created for—a deep, abiding, consuming love for God—eludes us while we busy ourselves with avoiding greed, pride, lust, anger, impatience, and a host of other sinful traits. We mistakenly think that the battle is fought on these fronts, so we spend our energy fighting symptoms when the ultimate source of our sickness is a loveless heart toward God, the most grievous sin of all.

"To love God is something greater than to know Him."
—Thomas Aquinas

In Deed True discipleship is an outgrowth of love for Him. After years of trying to follow in Jesus' steps, we may discover, like Peter, that Jesus values our affections even more than our works, for only out of the former do the latter flow. We find that to fail at this point is to experience ultimate failure, but to have our love for Him revived is to experience ultimate joy. Does Jesus' piercing question hit home? Ask Him to kindle in your heart an abiding love for Him.

Our Work

"Feed my sheep." (John 21:17)

In Word Just as the question in this verse—"Do you love me?"—reminds us of the great commandment to love God with everything that is in us, the imperative of the verse—"Feed my sheep"—reminds us that there is a second great commandment to love our neighbors as ourselves. According to Jesus, those two commandments summarize the law and the prophets. So His dialogue with Peter before the other disciples here is an appropriate closure to His ministry in the gospel of John. It, too, is a summary of the law and the prophets, a summary of every believer's call to ministry—to love Jesus and to feed His sheep.

The correlation between the question and the imperative is clear. To have a heart for God is also to have a heart for that which concerns Him. And God has made it known throughout Scripture that He is passionately concerned for His people. The great shepherd tends to His sheep. He watches them, He feeds them, He protects them. He makes them lie down in green pastures and leads them beside still waters. He cares more deeply than we can know.

"If we do not show love to one another, the world has a right to question whether Christianity is true."

—Francis Schaeffer

In Deed Do we also have the heart of a shepherd? Are we passionate about the welfare of others? Do we tend to one another with the same concern with which the Great Shepherd tends to us?

Too often we envision our love for God as a separate endeavor from our love for others. But the two are intertwined. The first, if genuine, inevitably leads to the second. John spells this out in his first letter. To love God is to love our brother. If we are to have any genuine relationship with God at all, we must feed His sheep.

At His Feet

"Martha . . . you are worried and upset about many things, but only one thing is needed." (Luke 10:41-42)

In Word We are called to serve God. There is no dispute among believers about this; the Bible is very clear. He has made us for Himself, and Jesus frequently calls us to obedience and service. So Jesus' words to Martha may seem strange to us. Why does someone who has called us to obedience tell His servant to stop working, sit down, and listen?

The answer lies in God's priority for us. Nowhere in the Bible are we told to serve Him at the expense of knowing Him. Having made us for Himself, He does not at first fashion us for usefulness. He fashions us for knowing Him.

This is far removed from utilitarian thinking. When we make something, we usually make it for a practical purpose. Our only occasion to make something for the sake of its own beauty is when we are being creative and artistic. Parents can relate; few of us have children in order to have more help around the house. We have children to know them and enjoy them. So it is with God. He is first and foremost an Artist, a Craftsman, and a Father who enjoys His children. He is not a factory worker manufacturing a product.

Is this hard to grasp? We often see our Creator as a utilitarian God looking for an end result—a *practical* end result. We view Him in terms of obedience and service. It's easier for us—that's how we would look at things if we were in His place. We are great fans of usefulness; when things are no longer useful, we usually throw them away.

"Oh, the fullness, pleasure, sheer excitement of knowing God on Earth!"
—Jim Elliot

In Deed What is God's view toward you? Is He only after your usefulness? No, the Artist wants to enjoy His work. He seeks satisfaction in His technique and creativity—processes which continue on in your life every day. He will use you well, but not before He has enjoyed your company.

What is God's will for you? Jesus' words to Martha give us deep insight into His heart. He first wants us at His feet. Above all, He wants us to learn from Him.

Ears to Hear

"He who has ears to hear, let him hear." (Luke 8:8)

In Word Jesus uses this imperative 14 times in the Gospels and Revelation. It is a common but curious command in His teachings. And it raises a lot of questions for us. Why, for example, would the One who was sent to seek and to save us seem so casual about who hears and obeys? Why is He not pleading with the obstinate to repent?

We may never know some of the intricacies of God's salvation—why some believe while others don't. The reasons are mysterious to us. But one thing is clear: Jesus comes with the expectation that some will be ready to receive His message enthusiastically. And with that clear expectation comes the negative implication: Some will not. There are stubborn hearts in this world, listeners "without ears," those who will not open themselves to the possibility of the truth of the Gospel. Even among believers, Jesus faced this resistance. Many who accepted His claims could not—or simply would not—accept all of His teachings (see John 6:60-66, for example). Then and now, we see a strange phenomenon—priceless, eternal truth is often not welcome in human hearts.

"He who has Christ's Spirit will find in [His teaching] a hidden manna."

—Thomas à Kempis

In Deed This ability to hear has profound implications for unbelievers. Rebellious souls cannot hear the words of Jesus—really hear them—until they recognize and acknowledge their own insufficiency. (One of the greatest ironies of our age is that those who most often claim open-mindedness and the potentials of human enlightenment have completely shut their ears to Jesus.) But this concept also has profound implications for us. We, too, must always be on guard and aware of our insufficiency. Human nature gravitates toward rebellion and its inevitable result—deafness.

Jesus almost always uses this phrase after a difficult message. His hard teachings are often a stumbling block, but we can use them as a true test of the openness of our hearts. When Jesus' words grate against our natural inclinations, we must ask ourselves, "Do I have ears to hear?" How we respond will indicate the condition of our hearts.

His Father's House

"Didn't you know I had to be in my Father's house?"

(Luke 2:49)

In Word Mary and Joseph were perhaps given history's most sacred charge: parenting the Son of God. And they lost Him! For more than three excruciating days, He was missing. They looked among their traveling companions. They searched all over Jerusalem. Surely their thoughts vacillated between trust in the sovereignty of God over His own Son—after all, the divine plan revolved around Him alone—and the frantic anxiety any parent would feel when a child is missing. When they finally found Him, He calmly reassured them: Where else would He be? The temple is His home.

Don't we also search for Jesus? Even though we are assured of His presence, He often seems awfully absent. For days or weeks we may seek Him. Like Mary and Joseph, our thoughts may vacillate between resting in God's sovereignty with the knowledge of Jesus' presence, and anxiously seeking the invisible Son. "Though you have not seen Him, you love Him" (1 Peter 1:8). While such love results in "inexpressible and glorious joy," it also stirs an unquenchable longing in our hearts.

In Deed Jesus does not leave us to despair. What greater commitment could He make than this: "Didn't you know I had to be in my Father's house?" We do not need to wonder where He is. He is always about His Father's business.

Knowing that His Father's business is to dwell in and work out His plan in believers, we need not fret over His absence. In light of the post-resurrection fact that our bodies are His temple—both individually and corporately (1 Corinthians 3:16 and 6:19; 2 Corinthians 6:16; Ephesians 2:21-22)—what greater assurance of His presence can He give? His own nature compels Him. He *must* be in His Father's house, and His Father's house is us.

"To believe in the God over us and around us and not in the God within us—that would be a powerless and fruitless faith."

—Phillips Brooks

Faith and Worry

"Why were you searching for me?" (Luke 2:49)

In Word The young Jesus was missing for three days, a painfully long time for a mother and father who don't know where their child is. It wasn't the only time Jesus would be missing for three days, and each event prompted a similar response from His loved ones, as well as a similar response from Him. Both times—when He calmly sat in the temple discussing theology and when He lay in the grave—His loved ones were thrown into a panic. No one ever seemed to look in the right places for Him.

There is no faith evident in either of these two incidents—Mary and Joseph turned Jerusalem upside down looking for the young Jesus; and His relatives, disciples, and friends scattered and hid while He lay in the grave, then wondered who had taken His body. In both cases, they fundamentally misunderstood who Jesus was.

Both of these events were catastrophic. But not to Jesus. Both times, Jesus calmly gives reassurance. *Faith is the appropriate response,* He seems to imply in His gentle rebukes. God remains on His throne, Jesus is Lord, and the situation at hand—whatever it is—isn't nearly as critical as it seems.

"Anxiety is the natural result when our hopes are centered in anything short of God and His will for us."

—Billy Graham

In Deed Isn't that an accurate portrayal of our reaction and His response in a crisis? We often run around in a panic because a given situation isn't quite what we planned, or perhaps it even appears disastrous. All the while, Jesus calmly awaits our discovery that God is in fact sovereign, and Jesus Himself does in fact remain Lord. Neither death nor frantic parents are beyond His reach.

Are you in a crisis? Hear Him asking "Why were you searching for me?" and know that your situation is much larger to you than it is to Him.

Love for All

"Love your enemies and pray for those who persecute you." (Matthew 5:44)

In Word This command is so contrary to human nature that even those of us who have said for years that we are followers of Christ have usually not followed Him very far on this point Loving anyone beyond our close circle of family and friends is difficult; we can manage if we try. But this command is more difficult than loving those people close to us who annoy us a little bit. It is more difficult than loving passing acquaintances and even complete strangers. This tells us to love those who actively seek to do us harm, those who have nothing but ill will for us and will likely mock any attempt we make to reconcile with them. There is absolutely nothing in it for us, at least on the surface. And yet it is not just a suggestion; it is a command.

"I am determined that I am going to love everybody, even if it kills me! I have set my heart on it. I am going to do it."

—A. W. Tozer

In Deed We are prone to withhold love from those who get on our bad side. We often use our love as leverage—a reward for those we like and a lost privilege for those we don't like. But Jesus gives us no allowance for this. There is no one on the planet from whom we are told to withhold love.

Think about those whom you can consider enemies, or who have declared themselves your opponents. Perhaps they disagree with your faith or your politics; perhaps they have betrayed your confidence; perhaps it's just a personality conflict. Make a list. Then review the list with an understanding that everyone on it is to be the object of your love.

Is this possible? Humanly speaking, no. We can no more manufacture love than we could save ourselves from sin. Ask God, the author of all love, to love them through you.

Light and Truth

"I have come into the world as a light, so that no one who believes in me should stay in darkness."

(John 12:46)

In Word We live in a dark kingdom (Colossians 1:13). The Bible is very clear and consistent about that. Our understanding was darkened (Ephesians 4:18); we are surrounded by powers of darkness (Ephesians 6:12); we ourselves have done deeds of darkness (Romans 13:12); our motives are dark (1 Corinthians 4:5); and even when we see God, we see Him very dimly (1 Corinthians 13:12). In fact, Paul goes so far as to say that we *were* darkness (Ephesians 5:8).

This is insulting to the human ego, to say the least. We think we're fairly well-educated and wise. We even have an intellectual era we refer to as the Enlightenment. So when Jesus implies that He has come into the darkness, we might wonder where all this alleged darkness is. Aren't we pretty bright folks?

No, Jesus really is the only light this world has ever seen. We can't find illumination anywhere else. He's the One through whom God once said "Let there be light," and there was light. We're the ones who shrouded this planet in a sinful haze of spiritual blindness. He came back into it with all the radiance of a million suns.

In Deed Plato told an allegory of people in a cave who saw each other as shadows. They thought they could see clearly enough, because shadows were all they knew. Like Plato's cave-dwellers, we think we're well-informed; and when we encounter light, we feel the pain of brightness in our maladapted eyes. We turn back to the darkness we're so comfortable with.

Do not dabble in the wisdom of the world. This world no longer has anything to offer you. Its interpretations of life are but shadows; its knowledge is untouched by the light of truth. Reject it. Do you really want understanding? Open your mind exclusively to Jesus and let Him shine.

"I believe in Christianity as I believe the sun has risen, not only because I see it, but because by it I see everything else."

–C. S. Lewis

Ask and Receive

"What do you want me to do for you?" (Mark 10:51)

In Word Why did Jesus ask this? A blind man is screaming at the top of his lungs for Jesus to have mercy on him. The need seems pretty obvious. But the Son of the Omniscient, the very One who had "seen" the entire sordid past of a woman at a well, asked the noisy blind fellow what he wanted. Why?

Because it is important for the blind man, and for us, to ask for His help. To assume that God will meet our needs without our asking, even though He often does, is to desire a Savior and Provider without the "bother" of a relationship with Him.

"You do not have because you do not ask God," writes James (4:2). Jesus says clearly, "Everyone who asks receives" (Matthew 7:8). In fact, many of His parables are about asking—persistent, bold, specific asking. Just as many rebuked blind Bartimaeus and told Him to be quiet, many will tell us that being specific in prayer is unspiritual, or theologically misguided. With Bartimaeus, and with us, Jesus overrules their objection.

"Whether we like it or not, asking is the rule of the kingdom."

—Charles Spurgeon

In Deed So Jesus insists on specific requests, even though He knows all of our needs before we even ask. Perhaps He insists so we'll recognize His answer when it comes—a gift specifically from Him and specifically for us. Perhaps it is so that when the answer comes we will clearly see how His will differs from our own limited vision. Perhaps it is so we will remember, having voiced our request, to give thanks when it is granted. Perhaps the asking and receiving witness to the world in a way that the presumption of providence would not.

We wonder sometimes why God has not met a certain need. Our first step, often neglected, is to be specific. We must ask.

God Alone

"You cannot serve both God and Money." (Matthew 6:24)

In Word We may consider ourselves far beyond materialism. "Jesus doesn't mean that wealth is bad, He only means that we cannot be attached to it." This is the mantra that Christians often quote when confronted with verses about materialism. But in so quoting, we often betray the fact that we *are* attached. We will so quickly offer caveats to Jesus' statements about money that we demonstrate ourselves suspiciously wedded to our materialism. The more we deny His judgments against "things," the more we show ourselves to be possessed by them. "Jesus isn't *really* asking the rich young ruler to sell his possessions, He is only pinpointing the young man's idols," we say hastily. "Jesus doesn't mean that we *can't* lay up treasures on earth, He just means that shouldn't be our *priority*." We are exactly right in these interpretations. But our vigorous defense of them is suspicious.

"The golden age only comes to men when they have forgotten gold."

—G. K. Chesterton

In Deed Our understanding of this verse really should go in the other direction. Instead of apologetics for Jesus' severity toward money, we must apply His judgment to even other areas. "You cannot serve both God and _______." He may as well have let us fill in the blank ourselves, and He indicates as much in the first part of this verse. Having two masters is always an inappropriate situation. It leads to double-mindedness and neglect of at least one, if not both.

Does Jesus contend with any rivals in our lives? Do we have any "gods" before Him? We may not know the answer to this until He asks us to give one up. Like the rich young ruler (Luke 18:18-23), we often don't know our idols until they are threatened. Try this exercise: Let someone fill in the blank above with every rival he or she can think of and then measure the defensiveness of your reaction. This may show where God wants to work in your life.

Our First Command

"Go home to your family and tell them how much the Lord has done for you, and how he has had mercy on you." (Mark 5:19)

In Word Who is the first person in the Gospels whom Jesus commissions to be a witness of His mercy? A disciple who trained with Him for three years? A seminarian of the day? A centurion, government official, or converted Pharisee? No, it was the Gerasene demoniac. The man in whom a legion of evil spirits dwelt. A beast-like creature with superhuman strength who lived among the tombs. The village sideshow.

Children would have been warned by their mothers not to go too close to the cemetery, but they probably went anyway, lurking in the distance to catch a glimpse of him. He was the equivalent of the modern-day haunted house, the village enigma who defied explanation. He defied explanation even more after his encounter with Jesus, as he sat there dressed and calm, in his right mind. He begged to become a disciple, but Jesus called him to be a missionary to his hometown. "And all the people were amazed" (v. 20).

"The Church has nothing to do but to save souls; therefore spend and be spent in this work."

—John Wesley

In Deed We often think we need years of preparation and experience before we are useful to God. We don't. We often think God needs His witnesses to have sterling reputations. He doesn't. All that's required is this: an encounter with Jesus and the will to tell about it. How we complicate things! We study apologetics, we wait for a call, we seek so much direction. These things are helpful, but not prerequisites. Like the ex-demoniac, all we're asked to do is to "tell them how much the Lord has done" for us. It's that simple.

Willing and Able

A man with leprosy came to him and begged him on his knees, "If you are willing, you can make me clean." Filled with compassion, Jesus reached out his hand and touched the man. "I am willing," he said. "Be clean!"

(Mark 1:40-41)

"If you can do anything, take pity on us and help us." "'If you can'?" said Jesus. "Everything is possible for him who believes." (Mark 9:22-23)

"Birds lack faith. They fly away when I enter the orchard, though I mean them no ill. Even so do we lack faith in God.

—Martin Luther

In Word When we pray, we know in our minds that God is limited neither in His power nor love; yet in our hearts, we question both. How did Jesus respond to such questions? To the leper who said "If you are willing," Jesus affirmed His willingness. To the father who said "If you can," Jesus affirmed His power, especially when it is invoked in faith.

Haven't those questions been the cry of this world against "the problem of evil"? In light of all the suffering in the world, the great philosophers say that God is either able to help and not willing, or willing to help and not able. Jesus will have none of that argument. The problem is not with God's power and it is not with His love; it is with our faith.

In Deed When God doesn't resolve a situation to our liking, especially a situation in which the suffering is great, we are tempted to accuse Him of either impotence or negligence. And Jesus' response tells us to look within.

Unanswered prayer is a call to come closer, look deeper, know God better, and seek His will further. It is a call to be transformed as a disciple and to be conformed to the image of Christ. By such the Father separates those who desire to test Him from those who desire to know Him.

Supernatural Unity

"I in them and you in me. May they be brought to complete unity to let the world know that you sent me and have loved them even as you have loved me."

(John 17:23)

In Word What does Jesus look for in His bride? A thorough reading of His priestly prayer in John 17 reveals His desire for believers' protection, sanctity, and joy. But above all, the overriding theme of His prayer is their unity. Complete unity. The kind of unity that He has with His Father.

Isn't He a little unrealistic here? A united front is attainable, perhaps, but the same kind of unity He has with His Father? Perfect oneness from within the Trinity? Look at our churches; there is division between them and within them. How could the Son of God, One with the Father, have such unanswered prayer?

Jesus is no fool. He knows well what He is doing when He lays before His Father and before us this humanly impossible ideal. The unity of sinful human beings is utterly unattainable but for one thing: His presence. His aim—aside from His Father's supernatural intervention in our fellowship—is for believers to hear or read these words and know beyond any doubt that we *must* depend on Him. There is no other way.

"Unity in Christ is not something to be achieved; it is something to be recognized."
—A. W. Tozer

In Deed Examine the characteristics of the disciples: antagonistic political opinions, different levels of education, diverse professions, varying temperaments. They had plenty of reason to argue with one another, and sometimes did (Matthew 20:24; Mark 9:34). After three years with Jesus and an outpouring of His Spirit they were "one in heart and mind" (Acts 4:32). What pulled them together? A common background? Not even close. A common goal? Not entirely. Just Him. His very, very real presence. This impossible standard of unity has only one solution: absolute dependence on Him.

Real Evangelism

"I in them and you in me. May they be brought to complete unity to let the world know that you sent me and have loved them even as you have loved me."

(John 17:23)

In Word What is the greatest evangelistic tool of all time? Crusades? Short-term or long-term missions? Tracts? Door-to-door or neighbor-to-neighbor witnessing? Lifestyle evangelism? TV and radio? Films? Technology? All have been used by God, sometimes quite dramatically, to spread His Gospel into the world. But none of them are highlighted in Scripture as the key to pointing to the Christ as God's Son. That honor goes to unity.

Most evangelistic training manuals and classes do not include a session on the unity of the church. But Jesus prays for His believers to be one—completely united—*in order "to let the world know that you sent me."* Such unity stands out because true, loving fellowship is alien to this world. "By this all men will know that you are my disciples, if you love one another" (John 13:35). The implication is clear: If we don't love one another, the world won't know.

"Love for the brethren is far more than an agreeable society whose views are the same."

—A. W. Pink

In Deed Have you ever been in a fellowship in which "all the believers were one in heart and mind" (Acts 4:32)? If you have, you know that such a fellowship acts as a magnet to everyone around it. It grows deeper and often larger. People are drawn to something they know to be supernatural; they marvel at unity because it does not come from human impulse.

And the reverse is true. No one is drawn to a church that bickers. Chronic strife is a clear sign that Jesus is not acknowledged as Lord in that place. The genuine unity of the saints is the greatest tool of evangelism God has given us. Do not seek others for the kingdom without seeking this as well.

Joyful Blessing

"The younger [son] said to his father, 'Father, give me my share of the estate.'" (Luke 15:12)

In Word There is more than one way to ask for a blessing from God. When many people think of asking God to bless them, they assume it implies the kind of insolence with which the Prodigal Son approached his father. Though the father is even gracious enough to honor this insult with blessing, the offensiveness of the request is easy to see.

But what father would deny a son who sincerely comes to him for blessing? Not only would he bestow abundance and fullness on his son, he would do so with great excitement and joy. He would be filled with compassion. "If you, then, though you are evil, know how to give good gifts to your children," Jesus says, "how much more will your Father in heaven give good gifts to those who ask Him!" (Matthew 7:11). Blessing children is natural even for those of us who are tainted with impurity. How much greater the blessing from the One who is pure love!

"The purpose of all prayer is to find God's will and make that will our prayer."

—Catherine Marshall

In Deed When we ask God for His blessing, do we ask with the arrogance of the Prodigal Son? Or do we get on our knees before the Father and humbly ask that His highest will for us be made real? Do we ask without regard to the Father's character, will, or feelings? Or do we know Him personally enough to ask with the respect He deserves?

God is a blesser by nature. How rarely we take this into account when we approach Him! We assume reluctance on His part, as though He would begrudge us anything. Not so, says Psalm 84:11—"No good thing does he withhold from those whose walk is blameless." Even when we take His goodness for granted, He often blesses. How much more joyfully He blesses when the request is honoring to Him.

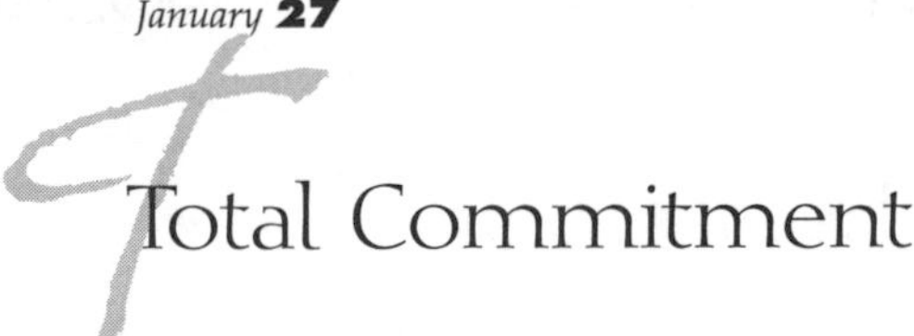

Total Commitment

Peter said to him, "We have left all we had to follow you!" "I tell you the truth," Jesus said to them, "no one who has left home or wife or brothers or parents or children for the sake of the kingdom of God will fail to receive many times as much in this age and, in the age to come, eternal life."

(Luke 18:28-30)

In Word A religious leader was recently quoted criticizing a cult for expecting "total commitment" from its followers. The cult's false doctrines could have been easily exposed and would have made a better target, but the critic didn't care about doctrine. What rubbed her the wrong way was the level of commitment expected.

Many consider total allegiance a characteristic only of cults, not of Christianity. Our society respects those who dabble in religious belief but reviles those who are wholeheartedly committed—especially if the object of commitment is Christ. It has been observed that in our culture it is respectable to say we are seeking, but arrogant to say we have found. We may be considered naive, unscientific, intolerant of others' beliefs, imbalanced, or any one of a number of other suspicious complaints. Throughout history, those who have "left everything" to follow Christ have often been considered fools.

In Deed Have we come to view total commitment as an option? Or worse, is it to be avoided as an unrealistic demand? Where in Scripture does Jesus expect of His disciples anything less than total devotion? Jesus is perfectly clear in His absolute call to discipleship. We are to abandon all that we are to Him.

Lord, grant that we might not be afraid of radical commitment, even if we are ostracized by a world that doesn't understand it.

"If we were willing to learn the meaning of real discipleship . . . the resultant impact on society would be staggering."

—David Watson

The Devil's Test

"The devil will put some of you in prison to test you, and you will suffer persecution for ten days. Be faithful, even to the point of death, and I will give you the crown of life." (Revelation 2:10)

"The things of earth will grow strangely dim in the light of His glory and grace."

—Helen H. Lemmel

In Word Jesus has something specific in mind for the church in Smyrna when He says this, but it applies to us as well. Satan's persecution has never been an isolated incident among one segment of Christ's body. It is targeted at all Christians of all times, in one way or another.

Why this vendetta? Why won't he just let it go? Satan is a creature of vengeance. Above all else, He wants to interrupt your worship of God. If he can't stop it, he'll try to distort it, degrade it, diminish it, distract from it, and defuse it in any way possible. He hates it. It's the worship he craves, and it is directed toward his worst Enemy. The Most High God basks in the glory of our praises. The most low creature finds that utterly revolting.

Our response, whether in good times or bad, whether in ease or difficulty, whether in fruitfulness or barrenness, is to worship. It is never inappropriate. God is worthy at all times and in all places. The fact that we can't always see the reasons doesn't mean they aren't there. To withhold praise of the eternal God when we don't feel like praising Him is to agree with our limited vision rather than the inviolable Word. It's to exalt our fickle emotions over truth. Don't fall for that trap.

In Deed Are you suffering? Be faithful and worship. Are you persecuted? Be faithful and worship. Are you dying? Be faithful and worship. Just like Paul and Silas in the depths of a Philippian prison (Acts 16), just like Jehoshaphat surrounded by hostile armies (2 Chronicles 20), be faithful. Turn your eyes upon Jesus and worship. Let the crown of life loom larger to you than the trials at hand. Let the devil's test fail. In your life and your testimony, reflect God's glory clearly.

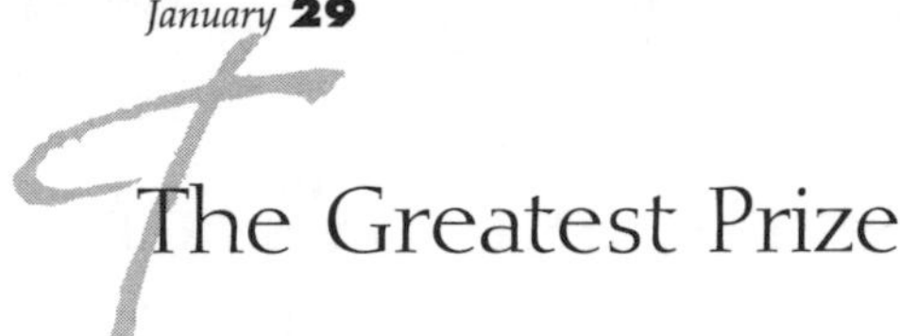

The Greatest Prize

"The kingdom of heaven is like a merchant looking for fine pearls. When he found one of great value, he went away and sold everything he had and bought it."

(Matthew 13:45-46)

In Word There are several ways to approach this parable, but one of them is to understand Christ as the pearl and us lost human beings as the searching merchants. The implication is that when the Gospel comes into a person's life, it is *everything*. It is not a philosophy to add to the mix, or an access to God that will help us accomplish our goals. It is a radical rearrangement of all of life.

We have examples of this in the twelve disciples. They left careers and families in order to follow Jesus and the promise of His kingdom. We also have a clear example in Paul. "But whatever was to my profit I now consider loss for the sake of Christ. What is more, I consider everything a loss compared to the surpassing greatness of knowing Christ Jesus my Lord, for whose sake I have lost all things. I consider them rubbish, that I may gain Christ and be found in him, not having a righteousness of my own that comes from the law, but that which is through faith in Christ—the righteousness that comes from God and is by faith. I want to know Christ" (Philippians 3:7-10).

"Anything that takes God's place is out of place."

—Abe Van der Puy

In Deed Is Jesus *everything* to us? Or one loyalty among several? If someone asked us how much we would give up in order to know Him, is there anything we would hold back? Do we believe only when it doesn't cost us too much? It's easy to know the right answer to these questions; a wholehearted abandonment to Christ is more difficult and more profound. What is the pearl of your life?

Our Dangerous Mission

"Go! I am sending you out like lambs among wolves."
(Luke 10:3)

In Word What good shepherd in his right mind would send his sheep into a pack of wolves? And yet this is exactly what our Good Shepherd tells us. It is not just a suggestion. It is an emphatic command. *"Go!"*

Why would our Shepherd do this? Doesn't He lead us beside still waters and into green pastures? Doesn't He know how dangerous the wolves are? Of course He does. He, whose own body would not survive the wolfpack, knows exactly what He is commanding. Why then does He do it?

There can only be one answer. The plentiful harvest He has just mentioned is worth the cost of His lambs. The price of not going into the wolves is substantially more than the cost of going, even if the lambs are sacrificed there. Our Savior is the same Shepherd who leaves the 99 behind for the one, and He bids His disciples to have the same all-or-nothing spirit. These lambs do, in fact, return to Him safely after this trip into the wolfpack, but there will be times in the future when they won't. And He knows this.

"Nothing is really lost by a life of sacrifice; everything is lost by failure to obey God's call."

—Henry Parry Liddon

In Deed What excuses do we have for avoiding the wolves? We might prefer the company of lambs, but the wolves are needier. We don't feel called to serve a wolf population, perhaps, but indeed we are—the Shepherd has called us Himself. They are too dangerous, we object, and we are right. But still our Shepherd says, "Go!" There must be a reason. The harvest must be incredibly valuable to risk so much.

He who was sent into a ravenous world to die sends His own lambs into the midst of wolves. As the Father has sent Him, so He sends us. But not alone. Be encouraged. This Shepherd doesn't send us without a promise—"I am with you always" (Matthew 28:20).

Our Deepest Love

"Anyone who loves his father or mother more than me is not worthy of me; anyone who loves his son or daughter more than me is not worthy of me; and anyone who does not take his cross and follow me is not worthy of me." (Matthew 10:37-38)

In Word We might be tempted to think these verses are only about us and our obligations. But they tell us more about God. God's desire is for us to know Him in Christ, but how can we if our love is focused elsewhere?

We pursue knowledge of that which we love. Those who love literature get academic degrees in it. Those who love gardening read up on techniques. Those who love photography study the art. If we do not love these things, we will not get to know them well. We do not zealously invest in that which does not interest us. Our greatest love shapes all our other affections and determines our path.

Isn't it the same in our relationship with God? Can we really know Him if other loves are greater rivals? His desire is for our single-hearted devotion. This is not the voice of an egocentric god who demands worship. It is the voice of a loving God who knows we will only be fulfilled if He blesses us with Himself.

"To cherish true love for God is to be constrained by love to yield one's ego with all that it is and has, and to let God be God again."

—Abraham Kuyper

In Deed Consider a God who would ask us to love Him more than our deepest human relationships. He is the same God who commanded us to love others. But He knows that our most subtle idolatries are in making the command of God greater than God Himself. They are subtle because they begin with righteousness and obedience to the law of love, but end in disproportionate affections that dishonor Him. Let us be mindful that if He tests us in these loves, it is only because we were created to know Him intimately.

Jesus' Rivals

"Anyone who loves his father or mother more than me is not worthy of me; anyone who loves his son or daughter more than me is not worthy of me; and anyone who does not take his cross and follow me is not worthy of me." (Matthew 10:37-38)

In Word These are startling words from Jesus. And in a sense we can dismiss them with a disclaimer: "None of us is worthy of Him anyway; that's why we call it grace." Acknowledging our universal unworthiness, we can move on without dealing with this radical call. But we must linger at these words longer if we really want to know the mind of Christ.

When we consider these verses in the context of the whole Bible, we know that Jesus does not oppose love for family. Rather, He opposes disproportionate love—that which depreciates His desire to have us love Him wholeheartedly. He can have no rivals in our hearts, not even good ones.

"Whatever a man seeks, honors, or exalts more than God, this is the god of idolatry."
—William Ullathorne

In Deed Jesus only asks us to be realists. In reality, He is more valuable than any other person or thing in all of existence. In fact, all existence—other than the self-existing Godhead—came through Him (Colossians 1:16). He is where true worth lies. When we value others more, we are not living in truth. Instead, we deny truth, attributing greatest importance to someone or something less important than Him. This is the unworthiness of disproportionate love. We deny the reality of who Jesus is.

Try this exercise: Make a list in one column of all of your relationships, possessions, and plans. Then in another column write "Jesus." Look at your columns like an accounting sheet. Which weighs more to you? On which column do you place the most value? The answer will tell you how much you value the Gospel's worthiness.

Always on the Road

"Foxes have holes and the birds of the air have nests, but the Son of Man has no place to lay his head."

(Luke 9:58)

"I do not pray for success. I pray for faithfulness."
—Mother Teresa

In Word We might cringe if we heard a preacher give such a discouraging call to discipleship. Isn't the kingdom of God a little more attractive than that? Isn't this likely to drive folks away? And what's wrong with nests, anyway? Nothing, except that Jesus knows our tendency to focus on making a home for ourselves.

Try this little exercise: Compare, on the one hand, the amount of time we spend with our eyes focused on getting an education, earning a living, establishing a career, building a home, staying healthy, and achieving our goals; and, on the other hand, the amount of time we spend with our eyes focused on our Master and His mission.

Yet which is more important? Our answer to that defines whether or not we are disciples. Not that the elements of each option are always incompatible—it isn't wrong to earn a living, build a home, or stay healthy. Jesus' followers just cannot make priorities of those endeavors. When they do, their lives are out of order.

In Deed Discipleship isn't about making a home in this world, it's about preparing for another. Discipleship is all about investing in the kingdom of God rather than the kingdom of this world. Following the example of Abraham, it is a forward focus on the city of God (Hebrews 11:10).

Jesus wants to make this clear to His followers. Anytime we face a choice between settling into this life and striving for a kingdom still in formation, we must choose the latter. We simply cannot settle here; we're on a journey.

A New Family

"Everyone who has left houses or brothers or sisters or father or mother or children or fields for my sake will receive a hundred times as much and will inherit eternal life." (Matthew 19:29)

"When we take God for our God, we take His people for our people."
—Matthew Henry

In Word "Blood is thicker than water," the saying goes. The assumption is that our deepest human loyalties lie with our blood relatives. But this is not so in the kingdom of God. "Whoever does the will of my Father in heaven is my brother and sister and mother," Jesus says (Matthew 12:50). The Spirit is thicker than blood in the kingdom. The covenant of the kingdom ties us together in ways that genetics never will. Jesus explains in Matthew 10:35-36—"I have come to turn 'a man against his father, a daughter against her mother, a daughter-in-law against her mother-in-law. A man's enemies will be the members of his own household.'" Families will divide over Him; a new family will be formed.

There is a wonderful illustration of this in the Old Testament. In marriage, man and woman leave father and mother and cleave to one another. In God's plan, the bonds of covenant take priority over the bonds of blood kinship. And now, according to Scripture, we are the bride of Christ. Aren't we glad for the depths of spiritual union over blood-relatedness? If this were not so, we would be forever related to Adam and never to Christ.

In Deed Over and over again, Jesus calls His disciples to place their relationships in the Spirit above their relationships in the flesh. Our ties to Christian brothers and sisters are infinitely more substantial than those to our blood relatives. We gain hundreds of brothers, sisters, mothers, fathers, and children in the Spirit because the Spirit is thicker than blood. We are bound together with Christ, and through Christ to one another. May we glory in the family that is now ours.

No Greater Reward

"Everyone who has left houses or brothers or sisters or father or mother or children or fields for my sake will receive a hundred times as much and will inherit eternal life." (Matthew 19:29)

In Word There is a false spirituality in the church that insists that we are never to serve God with an eye on the reward. Yet over and over again, Jesus uses reward as an incentive for His disciples to follow Him at all costs (at least nine times in the Sermon on the Mount alone—see Matthew 10:42, 16:27 and Luke 6:23 for other examples). He would not tell us about it if we were not supposed to consider it.

Jesus assures us that even though the costs of discipleship are great, they will never outweigh the benefits. We serve Him knowing that there is surpassing value in our service and in the rewards we will reap from it. God is no one's debtor. He is extravagant in His promises.

The message in this verse is clear: Jesus expects His disciples to leave *everything* behind. But it's another of the many paradoxes of the Gospel. In losing everything, we gain everything *and more!*

"Theirs is an endless road, a hopeless maze, who seek for goods before they seek for God."

—Bernard of Clairvaux

In Deed Though we invest much of our lives in houses, property, and relationships with friends and relatives—all good things—the Gospel is of inestimably greater worth. Jesus would have us value our relationships, but He would have us value the Gospel more—so much more, in fact, that He assumes many will leave even their closest relatives behind for His sake. The Gospel, if we accept it, will loosen our grip on all our attachments while making our attachment to Christ supreme. The cost of that is huge, but the reward is greater still.

Remind yourself that costly discipleship is really to our benefit—an investment with unparalleled returns. We are to humbly accept the extravagance of His promises.

Blessing in Service

"Now that you know these things, you will be blessed if you do them." (John 13:17)

"Faithful service in a lowly place is true spiritual greatness." —D. Jackman

In Word Many of us have sought a blessing from God. In fact, most adherents of most religions seek a blessing from their deity or founder. It's common to all humanity; we want to be blessed. There's nothing wrong with that, as long as we seek it from the right source. The Bible is full of promises that God will bless His people. He is, by nature, an extravagant giver. It is not selfish to ask His blessing according to His nature. In fact, it is expected. There are at least 25 references in the Gospels to Jesus offering blessing those who followed Him.

But many of God's blessings carry prerequisites. We forget them easily. We ask God for His favor, but we neglect the conditions on which He has already promised it. Haven't you noticed that? Something goes wrong and we cry out to God to fix it, or to restore His favor. But do we examine our own condition first? Jesus was very clear: His followers *will* be blessed—if they are poor in spirit, if they are meek, if they have ears to hear, if they have a certain attitude or obey a certain command. Here in John 13, He promises a blessing for those who follow His example of service: washing others' feet. Those who give themselves to service in Jesus' name will receive God's favor. It is an inviolable spiritual law.

In Deed Does God's blessing seem to be far from you? First realize that you have already been blessed, and be thankful. Then examine His Word. There are conditions that will carry further blessing when fulfilled. Obedience is one of them (Luke 11:28). So is godly character (Matthew 5:3-10). And humble service, often neglected among sincere believers, never goes unrewarded by the One who sees in secret.

The Master served His disciples. We are not greater than He is; we must be servants, too. In so doing, we will bless others, and He will bless us in return.

Channels of Blessing

"Now that you know these things, you will be blessed if you do them." (John 13:17)

In Word The blessedness of service is an enigmatic thing. We know that if the only motive for our service is getting a reward, we would really be self-serving, not selfless, so we rightly seek other motives. Nevertheless, Jesus holds God's favor out there as a promise for those who will serve others in His name. Why?

There is a spiritual principle at work when we do anything in the Spirit, character, and name of Jesus. A dammed lake that has little outflow can receive little inflow. But when its floodgates are opened, it can accommodate rivers flowing into it. Likewise, we were not created to be untapped reservoirs of His grace. We cannot store it up, and we cannot legitimately withhold it from others. But when we serve in humility, willingly taking a role that's inferior to the ones to whom we minister, we become like Jesus. In effect, we become channels of His blessing. His mercy flows out, and we are emptied enough to receive more of His mercy.

"We may easily be too big for God to use, but never too small."
—Dwight L. Moody

This is how Jesus does His work in this world. The church is His body; its members must do the things that He would do if He were here in the flesh. Our works must look a lot like the things He did during His earthly ministry. If His Spirit is in us, we will be like Him and we will act like Him. His Spirit will flow from us to a needy world; and His Spirit will flow into us because we have not been stingy with His grace. We receive blessing because we have become blessers.

In Deed Do you seem to have little of Jesus' Spirit? Perhaps it is because you are not sharing what you do have of Him with others. Begin to serve, and you will begin to see Him serving through you. The blessing you give will be the blessing you receive in even greater measure. Only when you've emptied yourself can you be filled.

Above Our Worries

"Do not worry about your life . . . Seek first his kingdom and his righteousness, and all these things will be given to you as well."

(Matthew 6:25, 33)

In Word We most often read the instructions of Jesus as messages about us. But there is another meaning to them all. They are all messages about God as well. We know what this statement says about us—that we are worriers by nature. But what does it say about God? That if Jesus is in a position to tell us not to worry, it must mean that His Father is aware of our needs and our future, and able to do something about them both.

We often get such advice from friends. "Don't worry. It will be OK." But this is just advice, encouraging words meant to help us keep a positive outlook. They can really do nothing to change a stressful situation other than be with us as we walk through it. Jesus can do more than this. His encouragement comes from His intimate knowledge of the Father. His words are more than gentle advice. He knows something we don't know.

"If you would voyage Godward, you must see to it that the rudder of thought is right."

—W. J. Dawson

In Deed What Jesus knows is this: God feeds and clothes His children. No one who trusts in Him is abandoned by Him. They may go through hardship; they may even die. But never before He specifically allows it in His own timing. Never is their provision beyond His purview. While the pagan world takes provision as each individual's responsibility, Jesus says the initiative is God's.

Above our worries is an active Provider with a perfect sense of timing. He is in control, even when we aren't sure how tomorrow's needs will be met. When we run after provision we are running after the wrong thing, something that God has claimed as His domain. We are to run after His kingdom and righteousness. That's what we were made for.

First Things First

"Is not life more important than food, and the body more important than clothes?"

(Matthew 6:25)

"You can't get second things by putting them first. You can get second things only by putting first things first."

—C. S. Lewis

In Word If other people were to calculate how we spend our time, or the allocations in our checkbook, what would they say about our priorities? Would they say the kingdom of God is our priority? Would they say we truly know what life is about?

We are told not to worry about what we will eat or drink. Why do we have that tendency? And why would God turn our attention away from it? The answer to the first "why" is that we get our priorities mixed up. We spend all our time trying to sustain ourselves so that we might experience and enjoy life. But we never get around to experiencing and enjoying life, because we're spending all our time on sustaining it. Our priorities are wrong.

The answer to the second "why" is that God wants us to invest in what is valuable. In spite of all the obsessiveness about food in our culture, and in spite of all the billions spent on marketing the latest "look," these things are temporary. In the eternal scheme of things, food and clothes and other externals have no significance. They are not valuable. They only support what is valuable—life. We act as though the wrapping is more important than the gift. We don't recognize real value.

In Deed What are we to do with mixed-up priorities and misplaced values? Lay them aside. Look at what God does with His birds and His lilies. They spend all their lives just "being" for the glory of God. We spend all our lives just "doing," usually for the glory of ourselves. We need Jesus to come along and radically revise our conception of things. He takes our upside-down thinking here and turns it upright, the way God intended it. Let us measure our priorities with those God has for us.

The Mistrust of Anxiety

"Do not worry about your life." (Matthew 6:25)

In Word Words of encouragement from the Master are always welcome. The stresses of life come upon us and a brother or sister in Christ reminds us that He is in control. He is sovereign, He knows when the sparrow falls, He numbers the hairs on our heads, He clothes the lilies of the field. He says not to worry about our life, and we welcome the suggestion as an encouraging pat on the back.

But how often do we view this verse as a commandment from on high? It may not carry the force of a "Thou shalt not," and it may not have the emphasis of a "Go into all the world," but it is written as an imperative nonetheless. "Do not," Jesus says, and Paul echoes this injunction in Philippians: "Be anxious for nothing" (4:6). These are our liberating orders. We are told not to do something we hate doing anyway. Why?

"Anxiety does not empty tomorrow of its sorrows, but only empties today of its strength."

—Charles Spurgeon

In Deed Consider what our worry says of our opinion of God. When we stress and strain over a situation, are we affirming His providence and abundance? Are we embracing His grace? No, our anxiety reveals our mistrust of God's sovereignty; it is an emotional slander of His character. We may justify our worry by observing all of the tragedies in the world around us, knowing that such may befall us as well. Yet God promises His sovereignty even over these, as well as His presence with us in the midst of them.

Dare we suggest by our worry that some catastrophe may slip by without His notice? No, "tragedies" befell Joseph, Moses, David, Jesus, Paul, and others, and God ordained them all for good. All of these surely could have worried, examining their circumstances while going through them. But looking back, we see God's perfect plan unfolding. Therefore Jesus urges, even commands: Do not worry.

God's Pleasure in Persistence

"Because of the man's boldness he will get up and give him as much as he needs."

(Luke 11:8)

In Word "Blessed are the meek," Jesus tells us (Matthew 5:5). But there are some circumstances in which He calls for brashness. In this parable on persistence in Luke 11, a man seeks help from his neighbor on behalf of his friends, knocking repeatedly on the neighbor's door at midnight with an unusual request for bread. It was an unlikely and inconvenient time for such a request. But because of his perseverance, the neighbor answers.

A story in Luke 5:17-26 relates a similar persistence. Several men carried their crippled friend to Jesus on a stretcher, lowering it through the roof so that the Healer could not avoid seeing him. Like the man in the parable, they are tenacious—all of them are zealous for the welfare of their friends. Our Western sensibilities make us want to tell the stretcher-bearers to get in line, or to tell the man to quit pestering his neighbor at inappropriate hours.

"We are never more like Christ than in prayers of intercession."
—Austin Phelps

Jesus has no such rebuke for them. Their brazenness honors Him. This is how the Father is to be sought—with a clear knowledge that it is His nature to meet needs. If we are zealous to have others' needs met, certainly He is even more zealous.

In Deed How persistent are we in seeking God's help for the needs of others? When we are told to "bear one another's burdens" (Colossians 3:13), do we interpret that as a brief mention in a prayer meeting? Or are we zealous and bold in our approach to God? Far from offending God, this boldness pleases Him. In this parable, He almost begs His disciples to pester Him. Let us consider our zeal on behalf of our brothers and sisters in Christ. Does it equal the boldness of the persistent neighbor?

Witnesses of the Resurrection

"This is what is written: The Christ will suffer and rise from the dead on the third day, and repentance and forgiveness of sins will be preached in his name to all nations, beginning at Jerusalem. You are witnesses of these things."

(Luke 24:46-48)

In Word We have been entrusted with the greatest truth the world has ever known. The disciples were the first hearers of this incredible commission. At the apex of history, the Christ died and was raised—the age of resurrection had begun. The fulfillment of the sacrificial system had come, sins had been forgiven through Him, and the whole world was to be the audience of this story. It is an incomparable story; no man-made religion has ever come close to matching it. No others have claimed resurrection to back up their teaching. The disciples, as witnesses, were entrusted as guardians of this truth.

We, too, are witnesses of the resurrection. We haven't seen it in the same way the disciples did, but we have certainly witnessed it, if He lives within us by faith. And like them, we have been radically changed by this resurrection. No one who has encountered the risen Christ can remain the same; we are compelled by His Spirit within us—His relentlessly searching Spirit—to go and tell.

In Deed This mission has been handed down to us: Having been freed from a prison of shame and incomprehensible guilt, we have been told to walk right back into the courtroom where we were once convicted. As witnesses in the trial of this world, we are told to testify of what we've seen. There is no hope for these defendants other than this evidence of Christ's death, resurrection, and forgiveness of sins—just as there was once no hope for us. The charge against this world is sin, and we know of evidence that changed everything for us. That's the truth we're called to tell.

"The Spirit of Christ is the spirit of missions, and the nearer we get to Him the more intensely missionary we must become."

—Henry Martyn

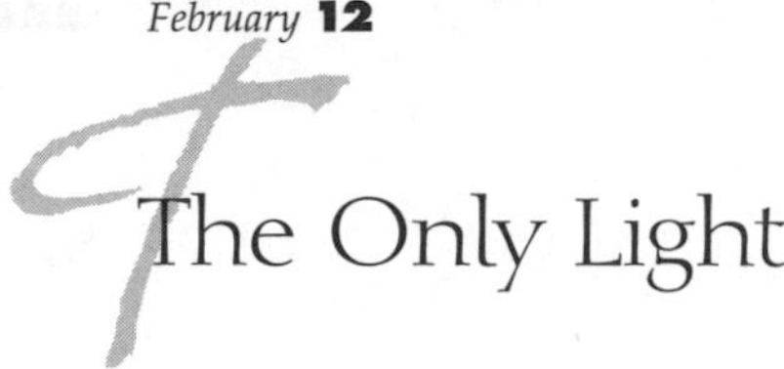

The Only Light

"I am the light of the world." (John 8:12)

In Word How the world wants to change this claim of Jesus! One little word would satisfy all of the religious pluralists in our culture. If only Jesus had said "I am *a* light of the world," few would disagree. We live in an age when people like to grab a little light from here, a little from there, and even a little from Jesus Himself. For most, He is one source of illumination among many.

Adherents of most of the world's religions have a remarkable admiration for Jesus, as long as He is *a* light. As soon as we remind a nonbeliever that His claim is far more exclusive—He is *the* light—we are accused of arrogance and intolerance, as though we were the ones who put those words in Jesus' mouth. No, these are His words, not ours. The claim is His, and whoever has an argument with this exclusivity has an argument with Him.

"When God spoke to humanity in Jesus, He said the last thing He has to say."

—G. Campbell Morgan

In Deed Do we ourselves heed these words? Aren't we also sometimes guilty of seeking illumination from other sources? A little secular philosophy and psychology here, a little humanism and spiritism there? Or, perhaps a little closer to home, what about the editorials and advice columns in the morning paper? Or the mind and body experts? Does it all measure up to Christ?

Surely there is truth in some of mankind's research and findings, we would counter, and we are probably right; many have discovered some elements of truth, even apart from Christ. But it must all be measured by Him. Only He may validate for us what is—and is not—light and truth. Ask yourself this: Is Jesus my only source of light? Does my view of His exclusivity measure up to His claim?

The Mystery of Discipleship

"No one pours new wine into old wineskins."

(Mark 2:22

In Word We are too familiar with the context of this saying. We know that Jesus is the new wine. And we know that the Pharisees' legalistic belief system is the old wineskin that will not contain Jesus. But do we take the time to ponder which of our own wineskins have attempted to accommodate Jesus and failed?

The life of a disciple may be rigorous, but it is never rigid. Jesus is too inscrutable for that. "The wind blows wherever it pleases" (John 3:8). This is the uncertain way of discipleship; to be convinced of this, one must only observe how often the disciples lapsed into confusion as they followed the Savior. They had expectations that He frequently defied.

On what points are we rigid? Where do our expectations lie? Do we insist that Jesus bring about our own vision for the future? Do we try to constrain Him to our church structures? Do we rely on a methodology in our ministry? The structures, the vision, the methodology may be good, but Jesus will not fit. He defies constraint. The Lion of Judah cannot be tamed.

"We know God easily, if we do not constrain ourselves to define Him."

—Joseph Joubert

In Deed How then may we know Him? This is exactly the point. He refuses to be known in a method, system, or structure—even good ones—because He wants a relationship. We do not know our spouses, children, parents, siblings, or fellow believers by our formulas—we know them as they relate to us. Neither do we know Jesus by our formulas. We may plan for our future, systematize our theology, and program our ministries, but Jesus will often stretch us in other directions. Though we can certainly expect Him to be constant, we cannot expect Him to be predictable. Our wineskins, no matter how reliable, are not part of our discipleship gear. Disciples must always accommodate new wine.

A Friend in Sorrow

"I tell you the truth, one of you is going to betray me." (John 13:21)

In Word As John, "the disciple whom Jesus loved," reclined against Jesus at the Last Supper, he surely felt the comfort and joy that not only accompanies a close human relationship but that comes only from knowing divine companionship. Perhaps the other disciples, while enjoying the company of Jesus, envied John's closeness with Him. We, too, long to recline at the table with Jesus. We crave that familiarity. So we draw near to Him, and pray that He draws near to us. And what do we expect to find? Like John, do we hope to feel the comfort and joy of this human yet divine companionship? We are right to think so. But there is more. Piercing the moment is this sorrowful revelation: "One of you is going to betray me."

Divine intimacies bring not only joy but sorrow. Do we want fellowship with Christ? We may have it, but with all of its magnificent rewards comes a cost—partaking in His sufferings. Paul knew it, too. He wanted to know not only the power of the resurrection but also "the fellowship of sharing in his sufferings, becoming like him in his death" (Philippians 3:10).

"A Christian is someone who shares the sufferings of God in the world."

—Dietrich Bonhoeffer

In Deed If we are to reach any depth of maturity in Christ, we must know that He and this world do not mix. There is enmity between them. We tend to avoid pain at all costs, but we are unrealistic and deny His call when we expect to know Him without knowing the grief of His rejection. When we recline and dine with Christ, we are choosing the magnificence of His incomparable glory. But, like John, we are close enough to know His pain. As He warns us, "In this world you will have trouble. But take heart! I have overcome the world" (John 16:33).

Judge Not

"Whoever believes in him is not condemned."

(John 3:18)

In Word One of the hardest truths for Christians to grasp is that we who believe in Him are not condemned. We generally have no trouble telling an unbeliever this wonderful truth. Our difficulty most often comes in applying it to fellow believers. How prone we are to notice others' sins, and even to hold those sins against them! The grace we proclaim to the world is unconditional, just as God has said. But the grace we proclaim to Christian brothers and sisters seems awfully conditional sometimes, depending on how well they embody biblical truth as we see it.

We actually enjoy hearing the testimonies of those who lived in gross rebellion, only to encounter Christ and be radically transformed. Praise God for those testimonies! They are trophies of God's grace, and we are right to rejoice in their radical conversions. But we often shun those who struggle with sin *after* professing Christ, as though sanctification is an instantaneous event. We forget that grace is ongoing. Sin is so deeply embedded in us that the vestiges of it will be manifested frequently for the rest of our lives. Or, as is often said, we all walk with a limp.

"Grace is what the New Testament is all about."

—J. I. Packer

In Deed The good news of the Gospel is simply this—there is no condemnation for those who are in Christ. Our sins were buried with Him long ago. This is a wonderful truth we claim for ourselves; do we apply it to others? We are often like hospital patients in post-op, pointing out each other's scars. Or members of a recovery group who see everyone's dysfunction but our own. Have we forgotten? We are all dysfunctional, though recovering; all scarred, but healed; all buried, but raised up. No sins are held against us in this resurrection. Any other "gospel" is not good news. Ask God to give you a ministry of grace.

Truly Good News

"Whoever believes in him is not condemned." (John 3:18)

In Word Christians have earned a reputation for condemning others. Some of this is simply that we stand up for what is right and proclaim what the Bible says about sin. We enter political and social discourse on the volatile issues of abortion, euthanasia, morality of public figures, bioethics, and the secularization of public education, among others. We stand against what we know to be evil in this world. And we should.

But some of our reputation is warranted. We often wrap up within our proclamation of truth an indictment of those who don't live up to it. We condemn those who do evil, even though we know that with hearts full of human nature and not of Christ, they can do nothing else. Jesus never asked us to condemn. His Gospel is profoundly simple. "God did not send his Son into the world to condemn the world, but to save the world through him. Whoever believes in him is not condemned" (John 3:17-18). If He did not come to condemn, and we are called to be like Him, why do we condemn?

"Cry the Gospel with your whole life."

—Charles de Foucauld

In Deed Again we must ask ourselves: Does our mission match the message of Jesus? In proclaiming the Gospel to the world, are we like Him at all? Are we hard on self-righteousness but merciful toward sinners? If not, we are not like Him. And if we are not like Him, we must question how much we have let His words and His life saturate our minds. In trying to do the work of the Holy Spirit by convicting the world of sin, we may be demonstrating mistrust that God will do as He said. It is His responsibility to convict of sin. The *only* Gospel Jesus sends us into the world to preach is truly good news: forgiveness of sins by the abundant grace of God to all who believe.

Jesus the Liberator

"He has sent me to proclaim freedom for the prisoners." (Luke 4:18)

In Word Jesus the freedom fighter. The liberator. The defender of all who are oppressed. The image conjures up a khaki-clothed Marxist in a third-world jungle. This Jesus has, in fact, been adopted by some freedom movements around the world, but it isn't a portrayal the evangelical church normally embraces.

But let's reconsider that. Take the image of this freedom fighter out of a socio-political context and define oppression as the spiritual enslavement that it truly is, and we may be on to something. The oppressive government of the ruler of this age (2 Corinthians 4:4) reaches into suburban neighborhoods as much as slums; into downtown office suites as much as jungle outposts; into education and religion as much as politics and economics. And we need liberating. Whether we are the diseased or the doctors, beggars or barons, ignorant or educated, we are prisoners in a fallen kingdom.

"Sin is a power in our life: Let us fairly understand that it can only be met by another power."
—Henry Drummond

In Deed This is extremely relevant for the average Christian. We know we have been freed from the penalty of sin, but how often we feel enslaved by it! We know we have eternal life, but how often we feel imprisoned in a body of death! We can easily feel trapped in mundane, uneventful lives. We are so frequently stuffed back into our shackles that the excitement of our freedom seems a distant memory.

Focus today on Christ as Deliverer. Think of what robs your joy in Christ and makes you feel imprisoned. Know that whatever it is—whether it is within your heart or some external constraint—Christ is victor over it. Consider how an imprisoned Paul and Silas sang joyful hymns to God and how a dying Stephen saw heaven opened. None were bound by their surroundings. What binds you? Circumstances? Discouragement? Sin? Ask God to reopen your eyes to Jesus the Liberator.

Jesus and Our Need

"But what about you?...Who do you say I am?"

(Mark 8:29)

In Word We have heard the common answers to this question—good teacher, moral leader, tragic hero, well-intentioned martyr, etc.—and most of us have found them to be insufficient. He is the Messiah, the Christ, the Son of the living God. As a matter of the witness of Scripture and the faith we hold dear, we know this to be true. Many of us have even boldly proclaimed it to others.

But we must ask ourselves this very question. Who do we say He is? Perhaps an even better question would be this: Who do we really—deep in our hearts—believe He is? We must go beyond the pew and the pulpit and into our living rooms and offices for the answer. We must wonder if this is true for us on Wednesdays just as it is on Sundays. We must come down from the mountaintops and answer from the valleys. Why? Because regardless of how long we have been Christians, this answer must be more than theology in our heads; it must be the truth that grips our hearts.

"I have a great need for Christ; I have a great Christ for my need."

–Charles Spurgeon

In Deed When your situation is dire—a relationship has broken, finances are looking impossibly bleak, a disease is pronounced incurable, or tragedy strikes a loved one—who is He? Is He a theological tenet or really *your* Savior, *your* Provider, *your* Healer and Friend? When you are tempted beyond your strength—immoral desires are running rampant, an ethical compromise would seem so easy, or you are pressured to conform to the world's expectations—who is He? An ancient biblical character or *your* Righteousness, *your* Strength and *your* Refuge?

Know Him in your innermost being. Jesus doesn't help us much as the center of our theology; He helps us as the center of our lives.

Saying and Doing

"Why do you call me, 'Lord, Lord,' and do not do what I say?" (Luke 6:46)

In Word It is a penetrating question. The Lord of all creation has put His finger on the inconsistency that invades all of our hearts. There is always a discrepancy between what we say and what we really believe. For some of us, it is a slight discrepancy; for others it is vast. For all of us, "Lord" has not always meant what it should.

God has a way of testing His lordship in our lives. Just ask Abraham; the excruciating walk up the mountain of Moriah for the sacrifice of his only son, Isaac, was the ultimate test of lordship. Like us, Abraham had known what it was like earlier in his life to mistrust God. This time he passed the test.

Jonah failed his test. Though God exercised His lordship anyway, Jonah was less than cooperative. He had limits to God's rule in his life, places where he would draw the line on God's authority. He maintained a little autonomy, holding on to some illusion that he had the right to govern himself. God's people don't have that right, nor should we even want it. (It's a huge burden to try to govern ourselves when we have so little information about our true selves and our future directions.) But, like us, Jonah wanted a measure of independence. He wanted the privilege of being God's own possession without the responsibility it entails.

"The best measure of a spiritual life is not its ecstasies but its obedience."

—Oswald Chambers

In Deed What would Jesus say about His lordship in your life? Have you set limits on His authority in your affairs? If you have determined aspects of your future by saying, "I would never do that," or "I would never go there," then you have placed limits on God. Expect Him to test them. He will always try to stretch you out of your assumption that you are in control of your life.

It is good to have direction. It is not good to have self-direction that dictates where you will allow God to place you or what He will have you do. Discern the difference. Don't just call Him "Lord." Make sure you do what He says.

An Uncomfortable Lordship

"Why do you call me 'Lord, Lord,' and do not do what I say?" (Luke 6:46)

In Word How often we try to affirm the lordship of Christ with as little discomfort as possible! Even nonbelievers have noticed a curious phenomenon: Many Christians make very little effort to actually apply the teachings of Jesus to their lives. We ask Him to save us but may not expect Him to transform us. We call Him "Lord" but just *know* He wouldn't challenge our innermost being. We find exceptions to almost all of His commands. "Go into all the world" (Mark 16:15). But not *there,* we assume. "Love your enemies" (Matthew 5:44). But not *him,* we suppose. "Any of you who does not give up everything he has cannot be my disciple" (Luke 14:33). But surely not really *everything.*

We forget that the nature of God in Christ is radically contrary to the nature of man in Adam. If it were not so, we could have adapted to the holiness of God and saved ourselves. But we could not; it was not in our nature to do so. And it is not in our nature to conform to the lordship of Christ. His authority often does violence to the self we've cultivated.

"The beginning of self-mastery is to be mastered by Christ."
–D. G. Kehl

In Deed Let's not misunderstand—His lordship isn't another external law placed upon our unwilling hearts. He gets inside us. He transforms us from within. His work may be uncomfortable, but there is an overcoming—and loving—power in it.

So what is the answer to His question? Why do we call Him "Lord" and do not do what He says? Perhaps we do not know how thoroughly He plans to change us. Perhaps we do not ask Him to change us from within. Or maybe we have asked but don't really believe He can overcome our obstinacy. We know ourselves too well, and Him not enough.

Understand, ask, and believe. Change is the heart of His Gospel.

A Blessed Conformity

"Love your enemies, do good to those who hate you, bless those who curse you, pray for those who mistreat you." (Luke 6:27-28)

In Word We are tempted to conform to this world in our relationships with others perhaps more than in any other arena of life. We feel compelled to respond to others as they have dealt with us. When we have been cursed, we curse back—or at least let ourselves feel resentment about the insult. When we have been mistreated, we cultivate a bitterness about the experience. And Jesus *never* says that these are not genuine or legitimate feelings. Nowhere does the Savior say, "No, you haven't been slighted as you thought; you haven't actually been mistreated, it only feels that way."

No, Jesus gives no attention to whether our feelings are legitimate. That is not the point. Our feelings may be entirely accurate. What Jesus calls for, instead, is absolutely counterintuitive to the human experience: a rejection of our resentments and bitterness, no matter how appropriate they are. We are to love even when love grates against our souls. While we hope for the downfall of our enemies, Jesus actually expects us to pray for blessings to rain down upon them. Why?

In Deed The Bible says we were once enemies of God (Romans 5:10; Colossians 1:21). And His response was to rain blessings upon us—the gift of salvation. Did this give us victory over God? Did it make us haughty? Quite the contrary. God's blessing, in spite of our enmity with Him, subdued us. It made us humble. Neither will our blessing of our enemies give them the victory we think it will. Rather, it will demonstrate the grace of God. And we will be one step closer to being like Him.

"Never cease loving a person, and never give up hope for him, for even the Prodigal Son who had fallen most low could still be saved."

—Søren Kierkegaard

Waiting on God

"Do not leave Jerusalem, but wait for the gift my Father promised." (Acts 1:4)

"You will be my witnesses . . . to the ends of the earth." (Acts 1:8)

In Word At times, being a disciple is confusing. Jesus may tell us on one occasion not to take with us a purse or bag (Luke 10:4), and on another occasion to take a purse and a bag (Luke 22:36). We are told that we cannot find our life without losing it, and we cannot become great without being a servant. The Gospel abounds with paradoxes and context-specific instructions.

Here the disciples are told to stay in Jerusalem—and also that they will be His witnesses to the ends of the earth. What should they make of this ambiguity? They are looking for the kingdom of God, even willing to march into service; they are looking for guidance. And Jesus gives them virtually no information to go on. "Wait." "It is not for you to know." All they are told is to see what God does.

"A holy, joyful expectancy is of the very essence of true waiting."

–Andrew Murray

In Deed Often we look for God's direction in a matter—a career choice, a business decision, or maybe a relationship issue. We are willing to act. We'll do whatever He says. We just need to know what it is. We don't hear from Him, and then we grow impatient. And just when it seems that God has left us in a state of perpetual ambiguity, He acts. We were to wait and watch, because, like the disciples, we were yet unequipped.

Waiting is perhaps the most difficult aspect of a believer's relationship with God. Our culture emphasizes speed, efficiency, and instant gratification. We pray and then wonder at God's "silence" when His response isn't immediate. We forget the stories of Joseph, Moses, and many others who spent years in preparation for God's timing.

When we find ourselves impatient and directionless, we must remember that all of His work is done on His initiative and that He takes time to prepare us for it. Like the disciples, we are to wait and watch.

Blessed Like a Child

"And he took the children in his arms, put his hands on them and blessed them." (Mark 10:16)

In Word What is the blessing of God? It would take volumes to explore His manifold blessings. But Jesus gives us some hints as to the shape they take and who may receive them.

Is God's blessing spiritual? Absolutely. There is a whole set of beatitudes that spell out our blessing in Matthew 5 and Luke 6. It begins with the character God works into us, continues with Him using us to bless others, and ends with knowing Him and inheriting His kingdom. Hardship is involved, but the blessing is infinitely greater because the chief blessing is Himself.

Is it *only* spiritual? Absolutely not. Material wealth is not a blanket promise in the Bible, but the comfort of knowing we will be provided for is assured. The earth and all that is in it belongs to the Lord. He bestows blessing on His children from His wealth. And there's more. God's blessing is psychological, emotional, relational, and physical. And eternal. It covers every area of our lives where our lives really have substance. It is *His* definition of blessing—fuller, deeper, and longer than the temporal expectations we often pursue.

"Never undertake anything for which you wouldn't have the courage to ask the blessings of heaven."

—George C. Lichtenberg

In Deed Who receives blessing in the Gospels? Those who are poor in spirit, meek, merciful, and persecuted (Matthew 5). Those who invite the poor and the lame to their banquets (Luke 14:13). Children (Mark 10:16). Those who hear the Word of God and obey it (Luke 11:28). Those who do not fall away (Luke 7:23). Those who are invited to the wedding supper of the Lamb (Revelation 19:9). In short, those who trust God and who grow to be like Him. And most of all, those who, like a child, receive His mercies in *whatever* form He wants to give them.

Truly Lord

"You call me 'Teacher' and 'Lord,' and rightly so, for that is what I am." (John 13:13)

In Word All religious systems can attest to a curious phenomenon: Many "believers" make little effort to live up to their beliefs. There are "Buddhists" who do not follow the teachings of Buddha, "Muslims" who do not follow the teachings of the Koran, and "Hindus" who do not practice Hinduism, among numerous other examples. This is not a rarity; it is widespread in every faith—even ours. There is very often a wide gap between what a Christian says he or she believes and what he or she actually practices.

"Jesus Christ will be Lord of all or He will not be Lord at all."

—St. Augustine of Hippo

Jesus was well aware of this human tendency. He once asked His disciples: "Why do you call me, 'Lord, Lord,' and do not do what I say?" (Luke 6:46). Here in John 13, His implication is clear: If the disciples are genuine in their belief, they will follow His example.

All of us have inconsistencies in our faith. But how numerous those inconsistencies can be! We who claim the name of Jesus often do not serve as He served, heal as He healed, forgive as He forgave, pray as He prayed, or sacrifice as He sacrificed. He emphatically tells us to believe, love, and watch for His coming again; but we can be awfully casual about these commands. He has called all who follow Him to a radical lifestyle; but how many Christians do you know who are radically different from their culture?

In Deed It is folly to call Jesus "Teacher," "Lord," or any other title that presumes His authority, and then to be casual about His authority in our lives. But such folly is so consistent with human nature. We can be fickle and apathetic. We convince ourselves that we believe something, even while our actions demonstrate otherwise.

Examine the relationship between your faith and your way of life. Are they consistent? Are Jesus' radical words your driving force? Let them shape you, no matter the cost. Let Him truly be your Lord.

Our Mercy

"I have not come to call the righteous, but sinners."

(Matthew 9:13)

In Word As we learn the mind of God, we must conform to it. It is one thing to understand and appreciate God's revelation of Himself. It is quite another to know that He expects us to become like Him. When we learn of God with this in mind, we are dumbfounded. How can we have such character? How can we even approach such perfection? We have the promise of Christ that He will come to live within us. He will do this conforming work Himself. All He asks of us is our cooperation.

So what may we expect of Him? If He is extravagantly merciful, so must we be. If He prefers the company of those who know their sinfulness over the company of those who don't, so must we. If He dines with the unlovable, He will put it within us to do likewise.

"We cannot help conforming ourselves to what we love."

—Francis de Sales

In Deed This God showed up on our planet in the form of a merciful Savior. He offers grace without rebuke to those who know they need it. His rebukes are saved for those who won't acknowledge their need. He is purity that pursues the corrupt; mercy that hounds the needy; grace that demands only belief.

"And we, who with unveiled faces all reflect the Lord's glory, are being transformed into his likeness with ever-increasing glory"(2 Corinthians 3:18). Let us meditate on how well the Savior's character is becoming a part of our lives. As we are conformed to His image, we should see in ourselves the characteristics that He displayed. We should sit at the table with "tax collectors and sinners" with their need for healing in mind.

Are we like Him? Do we have extravagant mercy? When people describe us, does their description reflect in some small way His winsome call? "I am here for sinners."

Sharing Mercy

"I have not come to call the righteous, but sinners."
(Matthew 9:13)

"Mercy imitates God and disappoints Satan."
—John Chrysostom

In Word How much like our Master are we in this regard? Are we more zealous for our reputation than we are for His lost sheep? With whom do we fellowship? If we placed ourselves at this dinner at Matthew's house, would we be more likely to react like the Pharisees or like the Savior? Our answer to these questions tells us whether or not we have forgotten where we came from.

Jesus ate with tax collectors—traitors to Jews, treacherous money-grubbing extortionists. He also mingled with prostitutes and other unsavory characters, so much so that He was accused of gluttony and drunkenness. Why would the Messiah allow His reputation to be so tarnished? Because the Gospel was meant for such as these.

Is it meant for us, too? What about those of us who claim no such degradation in our past? It's there. It may be buried deep within us, and we may have covered it well, but if we don't know it's in there we're likely to become like the Pharisees at Matthew's table. We've forgotten that it was once just as offensive for Jesus to dine with us.

In Deed Anyone who is appalled at the depravity of someone else doesn't understand the Gospel. In order to understand the Gospel, we must begin by knowing that we are all children of Adam, and as such, are partakers in the rebellion common to man. That this rebellion manifests itself in one person as murder and in another as a selfish fib is no matter—it all comes from the same seed. Some sinners are more whitewashed than others, but rebellion is at the core of us all. Knowing this does not leave room for the mind of a Pharisee—it casts us on our faces, grateful for His mercy. Know this Gospel of mercy, savor it, never forget it. And welcome others into it.

Whom God Uses

"I have not come to call the righteous, but sinners."

(Matthew 9:13)

In Word It's quite an intimidating list, if you think about it.

- Abraham the man of faith
- Moses the lawgiver
- David, a man after God's own heart
- Elijah the prophet
- Peter the rock
- Paul the evangelist

Heroes of our faith. God's anointed. Role models we can never live up to. Or so we think. It is profoundly encouraging that the great examples of faith and godliness in the Bible are not really the superhuman spiritual giants we've traditionally made them to be. If they were, few of us would be eligible for God's service. We just can't relate to their spiritual stature.

"Grace is love that cares and stoops and rescues."

—John R. W. Stott

Let's take another look at that list.

- Abraham the liar (Genesis 12:13) and the impatient one (Genesis 16:2)
- Moses the murderer (Exodus 2:12)
- David the adulterer (2 Samuel 11:2-5)
- Elijah, prone to despair and suicide (1 Kings 19:3-4)
- Peter the denier (Matthew 26:69-75)
- Paul the persecutor (Acts 8:3)

And the list goes on: Jonah the disobedient complainer, Matthew the tax collector, Rahab the prostitute, Jacob the deceiver and many, many more. What churches or ministries today would accept them for service? God did. Not only did He use them in His service, He showcases them in His Word. They are trophies of His grace.

In Deed So are we. Who can claim to be beyond His grace? Even more, who can claim to be beyond His service? God delights in overcoming our flaws, in showing His power through our weakness. Rejoice in the encouragement of God, who gave us in His Word examples of faith who were as human as we are. And know this—that if His call was meant for such as these, it is meant for us.

Blessed for a Purpose

"Return home and tell how much God has done for you." (Luke 8:39)

In Word Why has God been good to us? Because He loves us? Of course this is true. But there is more. He has been good to us because He loves others, too. He wants us to tell of His goodness. His mercy has been given that we might speak of His mercy; His patience that we might speak of His patience; His blessings that we might tell others that He is a God who blesses. All of His goodness toward us is for us, yes, but also for others. It is for the reputation and glory of His name.

This is not new—it is how He has made His name known from the beginning. "I will bless those who bless you . . . and all peoples on earth will be blessed through you" (Genesis 12:3). "You sent miraculous signs and wonders against Pharaoh . . . You made a name for yourself, which remains to this day" (Nehemiah 9:10). This is our story, too. God has been good to us not for our glory, but for His.

"The Gospel is not a secret to be hoarded but a story to be heralded."

—Vance Havner

In Deed Pledge to tell others what the Lord has done for you. Learn to say, "Let me tell you about God's patience. He is so patient that He __________," and fill in the blank with a story of how He has dealt with you. Learn to say, "God is so merciful that He ________," and tell someone of His mercy toward you.

This may seem difficult because it will require honesty and transparency on our part. The Gerasene from this text must say he is an ex-demoniac when he tells the story. We may have to confess why we needed mercy, or why God had to be patient with us. This often doesn't reflect well on us. But it *does* reflect well on Him, and His glory—not ours—is the ultimate purpose of all creation.

Give Him glory. Tell what He has done for you.

Toward Transparency

"There is nothing concealed that will not be disclosed."

(Luke 12:2)

"Friends, if we be honest with ourselves, we shall be honest with each other."

—George MacDonald

In Word Most of us have a well-cultivated private side. There are things we don't want others to know about us. Some of those things would perhaps reflect badly on us; others are simply personal and private. While some people are more open than others, none of us is a completely open book.

Or are we? The book may be closed now, but it will eventually be opened. God already sees all. He sees into our hearts even more clearly than we do. The private things we think as we're lying down to sleep at night are not hidden from Him; He even knows the motives and causes behind them. And one day, all sin will be exposed. That's frightening.

We can take comfort in the fact that Colossians says our lives are hidden with Christ in God (3:3). Sin that has been cleansed by the blood of Jesus is cleansed indeed, removed from the mind of God farther than the east is from the west. Still, Jesus' point is sobering: No hypocrisy known to man will be concealed. All will be exposed.

This is a problem for minds well-trained by our culture. We've been taught to think that our personal behavior is . . . well, personal. "As long as it's not harming anyone . . . ," right? We've heard it far too often. But sin always has corporate ramifications. It affects our society, and for Christians, it affects the body of Christ. It is inconceivable that one part of the body would be so painfully infected while others are untouched. No, when the body is revealed, so will all its members—and its diseases—be revealed

In Deed Jesus speaks of hypocrisy more harshly than any other sin. The cost of hiding our secrets is higher than the cost of confessing them. The question we must all ask ourselves is this: How honestly are we living within the body of Christ. Are we really genuine with others? We might as well be transparent now; one day, whether we like it or not, we will be.

The Paramount Plan

"How then would the Scriptures be fulfilled that say it must happen in this way?" (Matthew 26:54)

In Word In the garden, Jesus has been praying with deep sorrow and an overwhelmed spirit. He knows what He faces the next day—torture and death. Ridicule and shame. The sins of the world on His human shoulders. If ever there was a time to be self-absorbed, this was it.

At His moment of crisis, when the betrayer and the mob walked up to Him with treachery in their hearts, Jesus thought first of the Scriptures being fulfilled. Forget personal consequences. The Word was at stake. It absolutely *must* happen this way. The incarnate Word and the written Word must not conflict. The promise of God is more important—and more real—than any personal threat.

"The whole science of the saints consists in finding out and following God's will."

—Isidore of Seville

How was Jesus able to say such a thing at a moment of such danger? He had prayed. Not just that night in the garden, but also for extended periods throughout His ministry and His younger life. The will of God was no guessing game for Him. He was reluctant because of the pain, but He was not uncertain. His fellowship with the Father led Him in exactly the ordained way—even when it hurt.

How can we say such a thing in our moments of crisis? Only by having already been immersed in the ways of God through prayer, the Word, and our faith. Only by having extended periods of time seeking God's will regardless of its cost to ourselves. No self-centered mind can arrive at that point; it's only for a God-saturated life.

In Deed What is your priority in your moment of crisis? Is it that God's will be fulfilled? Is it that the promises be proved and the plan lived out? Or is it safety, convenience, expedience, ambition, or comfort? We have a multitude of voices distracting us from the hard way of God's Word; and only one keeping us there. But it's the essential voice. It's the same one Jesus heard in the garden that night, and it never leads us astray.

Be Prepared

"Keep watch, because you do not know the day or the hour." (Matthew 25:13)

In Word The parable of the virgins is one of three Jesus gives us in Matthew 25 about His second coming. That glorious event cannot be described in words, nor can our reaction to it. The best He can give us is pictures. This one is about ten bridesmaids who waited a very long time for their bridegroom to come. Five were prepared for such a long wait, five were not. Those who were prepared are called wise; those who were not are called fools.

"Heaven is a prepared place for a prepared people."

—Lewis Sperry Chafer

There is no hint in Jesus' story that the Bridegroom will say to those who were not prepared: "I know it was a long time, and I know you gave it a good shot. Your love for me is all I could ask; you just miscalculated the timing. Enter into the wedding banquet." No, Jesus gives surprisingly little grace to those who were willing to be brides, but were half-hearted about their preparation. The truth behind this parable is sobering: True love does not come unprepared. It does not calculate timing in case a back-up plan is necessary; it does not give up and go home; it does not come with a set of expectations. It stakes everything on its object and waits until He comes, even if He comes at midnight. It says, "This isn't my best option, it's my *only* option." True love waits.

In Deed Many Christians are half-hearted about the Bridegroom's return. Jesus' words to them are frightening: "I don't know you" (v. 12). Those who really love Him don't know the day or the hour any better than those who do not. They *do* know, however, that the day or hour doesn't matter to them. All that matters is that He is coming. As long as it takes, they will be waiting. However late the hour, they will be prepared. This blessed event means *everything* to them.

What does Jesus' return mean to you? Does it impact your activities today? Consider the question carefully. And consider the wonderful union you will have if you are ready and waiting when He comes.

Be Trustworthy

"You should have put my money on deposit with the bankers, so that when I returned I would have received it back with interest." (Matthew 25:27)

In Word What do you do with the things God has given you? Thank Him for them? That's a good start. But there is more. The parable of the talents gives us clear evidence of what God expects from us. Whatever He has given us, we are to do something with it. If He's given us much, we are to do much. If He's given us little, we are to do at least something. If He's given us nothing . . . well, that just does not apply. In spite of the feeling of many that God has not really blessed them at all, He has. There is always something from His hand that He has trusted us to steward properly.

The gifts of God are not given for us to hoard. They are not even given for us to save wisely. They are given for us to invest. There will always be some risk of loss involved, and there will always be some loss of ownership on our part. But the alternative is for us to take what God has given—time, talents, skills, money, property, relationships, and more—and do absolutely nothing lasting with them. This grieves God and it shames us. Temporal blessings are *always* to be invested in some eternal profit. That's what kingdom resources are all about. If we find ourselves lacking in them, we've probably failed to use them for lasting purposes. We would have been given more according to our investments. Our urge to "stock up" can cost us everything.

"God will not merely judge us on the basis of what we gave, but also on the basis of what we did with what we kept."

—Erwin Lutzer

In Deed Do you see the difference between saving and investing? Saving preserves; investing multiplies. God is interested in multiplying. Since He owns everything already, He is not interested in our preserving what we have. He is interested in our using it for better purposes. We are to invest, to multiply, to see the kingdom expand—even at great risk to ourselves. The Master will return for an accounting. What will you do with His resources today?

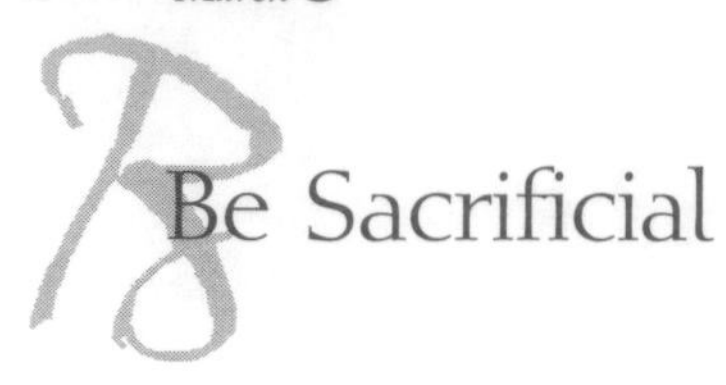

Be Sacrificial

"Whatever you did for one of the least of these brothers of mine, you did for me." (Matthew 25:40)

In Word The third picture of the Second Coming in Matthew 25 is perhaps the best known. It has been used to urge us to ministries of mercy for all who are in need around the world. Some scholars say it commands us to care for the "brothers" of Jesus—the Jews—during the tribulation. Others say that faith during the tribulation will be defined as taking care of a different set of "brothers" of Jesus—suffering believers. Still others say that the parable commands all Christians everywhere to care for the needs of a needy world.

Whatever the interpretation, the Lord who blesses those who give a cup of cold water in His name means for us to care deeply about those who suffer. As the lead Sufferer, He takes it personally when we don't. James says pure religion is looking after "orphans and widows in their distress" (James 1:27). John says that if anyone has material possessions, sees a brother in need, and does nothing, he does not have the love of God in him (1 John 3:17). The God of healing, deliverance, and providence cannot be any more clear: Those who are not deeply concerned for those who suffer are not like Him at all. The return of Jesus will expose us. We either care for people in His name or we don't. The difference from this side of eternity is noticeable. The difference on the other side is just staggering.

"To go to people and say 'Jesus loves you!' and yet do nothing to help change their circumstances is not a complete message."
—John Wimber

In Deed We live in an age of global communication. There is therefore no escape clause for us in 1 John 3:17; we always are able to see a brother in need. The question for us, once we've seen the desperation of this world, is whether we will be like God or not. Will we recognize that suffering grieves the heart of the Rescuer God? Will we let the Savior save through us? Will the body of Christ reflect the mind of Christ? We will have to answer these things at His coming. How will you answer them today?

Eternal Perspective

"Those eighteen who died when the tower in Siloam fell on them—do you think they were more guilty than all the others living in Jerusalem? I tell you, no! But unless you repent, you too will all perish."

(Luke 13:4-5)

"We have all eternity to celebrate our victories, but only one short hour before sunset in which to win them."

—Robert Moffatt

In Word In this world, towers fall. People die. Survivors mourn. And we all think about the coming day we slip away from this visible world to whatever lies beyond. As Christians, we know what lies beyond; it is the secular world that panics at the thought. Yet even we are shocked when this world is rocked.

The current events of Jesus' day were no less alarming. Pilate killed some Galileans as they worshiped (v. 1). A disastrous collapse of a tower killed 18 residents of Jerusalem (v. 4). And Jesus' spin on the headlines of the day was, in effect, to say this: "Everyone will die, whether 'prematurely' or from old age. Have you prepared for that by repenting?"

Jesus points to the real issue—the eternal tragedy that many die without acknowledging their need for the Savior. This eternal tragedy far outstrips anything this world can dish out. The number of the dead is higher than in our disasters—billions, not thousands; and the consequences are infinitely more profound—not just a funeral service but eternal isolation from God and true life. There is no resurrection, no rebuilding, no reprieve in an eternity without Christ. It is forever.

In Deed We need to view life and death—and our neighbors—with an eternal perspective. We must understand that physical death separates us from those we love for a short time, but death without Christ separates those we love from the presence of God forever. May a passion for God and an awareness of eternal realities compel us to live and to preach the Gospel. Speak about it to someone today.

Be Ready

"Be dressed ready for service and keep your lamps burning." (Luke 12:35)

In Word We are told at nearly every turn that we are products of our past. Our biological makeup and much of our personalities result from the genetic material of our ancestors. Our decisions, our flaws, and our preferences are the result of our childhood and our social environments. Everything we are, according to the psychologists and the geneticists, comes from a previous condition.

No, says Jesus. Our behavior today is to be based on our future. Our new nature has come from Him, we are being conformed to His likeness, and our deeds today are to be determined by the fact that He is coming again. We are products of a coming kingdom, not a conditioning past.

"We are not a post-war generation but a pre-peace generation. Jesus is coming."
—Corrie ten Boom

Jesus tells His disciples to be ready at all times, like servants prepared for a returning master. We are to be dressed like servants, clothed in the garments He has given us. Even in the dark hours, when we see unclearly and grow discouraged, we are to keep our lamps burning. We should not grow despondent if He delays. We are to serve in His household while He is away, keeping our eyes open to see Him when He returns.

In Deed Are we ready for His return? If we are living according to our past, which is based on a corrupt inheritance, we are not. But if we are living according to our future as fellow heirs with Christ and sons of the living God, then we can know that we are ready.

Let your future guide your present. Remember who you are in Christ. Remember who He promises you will be for all eternity. Base your actions today on the fact that you are being conformed to His image and when you see Him you will be like Him (1 John 3:2). Don't let the past define you. Know that He is coming again and your future will be fulfilled. And be ready.

Be Wise

"Who then is the faithful and wise manager?"

(Luke 12:42)

In Word Jesus is coming again. He said so repeatedly, and His followers throughout history have believed it. But 2000 years after He said He would come, He still tarries. And how we live today reflects what we think about that.

Many Christians believe that Jesus is coming again but do not live with the urgency that indicates that it is a real belief. But there is a reason Jesus told His disciples to be ready and then waited 2000 years. He intends for us to live every day with an eternal perspective, sowing seeds that will bear everlasting fruit. He wants us to be single-minded in our service, preparing His household in the same way we would if He were standing beside us telling us what to do. He sees who has taken His interests to heart and who has not. Those who love Him serve Him well. Those who give Him mere lip service will get up and act busy when He comes through the door.

"The return of our Lord is the great Bible argument for a pure, devoted, active life of service."

—R. A. Torrey

In Deed Does Jesus' return guide your life today? Or is His return on the back burner, a distant thought while you live out the demands of the present? Be careful of the answer. According to Jesus, it's the difference between being wise and foolish.

Jesus' encouragement to be prepared contains some of the most sobering words in the Bible. The alternative to being ready is extremely harsh treatment from the Master. Faithful and wise managers have nothing to fear, but those who do not live according to the Master's principles are judged severely—beaten and cut up, in fact—and assigned a place with the unbelievers. Why? Because disobedience *is* unbelief.

Be dressed and be ready. Keep the lamps burning. Watch for the Master's return and be wise. He is coming.

Anxiously Awaiting

"When these things begin to take place, stand up and lift up your heads, because your redemption is drawing near."
(Luke 21:28)

In Word Perhaps we have relegated this instruction to a future time we know not of. It is out there somewhere, a revelation for a generation that will one day see the heavens and earth shaken and shattered. We see no signs of the apocalypse, so we don't stand up, lift up our heads, and savor the nearness of our redemption.

Why not? Isn't this the appropriate posture for any Christian at any time? Perhaps our redemption is not yet here in the sense of Jesus' second coming. But which of us knows when we will meet Him face to face? Regardless of our proximity to the revelation of Jesus in the air, our proximity to our last day in this body is always imminent. We do not know when we will die, so we must always be prepared.

This is no morbid exercise for the believer who knows his or her standing in Christ. We who have been washed clean by the blood of Jesus can take a welcoming stand, with heads lifted high, in anxious anticipation of seeing His glory. We have nothing to fear but sin, and since we believe He has saved us fully, we have nothing to fear at all. It's true for any of us, wherever we are: Our redemption *is* drawing near.

"Other men see only a hopeless end, but the Christian rejoices in an endless hope."
—Gilbert Brenken

In Deed Few Christians hold this posture, and even fewer seek it. For some reason, many of us are not all that eager about our encounter with Jesus. Have we let guilt weigh us down? Consider the cleansing blood of Jesus. Have we let fear of death rob us of the joy of eternity? His perfect love casts out all of our fear (1 John 4:18). Have we let His holiness distance us? We have permission to draw near (Hebrews 4:16). Regardless of what confronts us—tribulation, distress, guilt, or death—a greater reality also confronts us: the glory of our merciful Savior. The final redemption is nothing to hide from. Let it draw near.

A Certain Peace

"Do not let your hearts be troubled and do not be afraid." (John 14:27)

In Word We live in an unsettling world. There is no such thing as security here. Thieves break in, accidents happen, illness strikes, terror assaults, and death comes to all—no one is immune. No human institution can guarantee our safety. The locks on our doors, the airbags in our cars, the medicines on our shelves—they may help us, but they do not come with promises. We walk on shaky ground.

On the night He was betrayed, Jesus reminds His disciples of this certain truth. Even He, the Son of God, will experience the uncompromising danger of a fallen world. But He leaves them with a promise: peace. They may breathe a sigh of relief. There is a sure foundation for security, not in this place, but in the One who transcends it. They need never be troubled if they rest secure in Him.

Some of the world's strongest faith-filled Christians became so in battlefields, torture chambers, cross-fires, and crime-ridden neighborhoods—the places on this planet where conflict rages and death can come in an instant. One of the many paradoxes of the Gospel is that those who have no security in this world can be the most secure of all. They have found it elsewhere—in the promises of the One who overcomes the world. The King whose kingdom is never shaken has assured them that they need not let their hearts be troubled. They are beaming examples of peace in the presence of God.

"Peace comes not from the absence of trouble, but from the presence of God."
—Alexander Maclaren

In Deed We fill ourselves with false securities. We surround ourselves with safety measures, especially protecting our physical lives. But the world is fraught with hazards, not just physical, but also spiritual and emotional. Who can protect us? Real security can only be found in Christ—all else is sinking ground. It does not matter what threatens us if we know He is with us. He, and no one else, has promised us peace. And His promises are certain.

Take Heart

"In this world you will have trouble. But take heart! I have overcome the world." (John 16:33)

In Word Jesus has no illusions about human nature. He who came to redeem a fallen race knows that race's capabilities. He who set His mind on the Cross knows the violence men can do. And nowhere in the Gospels does Jesus promise to shelter His disciples from the brutality of this world. Nowhere does He suggest that they can escape suffering. He offers something infinitely better than escape. He offers an overcoming peace.

All human beings will suffer sometimes. It's part of living in a fallen world. Disciples of Jesus will have an additional aspect to their suffering: persecution and rejection. Yet Jesus promises peace. How can He do this? How can He say, on the one hand, that His disciples will grieve and know the same rejection that He experiences, and, on the other hand, tell them to be encouraged?

"This world is our passage, not our portion."
—Matthew Henry

In Deed Seeds are buried in the ground. Caterpillars are confined in a cocoon. Grain is pummeled into flour. But each one has a higher purpose and another world to experience or function to fulfill. So do we. We can easily make the mistake of thinking that God's primary purpose for us is a matter of our lifetime on earth, while His heavenly kingdom is an afterthought. But the kingdom is the main event. Like the seeds, the caterpillars, and the grain, we are in an elemental form, being shaped by the Father for a greater, lasting purpose.

The world is the arena in which we are trained. As God shapes us for His kingdom, He uses many means. One of them is the tribulation that our world naturally dishes out. But our trouble is not meaningless; we can take heart. Peace is found in seeing beyond the training ground that so often distresses us. It is found in placing all hopes in the One who overcomes the world.

The Blind Who See

"For judgment I have come into this world, so that the blind will see and those who see will become blind."

(John 9:39)

In Word Jesus is the deciding moment of history. He does not say that He came to pronounce judgment—not in His first coming, anyway. He came that the world might judge itself. Those who believe in Him have judged themselves in need of a Savior. Those who will not believe Him have judged themselves able, at some level, of working out their own means to God—through enlightenment, through good works, through a naive trust that their sin is not so bad. Whatever the attempt, it is a denial of the Savior's mission. As Jesus clearly spelled out in John 3:18: "Whoever does not believe stands condemned already because he has not believed in the name of God's one and only Son." Judgment is self-inflicted.

This self-judgment that proclaims a person's ability to find his or her way to God seems to be visionary in the eyes of this world. Media laud the prominent spiritual seekers among us. The gurus who help people find their inner path—to God, to healing, to whatever—are highly esteemed in our culture. But what does Jesus say of them? "Those who see will become blind." They have neglected the litmus test of wisdom. They have refused the exclusive claims of Jesus.

"The coming of Jesus into the world is the most stupendous event in human history."

—Malcolm Muggeridge

In Deed Do you see Jesus? There is a prerequisite: We must first have been acutely aware of our blindness. Jesus does not cater to the human illusion that we might discover truth. We never discover truth. It is always revealed. This was our means of understanding the Gospel in the first place, and it is our means of progress in the life of discipleship. We cannot follow Him well unless we know: Truth is a gift. Just as we were saved by grace and therefore live by grace, we were awakened by revelation and are now taught by revelation. We can never forget this. It is the only way to see.

God Provides

"They do not need to go away. You give them something to eat." (Matthew 14:16)

In Word The disciples had not even considered that Jesus might be able to meet the needs of so many. More than 5,000 people were gathered to hear Him and to receive healing from Him. As evening approached and people began to grow hungry, the disciples urged the incarnate Provider to send people away to buy food. The same God who had poured manna from heaven for millions in the wilderness was now being encouraged to send people off to find their own provision. And He could have done so; there were villages nearby (v. 15). But He did not. They needed to know that He is the Provider, the God of deserted places.

We tend to see our need as either too large to even ask God to handle or too small for Him to be concerned with. We are forgetful. Like the disciples, we must be reminded of the God of history. He is the Provider who clothes the lilies and who sustained an entire generation with water and food in a barren wilderness. Too small for God to address? He is the God of five loaves and two fish. Too large? He is the Creator and Sustainer of all that is—is anything too difficult for Him?

"Man's extremity is God's opportunity of helping and saving."
—Matthew Henry

In Deed What is your need? Whatever it is, it is entirely God's concern. He may instruct you in it ("You give them something to eat"), and the obedience is yours to carry out; but the provision is His. When given the opportunity to stress self-sufficiency or dependence on God, Jesus chose the latter. Let neither the enemy nor your own limited vision talk you out of dependence on Him. Contrary to the voices in our heads, no need is too small, and none is too large. He is the God of compassion (v. 14) and the God of abundance (v. 20), and best of all, He is our Father.

Through Us

"They do not need to go away. You give them something to eat." (Matthew 14:16)

In Word Just as we underestimate God's ability to provide in our hour of great need, we also often underestimate the role He assigns us. We pray for the world, our country, our families, our friends. We pray for the salvation of others. We ask God to bless them. We ask Him to heal hurts and bind wounds, and to lift up the brokenhearted and help the needy. But we may be blind to our role.

Are we missing something? Is there a piece to this puzzle that we're overlooking? Is Jesus waiting for us, perhaps, to offer our meager loaves and fishes? In spite of His ability to act alone, does He say to us, in effect, "You give them something to eat"? God brought the Israelites through the Red Sea, but only after Moses lifted up the staff. God brought down the wall of Jericho, but only after Joshua led His people through the right steps. God conquered Goliath, but only after David stepped onto the battlefield. And Jesus kept Peter afloat, but only after Peter got out of the boat.

"God's blessings are not limited to the human resources available."

—Tom Elliff

In Deed The great works of God that come about through our faith usually do not come without an initial offering from us. The offering may be pitifully small—so much the better to display God's power—but it still must be given. Every miraculous work begins with an act of faith, a stepping out of God's people on the limb of trust. In handing the five loaves and two fishes to Jesus, the disciples were not for a moment thinking this human effort would meet the needs of the crowd; they were only giving what they had.

That's where miracles begin. Our abilities are too paltry to meet the overwhelming needs of this world. But when Jesus gets through with them, they are powerfully sufficient. Do we want Him to work through us? We must give Him what we have.

Real Safety

"They will put some of you to death . . . But not a hair of your head will perish." (Luke 21:16, 18)

In Word In many places in the world, Christians are put to death for no other reason than being Christians. This is no surprise; Jesus said it would be so. American Christians usually aren't quite sure how to relate to this, because we aren't often threatened with death for our beliefs. But it happens. According to recent statistics, Christians are the most persecuted religious group in the world.

Still, there is something comforting in Jesus' words. "Not a hair of your head will perish." He has just told them that some will die, yet not a hair of their head will perish. How can this be?

Jesus doesn't define death as genuine harm. As frightening as death is to most of us, and as tragic as early death seems to us, we can all expect to die. Death is a universal experience, whether we are being persecuted for our faith or our bodies fail us for some other reason. Yet Jesus assures us that if we stand firm with Him (v. 19), not a hair will perish. No real harm will come to us, because death in Christ is not real harm. "Do not be afraid of those who kill the body and after that can do no more" (Luke 12:4).

"If the Father has the kingdom ready for us, He will take care of us on the way."

—Andrew Bonar

In Deed Where does your security lie? Do you seek security in your physical well-being? That would be insecure indeed, according to Jesus. No, real safety is found in standing firm with Him. He is our protector and defender. Even when we walk through the valley of the shadow of death, we need not fear any evil; the Good Shepherd is with us. Our safety is contingent only on our faith in Him (Luke 12:8-9).

Let God redefine your understanding of security to be consistent with Jesus' words. Know that even when you die, not a hair of your head will perish.

God's Possibilities

"All things are possible with God." (Mark 10:27)

In Word How easily we forget this! Whether the issue is salvation for those who are far from God, as in this passage, or some other matter of faith, the principle is the same: All things are possible with God.

We often limit our vision to what we know to be within the realm of possibility—not as God defines possibility, but as we define it. We set ambitious—but realistic—goals. We pray for impressive—but conceivable—miracles. We hope for divine—but plausible—resolutions to our problems. But we forget and need to hear it again: All things are possible with God.

"God is the God of promise. He keeps His word, even when that seems impossible."
—Colin Urquhart

Our Bible is full of impossible situations. A nation camped at the edge of a sea with a hostile army behind them. An inexperienced band of fighters faced an impenetrable, walled city. A shepherd boy stood before an armed and angry giant. A worshiper faced a lion's den. "Dry bones" rotted in a valley. And our only hope of salvation lay in a sealed tomb.

In Deed Have you reached a dead end? Is it more dire than anything God has dealt with before? Is He confounded by your hopeless situation? We can take comfort in His many promises. "Surely the arm of the Lord is not too short to save, nor his ear too dull to hear" (Isaiah 59:1). "I am the Lord, the God of all mankind; is anything too hard for me?" (Jeremiah 32:27). "Call upon me in the day of trouble; I will deliver you, and you will honor me" (Psalm 50:15).

God does not promise to grant us everything on our agenda, but He does promise to meet real needs and to support real ministry in response to real faith. His track record is impressive. Never have His purposes been thwarted by circumstances too demanding. Never has His strength fallen short of the need. This is the promise we have in our Savior: All things are possible with God.

God at Work

"It is the Father, living in me, who is doing his work."

(John 14:10)

In Word Philip asks to see the Father, and Jesus answers that Philip has, in fact, been seeing the Father in Himself. Once again, we have an affirmation of the divinity of the Christ. That's good to know, but what does that mean to us practically?

As followers of Christ, we may have trouble separating the attributes He is modeling for us from the ones that are unique to Him. This attribute—the work of God in Him—is an example for us to learn from. Jesus clearly says so: "Anyone who has faith in me will do what I have been doing" (v. 12). He promises that the Holy Spirit will be in them (v. 17).

We gratefully accept this wonderful promise in principle, but we know that we continue to sin. We are still feeble in faith and in service. We persist in our own agendas and follies. We sometimes see a huge discrepancy between the glory of the promise and the reality of our experience.

"God never made a promise that was too good to be true."

—Dwight L. Moody

In Deed On one hand, we should be wonderfully encouraged by this verse. God, the Architect of incomprehensibly vast expanses and of amazingly intricate complexities, intends to dwell within us in the same power with which He indwelt Christ. Think about that. Let it sink in. It is a glorious truth of which Paul was well aware: "It is God who works in you to will and to act according to his good purpose" (Philippians 2:13).

On the other hand, this verse should greatly unsettle us. We know, deep in our hearts, that we do not experience it as often and as fully as we should. Let it do its unsettling work. Be bothered. Be persistent in prayer toward this end. Ask God to satisfy this truth in you, and do not rest until He does. His promises are not false advertising; they are there to be fulfilled.

An Eternal Obsession

"Our Father in heaven, hallowed be your name."

(Matthew 6:9)

In Word Occasionally in the Old Testament, God is referred to as Father, but He is never addressed in prayer as Father. Jesus' intimate opening to prayer may have stunned His listeners. They might not have been surprised to hear Him say "My Father," since He clearly had some special relationship with the Almighty. But to instruct His disciples to address God this way? That level of familiarity made God out to be accessible and affectionate—not easy concepts for those of us steeped in formal religion.

"We are called to an everlasting preoccupation with God."
—A. W. Tozer

As soon as Jesus tells us of the intimacy with God that is available to us, He stresses the utter transcendence and "otherness" of God—His holiness. "Hallowed be your name," He says. In two brief phrases, He has captured the essence of our relationship with God. It is at once intimate and unfathomable; familiar yet mysterious. Though we may know Him deeply, we will never know Him fully.

We often take this opening to the Lord's Prayer to be a prelude, similar to the salutation of a letter. But this particular salutation is actually the substance of our faith. It is full of mystery and intrigue. We're waiting to get to the good part of the prayer—the part about us—but this opening line *is* the good part. It contains the truths that will preoccupy us for eternity in His presence. It captures both the closeness of God and His unreachable distance. We will explore such mysteries forever, always growing in intimate knowledge of Him, but never exhausting the exhilaration of new discovery.

In Deed This verse is too often considered the opening formality of the prayer that Jesus taught, and we are prone to skim over formalities. We cannot afford to skim over this. It will be our eternal obsession, the truth that fills the depths of our souls. Meditate on its riches. The greatest commandment—to love our transcendent Father with all of our being—begins here.

Whose Will?

"This, then, is how you should pray . . . 'Your will be done.' " (Matthew 6:9-10)

"Ask whatever you wish, and it will be given you." (John 15:7)

In Word In our prayers, we often feel a tension between two teachings. Jesus tells us to pray for the Father's will (Matthew 6:10). He also tells us to pray for *our* will (Mark 11:24; John 14:13; 15:7). Which does He want us to do?

On the side of asking for *His* will, consider this: If God's will is perfect; if He loves us even more than we love ourselves; if He knows everything about us and everything about our future; if He crafted us Himself; if He is powerful, able to do beyond what we can even ask or think (Ephesians 3:20); if He desires to bless us with the best (Psalm 84:11; Matthew 7:11); if His desires for us are infinitely better than our requests for ourselves; why—for any reason—would we ever ask anything other than His will?

"A man's heart is right when he wills what God wills."

—Thomas Aquinas

On the other hand, Jesus is quite specific: If we remain in Him and His words remain in us, we are to ask whatever *we* will, and it will be given (John 15:7). Why the difference? Why would Jesus tell us to ask what *we* wish when He knows it will be inferior to what God wishes?

In Deed When we break down the question this way, we are focusing on the object of our prayer—the answers we expect to receive. But prayer is a relationship. Jesus has more in mind for us than the cause and effect of requesting. He wants to bring us into union with the Father in the arena of our wills. Yes, He wants us to ask for God's will. He also wants us to ask for our will to be done. He wants those two wills to be one and the same.

Are they? Are we finding that our hearts burn more and more with a passion to see God's kingdom come, His will to be done? If not, this should be our first request—that God would conform our hearts, drawing us up to the level of His will and His ways.

The Goodness of His Will

"Your will be done." (Matthew 6:10)

In Word We know that we should pray for God's will to be done, but we're often afraid to. Why? Because we do not trust that His will is best for us. We think His agenda and ours are by nature at odds with one another. Because of our corruption, they may in fact be at odds. But if we could see the whole picture, we would understand that it is our own will that falls short of fulfilling our well-being, not His. If we really understood, we would know that when His will and ours contradict, His is by far the better of the two, not just for His own purposes, but also for our happiness and eternal blessing. If we could see as well as He does, we would choose His will over ours every time—not because we're mature, selfless and God-centered, but even for our own self-interest. What He wants is always best for us.

"There are no disappointments to those whose wills are buried in the will of God."

—Frederick Faber

Why is this so hard for us? Because we're accustomed to human relationships between equals, in which a contradiction between two wills is almost always a contradiction between two self-interests. But our relationship with God is closer to the parent-child relationship in which the parent knows what's best for the child and the child only thinks he knows what's best for him. Both parent and child are zealous about the child's well-being. But the parent is better qualified to define it properly. The child's vision is too limited.

In Deed Do you realize that when you pray for God's will to be done, you are actually praying for your own best interests to be accomplished? In a sense, it is a very self-promoting prayer—not as a license for selfishness, but because God's will for us never contradicts our own desire for blessing. He may lead us through hard times, but there will be greater blessing in the end. His eternal perspective eminently qualifies Him to take us through difficult places when He knows the ultimate outcome will fulfill our heart's desires. Our vision is too limited to see this, so we hesitate to pray as Jesus instructed. But we will never be disappointed when we do.

A Call to Arms

"Your will be done." (Matthew 6:10)

In Word When Jesus instructed His disciples to pray that God's will be done, He never intended it as the feeble resignation to some mysterious will that we can't quite comprehend. We too often use this phrase as a caveat to those who hear us, in effect saying, "I really don't know what God's will is, but let's see if this prayer hits the mark."

No, when we say "Thy will be done," it is to be an assault on the gates of hell. It is an offensive march against the evil of this world. There is nothing defensive or ambiguous about it. It calls for God to make His kingdom manifest in this enemy territory, taking ground that the adversary has stolen. It is specific and assertive, a battle cry against everything that is not His will. It is war.

Observe the Master who gave us this instruction. When did He pray "Your will be done"? It was before the ultimate battle against His human nature and the powers of darkness, as He pondered the coming Cross in the Garden of Gethsemane (Luke 22:42).

> "God's will is not an itinerary but an attitude."
> —Andrew Dhuse

In Deed This request is not to be a statement of our resignation or the fine print at the bottom of our prayers that takes our will out of the situation. We are right to be suspicious of our own wills and defer to the Father's. But while this request is an appropriate deferral to His higher plan, it is much more. It is a conscious appeal to bring God's kingdom into victorious conflict with the hostility and depravity of our world. We are not only saying "not my will," we are also saying "not the enemy's will."

Wherever human tendencies or a corrupt world come into conflict with the revealed will of God, we are to pray "Thy will be done." We *know* what His will is with regard to our own hearts, sin, evil and violence, salvation, and much more. Shall we be tentative in these areas? No, Jesus gives us a call to arms: Pray that God's will be done.

Bad Investments

"A man's life does not consist in the abundance of his possessions." (Luke 12:15)

In Word The many ruins and relics of antiquity testify that earthly empires do not last. Mausoleums and memorials reveal the transience of life. The inability of governments to solve the world's problems persuade us that politics is not the answer. Volatile markets and monthly statements show us the corruptibility and futility of wealth.

Still, the tendency of mankind is to invest in earthly things. So few people know so little of the coming kingdom that it becomes an afterthought. Six days a week we plan for life by investing in houses and goods—insuring them all—and perhaps give one day's thought to eternity. We research human answers to human problems and neglect the divine privilege of dependence on a transcendent God. Both as individuals and societies, we so focus on the here and now that we grow blind to the there and then. While all eternity lies before us, our vision extends but a few decades. But as in Jesus' parable of the rich fool, human plans can be interrupted in one surprising moment, and what we have valued most may no longer matter at all.

"The real value of a thing is the price it will bring in eternity."
—John Wesley

In Deed Where do you invest your life? In trying to maintain security and comfort in the next few decades, or in knowing the security and incorruptible glory of eternity? Millions will one day look back at their incredible lack of logic, remembering the months and years they spent on temporal comforts compared with the scarce attention they gave to everlasting realities. What a tragedy! What a waste. What a heartbreak for those who have missed the big picture and who see all of their life's labor come to nothing. By contrast, what a blessing for those who are rich toward God (v. 21)! Consider the long term and examine where your investments lie. Use your resources for the coming kingdom.

The Cost of Discipleship

"Anyone who does not carry his cross and follow me cannot be my disciple." (Luke 14:27)

In Word Human nature, especially in our age, is to avoid carrying crosses at all costs. Though many people historically have made great sacrifices for a greater good, and some undoubtedly still do, we are more likely to act as if avoiding sacrifice *is* the greater good. We seek safety, comfort, security, and pleasure, often at the expense of doing God's will. "Let the true zealots—the missionaries and the ministers—live consecrated lives on our behalf," many might say. "Their sacrifices are the exception, not the rule." We risk compromising God's mission for the path of least resistance. We're not willing to pay the price of impacting the world.

We read a New Testament full of crosses and chains, stonings and scars, beatings and bondservants, and we thank God that those days are gone. But they are only gone because we have learned to tiptoe around the "excesses" of New Testament zeal.

"Give me a hundred men who fear nothing but sin and desire nothing but God, and I will shake the world."

—John Wesley

In Deed Jesus offers us no such option. We are not allowed to fit God's mission in around our higher priorities. We may choose safety or Christ, but not both. We may pursue the American dream or the kingdom of God, but not both. We may "give up everything" (v. 33) or not give up everything, but not both. Christ compels us to choose.

Let's break out of our comfort zone. The life of discipleship is not about comfortable pews and golden crosses; it is about a clash of kingdoms. It is not about protecting ourselves; it is about signing up for the war. Imagine standing before the throne of our Protector one day and telling Him, "Sorry, Lord, I would have done Your will, but it wasn't safe." Self-preservation at the expense of obedience always has grave consequences in the Bible. Let's recognize where eternal safety lies and abandon ourselves to the Christ who calls us to carry our crosses and sacrifice all we have.

The Cost of Non-Discipleship

"What good will it be for a man if he gains the whole world, yet forfeits his soul?"

(Matthew 16:26)

In Word The cost of discipleship is great. Jesus makes that point over and over again. Unlike some ministries today that almost beg people to entrust their lives to Christ, appropriate as the appeal may be, Jesus discouraged people from following Him if they could not do it wholeheartedly. He called for a willingness to deny oneself and take up a cross. He called them to suffer the cost.

But the cost of *not* following Jesus is even greater than the cost of discipleship. Those who do not follow Him—even those who follow Him, *but not wholeheartedly*—miss all of the blessings and benefits of being completely sold out to Christ. They miss intimate fellowship with the Creator of all that is; they miss the power of God at work in their lives; they miss the peace and fullness of knowing they are right with God. And they will miss great eternal rewards.

"He is no fool who gives what he cannot keep to gain what he cannot lose."

–Jim Elliot

Every human being pays an extremely high price—either the cost of discipleship or the cost of opting out of it. The cost of opting out is greater. In fact, it's infinitely greater. Holding on to a little bit of sin and self destroys intimacy with God and renders a life relatively fruitless. Maintaining one's own agenda regardless of God's will means missing the blessing of walking in His steps in the power of His Spirit. That's costly.

In Deed "What good will it be for a man if he gains the whole world, yet forfeits his soul?" Jesus asks. In other words, having just revealed the cost of following Him, He now asks: "Are you willing to pay the price of *not* following Me?" Too many Christians have held back a little from Christ, thinking the cost of all-out abandonment to a self-denying Savior is too costly. It is too radical, too zealous. But think about the alternative, and compare the costs. Either way, there is a price to pay. All things considered, it's a pretty easy choice.

Our Rebel Leader

"Am I leading a rebellion?" (Mark 14:48)

In Word The scene is almost ludicrous. Jesus, the Prince of Peace, was surrounded by a hostile, armed crowd. He had been walking weaponless throughout the streets of Jerusalem with compassion in His voice and healing in His wings, but compassion and healing are a little too suspicious for powerful people. So they come, burning with anger and betrayal.

The Son of God apparently knows about sarcasm: "Am I leading a rebellion . . . that you have come out with swords and clubs to capture me?" But the question is more loaded than the sarcasm on the surface would indicate. He *is* leading a rebellion. He is leading a rebellion against the human rebellion, which was instigated by the angelic rebellion. He is leading a rebellion against the ways of this world and against all the enemies of the kingdom of God. He is leading a rebellion against the culture of hate, anger, and enmity and against the culture of lust, greed, and idolatry. There is a war behind the scenes of this battle. The commander of this traitorous world is now being cast out (John 12:31). Jesus knows exactly who has surrounded Him. On the surface, it looks like spiteful Jews under the authority of spiteful Gentiles. But Jesus has already told His disciples: "The prince of this world is coming" (John 14:30). Yes, by all means, this is a rebellion.

"Anyone who witnesses to the grace of God revealed in Christ is undertaking a direct assault against Satan's dominion."

—Thomas Cosmades

In Deed As descendants of Adam and Eve, we have all been participants in a rebellion. We have committed treason against the High King of heaven. We're not sure what we were thinking at the time, but somewhere back there we joined in. Now we have a golden opportunity to join the quashing of our former uprising. Wherever we see injustice, we can right it. Wherever we see pain, we can soothe it. Wherever we encounter the wounded, we can help them heal. The passing prince of this world is being cast out; the time has come for us to join in. Are you waist-deep in this war, or are you just passively sitting by? Join the battle. Join the rebellion wherever you can.

Our Weapons

"No more of this!" (Luke 22:51)

In Word We are members of a rebellion against the prince of this world. It is led by the Owner of this world, so we are sure of victory—it has already been secured. But having come from the enemy camp, we are used to weapons of destruction when we fight. We do not at first realize that we have been given a different set of weapons.

Paul says our weapons are not of this world. They are not even *like* the weapons of this world. "On the contrary, they have divine power to demolish strongholds" (2 Corinthians 10:4). Jesus let Peter know immediately that his type of warfare was out of place. Peter cut off a servant's ear. "No more of this!" Jesus responded, and followed it up with healing. That's the key: The weapons of our warfare are not *de*structive, they are *con*structive. They include things like humility, forgiveness, resisting good with evil, holy attitudes, the Holy Spirit within us, and the even more offensive ones—the Cross of Christ, the Word of God, and the prayers of the saints.

"Prayer is the mightiest of all weapons that created natures can wield."
-Martin Luther

Jesus won this showdown in the Garden of Gethsemane. No one really knew that but Jesus. His victory didn't look like a victory. Neither do ours. When we turn the other cheek, offer to go the extra mile, forgive someone a thousand times, humble ourselves in the sight of men and God, pray on our knees, and quote from the Word, it doesn't look like we win. But we do. The enemy trembles. He would much prefer that we go back to his style of battle—evil for evil, sword for sword, spite for spite. He knows how to fight on those terms. He has no idea what to do when his greatest offenses become the showcase for God's greatest mercies.

In Deed How do you fight the good fight? Are your battles a reflection of the Spirit of God within you? Or are they consistent with the spirit of this world? One will lead you to victory, the other into darkness. You will encounter a battle today, as you do every day. How will you respond? Make sure you look a lot like Jesus in the Garden.

A Beautiful Thing

"She has done a very beautiful thing to me."

(Mark 14:6

In Word The story is a familiar one to many: In the days preceding His death, a woman breaks open a clay jar of expensiv perfume and anoints Jesus with it. It is an appropriate preparatio for His burial, Jesus says, despite the protests of some at this dinner party. The formality of the dinner is not relevant, and neither is the "waste" of the precious perfume, He says. She has done a beautiful thing.

Not only has this woman (Mary of Bethany, according to John 12:3) done a beautiful thing in anointing Jesus for burial with a precious fragrance, she has done a beautiful thing by giving us an accurate illustration of the life of a believer. Like the vessel of nard, we are also to be broken and poured out at the feet of the Savior, as He was broken and emptied for us.

The illustration is a running theme in the New Testament. "We have this treasure in jars of clay," Paul says in 2 Corinthians 4:7, emphasizing later that he is being poured out for the sake of the Gospel (Philippians 2; 2 Timothy 4). Your life as a believer is to be a life of your most valuable treasures being emptied at the feet of the Lord. It is not a waste. It is a fragrant offering.

> *"The oil of the lamp in the temple burnt away in giving light; so should we."*
>
> —Robert Murray M'Cheyne

In Deed We may be tempted at times to feel like our service for the Lord is a waste of time and resources. Like Mary's act of service, ours may bear no visible fruit and it may impress no one else at the party. But motivation is the key. Is it done in pure devotion? Is it an offering of the best we have for the One we treasure most? Is it prompted by a passion for the character and work of our Savior? Then it is not a waste. A vessel broken so that its treasure might be devoted to Jesus is the kind of sacrifice that pleases Him most. It is what He asks of us and it is a fragrant aroma to Him. It is a beautiful thing.

Sinners at the Cross

"This is my blood of the covenant, which is poured out for many for the forgiveness of sins." (Matthew 26:28)

In Word Our human responses to sin would be amusing if they weren't so contrary to truth:

- We cover it up, like Adam and Eve in the garden. We know it's there, but we don't admit it to God, and we certainly don't let others see it—that would be too humiliating.
- We deny it's there. We come up with justifications like "Everyone is basically good," and "I'm OK, you're OK." We relegate sin to the aberrant folks who end up in prisons and psychiatric wards.
- We redefine it. It's not sin—it's a weakness, a character flaw, human nature.
- We try to compensate God for it. We do good works, we come up with all sorts of religions and rituals, we make vows of obedience for tomorrow to make up for disobedience yesterday. We try to make the good in us outweigh the bad.

At Calvary, the naked truth is staring down at us, challenging us to drop the pose and own the truth."

–Roy Hession

In Deed But the Cross—the disfigured, bloody form on the tree, the picture of the penalty we deserved—undoes all of our approaches to the problem. There, in plain daylight, the innocent sacrifice takes our shame upon Himself. We can either own up to the need for that sacrifice, or we can persist in one of the pitiful solutions above. But when we really see God's assessment of our situation—that we were worthy of this brutality, this ultimate ransom for our rebellion—how can we degrade the sacrifice with our shallow attempts to deny our need? "How shall we escape if we ignore such a great salvation?" (Hebrews 2:3)

We can't. No, at the Cross we see who we are, and we are humbled. We see the ugliness of our sin and we are speechless. We know we can make no claim of our own righteousness before God. But Jesus is our claim. We bow before Him. We know He is there for us.

God at the Cross

"This is my blood of the covenant, which is poured out for many for the forgiveness of sins." (Matthew 26:28

In Word God's response to our sin pulls no punches. It is a graver assessment than we thought. The righteous God of Israel who spent thousands of years of Old Testament history condemning disobedience and idolatry, finally unleashes His full wrath for the human rebellion—on His own perfect Son. The observers in the heavenlies—angels, demons, and anyone else who sees God more clearly than we do—must have staggered at the sight. The enemy had tirelessly worked for centuries corrupting the creation and the creation willfully went along with his treason. All the while, God stored up His anger. Yet when God's judgment came, He had already sent an innocent Deliverer to stand in front of the Judge's fury.

The Cross is God's wrath made plain. It is also God's love made plain. No man-made religion can claim such a God. All other deities are either so angry that they can't be appeased, or so innocuous that they are meaningless. Nowhere else in the universe—even in fertile imaginations—have justice and grace been reconciled so completely.

"As you sit and gaze, it will be born in you that only a crucified Savior could meet your need."

—William Sangster

In Deed No human being could have come up with this plan. No human religion could have laid down a centuries-old sacrificial system to so perfectly foreshadow what would be fulfilled in one individual—the same individual who also happened to deliver the most profound teachings that the world has ever heard. No, the blood of the covenant poured out at the Cross comes from the hand of God—in judgment and in love.

Meditate on the judgment of God. It was harsh and heavy. It is a true assessment of our offense. Meditate also on the grace of God. It is a love far above our understanding that pays so high a price for so unworthy a purchase. Meditate and marvel at the staggering plan of God.

The Resurrection Promise

"The Son of Man is going to be betrayed into the hands of men. They will kill him, and after three days he will rise." (Mark 9:31)

In Word Death surrounds us. It is on our TVs and in our newspapers. It has taken family members and friends. It will come to each of us. For all who are crushed by the reality of the Fall, Jesus gives this promise. There is a resurrection.

Perhaps we have heard this from the pulpit so often that we have lost a sense of amazement over this impossible claim. But think about it. This just does not happen, at least not visibly. Most religions have some concept of an afterlife, but a man being physically raised from the dead? No one ever made such a claim. Except Jesus. Even His disciples, who had seen Him raise Lazarus, a widow's son, and a little girl, were dumbfounded (v. 32). They didn't know what to make of this prediction, because it was beyond the realm of possibility. People die and they are buried. Period.

"Death died when Christ rose."
—Anonymous

But Jesus erased the period. His resurrection, far from being an exclusive privilege of the Son of God, means everything for us. It reversed the curse of death that we brought upon ourselves at the Fall. It is the re-genesis—the beginning of a new creation. And we are invited to be a part of it.

In Deed The promise of this resurrection is astounding. Every privilege of the risen Jesus, in all of His glory, is offered to us to partake in. It is the reality of the eternal promises of God. In His resurrection, He intercedes for us at the right hand of God (Hebrews 7:25); He lives in us (John 14:20; Galatians 2:20); and He exercises all authority in heaven and on earth (Matthew 28:18). Not only is He exalted, but we are seated with Him in heavenly places (Ephesians 2:6); we are fellow heirs of His inheritance (Romans 8:17); and we have eternal life (John 6:40).

These are magnificent and astonishing truths. We could spend a lifetime—make that an eternity—letting them sink in. Today, meditate and marvel at the promise of the resurrection.

Exchanged Lives

"I am the resurrection and the life." (John 11:25)

In Word The death of Jesus is for the believer everything we need for the forgiveness of our sins. In a sense, we and all of our sin died with Jesus on the cross. His death is the penalty of our rebellion and the price of our pardon. The wrath of God is satisfied in the Cross, and we are free from that awful, awful burden.

But the story of the Christian life does not end with forgiveness. If we and all of our sin died with Jesus on the cross, who then lives? We cannot say on the one hand that we died with Him and on the other hand that we are still alive in our natural selves. We must choose—our old life or its death. And if we choose its death, then how do we live on?

Paul gives us the glorious answer: "I no longer live, but Christ lives in me" (Galatians 2:20). The life that we live by faith is an exchanged life—everything that we were went with Jesus on the cross; everything that He is was raised from the tomb and is given to us. We gave up everything in our old nature, in all of our lostness, to have that substitute on the cross. In return, we gained the life of the everlasting Son of the living God, with all of His privileges and power. What an exchange!

"Because of the Resurrection, everything changes."
—Max Lucado

In Deed The sad truth about this exchange—and it is the only sad thing about it—is that we are forgetful creatures. Having accepted the Cross as our payment for sin, we forget to live in the Resurrection that follows. Our old natures want to ignore their death certificate. Their demise is a legal fact, not a biological reality (yet). They remind us of what we were before the Cross. And we listen.

Yet Jesus is the Resurrection and the Life. He offers to fill us with His glorified self. The substitution of the Cross is not just in death, but in resurrection. We may now live in the power that raised Him. But only if we live by faith. Are you living that life? Or better yet, is He living that life in you? Believe it. Believe in the Resurrection and the Life. And be reminded daily: "I no longer live, but Christ lives in me."

The Indwelling Christ

"On that day you will realize that I am in my Father, and you are in me, and I am in you."

(John 14:20)

In Word Think of that. This historical Jesus who walked Palestine nearly 2000 years ago, who impacted the world like no other teacher ever has, who performed amazing feats of healing, deliverance, and provision, and who is the giver of eternal life, is the same person who pledges to live in us who believe in Him. Are we conscious of His presence? Do we realize the incredible treasure that we have within us? Or do we keep Him buried deep down inside, unaware of the power and the pleasure that's available in His promise?

The eternal Godhead is somehow present, not in our natural selves, which are corrupt and lifeless, but in our born-again natures that are alive to God through faith. The Holy Spirit can make us aware of His presence in our conflicts with others; we can be aware of His presence in our hours of great need; and we can be aware of His presence in the routines of daily life. We might sometimes make this reality practically irrelevant by ignoring its implications, but His promise is real. He is there to be known and to be seen.

"To possess a Spirit-indwelt mind is the Christian's privilege under grace."

—A. W. Tozer

In Deed How can we know His presence? By love and obedience—two sides of the same coin that Jesus sets before His disciples in verse 21. To obey Him is to love Him, and to love Him is to know His presence in a deeper, fuller way than many Christians ever experience.

The people who are most aware of God's presence in their lives are the ones who love Jesus with a passion and who have abandoned all disobedience to Him. God uses them without reservation. He is "able to do immeasurably more than all we ask or imagine, according to his power at work within us" (Ephesians 3:20). May we each find this to be true in ourselves.

Bread of Life

"I am the bread of life. He who comes to me will never go hungry, and he who believes in me will never be thirsty."

(John 6:35)

"The heart of man is restless until it finds its rest in Thee."

—St. Augustine

In Word "Blessed are those who hunger and thirst for righteousness, for they will be filled," Jesus had said (Matthew 5:6). Now He tells us how. We will be filled with Him. He is the righteousness. He is the object of everything for which we truly hunger and thirst. He is the Manna the Father sent, the Bread that satisfies our souls.

Yet even today many believers seem hungry and thirsty. Jesus often seems absent from their lives.

Perhaps we hunger for the wrong kind of bread. Jesus says, "He who comes to *me* will never go hungry." Many of us appeal to Jesus for the goods of this world, the fulfillment of our own agendas, or the circumstances we would like to have. To us, Jesus is a means to another end—our goals. If this is our story, Jesus is never satisfying.

Perhaps we hunger for the right kind of bread but don't meet Jesus' conditions for receiving it. Jesus says, "He who *comes,* . . . he who *believes.*" Both of these conditions imply that we meet Him on His terms, not ours. We try to come with part of ourselves, but not all. We believe in some of His teaching, but not all. We want the benefits of the Son of God without abandoning ourselves to Him. If this is our story, Jesus is never satisfying to us, either.

In Deed But to those who hunger and thirst for righteousness and who come to Him without reservation, trusting in Him as the source of all righteousness and strength, He satisfies. Those whose whole life is reoriented around Him and who desire nothing else will never want for anything. He is not our means to get bread; He *is* the Bread.

When we follow Him by faith with nothing else to rely on, He provides. And we are filled.

Living Water

"If anyone is thirsty, let him come to me and drink."

(John 7:37)

In Word "I will pour water on the thirsty land, and streams on the dry ground; I will pour out my Spirit on your offspring, and my blessing on your descendants." So said the Lord through the prophet Isaiah (44:3). The fulfillment of God's promise came 700 years later. At a ceremonial outpouring of water, Jesus proclaimed Himself to be the source of the living water foretold by the prophets.

People thirst in our day, too. Many are unbelievers searching for the truth. Many, however, are within the Christian family. Heaven's resources are available to us in abundance, and we still may not experience them. The presence of God's Spirit is assured, but we may wonder if He is with us. We read of God's miraculous, exciting dealings with His people, and we often struggle with our mundane lives. Like the woman at the well, we ask where we can get this living water (John 4:11). We really want to know. To whom is it given?

"The Holy Spirit may be had for the asking." —R. B. Kuiper

Jesus' conditions for this gift are few and basic. We must thirst, we must come, and we must drink. That's it. All that is required of us is to need it badly and come to the source. It's that simple.

In Deed Many approach the subject of living water with a mild interest. But if we really want it, we must be truly thirsty. We must search the Scriptures and apply them to our hearts, asking God to give us this water. And we must truly come to Jesus, not casually and with reservation, but with enthusiasm, openness, and trust. We must prepare our hearts for the overflowing tide, always looking to Him in faith. We must excitedly expect Him to fulfill His promise.

For those who really thirst, who really come, and who really drink, the water gushes. The Spirit is poured out. And dry ground becomes a well-watered garden.

Love Like His

"Love your enemies and pray for those who persecute you, that you may be sons of your Father in heaven."
(Matthew 5:44-45

"We are not merely to serve Christ, we are to be like Him."
—Derek Copley

In Word The imperative of this passage is well-known, often from very early in our discipleship. We are to love our enemies. But what about the "why" of this verse? It is often left out of the discussion. We are to love our enemies and pray for them *because we are to be sons of our Father.* Does this mean we are saved by our ability to love, and therefore by works? Other passages of Scripture make it clear that this is not so—our salvation is by grace through faith alone. So how might we be children of God by our love in the face of hate? Because that is what God is like. God loves His enemies and He intercedes for those who persecute Him. By this act of loving and praying for our enemies, we become "chips off the old block." We grow into conformity with God.

In Deed This raises a larger issue for us. Not only in loving our enemies and praying for those who persecute us are we to be like God—children conformed to His image. We are to be like Him in all character issues. Whom God loves, we are also to love. Those impurities in ourselves that God despises, we are also to despise. Whom God seeks for His own, we are also to seek. His way is to become our way.

Study God's character in Scripture. Examine His tenderness and compassion, His holiness, His hatred of evil, His mercy, and His love. He calls us to be like Him (2 Corinthians 3:18; Ephesians 5:1; 1 Peter 1:16). As we see Him as our standard, let us also see the radical transformation that must take place in us as we, His children, grow to be like Him.

Made for Worship

"A time is coming and has now come when the true worshipers will worship the Father in spirit and truth, for they are the kind of worshipers the Father seeks."

(John 4:23)

In Word When we consider God's will for our lives, we usually are thinking in terms of a career direction or a major family or financial decision. God wants to direct us in these, but He has a higher priority. What is God's will for us? Worship.

Jesus calls for obedient followers. He asks us to pray that laborers be sent into the harvest. But above all of these callings of service is a prior calling: to worship Him in spirit and in truth. This is our ultimate purpose. When all is said and done, when the Lord has returned, when the multitudes are gathered before His throne, we will know we exist only for worship. It is the last picture given in Scripture of the saints in heaven (Revelation 19).

It stands to reason, then, that this is what God's creation is all about. When we focus on accomplishments and service, we are missing the point if these are not acts of worship themselves. When we seek His guidance, we may not get it if we've neglected His first purpose for us. We must major on worship and let everything else support that vision.

"If you will not worship God seven days a week, you do not worship Him one day a week."

—A. W. Tozer

In Deed Every workman knows you need the right tool for the right job. Human resources managers know how to assign people appropriate tasks. But in our relationship with God, we sometimes miss the point that we are created for His glory. We find ourselves as misapplied tools or employment misfits in the kingdom of God because we don't see our proper role.

Above all else, Christians' lives must be characterized by worship. There is a reason Jesus pointed to our love for God as the greatest commandment (Matthew 22:37). It fulfills our purpose. We were designed for worship, and the Father is seeking those who know that.

The Humble God

"Unless I wash you, you have no part with me."

(John 13:8)

In Word Jesus' illustration of the incarnation must have made little sense to the disciples at the time. Peter resisted the foot-washing, and his words probably expressed the sentiments of the others. What was Jesus doing? They had spent three years coming to a realization of His greatness; now He was redefining what greatness is. It didn't look anything like what a victorious, reigning Messiah ought to look like.

And think about the subjects—those dirty, sinful feet. The treacherous feet of Judas, carrying him to the dark, secret places of Jerusalem on wicked business. The stubborn feet of Peter, standing resolute in the courtyard while his cowardly mouth denied any association with Jesus. The fleeing feet of everyone else for whom the Cross was just too much to take. They were dirty in more ways than one. But Jesus knelt before them and washed them. He served them with humility.

We can entertain no personal indignation in the face of Jesus' example. How can frail humans look down on others when even the King of kings would not? How can we hold others in contempt when the Alpha and Omega carefully held the most contemptible extremities of these earthen vessels in His hands and cleaned them? How can we maintain human pride when the exalted Lord refused to?

"Jesus' life began in a borrowed stable and ended in a borrowed tomb."

—Alfred Plummer

In Deed We praise this high and holy God for His power and majesty. Do we also praise Him for His humility? We can; we serve a humble God. He did not ride into this world on a gilded chariot. He was born in a stable. He left His radiant appearance to be clothed in a human body subject to temptation and pain. We are not worthy to utter His name, but He tells us to call Him Father and Friend.

Do you suffer from the illusion of an unknowable God? You know what the Bible says, that He is loving and forgiving; but has that really sunk into your heart? Consider the humility of God. The high and holy One is never inaccessible to someone with a contrite spirit. He encourages your intimacy with Him. He'll even wash your feet.

A Different Love

"A new command I give you: Love one another. As I have loved you, so you must love one another."

(John 13:34)

In Word Have you ever asked yourself what is new about this commandment? Jesus says it is new, but what element of it was not already given in the Old Testament? The commandment to love our neighbors as ourselves was prominent in Jewish theology before Jesus came. It's scriptural from all the way back in Leviticus (19:18). So what's new?

Jesus clarifies after His initial statement: We are to love one another *as He has loved us*. That's what is different. That's more than loving our neighbors as ourselves. That's making deep, painful sacrifices for them. It is a matter of seeking their good above our own. No prior commandment has made such specific claims on us, defining for us what real love is. No definition will suffice in teaching us what kind of love this is; only an illustration will do. And the illustration is Jesus. The way He loved others is the way we are to love others.

"I have found the paradox that if I love until it hurts, then there is no hurt, but only more love."

—Mother Teresa

We are reluctant to embrace such love. We know it will make radical, life-altering claims on us. We will not be able to walk down the road and pretend we don't see the beaten Samaritan lying beside it, as Jesus' earlier parable illustrates. Whatever form the beaten Samaritan takes in our lives—an emotionally wounded friend, a homeless vagrant, an outcast of our culture, a disease-ridden sinner—we are to love as Jesus loved. That's new, and that's hard.

In Deed Do we take these words of Jesus seriously? Perhaps the historical portrayal of Jesus as a man who went about doing good and helping people has made us think simply of increasing our level of generosity. But Jesus asks more of us than that. We are first to realize how radical His love is; and then we are to embrace it as our own. We receive it and we give it—even, as Jesus did, to people who do not deserve it. This is indeed a new commandment. It has the power to change everything about us.

A Clash of Kingdoms

"Blessed are the poor in spirit . . . those who mourn . . . the meek . . . those who hunger and thirst for righteousness . . . the merciful . . . the pure in heart . . . the peacemakers . . . those who are persecuted."

(Matthew 5:3-1(

In Word Have you ever observed how these descriptions of our blessedness clash with the world? For every beatitude there is a conflicting value more virtuous in society's eyes.

- Our world sells us "a higher plane" with self-help materials from spiritual gurus. Poverty in spirit is a weakness.
- Our culture values "the pursuit of happiness" and "the right t party," not mourning the sin of the world.
- The meek are scorned by the self-sufficient. Over-assertive, egocentric athletes, entertainers, and politicians are the most highly praised members of our society.
- Those who desire righteousness are considered too repressed and dysfunctional to enjoy liberated lives.
- Mercy? We live in the most litigious society in history; moderr man is astoundingly creative in formulating lawsuits of retribution.
- Purity in heart is an unrealistic, holier-than-thou goal; "we're only human," after all.
- Peacemakers may be awarded Nobel Prizes in international affairs, but asserting one's individual rights is highly valued. Personality conflicts, divorces, and contract disagreements abound; political contests are nastier than ever.
- Our culture honors the successful, not the persecuted.

"The Christian should stand out like a sparkling diamond."
—Billy Graham

In Deed No wonder Jesus follows up the Beatitudes by expounding on persecution! With such a clash in values betweer an aggressive world and a peace-loving Kingdom, persecution is inevitable. There is no fellowship between the two. The Beatitudes serve as an emphatic imperative: Live in the world where God placed you, but never, ever blend in.

Swimming Upstream

"Blessed are the poor in spirit . . . those who mourn . . . the meek . . . those who hunger and thirst for righteousness . . . the merciful . . . the pure in heart . . . the peacemakers . . . those who are persecuted."

(Matthew 5:3-10)

"Persecution is one of the surest signs of the genuineness of our Christianity."

—Benjamin E. Fernando

In Word How difficult it is to live contrary to our culture! We are called to be in the world but not of the world. We are to be salt and light in our society, not isolated from it, but mingling with it in order to display the good news of a transformed life in Christ.

It is a message that society doesn't welcome—hence the persecution—though it should welcome that message above all others. We are called to display the most benign of all characters in the most vicious of all contexts. Our Master was a lamb in the slaughterhouse, and calls us to follow Him. How reluctant we are! A little conformity here, a little compromise there, and suddenly we are inoffensive Christians in an offensive crowd. We simply seek survival—our natural instinct—knowing deep down that we were not called to survive, but to die daily (Matthew 16:25; Luke 14:27; 1 Corinthians 15:31).

In Deed We're not called simply to swim upstream in a gently flowing brook. We must swim upstream in the raging rapids. That is the nature of the unbelieving world—it is radically opposed to the Gospel, and the Gospel is radically opposed to it. This is often too harsh to the modern ear, isn't it? God is love, we say, not radical opposition. But true love gives a true assessment, and Jesus tells us that the reality of eternal values lies in dramatic contradiction to cultural trends.

Are you discouraged in this upstream journey? Be encouraged. We will fit perfectly in the coming kingdom, and living by its principles, we will draw others into it.

Inevitable Insults

"Blessed are you when people insult you, persecute you and falsely say all kinds of evil against you because of me."
(Matthew 5:11

In Word Notice that Jesus doesn't say, "Blessed are you *if* people insult you." He says "*when*." It is a given. Those who live as disciples in this world will get on the nerves of their culture. There is an inherently abrasive relationship between the kingdom of God and the kingdoms of men. Why? Because God and men are rivals for the same throne.

Jesus is an offense to the ego of this world. In our natural selves, we see ourselves as lords of our own lives. When those lives are dysfunctional, we seek to mend them. We apply self-help techniques, psychological therapies, religious philosophies—anything to pull ourselves up. We think we need improvement and that we can do it ourselves or with a little help from our friends.

"Scars are the price which every believer pays for his loyalty to Christ."
—William Hendriksen

But Jesus did not come into the world to improve us. He came to rescue those who are lost, broken, and helpless. Therein lies the offense. The world cannot accept a Savior until it admits it needs saving. To live compatibly with the Christ violates the human ego.

In Deed Our gospel message should have no offense but Christ Himself—it should always be presented in a winsome way on our part. But even so, though some are saved, much of the world will rail against the Gospel. It challenges man's authority in his own life and insists that there is another Lord fa more worthy. "Do not be surprised at the painful trial you are suffering," Peter says (1 Peter 4:12). Know that our Savior is a threat to the prideful self-sufficiency of man. Expecting nothing else, we will be well-equipped when such trials come.

A Higher Purpose

"You will always have the poor among you, but you will not always have me." (John 12:8)

In Word Judas was surprised that his logic didn't work on Jesus. As Mary poured expensive perfume over Jesus' feet, Judas objected. He was the treasurer, and he apparently had a keen interest in the amount of money allowed to flow through his hands. And, on some pay scales, this would have been a full year's wages! Surely an appeal to the needs of the poor would persuade Jesus to tell Mary to invest her resources more wisely. But no. Judas received a surprising response.

The response may be surprising to us, as well. Didn't Jesus care deeply for the poor? Didn't He identify with the needy? Wouldn't He prefer that valuable resources feed the hungry rather than lavishly anoint His feet? It is in His nature to make huge sacrifices—His own life, in fact—for those who need Him. Why would He not gladly sacrifice the luxury of this perfume?

There is a clear statement of values in Jesus' response. The Cross is everything. The death, resurrection, and exaltation of the Son is paramount. It is the pinnacle of all history, the turning point of all creation. It is important—vital, in fact—to take care of the poor, as Scripture consistently says. But the poor have always been present and will always be present. The glorification of the Son in His supreme sacrifice for our salvation was a one-time event. *Everything* in the universe should point to it. It is the highest of all values.

"The divine priority is worship first and service second."
—Richard Foster

In Deed We often raise our work for Jesus—like feeding the poor—above the Person of Jesus. When we do, we subvert the proper order. Our values are distorted, and our works become empty. Worship is to come first. It is paramount. There is no praise and no perfume too lavish for Jesus. He is the highest priority, ultimately valuable above all other concerns. Do you want to reflect true worth? Let your work flow out of a heart enamored with Him.

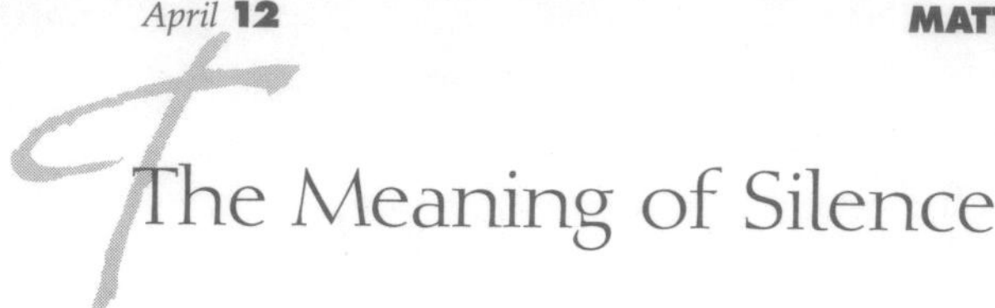

The Meaning of Silence

Jesus did not answer a word. (Matthew 15:23)

In Word What are we to make of a Savior who does not answer? The request of the woman whose daughter was demon-possessed was legitimate. Her acknowledgment of Jesus as Lord was accurate; her understanding of His will was appropriate. And yet, as with many of our seemingly appropriate prayer requests, He does not answer "a word."

Our response to His silence is often too timid. We backpedal, saying that perhaps our request was not in line with His will, or maybe we assume that we didn't have enough faith, because, if we ask anything—even the removal of a mountain—and do not doubt, it will be done (Matthew 21:21). So we drop the request and do all sorts of interpretive gymnastics to justify the fact that God has not answered our prayer. But deep inside we know that His promises are certain and that we water down Scripture by explaining why we did not experience them.

"The great point is never to give up until the answer comes."

—George Müller

Children learn much about their friends by playing hide-and-seek. They experience how their friends' minds work. They don't give up when they can't find them at first; an exciting encounter will take place if they keep looking. Might God's silence prepare us for an encounter with Him?

In Deed We need to contemplate this silence of Jesus in the Gentile woman's hour of great need. We need to remember that none—not one—of His promises guarantees an immediate answer to prayer. In His silence, He expects her continuing response of faith. She must ask herself: Am I sure of His goodness and His mercy (v. 22)? Am I sure He is able and willing (v. 25)? Do I know that God's blessing is given freely, not earned (v. 27)?

God often does not answer us immediately, but He encourages our persistence. He invites us in the silence to explore His character, learn of His will, and gain a proper perspective of how we fit into His plans. He tells us to seek and we will find.

The Test of Silence

"I was sent only to the lost sheep of Israel."

(Matthew 15:24)

In Word From the very beginning of His relationship with Abraham, the father of Israel, God promised to bless all peoples through His chosen nation (Genesis 12:3). When Messiah Jesus came, an old man in the temple affirmed His global mission—He would be "a light for revelation to the Gentiles" (Luke 2:32). Jesus speaks of His "other sheep" and tells parables that shatter the concept of a Jewish-only Savior. The theme of God's mission to *all* peoples is so frequent and constant in Scripture that we are shocked when we hear His words: "I was sent only to the lost sheep of Israel."

So why does He say this to a Canaanite woman in this text? Does it contradict His will for all peoples to honor Him? No, it is a test. Not only does it test the faith of the Gentile woman, it tests the learning of His disciples. Only a few verses earlier, Jesus taught them of vain worship and false purity. Worship and purity are of the heart, He says, not of ritual or of genetics. Whether one is a Jew or not isn't the point. The heart is what matters.

The disciples were asking that this woman be sent away. Had their ethnic focus blinded them to the Messiah's mission? Jesus spoke harshly to show them the natural outcome of their faulty theology. If the disciples seriously thought the Messiah was a Jewish monopoly, this is what He would look like cal lous and compassionless.

"Man may dismiss compassion from his heart, but God will never."

—William Cowper

In Deed What about us? Are we blind to the needs of others? Are our prayer requests so focused on ourselves that no compassion is evident? Do our churches harbor an us-and-them mentality? Are we enamored about what God is doing with "us" and passionless about what God is doing with "them"? If so, imagine the Messiah responding according to our theology and see how badly it fits. Let Jesus expand your vision—as He expanded the disciples' vision—to extend grace to the unlikely and the unlovable.

High and Lifted Up

"I, when I am lifted up from the earth, will draw all men to myself." (John 12:32)

In Word How is Jesus lifted up?

- On the cross. John's commentary in verse 33 is clear: Jesus is indicating the means by which He would die.
- Like the serpent. In Numbers 21, God sent venomous snakes as a result of Israel's sin. Moses was told to put a serpent on his staff and lift it up. Whoever looked at the icon of the curse was spared from the result of the curse. Jesus became the curse for us; if we gaze at the curse on Him, we are spared from the curse on us (see John 3:14-15).
- As an example. Jesus asked the Father to glorify the Son, that the Son might glorify the Father (John 17:1). In His death, He was lifted up both literally and figuratively.
- By the Resurrection. From death to life, from the stench of the grave to the aroma of sacrifice, from a dark tomb to an eternal light—Jesus was lifted up above the archenemy of the human race: death.
- In the Ascension. He was taken up into heaven, lifted above all creation in glory.
- Through our praise. The most glorious scenes in the book of Revelation are of those who worship around His throne: "Worthy is the Lamb, who was slain, to receive power and wealth and wisdom and strength and honor and glory and praise!" (Revelation 5:12).

"The Cross is the ladder to heaven."
—Thomas Drake

In Deed Our Savior is the apex of all that is. There is nothing higher, no one greater. In the great condescension, He came down, clothed Himself in human flesh, and lived among us, only to be lifted up in as shameful a way as man can conceive. But that lifting up—the most evil thing humanity could have done—was the very thing that God uses to draw us to Himself. Our murder of the divine is the very act that God tells us to gaze at to see His judgment of our sin and His plan to redeem us. Never let yourself cease to be drawn to Him.

An Available Presence

"It is for your good that I am going away." (John 16:7)

In Word These words must have sounded absurd to the disciples. They sound absurd to us, too. Good that Jesus isn't with us? No one who has ever cried out, "Where are you, God?" can fathom such a statement. An absent Savior? Our only refuge and help—missing in action? The One with the words of eternal life—working silently behind the scenes? It seems ludicrous to us that there would be any benefit in the absence of the One on whom we have pinned all our hopes.

Jesus tells us why, of course. The next verse explains that the coming of the Holy Spirit is contingent on Jesus' departure. We know the benefit of His absence intellectually, and that the Holy Spirit is alive and present in our lives. But do we know this by experience? Do our minds tell us that the Holy Spirit is in us by faith while our hearts act as if the Spirit of Jesus is far away in a refuge called heaven? Many Christians lapse into knowing the Holy Spirit's help as a psychological advantage but not as a supernatural blessing. He's beneficial as a theological belief but difficult to know in experience.

"There is no human power that can replace the power of the Spirit."
—Lewi Pethrus

But it need not be so. Jesus promised His disciples that the Holy Spirit is a gift for those persistent enough to ask for Him (Luke 11:13). So ask.

In Deed Next time you're trying to understand God's Word or pray according to His will, next time you're trying to overcome sin, next time you're trying to make sense of your circumstances or relieve your pain, stop and remember the assistance available to you. He's the greatest power in the universe, and He makes Himself known through faith and persistent asking. Don't settle for a faint awareness that He is there somewhere, though you're not sure where. Pound on the doors of heaven—read Luke 11:5-13 if that concept bothers you—until He's a reality experienced in your heart. Remember that Jesus would not have left us in body unless He'd planned to come back to us in Spirit, deeper and fuller than we could have ever known Him otherwise.

The God Who Gives

"There was a man who had two sons. The younger one said to his father, 'Father, give me my share of the estate.' So he divided his property between them."

(Luke 15:11-12

In Word We call this the story of the Prodigal Son, but it is perhaps even more the story of a compassionate father. We are told that in the culture of Jesus' listeners, as in any Middle Eastern culture, the younger son's request is extremely offensive. Because estates are never distributed until a father's death, the son may as well have said, "I wish you were already dead so that I can do what I want with your possessions."

"God never tires of giving." —William Still

Isn't this an accurate picture of the human race? Haven't we all sought independence from God, calling His gifts—the body He gave us, the talents we were born with, the material goods He's allowed us to have—our own possessions to do with as we please? At some point in our lives, sinful pride has led us to go our own way, not acknowledging God in our hearts and living, for all practical purposes, as though He were dead. We, like the younger son and all the rest of humanity, have at least once acted as if He were not our Father.

To Jesus' first hearers, the offense of the younger son is stunning. But what is even more stunning is the response of the father. He gives. He knows the true nature of both of his sons, and he still gives them their inheritance.

In Deed Many of us live under the impression that receiving gifts from God is like pulling teeth. We pray and plead for this or that blessing, often ignoring the precious gifts he has already given. But God is a giver. He has already given to us abundantly. He will continue to give. It is a Father's nature.

The God Who Waits

"The younger son got together all he had, set off for a distant country and there squandered his wealth in wild living." (Luke 15:13)

In Word We were once citizens of a distant country. God didn't exile us there, we moved there on our own accord. Like the younger son, we were happy to be independent, away from the stifling presence of the father, though hypocritically satisfied with his wealth. We celebrated and squandered, thinking we were accountable only to ourselves and forfeiting any right we may have ever had to call ourselves His children.

Could there possibly be any better description of our generation than the escapades of the Prodigal Son? Many in our society act as if independence were the highest virtue. Many are living in a distant country and loving it. For now.

Meanwhile, our Father waits. He knows the futility of His children's independence; He knows it will bring them to ruin. But unless they see it themselves, they will not believe it. So He waits.

"God's favorite word is 'come!'"
—Robert L. Sterner

In Deed The waiting Father is a beautiful and welcome picture for those who are coming to believe in Him for the first time. But it is also meaningful for those of us who have long considered ourselves His children. We, too, are prone to live frivolous lives, squandering the benefits and neglecting the responsibilities of living in the Father's household. We, too, have a streak of independence that carries on in spite of our salvation by faith.

Many of us wonder if our failures have caused the Father to turn His back on us. We know He is righteous, and we know we are not. We may think we are no longer welcome in His house. But Jesus' illustration is clear. We have a Father who waits.

The God Who Runs

"But while he was still a long way off, his father saw him and was filled with compassion for him; he ran to his son, threw his arms around him and kissed him."

(Luke 15:2

"God is far more willing to save sinners than sinners are to be saved."
—J. C. Ryle

In Word No other religion pictures its deity like this. No other faith can claim a God who zealously pursues His children. All other deities are distant and elusive, demanding that their dis- ciples come to them, usually on a long and arduous path, often with arbitrary rituals of appeasement. But not the Father that Jesus portrays. He is a God who runs after His children. Never mind the child's past. All of his rebellious arrogance is no longer an issue. Neither are the rags and odor he's wearing when he returns. The return is all that matters, and the Father enthusiastically runs to His child and escorts him into His household.

Why does Jesus give us such a picture? It seems too good to be true. We know we are not worthy of such attention from the Father we've deeply offended. We know He has every right to close His door to us. We know this because, if we were in His position, that is exactly what we'd do.

In Deed Jesus' portrayal of the Father is contrary to human nature; this is no human father. He is contrary to our expectations, contrary to the man-made gods of this world, and contrary to the interpretations with which we and Jesus' hearers have understood God. Like Adam and Eve in the garden, we hid from Him. We know His anger should rightfully burn against us. We don't think He'll be glad to see us.

But our God runs to us. That's what the Incarnation and the Cross are all about. In spite of our rags, the lingering smell of the pig sty, the empty pockets, and the embarrassment that colors ou faces, He throws His arms around us and kisses us. There is nothing appealing about us that compels Him to do so; it is just His nature. May we daily give thanks for such a Father. We can base our lives on the knowledge that we are irrevocably His.

The God Who Celebrates

"But the father said to his servants, 'Quick! Bring the best robe and put it on him. Put a ring on his finger and sandals on his feet. Bring the fattened calf and kill it. Let's have a feast and celebrate.'" (Luke 15:22-23)

In Word The son had taken his leave of the father in order to have a life of riotous partying. Most human fathers would try to break him of this character flaw upon his return. But not the prodigal's father. His response? He throws a party.

No, it's not the same kind of celebration that the son first sought. That kind of celebration revels in unhealthy independence, doing harm to the body and the soul. It is what people do when their hearts are far from the father and they need a substitute for his love. But it leaves its participants alone and empty afterward. The father's party, however—that's a different celebration altogether. It rejoices in unity, building up the body and the soul. It soothes the conscience and deepens joy.

Joy is the serious business of heaven."

–C. S. Lewis

In Deed Do we enjoy our fellowship with the Father like this? We can. Yes, like the son, we know our credentials are unacceptable, our faithfulness is fickle, our return is of questionable motive, and we are not celebrating our victorious living. This party has a better theme.

Our party delights in the nature of our Father. He has taken us back in, He has told us not to worry, and He has given us hope for a future beyond all expectations. It is a celebration of His goodness. And we can and should get used to it; Jesus' description of the feast in this parable and His description of the feast of heaven in other parables say it again and again. Celebrating the Father's goodness is what His kingdom is all about.

The God Who Pleads

"The older brother became angry and refused to go in. So his father went out and pleaded with him."

(Luke 15:28)

In Word Many people think God is obscure, so shrouded in mystery that we may never figure Him out. Jesus' parable gives an entirely different picture. Our God is the God who pleads. He explains Himself and His ways. He seeks out those who don't understand Him or who don't agree with Him. Throughout history He has been revealing Himself, even coming in the form of a man to demonstrate His nature and to reconcile us to Himself.

"God had one Son and He made Him a missionary."
—Leighton Ford

The Bible is clear: God has manifested Himself in the majesty and intricacies of creation; in the moral impulse of all humanity; in His loving and miraculous dealings with His covenant people; in the authority of revealed Scripture; and, clearest of all, in the incarnation of Jesus Christ. No one on the planet has missed out on the pleading of God in *all* of these areas. Two or three, perhaps, but not all.

Many of those who still find God obscure are the older brother in this story. They find Him obscure because they do not accept what He has already said. They either do not want to know Him at all, or they have learned of Him and do not like His policies. They expect Him to be made in their image. But God hasn't cut them off; the Father still goes out to explain His purposes.

In Deed We may sometimes think that in our relationship with God, we were the pursuers and He was the recluse. Jesus, by His existence and His words, indicates that this is not so. Jesus is the pursuer incarnate. The Father goes to the older brothers of the world and pleads.

That's a model we should follow. We live in a world of many recluses, those who have not understood God and, in fact, refuse to understand Him. Still, the Father goes and pleads. He sent His Son for this purpose. And His Son sends us.

What We Need

"Friend, your sins are forgiven." (Luke 5:20)

In Word One of the greatest things a Christian can do for encouragement is to meditate on this verse. Many of us tend to beat ourselves up for our sins. We are right to take sin so seriously. When we are convicted by the Holy Spirit that we are not right in our relationship with God, we should immediately confess, repent, and accept forgiveness. But this last step is difficult for many. The thought of grieving and offending the eternal, sovereign Lord is hard to swallow.

To those who mourn over their sinfulness, Jesus speaks these words: "Friend, your sins are forgiven." The Friend of sinners always has words of comfort for those who know the gravity of sin. He did not come into the world to condemn but to save (John 3:17). Why would we think He might be unwilling to forgive us? These words address our greatest need.

"Christ comes with a blessing in each hand; forgiveness in one, holiness in the other."
—A. W. Pink

The paralytic in this passage came for another reason. Likewise, many Christians also think they have a more urgent need than their sinfulness. To these, Jesus' words also address the greatest need. They remind us of God's priority for us—rescuing us from our subtle but serious danger.

In Deed Wherever we are, this verse redirects us. Whether we come to Jesus under deep conviction for our sin or for something we think is a greater need, this is the best thing He could say to us. If we have a hard time forgiving ourselves for repeated offenses toward God—even though we have confessed and heard His forgiveness—we are at odds with Jesus. We need to see ourselves as He does—clean. If we come to Him with a casual attitude toward sin and what we perceive as a greater request, we are also at odds with Jesus. Then we too must see ourselves as He does—needy.

Do Jesus' words convict you? If so, let them; that was what He wanted you to hear. Do they comfort you? If so, let them; that, too, was what He wanted you to hear.

The Spirit of Life

"The Spirit gives life; the flesh counts for nothing."

(John 6:63

In Word In one terse response to His disciples, Jesus boil it all down. God's kingdom is so encompassing, so eternal, so all-consuming that it means everything. It is life—the source of life, the abundance of life, the destiny of life. All flesh—this world tha we see with our eyes and spend most of our lives obsessing about—means nothing as an end in itself. It exists as a very good part of God's creation, but it has no value—none at all—apart from life in the Spirit.

Disciples of Jesus must eat and drink of the eternal, absorbing everything that Jesus is as part of their daily diet. They must take on His spiritual nature and not give in to the flesh. They must liv with eternal perspectives, considering themselves citizens of a spiritual kingdom. They must understand that the Spirit gives life and that the flesh counts for nothing.

"The future life only brings to fruition the seed sown here."

—Geoffrey B. Wilson

In Deed This may be as hard to hear for us as it was fo Jesus' disciples. We are physically oriented. We must eat and drink of the earth in order to survive. We see the world around us clearly, while our faith in the promises of the kingdom is "ev dence of things not seen" (Hebrews 11:1 KJV). Though we set ou minds on Christ, our eyes are riveted on the things around us and how we will get by in our world. The flesh is compelling.

But Jesus tells us to partake of Him. His is the life that we must take upon ourselves; His words are the Spirit that give us His life (v. 63). We must daily reorient ourselves from the life of the flesh to the life of the Spirit. All of our decisions must be spiritually appraised from an eternal, kingdom-conscious perspective. Like Peter, we must acknowledge to Him: "You have the words of eternal life" (v. 68). Life can be found nowhere else

Servanthood

"The greatest among you should be like the youngest, and the one who rules like the one who serves."

(Luke 22:26)

In Word Would there be any division in the body of Christ if this verse were taken seriously? To our disappointment, our churches and ministries often resemble worldly institutions with their power structures, self-interest, and man-made methods. But the body of Christ is to be radically different. It is to be the one body on earth that subverts the fallen order. It is to be characterized by servanthood and humility.

Jesus modeled this for us. "I am among you as one who serves," He says (v. 27). And He demonstrated His servanthood in a number of ways: ministering to outcasts, washing the disciples' feet, and, most significantly, dying for our sins.

Yet despite the divine example, we often act in ways contrary to the Master. We are more like the disciples who argued about who was the greatest. Our arguments may not take that form—"whose ministry is bearing more fruit?" and "who is elevated to the most prominent leadership positions?" are questions we're more likely to ask—but they amount to the same spirit of contention. They reflect an unwillingness to be like Jesus, no matter how much we might call Him "Lord."

"There are no trivial assignments in the work of the Lord."

- Vance Havner

In Deed Does your church have too many people making themselves available for the most menial tasks? Does it have to turn away volunteers for the most thankless burdens of leadership? How often do we blow wind in the sails of other believers, giving them encouragement for the work they do? Not nearly enough to distinguish us from purely human institutions.

"Your attitude should be the same as that of Christ Jesus," Paul says (Philippians 2:5), before describing the humility of Christ. Christians that are characterized by that attitude glorify Him and demonstrate that they are not of this world.

The Folly of Bitterness

"Forgive, and you will be forgiven." (Luke 6:37

In Word Why do we hang on to bitterness the way we do? We nurse our resentments and cultivate them as though the are doing us a favor. We harbor grudges, often remembering offenses for years. We act as if our mental punishment of someone else somehow brings them to justice. But we deceive ourselves. Bitterness eats away at our lives, stealing our joy and eroding our sense of peace, while never—not once—hurting the one we resent.

This is such a pitiful human tendency, and yet we have all done it. We let offenses—large and small, real and imagined—rob us of the joy God means for us to have. How can we possibly understand God's forgiveness this way? When we focus on judgment and justice toward others, can we ever understand God's mercy toward us? Do we really imagine that those who have sinned against us have sinned greatly, while our offenses against God are minor and easy for Him to overlook? If so, we have it backward. Our sins against God, no matter how small, are offenses against the eternal, infinite Being. They therefore required an eternal, infinite sacrifice. Offenses against us pale in comparison.

"Forgiveness saves us the expense of anger, the cost of hatred, the waste of spirits."

—Hannah More

Jesus' parable of the man who owed the king the ridiculously large amount of 10,000 talents (Matthew 18:23-35) should hit home. He was forgiven his huge debt, only to go out and hold minor accounts against his debtors. His story is our story, least until we learn better. We underestimate the offense of our sins against God and overestimate the offenses of others agains us.

In Deed Far from being a legal prerequisite for our ow forgiveness, Jesus' command to forgive others prepares us to understand the Gospel. The God of extravagant mercy asks us only to get a glimpse of His grace. Do you hold any grudges against others? Get a glimpse of God's mercy by forgiving then

The Goal of History

"And this gospel of the kingdom will be preached in the whole world as a testimony to all nations, and then the end will come." (Matthew 24:14)

In Word Have you ever wondered what God's plan is? There is no clearer statement of the goal of history than this verse. Political scientists have written that the age of liberal democracy marks "the end of history," the fulfillment of political ideology. But history isn't about political evolution. New-Age Darwinists proclaim a next stage in evolution in which we become "superhuman." But history isn't about biological perfection. Economists plot ways to distribute the world's wealth equitably and profitably so that we can achieve material utopia. But history isn't about economics.

No, history is about the kingdom of God and its proclamation among all peoples. And when the kingdom has drawn its members from every people group, Jesus will announce the end of human history. All hopes for utopia—political, economic, human potential, etc.—will be found to have aimed far too low when He comes.

Many philosophers see no direction in history, and so the cultures they influence are directionless. But Jesus allows no such randomness in His followers' lives. We do not drift through history. We are given a goal. We are to point to Christ, the sum of all things (Colossians 1:16-18).

"The mission of the church is more important than the march of armies or the actions of the world's capitals."

-George Eldon Ladd

In Deed Where is your life pointed? Is it consistent with the goal of history that God has made plain? The beauty of His story is that we can be involved in history's progress toward its climax. We are allowed to be co-laborers with God in His plan for this world. Everything we do must be for the building up of His kingdom. Everyone must be involved in its proclamation to all peoples. Every eye must watch for His coming again. Leave it to others to speculate. We can choose the right direction because we know something the world doesn't know—how the story ends.

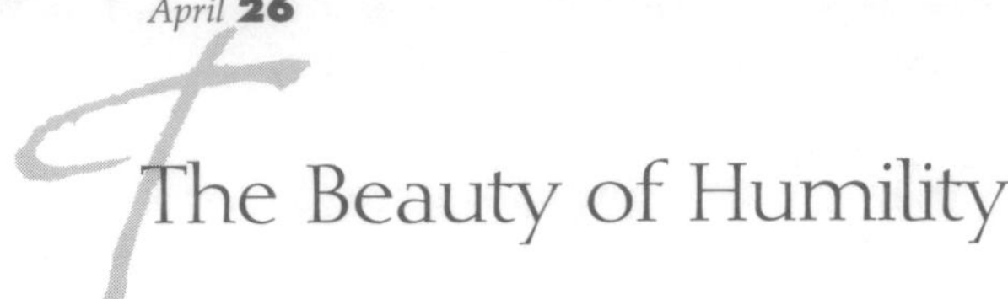

The Beauty of Humility

"Everyone who exalts himself will be humbled, and he who humbles himself will be exalted." (Luke 18:1

In Word Of all the sins known to man—quite a long list—the one condemned most emphatically in the Bible is pride. "God opposes the proud but gives grace to the humble," both Proverbs and James say. Jesus affirms this truth with a striking parable: The man who was too ashamed even to lift his eyes to heaven was the one God forgave. The beauty of humility and the offensiveness of pride are consistent themes in Scripture. Why?

Think about pride as the ultimate escape from reality. It deni that sin is a problem; it exalts self and self-effort; it denies a need for God and refuses His help; it attributes accomplishments to human ability rather than God's gifts; and it completely undermines God's effort to display His grace in the world.

"God can only fill valleys, not mountains."
—Roy Hession

Humility is based on truth. It acknowledges sin; it responds with grief; it sees God as the only hope; it invites Him into this fallen creation; and it allows Him to display His grace. The only difference between heaven and hell for an individual is whether or not one sees his or her brokenness and reacts to it with grief and repentance toward God. Only the humble do that. The prou never get that far.

In Deed Yet many Christians still try to put their best foot forward to make a good impression on the world (or on God). We think God displays Himself in our righteousness. But i it's self-righteousness, He is far from it. He displays Himself bett in our humility, where we are seen as needy and He is seen as merciful. *He* is the beauty in our humility. Christians who want t be exalted by their impressive accomplishments are headed in th wrong direction.

The incredible truth of the Gospel is that the way to be exalte is to fall face down in sorrow and repentance, crying out to God. It's OK to do that. It leaves nothing up to us and *everything* up to Him. There is no better place to be.

Grace to the Humble

"Everyone who exalts himself will be humbled, and he who humbles himself will be exalted." (Luke 18:14)

In Word Peter surely thought of these words of Jesus when he penned his first letter. "All of you, clothe yourselves with humility toward one another, because, 'God opposes the proud but gives grace to the humble.' Humble yourselves, therefore, under God's mighty hand, that he may lift you up in due time," Peter urged (5:5-6). He probably also remembered disputes the disciples had over who was the greatest, or his own unfounded brashness about his devotion to Christ. But years later, Jesus' words had finally sunk in.

Have we allowed them to sink in as well? Think about what this verse means. Not only is it an indictment of pride, it is also a remarkable encouragement to those who have allowed God to strip them of self-sufficiency. We may have walked a painful path when God began removing our false securities, but when He does so, He is there to support us.

"If you lay yourself at Christ's feet, He will take you into His arms."

-William Bridge

In Deed Many Christians go through an agonizing removal of pride. Peter did—he sank in the water when he took his eyes off Jesus, his fishing expertise was bested by the words of a carpenter, and he three times denied the Savior to whom he had just sworn undying allegiance. We are likewise stripped of self-sufficiency. God must do this to us, in fact, if we are to learn to lean on Him. Just as Peter learned this lesson well and urged others to count on God's grace to the humble, so must we.

This is the amazing mercy of our God: When we get to the helpless, hopeless end of ourselves, He is there. And not only is He there, *He exalts us!* He lifts us up, comforts us, and blesses us with the treasures of the kingdom and the gift of His Spirit. By undoing our pride, He equips us to serve Him; and there is no greater pleasure than serving Him. There is no higher calling and no more certain exaltation.

The Heart's Delight

" 'Love the Lord your God with all your heart and with all your soul and with all your mind.' This is the first and greatest commandment." (Matthew 22:37

In Word We live in an age in which many people think God is distant. We are amazed, then, when we learn that the relationship we are called to have with Him exceeds any other relationship in its level of intimacy. We are reluctant to believe such a truth. It is a theological proposition, perhaps, that God desires an intimate relationship with us—something that preachers say to convince us of His love, but that only the super-spiritual actually experience. We may wonder, deep in our hearts, if this is true for all of us.

"Our only business is to love and delight ourselves in God."

—Brother Lawrence

But not only is it true, it is one of the major emphases of the entire Bible. Not only does God love us and we are to love Him; He *delights* in us and we are to *delight* in Him. This is no sterile ac of our will—a love that must press on in spite of the coldness of our hearts. And God's love for us is not portrayed as a struggle for Him, either; He does not simply tolerate us in spite of His lac of feeling. No, the feeling is real. This relationship in its fullness i the most pleasurable relationship we could possible have—with anyone.

In Deed Meditate today on what Jesus says here in the context of two Old Testament verses: "Delight yourself in the LORD" (Psalm 37:4) and "He will take great delight in you, he w quiet you with his love, he will rejoice over you with singing" (Zephaniah 3:17). Think of that. God sings! Not just about anything, but about us! And He asks us to return the feeling. It's an amazing invitation.

Jesus intended this revolutionary truth to sink into our lives. is not just a pleasant pat on the back that will help us have a better day. It is the truth that shapes our hearts for a lifetime. An ete nal lifetime. Allow it to do its work in you, and see your relationship with God transformed.

The Heart's Contentment

" 'Love the Lord your God with all your heart and with all your soul and with all your mind.' This is the first and greatest commandment." (Matthew 22:37)

In Word Despite our extraordinary calling—to experience God's love and to love Him in return—we fill our lives with idols. Given the greatest invitation in the universe, we treat it as an obligation that we might be able to squeeze in around our other interests. Could anything be more ludicrous? The infinite, holy, jealous, merciful, mighty Ancient of Days makes a straight path for us into His heart of passion, and our response is so often to say, "We'll see; I've got some other things I'd like to do, too." The angels must be astonished at the squandering of such an opportunity.

The idols of our hearts grip us tightly. We are afraid to let go of them. We are, in imagery provided by C. S. Lewis, like children content to make mud pies in a slum because we can't imagine what is meant by the offer of a vacation at the beach. We hang on to what we know—our idols—because fellowship with God is too incredible for us to grasp.

Our idols are essentially one-night stands. They provide a moment of empty pleasure, but there is no lasting joy in them. They string us along with the offer of contentment, but contentment never comes. They rob us of something far more valuable—an intimacy of infinite depth with a Lover whose love has no limits.

In Deed The passions that draw us away from God can be intense. Jesus does not ask us to rid ourselves of passion, but to turn that passion toward God. When we realize this and break ourselves free from the illusions—or delusions—that make us think we can find fulfillment in anything other than Him, our lives begin to resemble watered, fruitful oases where there was once desert. Determine to pursue God in love as a response to His loving pursuit of you. Leave everything else behind.

We are half-hearted creatures, fooling about with drink and sex and ambition when infinite joy is offered us. We are far too easily pleased."

-C. S. Lewis

A World of Fear

"When you hear of wars and revolutions, do not be frightened." (Luke 21:

In Word One of the most controversial points of theolog among Christian denominations is our understanding of the end times. And though we'd prefer it if God had spelled things out more clearly for us, He seems intentionally ambiguous on many points. This verse is one of those points. Jesus does not say when wars and revolutions will take place, and specifically when the end will come in relation to the wars and revolutions. He simply says they will come. We can expect them. And we should not be afraid.

All of the signs Jesus gave as preconditions to "the end" hav been going on throughout the ages: wars, rumors of war, revolutions, earthquakes, famines, pestilence, persecution, false messiahs, and various other fearful events. Why was He not more specific? Theories abound, but we can be sure of one thing: Whe we observe the world around us, Jesus wants us to be ready. Christians at all times and in all ages should be ready. And not afraid at all.

> *"All fear is bondage."*
>
> *—Anonymous*

In Deed Today's world can be terrifying. So could the world in the age of Jesus and every era before and after. The sigr Jesus has given are the typical ways of the world. And every Christian's response in this world is to look beyond it to Jesus an His kingdom. We are to be entirely kingdom-focused. Fear indicates a belief somewhere deep inside us that we can be overcome by the ways of the world. We cannot.

Those who are in Christ are overcomers. He prevails, and we are in Him. He guarantees us tribulation in the world, but He als guarantees that He has overcome the world (John 16:33). Fear does battle with our faith. The two cannot coexist. When we fear we submit to the kingdom of this world. When we lift our eyes u in faith, we rise above it.

Just Like Lightning

"As lightning that comes from the east is visible even in the west, so will be the coming of the Son of Man."
(Matthew 24:27)

In Word The kingdom of God came in the person of Jesus, and He came like a seed planted in the ground (Matthew 13:31-32). A few noticed the tilling of the soil and the sowing of the seed, but many had no idea what was going on for years, until the stalk appeared and branches grew. Today, the legitimacy of the kingdom may be questioned by unbelievers, but its presence is not. The religion of Jesus is by no means obscure.

Jesus will not come again as He did the first time. There will be no birth in an obscure Judean stable. He will not live among us unrecognized by even His own brothers. He will not seek those who will consider the evidence and decide whether they will believe in Him. He will come for those who have already settled that question. His return will not be a process, it will be an instant.

Not only will it be sudden, it will be visible. Highly visible. Some rapidly growing cults assert that He has already come in the form of their particular founder. But if He did, He was terribly mistaken about the nature of His return. And we know, of course, that He who was right about so many things was never terribly mistaken about anything. When He comes, it will be sudden, and it will be clear to everyone.

The early Christians were looking not for a cleft in the ground called a grave, but for a cleavage in the sky called Glory."

–Alexander Maclaren

In Deed Many Christians wonder not only when Jesus' second coming will be—which we cannot know—but also what it will look like. Some may wonder if, in fact, He has already come. Will we recognize Him? Will He visit our neighborhood, our state, or even our continent? According to Jesus, *many* will try to deceive us about these things. But His prophecy is absolutely clear. His return will be glorious, everyone will know it, and no one will doubt whether it is the real event. Do not be deceived, and live each day in full anticipation of His sudden, visible return.

Joy or Dread?

"At that time the sign of the Son of Man will appear in the sky, and all the nations of the earth will mourn."
(Matthew 24:3

"The trump shall resound and the Lord shall descend; even so, it is well with my soul."
—Horatio G. Spafford

In Word The nations will deeply mourn at the sign of H coming. But why? We've been told by many that this evolving global culture, this maturing humanity that is learning unity and cooperation, will eventually achieve its full potential. Why woul a human race at its full potential mourn the arrival of its Creator and Savior?

Because all the nations of the world are on the wrong track. People in every nation will rejoice at His coming, but powerful governments will see a greater power, strong economies will see redefinition of what's valuable, and sacred cultural icons will be exposed for the idolatries that they are. When Jesus comes, every one's gig is up. The last will be first, and the first won't like it at all. Every one of the world's most treasured systems of power an status will suddenly realize that its foundations are unfounded.

Jesus' words here are about political and cultural groupings, but we as individuals also might take it to heart. Everyone has a natural reaction to the thought of Jesus coming soon. For some, it's joy. For others, it's dread. If you fit the latter description, it's time to figure out why. Soon.

In Deed Why would a Christian dread the coming of Christ? Perhaps he or she has not fully dealt with the issues of guilt and shame with which sin has infected us. Those feelings ca be deadly, but they can be healed at the Cross. Have you fully understood the implications of the cleansing blood of Jesus? If no let it be your first concern. Dwell on it, meditate on its power, and let it really sink in. Repair relationships, if necessary. Live with a clear conscience.

Others might dread His coming because of unfinished work to which they've been called. Realize that Jesus will not come when there's unfinished work to be done. If He comes, He's don working. And if He's done, so are you. There is *nothing* for a forgiven saint to fear when He appears. Let the nations mourn. We have only rejoicing ahead.

A Promise of Preservation

"I tell you the truth, this generation will certainly not pass away until all these things have happened."

(Matthew 24:34)

In Word Bible-believing Christians easily get hung up on this verse, especially when a critic comes along and tells us that Jesus was wrong about His understanding of the future. Don't get hung up on their arguments. Perhaps segments of the early church misunderstood Jesus' words in this verse, but the text does not necessarily mean that He would return before His hearers died.

The Greek word *genea,* translated in Matthew and Luke as "generation," may certainly mean that. But is it the generation Jesus is speaking to, or the generation that has seen the signs referred to previously in the discourse? That is open to interpretation.

But there's another way to approach the prediction. *Genea* may also mean a race of people, an ethnic group. Historians cannot explain exactly why the Jewish people have not gone the way of the other ancient tribes of the Middle East, but they haven't. They have persisted against all human odds and obstacles. Vastly outnumbered, often attacked, and widely scattered, the Hebraic culture is still around. It has not passed away. The physical people of Israel, as well as the spiritual entity of the church, are given a precious promise in Matthew 24:34, not a questionable prediction. The promise is that they will endure until the very end. Jesus will not let His people fade from the scene before He comes for their final redemption.

"Never be afraid to trust an unknown future to a known God."
—Corrie ten Boom

In Deed Don't let the skeptics mislead you. Jesus and His followers were not wrong about the end times. He has given us a promise. It is especially dear to those who are Jews outwardly, but it applies to those who are Jews inwardly (Romans 2:29) as well. God's people cannot become extinct. Take comfort in that. He will preserve us all, even if He has to move heaven and earth to do so.

Eat, but Understand

"As it was in the days of Noah, so it will be at the coming of the Son of Man." (Matthew 24:37)

In Word What was it like in the days of Noah? To the people that lived then, it was all probably pretty normal. People ate and drank as usual, and they made long-term arrangements like getting married. They worked, played, and laughed, just like we do. They grieved and worried, just like we do. From their frame of reference, it was probably a normal life. There was certainly no disaster on their horizon.

Surely Jesus is not implying that there is something inherently ungodly in eating and drinking and marrying, is He? Didn't He ordain all these things? Yes, but in their proper order. Life was never to consist of these things alone. They were all to be done in the context of a relationship with the living God.

That's what is so subtle about the coming of the Son of Man. Though it will be a dramatic event that all will recognize, the days leading up to it will not. People will eat and drink and marry, and most will not think anything about it. The difference between those who are ready and those who are not will not necessarily be the activities of their lives. We will all eat and drink, and many will marry. But those who are ready will see them as shadows of things to come. They will do them with a longing for the final redemption, with a holy hunger for a more permanent fulfillment. They will know that life—real life—has not yet been fully realized.

"Realize what is true: This world is in haste and the end approaches."

—Gregory the Great

In Deed Many think that being well-fed and well-connected *is* what a fully realized life is like. For them, there is no higher goal, nothing else on the horizon to be looking for. They will be stunned when He comes. The idea of a physically fulfilled life on earth as an ultimate goal will appear ridiculously foolish. As for those in the days of Noah, final judgment will burst upon the scene without warning. Like Noah himself, believers will know that the judgment has been amply foretold. More than that, we will have prepared well for the eternal banquet, longing for its better eating, better drinking, and the ultimate marriage.

Watch, but Wonder

"The Son of Man will come at an hour when you do not expect him." (Matthew 24:44)

In Word Right after Jesus tells His disciples to watch for the signs and to recognize them, to see and to know when the time is near, He tells them that He will come when they do not expect Him. What a curious mix of clarity and mystery! There will be signs and we should expect Him, but no one knows the day or the hour. We are commanded to keep watch but told we will be caught off guard. Is Jesus just pessimistic about our ability to heed His warnings? Or is He really trying to confuse us?

Nearly every generation of Christians has thought that it might be the last generation. Why? Because there have always been wars and rumors of war. There have always been false prophets. There have always been natural disasters that have rocked the world, or at least our corner of it. All of these are signs, and we are told they will be increasing—but we do not know how intensely and to what extent.

Confusion is one of the unfortunate results of Jesus' words predicting His second coming. Many throughout history have tried to specify the day and the hour, even though Jesus told us it could not be done. Many have envisioned elaborate scenarios of the end, though all we've been given are a few controversial signs to watch for. What is Jesus trying to accomplish with so much teaching yet so little certainty?

"Just look in your heart and see if there's room, 'cause Jesus Is coming soon."
—Keith Green

In Deed Jesus wants us to be on guard. He wants us to be able to tell, generally speaking, what events signal the end. But He does not want us to be definite about it. He does not even want us to be sure within ourselves that we are living in the end times. He has given us signs because He wants us to be ready. But He has given us ambiguous signs because He wants *every* generation to be ready. Readiness and a watchful eye are always the appropriate pose of the believer, in all times and in all places. Because of Jesus' words, the expectation has been building throughout church history. That is exactly how He wants it. We are to wait and to watch—and to be ready at any time.

Food That Endures

"Do not work for food that spoils, but for food that endures to eternal life." (John 6:27

"Learn to hold loosely all that is not eternal."

—Maud Royden

In Word One of the saddest moments in a person's life may be in facing later years and knowing deep inside that his or her life has been invested in passing things. Facing eternity, what will last? What has been invested in the real world, the kingdom of God?

We work hard, spend much money and time, and agonize over decisions that may only help us for a few decades, at best. And while we may have legitimate responsibilities in this life that keep us occupied, we too easily become absorbed in the here and now. All the while, we squander opportunities to invest in eternal treasures.

Other than God Himself, only two things are mentioned in Scripture as lasting forever: the Word of God and the souls of human beings. These two areas are where Jesus calls us to involve ourselves. No genuine investment in them will spoil; they are the "food that endures."

In Deed Once every few weeks, Christians should take inventory of their lives. How do we spend our time? How do we spend our money? Where is our energy going? What do we think about when we lie down at night and when we wake up in the morning? When we face our later years, what will we see that is lasting? When the world itself passes away, what of our work will remain? Answering these questions regularly will keep our lives on track and give us focus. They will direct us well.

Jesus gives us very clear instructions in approaching these questions. "Do not work for food that spoils," He tells us. Our lives should be entirely eternity-focused. We were created to bear fruit that lasts (John 15:16). When we invest ourselves in anything else, we are falling short of our purpose, missing the abiding joy of kingdom fruitfulness. Work for food that endures.

For His Glory

"This happened so that the work of God might be displayed in his life." (John 9:3)

In Word It is in the nature of man to ask why. We see tragedy in our world and we ask why. We encounter hardship in our lives, or suffer loss, and we ask why. We want to know the reason for it all, the unifying purpose behind this strange, needy world. Jesus reminds us: It is all for the glory of God. The universe exists to display His splendor.

We can see many specific examples in Scripture. The Israelites were kept as slaves in Egypt in order that God might be known as Deliverer (Exodus 11:9). He led them to near disaster at the edge of the Red Sea in order that He might gain glory (Exodus 14:4). Many psalms of David would never have been sung if not for his persecution. This man in John 9 was blind for his entire life "that the work of God might be displayed." Paul suffered in order that Christ's power might be seen (2 Corinthians 12:9-10).

But we are slow. We can't help but think this universe is about us, and when life is hard on us, it doesn't make sense.

We were made to be prisms refracting the light of God's glory into all of life."

–John Piper

In Deed If we remember that it is all about Him, we begin to see. It all makes sense. By our captivity He is known as Deliverer. By our sin He is known as Savior. By our weakness He is known as powerful. Next to our hatred, His love amazes. Every evil we can think of has the potential of being a platform for the goodness of God. It's all about Him.

Do we suffer and question God's goodness? Do we complain about our hardships? If so, we have forgotten that the universe is meant to glorify God, not us. Consider how His power might be made known in our trials. Redirect your prayers not to improve your situation but to have your situation demonstrate His glory. Thank Him for making Himself known.

Understanding Authority

The centurion replied, ". . . just say the word, and my servant will be healed. For I myself am a man under authority, with soldiers under me . . ." When Jesus heard this, he was astonished and said. . . ,"I tell you the truth, I have not found anyone in Israel with such great faith." (Matthew 8:8-10)

In Word Jesus promised His disciples authority (Luke 10:19). He said all authority had been given to Him, and He instructed His followers to use it. So why, in our prayer and service, do we experience so little power?

The centurion knows the key. He identifies himself as a man first and foremost *under* authority. Only then does he identify his own influence. His command over others has a prerequisite—his submission to a higher command.

If you wonder where to find the authority Jesus has given His people, examine your submission to His authority over you. Are you obedient? Even—or especially—in the small things? If not, understand the principles of authority. The authority of an ambassador flows from his compliance with his home government. The influence of a vice president flows from his consistency with his president. An employee is only authorized to act in the interests of his employer. It is no coincidence that Jesus was obedient unto death (Philippians 2:8) *and* that His ministry was so incredibly powerful.

"God doesn't give kingdom authority to rebels."

—Adrian Rogers

In Deed The kingdom authority that Jesus offers to His believers appeals to us when it is the authority we can exercise in our prayers and service over powers of darkness and evil influences. But authority is a two-sided coin, and we find far less appeal to Jesus' command over us. We call Him Lord, but find His lordship difficult, especially in what we consider "minor" matters of obedience. But the minor matters make a major difference. You will find that your experience of power over the enemy directly correlates to your experience of Jesus' power over you.

Withered Offerings

"Stretch out your hand." (Luke 6:10)

In Word A man with a withered hand had come to the synagogue. We'll never know this side of heaven how his infirmity had affected his relationship with God. Was he angry? Disillusioned? Content in the midst of suffering? We can only guess. We do know, however, that he was in the local place of worship on the regular day of worship. And that's where Jesus met him.

Jesus asks surprisingly little of the man with the withered hand. His purpose was to create a stage for Himself in front of unbelieving Pharisees. He does not wait for a demonstration of faith, as He does with other supplicants. He does not even wait for the man to approach Him. Jesus singles out the recipient of His mercy and gives him only two instructions: "Stand in front" (v. 8) and "Stretch out your hand."

Isn't this how God has dealt with many of us? We had very little to offer Him other than a desire to worship God. We had no great demonstration of faith, no noble and zealous pursuit of the Master, no clear awareness of His power. We were just there. He saw us and He told us what to do.

Even though we have so little to offer Him, He still requires something of us—a withered hand. We must take this sin-racked limb—the epitome of our fallen nature—and stretch it out to Him. Though we are wholly corrupt, withered in body and soul, we must nevertheless reach for Him at His call. Fallenness is all we have; in His mercy, it's all He asks of us.

"We have no power from God unless we live in the persuasion that we have none of our own."

—John Owen

In Deed Do you strive to offer your good hand to Jesus? He won't accept it. It's not the stuff of miracles. No, remember where He found you. Perhaps you've been overestimating your offerings to Him. When you do that, you are conversely underestimating His power in your life. You are contributing far too much. Own up to your withered hand, and let His strength be demonstrated in your weakness. It's the only way He'll show an unbelieving world the power of God.

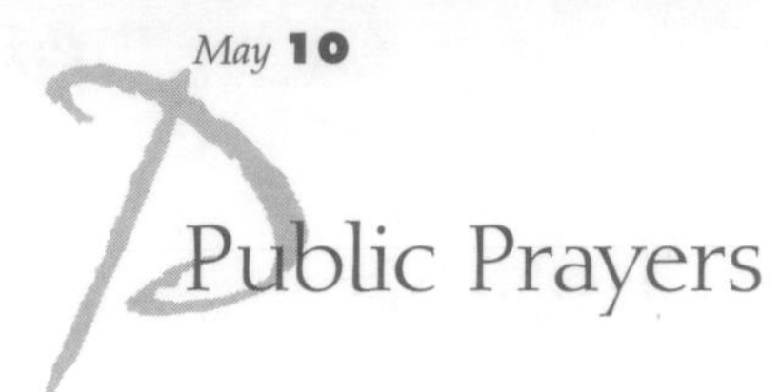

Public Prayers

"I knew that you always hear me, but I said this for the benefit of the people standing here, that they may believe that you sent me." (John 11:42)

In Word Too often our prayers are the private matter of our own hearts. That is, of course, where they begin. That is where God deals with us and speaks to us. But not all prayers are to be left there. The glory of God is a public matter, and nowhere on earth is God more glorified than when He is clearly at work. Miracles occur every day, but they often go unnoticed or are considered "coincidental" because no one heard the specific prayer of someone's heart that God answered in His mercy and power. When mercy and power come, the prayer needs to have already been on record. God is glorified as He responds to public requests.

Jesus spells this out for us. As He approaches the tomb of Lazarus, He is grateful for the public forum. He could have done this miracle with a minimum of onlookers and in the privacy of the tomb. He could have lifted up a silent prayer, leaving people to wonder whose prayers were answered. Was Lazarus raised because of Mary and Martha's goodness? Because of Lazarus' faithfulness? Because of a huge medical misunderstanding? No, it was a divine response to Jesus' prayer. It was, in essence, yet another sign from heaven saying, "This is my Son." It was validation that God was at work in Jesus, and that Jesus was doing God's work. How do we know? Because before Lazarus got up, Jesus prayed. Out loud.

"Large asking and large expectation on our part honor God."

—A. L. Stone

In Deed We're afraid to pray such risky prayers. That's understandable; we should only pray them after we've arrived at a position of faith and confidence in God's will and with sensitivity to His timing. But once we're there, we need to let God show His glory publicly. His demonstration of power is usually not a private, personal matter. It is more often a showcase for His mercy. When our prayers are witnessed by others, and then God answers, He receives honor and the faith of others is strengthened.

A Divine Privilege

"The knowledge of the secrets of the kingdom of heaven has been given to you." (Matthew 13:11)

In Word Have you ever wondered why a group of people can hear the exact same truth presented in exactly the same way, and half will believe and the other half won't? We might be inclined to attribute the phenomenon to the different personalities and backgrounds of the hearers, and that's probably part of the explanation. But there's more. The mysteries of the kingdom must be given. They cannot be discerned merely by human inquiry and logic. The kingdom is not made known by a scientific discovery, and it never will be. The intellect of mankind cannot and will not figure it out.

What is offered . . . is not truth concerning God, but the living God Himself."
–William Temple

That explains why some of our planet's greatest geniuses were clueless when it came to the things of God. Revelation is the key, and revelation is given to seeing eyes and hearing ears. In other words, hearts that are inclined to learn of God will learn; hearts that are inclined to explain Him away will remain utterly confounded and dark.

And consider the treasure that this revelation is. What a privilege! The answers to all of humanity's questions, the pursuit of the thinkers of all generations, the mysteries of the universe—all are given to those humble souls who will take up this Gospel and read it with a hunger in their heart to hear God speak. The answer to every *why* and *what for* is given not to the brilliant intellects but to the common seeker. Those who want to meet God on His terms and not their own will have divine mysteries opened up before them.

In Deed What a blessed treasure we've been entrusted with! What a sacred knowledge! We're no more entitled to glimpse divine mysteries than a vagrant is to sit in the Oval Office and discuss policy, yet we've been given a glimpse anyway. The relevant question for us is this: What will we do with that knowledge? It wasn't given for entertainment; it was given to pass on to those who will welcome it. Share it everywhere. The divine privilege is entrusted to those who know what to do with it.

Visions in the Storms

"It is I; don't be afraid." (John 6:20

In Word Sometimes terrifying circumstances come into our lives. And we, who fear the unknown, don't like the unexpected visions they bring. The disciples were terrified when, in the middle of a storm in the dark of night, a figure walking on th rough water approached their boat. They had never before encountered this, of course. Was it a ghost? Did it mean them harm? What are fishermen to do when out of the wind-blown waters comes a mysterious apparition?

Jesus allowed for the disciples' momentary panic, but He did not leave them in the dark, literally or figuratively. His identity was quickly revealed. "It is I; don't be afraid." His presence is the antidote to terror. Jesus calms storms, whether those storms rage outside the boat or inside our hearts. One way or another, He brings peace if we will only hear His words: "It is I."

Life is full of circumstances that are terrifying at first glance and can consume us with worries about the future. Financial crises, health crises, spiritual dilemmas, emotional needs, and any other vision that threatens us in a storm cause us much stress. Bu here is the lesson learned by the disciples: What initially made them panic was the very Person who brought them growth, faith, rest, and guidance.

"Jesus came treading the waves; and so He puts all the swelling tumults of life under His feet. Christians—why afraid?"

—St. Augustine

In Deed Our crises can do the same. Though our initial reaction may be panic, in reality Jesus may be coming to us with a crisis that heals, strengthens, encourages, or guides. To us, they are threatening. To God, they are often the very means to develop us as His disciples. They may bear eternal fruit that our terrified eyes cannot at first see.

Will we, like the disciples, take Jesus "into the boat" (v. 21)? When they did, John reports, they immediately reached the shore Their panic—like ours most often is—had been unfounded. Jesus brings them, and us, safely to solid ground.

Walk on Water

"You of little faith," he said. "Why did you doubt?"
(Matthew 14:31)

In Word If our ears are truly open to Jesus, we will probably hear such a rebuke daily. It is a gentle rebuke, coming from One who understands our frailties better than we understand them ourselves. But it is a firm reminder that the life we live is to be radically different than dependence on our human senses and reasoning that most of the world understands.

In this story, Peter has put Jesus to the test, in a sense. And Jesus lets him! "Come," He says, inviting Peter to walk on the water just as Jesus does. Peter's resulting experience mirrors ours. We hang in the balance between faith and unbelief, alternately fixing our gaze on Christ and then on the waves around us. Unfortunately, the latter frequently loom larger to us. We sometimes even obsess about this wind and these waves, which do not hesitate to tell us that we are doing the impossible—living supernatural lives. Frequently, we listen to them and we sink.

F.E.A.R.— False Evidence Appearing Real." —Anonymous

But the call of Jesus is this: "Come." We *are* to live supernatural lives. We may think we are being appropriately sensible when we measure the wind and waves and proceed with caution. But Jesus urges us to ignore them altogether and fix our eyes on Him. *He alone* is the true measure of our situation. When He tells us to step out on the water, *we can*, regardless of how many contrary warnings against it we have ever heard or imagined. His is the only voice we must hear.

In Deed The circumstances of our lives, whether unusual crises or everyday difficulties, batter our senses into believing untruths. We cower at the authority of these winds and waves—these very concrete illusions—as though their authority is real. It isn't. We must do what is extremely difficult for us human beings to do—ignore them. We must get to the point where we hear His voice alone and become deaf to all others. Then we will know what it's like to walk on water.

His Life, Not Ours

"Apart from me you can do nothing." (John 15:5

In Word This is one of the foundational truths of our discipleship. If we do not learn this early, we may spend years of frustration trying to be the Christians God calls us to be. Our natural tendency is to try hard, be sincere, study diligently, and trair ourselves to be the disciples we were meant to be. And there is a sense in which all of this is good—even necessary—if it is done with the knowledge that God is working in us all the while as ou enabler. But when we use all this self-effort to attain our own growth, we quickly find ourselves feeling like failures. We come to a startling conclusion: Only Jesus can live the Christian life; we can't. We can only have Him live that life in us.

Jesus is clear: He has not come to be just our Teacher, our Guide, our Savior, and our Lord. He is all of that and more. He is our Life. In a very real sense, we died with Him on the cross and He now lives in us (Galatians 2:20). He breathes His Spirit into us He sustains us, He bears His fruit in us, and He does His work ir us and through us. When we think we led others to Christ, we didn't. He did. When we think we've become more patient, loving, or joyful, we only became so because He did that in us. It is all His work.

"He who trusts in himself is lost. He who trusts in God can do all things."
—Alphonsus Liguori

In Deed Much of the Christian life is God stripping us o our self-effort so that He can live His life in us without our interference. We stress and strain over our discipleship, but God is after our relenting and our trust in His strength. When we find ourselves in circumstances that are beyond our control, frustratec from our lack of effectiveness, we can know with certainty that w are to realize our weakness and rely on His strength. God often places us in situations that are over our heads—even letting us fa miserably, sometimes—in order to teach us this. He must break u of self-reliance. We are never to depend on our own strength and strategies. We are to be utterly dependent on the power of God that works in us and in our circumstances.

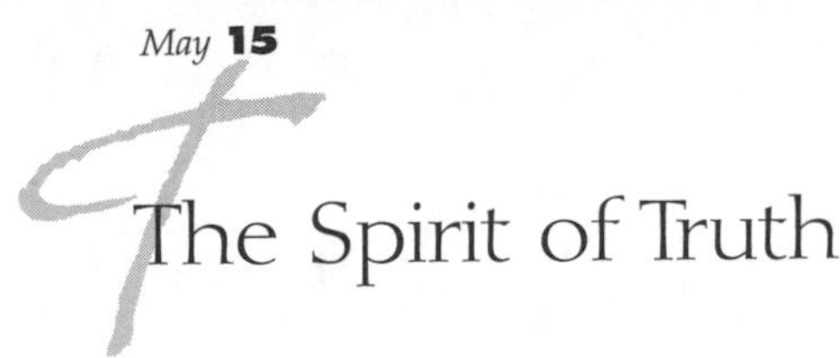

The Spirit of Truth

"You know him, for he lives with you and will be in you." (John 14:17)

In Word Jesus promises His disciples that they will be inhabited by His own Spirit. Such an extravagant promise should lead us to a very natural question, though many Christians never think to ask it: If His Spirit is in us, what will we be like? The answer is that we will be like Him.

How is it that many of us study the Holy Spirit in Scripture and never get around to relating the Spirit to the character of Christ? We look for signs of the clearly supernatural, and certainly they may be present. But above all of the highly visible manifestations of the Spirit is this more subtle supernatural work: The Holy Spirit makes us like Jesus. In our character and in our will, we grow to be like Him as the Spirit does His work.

"We know the truth, not only by the reason, but also by the heart."

—Blaise Pascal

This week we will examine this work of the Spirit—making us Christlike. And Jesus calls His Spirit "the Spirit of truth." What does it mean for us that "truth" is part of one of His revealed names? It means that He will remind us of Jesus' words, His teaching (14:26); He will guide us into all truth when we are confused and lack wisdom (16:13); and we ourselves will be known by our truthfulness, because He will infuse us with His pure, uncompromising nature.

In Deed There are some things in life that we can only know by revelation. Human wisdom is not enough for our understanding of God or for our daily decisions. But God reveals Himself and His will to us. We are not limited by our finite thinking. He works His truth into our minds.

We are also stewards of truth. We cannot become casual in our portrayal of truth, whether in the minor details of life or the proclamation of the eternal Gospel. We can't fudge the facts a little to make ourselves look better, or to get us out of difficult circumstances; and we can't soften the truths of the Gospel for a low-tolerance world. Those who are filled with His Spirit will be guided by—and always known for—uncompromising truth.

The Spirit of Compassion

"You know him, for he lives with you and will be in you."

(John 14:17)

In Word How often we read of Jesus having compassion on others. In Matthew 9:36, He had compassion on the crowds, who were like sheep without a shepherd. In Matthew 14:14, He had compassion on the sick. In Luke 7:13, He had compassion on the widow of Nain, whose only son (and means of support) had died. In John 11:35, He wept with Mary and Martha over the death of their brother. Mark 1:41 says He was "filled with compassion" for a leper. The sick, the hungry, the prodigals of this world are all objects of His concern.

In Jesus, we see the compassion of an infinite God in the heart of a human body. What an overflow of emotion! We feel the physical stress from our finite emotions and are overwhelmed by them. How much more does the compassion of God exceed the limits of human expression! We are amazed at the implications of boundless love incarnate. The infinite is expressed by the finite. The Son of God and the Son of Man are one.

"Every act of compassion done by anyone for his fellow Christian is done by Christ working in him."

—Julian of Norwich

In Deed The amazing thing about Jesus' compassion is not just that it is an expression of God's emotions in a human form. What is really amazing is that His emotions are also expressed through us when His Spirit reigns in our hearts. We have access to a love beyond ourselves. When we come across the really unlovable, we may ask Him to love them through us. When our human nature recoils at the offensiveness of others, we may trust the Holy Spirit to minister to them in spite of our own impulses.

Jesus' compassion reaches into lepers' wounds. It goes to the side of the road where victims lie. It sees needs and seeks to meet them. It welcomes offensive prodigals back home. If Jesus is love incarnate, and His Spirit is in us, we will love with His kind of compassion. This compassion will come from beyond ourselves. All we have to do is ask Him for it.

The Spirit of Comfort and Peace

"You know him, for he lives with you and will be in you." (John 14:17)

In Word When we base our contentment on our circumstances, we find that our lives have a way of repeating a cycle; we go through periods of peace punctuated by periods of turmoil. We enjoy the equilibrium, but we often become quite unsettled when the storms of life hit.

Jesus spoke to His disciples as a storm began to swell around Him. He knew their world would be rocked. He knew that the very next day after He spoke to His disciples about the Holy Spirit, their vision of helping the Messiah establish His earthly kingdom would die. Everything they had invested their lives in for the last three years would collapse in front of their very eyes. And this is what He told them as this storm began to blow: "Peace I leave with you; my peace I give you . . . Do not let your hearts be troubled and do not be afraid" (John 14:27).

"The world can create trouble in peace, but God can create peace in trouble."
—Thomas Watson

Jesus speaks often in John 14–16 about the Holy Spirit's comforting purpose. Where many translations use "Counselor," others use "Comforter." Both are appropriate. The word can be translated as either one; the Spirit is a comforting Counselor who promises us peace, and He is a counseling Comforter who promises to relieve our fears.

In Deed When we are unsettled, we ask a lot of "why" questions. "Why did this happen to me?" "Why does God seem so absent?" "Why doesn't God *do* something?" During these times, we must remember the promise of the Holy Spirit, a promise from a sovereign God who is "an ever-present help in trouble" (Psalm 46:1). Faith will make His presence—with all of His peace and comfort—real to us.

But what if this same Spirit lives within us? Not only will we have comfort and peace, we will minister to others in their trials. We will be comforting counselors and/or counseling comforters. We will represent "the God of all comfort" (2 Corinthians 1:3) as He ministers through us.

The Spirit of Missions

"You know him, for he lives with you and will be in you." (John 14:17

"The Holy Spirit is God the evangelist." —J. I. Packer

In Word Once again, we must consider how this verse plays out in our lives. If the Holy Spirit of God comes to live in us, what will we be like? He is a missionary Spirit, and we will be missionary people. Let's consider our missionary God:

- In His covenant with Abraham, He promises to bless *all people on earth* (Genesis 12:3).
- In affirming that covenant with Isaac and Jacob, He promises again to bless *all peoples on earth* (Genesis 26:4; 28:14).
- He gave Solomon wisdom so that *all nations* might hear of the wisdom of God (1 Kings 4:34).
- His grace to Israel is for *all nations'* salvation (Psalm 67:2).
- He blesses Israel's king for the sake of *all nations* (Psalm 72:11, 17).
- He desires praise from *all nations* (Psalm 148:7-11).
- His temple is established for the sake of *all nations* (Isaiah 2:2; 56:7; Jeremiah 3:17).
- He tells His disciples to go into *all nations* (Matthew 28:19).
- In the end, He will gather to Himself people of *all nations* (Isaiah 66:18; Revelation 7:9; 15:4).

In Deed Jesus confirms that God's Spirit pursues those who do not know Him: "When the Counselor comes, whom I will send to you from the Father, the Spirit of truth who goes ou from the Father, he will testify about me. And you also must testify, for you have been with me from the beginning" (John 15:26-27). If the Holy Spirit testifies, and that Spirit comes to live in us then we will testify. If we have a missionary God residing in our hearts, they will be missionary hearts.

Do we claim the blessing of His Holy Spirit and then act or think contrary to that Spirit? Then something is wrong. We must re-examine, repent, be refilled, and be refreshed—and be one with His purposes.

The Spirit of Sacrifice

"You know him, for he lives with you and will be in you." (John 14:17)

In Word Jesus' life can be described as a life of sacrifice. Not only on the cross did He pour out His blood to redeem us from our sins, but during His ministry He constantly worked long hours, washed others' feet, touched lepers' sores, suffered the threats of violent men, and dealt patiently with hard-hearted disciples. While we may be thankful that He "made himself nothing" (Philippians 2:7) on our behalf, we cannot escape the implications of His example: Our attitude should be exactly the same as His (Philippians 2:5).

Great victory has never been possible without great sacrifice."

-Samuel Zwemer

Self-sacrifice is not human nature. We are more inclined toward self-preservation. Yet in fundamental ways, the Gospel contradicts human nature. Human nature is the aberration that we fell into with our sin; it is a "fallen" nature. Why would we settle for it? God's intention for us is entirely contrary to our fallenness. It is to be like Him; we were made in His image, and through Christ He is conforming us to His image. So for those of us who say we have the love of Christ in us, how can we truly believe it if we are not willing to pour out our lives for others as He did? If His love is sacrificial, and His love is in us, then we will be sacrificial. If we are not, His love is not in us.

In Deed How does sacrifice play out in your life? Is your love the kind that the world has or that Jesus has? We too easily convince ourselves that we have the love of Christ within us when we love our friends and relatives deeply. And God does want us to have this kind of love. But we cannot be convinced that His love truly dwells within us until we see ourselves behaving like Him.

Do we love the unlovable? Do we sacrifice ourselves for others, for what God says is their good? Are we willing to pay any price—even to the point of death—that others might know His love? That is how His love behaves. It sacrifices.

The Mercy Gift

"Blessed are the merciful, for they will be shown mercy." (Matthew 5:7

In Word How do we know if we understand the mercy of God? How do we know if His gospel of grace has really sunk into our hearts and become a part of us? There's an easy test. Jesus summarizes it here: If you are the kind of person who show mercy, you are the kind of person who has experienced mercy. Merciful hearts grow from seeds of mercy sown in them. If we have really tasted forgiveness, we will lengthen its chain and offe it to others.

Jesus told a sobering parable to illustrate the point. A servan owed a king an impossibly huge sum of money. Not being able t pay it, the servant and his family were subject to being sold into slavery. But begging on his knees for patience, the servant drew sympathy from the king, who generously forgave the debt. Had the servant really experienced mercy? No, he had benefited from it, but he had not really understood it. He went out and demanded trivial payments from his debtors, bringing full charges against those who could not pay. Mercy had never sunk in. He had no clue what it meant.

"Do you wish to receive mercy? Show mercy to your neighbor."

—John Chrysostom

In Deed We're often the same way. Every time we judge another for forgetting to return a borrowed item, for cutting in front of us in traffic, for slighting us or assaulting our dignity, for careless words, or any other real or imagined insult, we have forgotten. The slights and insults, assaults and carelessness that we've heaped on God—and been forgiven for—are infinitely greater than anything we've ever been subjected to. And yet Jesu died for us *while we were still sinners!* That kind of grace is utterly amazing.

Human nature is hypocritical. We regard others' offenses much more highly than our own. Ours were simply oversights; theirs are insults. Don't buy into that double standard. Take this test: Are you judgmental toward others? Easily offended? Go bac to the Cross and meditate on the forgiveness God has given you. It will thoroughly cure you of any lack of mercy.

The Mercy Dilemma

"Blessed are the merciful, for they will be shown mercy." (Matthew 5:7)

In Word Have you ever noticed something odd about how we respond when people offend us? Have you ever really thought about our natural reaction? Our first gut feeling in such cases is to respond in kind, to return ill will for ill will, to rise to the same level of spite with which we've been treated. Why is that?

We know the options that are available to us. We could respond with equal offense; we could choose simply to not care; or we could respond with a demonstration of mercy. But almost invariably, our first reaction is to meet evil with evil. We are offended first, and then we have to talk ourselves into a gracious attitude and a merciful response. It is never the other way around, where we first feel merciful and wonder why we aren't more offended. The natural self has its preferences, and this is one of its strongest. The options are before us, but the impulses know of only one.

"The more godly any man is, the more merciful that man will be."
—Thomas Benton Brooks

Somehow, we must reverse the impulses. We must learn to think of mercy first. How can we do that? How can we alter something that is so ingrained, so unyielding a part of our sinful nature? How can mercy become more natural to us than our sense of vengeance?

In Deed The key is to ask the question that's really underneath the others: How can we be more like God? Moses asked for a glimpse of God, and as God passed by, He defined Himself as "the compassionate and gracious God, slow to anger, abounding in love and faithfulness, maintaining love to thousands, and forgiving wickedness, rebellion and sin" (Exodus 34:6-7). That's the core of who He is. That's what we're really asking here; how can we be more like that?

We have two options: We can try to reform the sinful human nature, or we can ask God for His nature. The former approach has never in history proven successful. You have probably already seen that for yourself, so give it up. Our only remaining option is to ask God. He offers us His nature. We must ask and believe He will give it. He always does.

Deeper Warfare

"When you stand praying, if you hold anything agains anyone, forgive him, so that your Father in heaven may forgive you your sins." (Mark 11:25

In Word There is a direct link between the forgiveness i our hearts and the efficacy of our prayers. Those who are relucta to forgive others are out of sync with God's character. Those whc know the depths of God's forgiveness for themselves apply that depth to their forgiveness of others, and are at one with the Father's purposes. They therefore pray consistently with godly character and are aware of God's purposes in the world. Their prayers avail much.

It is on this point that we often misstep. When we run into difficult people, we focus on resolving our relationships with them. We may believe that Satan's warfare against us is also focused on these relationships. If he can disrupt them, he wins battles; if we can maintain them, we think we win. But there is a deeper battle going on. The enemy uses contentious relationship as a tool toward a more profound warfare. If he can sow seeds o bitterness and resentment in our hearts, he hinders our prayers. And he is far more interested in hindering prayers than simply seeing people argue.

In Deed When we try to resolve broken relationships, w cannot afford to focus on the externals, seeking to preserve civili and keep the peace. There is a much more intense and high-stak war going on in our hearts. We must not only preserve peace wi our friends and enemies alike, we must also preserve peace in ou hearts. A restored relationship is fine with the evil one if we lose worshipful, joyful, prayerful, forgiving attitude in the process.

This is one reason God often puts His people in difficult and even oppressive circumstances. When we have learned to remai worshipful in an oppressive situation, we have won the battle, regardless of the outward resolution. This is the "standing firm" referred to in Ephesians 6:13. And our prayers can remain unhin dered.

> *"If there is the tiniest grudge in your mind against anyone, your spiritual penetration into the knowledge of God stops."*
>
> —Oswald Chambers

Discerning the Liar

"When he lies, he speaks his native language, for he is a liar and the father of lies." (John 8:44)

In Word The best lies are slight variations on the truth. Anyone can pick out an obvious counterfeit. The ones closest to reality are the most difficult to detect. So it is with the father of lies. He is only overt when no discerning eyes are around. But the more we discern, the more subtle he gets in his perversions of truth. He will taint the Gospel with the slightest of heresies—if we let him.

This is why some of the most deceptive cults have begun with Christianity as their starting point. The Gospel plus a bit of paganism or a dash of secularism is an appealing formula for the liar. We must *always* guard against anything that modifies the purity and simplicity of the message that Jesus died for our sins and was resurrected as our hope.

Our culture has fallen for the lies. It has no problem with our saying that Jesus is a way, a truth, and a life. It's when we say Jesus is the only way, the only truth, and the only life—the only way to the Father (John 14:6)—that the enemy gets uncomfortable. He hates the exclusivity of the Gospel, and he has inspired our culture to rebel against it. It is, and has always been, a scandalous proposition that there is only one way of salvation. The world rails against such particularity. It can tolerate anything but truth.

"The use of a counterfeit is Satan's most natural method of resisting the purpose of God."

-Stephen Slocum

In Deed Jesus tells us we are to be as wise as serpents but as innocent as doves (Matthew 10:16). Paul tells us that he is not—and neither should we be—ignorant of the enemy's schemes (2 Corinthians 2:11). And we are urged, even commanded, to put on the armor of God against the scheming weapons of the enemy (Ephesians 6:11).

It is a treacherous world, with deceptions scattered about like well-hidden land mines. The terrain is difficult. There is no way through it without strict adherence to the map. Let your mind absorb it; use it well and discern the lies.

Exposing the Liar

"When he lies, he speaks his native language, for he is a liar and the father of lies." (John 8:44

In Word The father of lies will try to deceive us in many ways. But he seems to have an overarching strategy that is twofold: 1) He wants to tell us we're more than we are; and 2) he wants to tell us God's less than He is.

There is a huge gap between sinful humanity and holy God. God bridged that gap with the perfect blend of justice and love—the Cross. Satan wants to bridge it in any alternate way he can. He elevates us and devalues God. If we can be reconciled with our Creator by our being a little bit better and by God being a little more reachable, then he has nullified our sense of need for the Cross. He has undermined the legitimate craving we have for reconciliation with the holy.

"The spiritual battle, the loss of victory, is always in the thought-world."
—Francis Schaeffer

How does the liar elevate us? He tells us that we're not as bad off as the Bible makes us out to be; or that sin isn't really that serious; or that sin doesn't really exist; or that we're able to overcome it with our good works; or, as in this passage, that our heredity is enough—we're of decent enough stock as children of Abraham or any other tradition.

And how does the liar devalue God? He can't, really, but he can change our perspective. He makes God appear unloving and distant, not worth pursuing; or so loving that He has no real concept of sin and tolerates all we do; or that He is pleased as long as our good works outweigh our bad; or, as in this passage, that our own thoughts and judgments seem so right to us that they must have come from God Himself. Regardless of the lie, our twisted perspective makes God the sanctioner of all we want Him to sanction.

In Deed Expose the liar. The gap between the infinitely holy and the utterly sinful can only be bridged by the blood of the Savior. Satan will do anything to convince us otherwise. He wants us to compromise the truth of the Gospel of salvation. But he lies. Always has, always will. Expose him everywhere you go.

Rejecting the Liar

"When he lies, he speaks his native language, for he is a liar and the father of lies." (John 8:44)

In Word Not only will Satan lie to us about ourselves; He will lie to us about God. Just as we may count on the fact that any search for fulfillment in something other than God and His gifts is futile, we may count on the fact that the enemy will lie to us about the character of the Father.

Have you heard Him? Any hint that God is not trustworthy came from him. Any nagging doubt that perhaps God's promises are not entirely reliable came from him. Any subtle thought that depicts a God made in the likeness of corruptible human beings, with petty thoughts and an unforgiving spirit, is his work. He is a liar and the father of lies. Nothing he says is legitimate.

Satan is out to distort God's image. He poisons our understanding by inspiring false philosophies, by offering false promises, and even by manipulating the Word of God to say what it doesn't really say. He is not so much interested in our thoughts and our captivity. He is interested in degrading the reputation of God on earth. In that pursuit, he is zealous.

Satan strikes either at the root of faith or at the root of diligence."

-John Livingstone

In Deed We let him get away with it, don't we? Any time we question God's goodness, distort His Word, pursue unbiblical insights, or craft our own image of God to suit our own purposes, we have fallen for the lies. The world is full of false deities. "God" has become the force, the embodiment of "love" (by our definition), the philosophical first cause, a distant observer, the opiate of the masses, a psychological crutch, and a host of other impersonal, unholy entities. Why? Because Satan is a liar and we far too often believe him.

The father of lies has many children. Where in this world can we turn for safety? To what bedrock may we anchor to avoid tossing around on the waves of phony concepts? Jesus gives us the answer: "You will know the truth, and the truth will set you free" (v. 32). This Truth is a person (John 14:6). Cling to Him and believe no one else.

Ignoring the Liar

"When he lies, he speaks his native language, for he is a liar and the father of lies." (John 8:4

"The best protection against Satan's lies is to know God's truth."
—Anonymous

In Word We try to fill our hearts with so much that is no of God. Advertisements tell us that we only need this or that product to feel better, look better, or be better. The world tells us that we can be fulfilled if we have enough romance, leisure, sex, entertainment, possessions, or money. Common wisdom tells us that if we don't have our health, we don't have anything. We are constantly telling ourselves that if we only had this kind of car, that size house, the job of our dreams, or the right family situation, that we would then be happy and content. Or, if we're inclined to be more spiritual about it, we might think we need some revelation or moving experience for us to finally get it all together. We have bought into all of this reasoning at one time or another. And in doing so, we have bought into lies.

Here Jesus tells us that Satan is the father of lies. He manipulates a world system that will tell us one myth after another to keep us chasing after the proverbial brass ring, searching for contentment but never finding it. We keep thinking the next fashion or trend will satisfy, only to find emptiness when we get there. If we buy into Satan's lies, we become like those of whom Paul warns: "They will turn their ears away from the truth and turn aside to myths" (2 Timothy 4:4). We will seek and never find, because our seeking will be based on illusions.

In Deed If our hearts are empty, they are empty only of God. He is the only real substance that can satisfy our cravings f fulfillment. Why do we press on after other things? Because we don't believe Jesus. We have bought into the lies of the evil one.

Any discontent, any ache, any emptiness should drive us to our knees in hunger for God, which He promises to fulfill. Let's seek Him in every situation, turning from the father of lies to the truth that sets us free.

Idols of Wealth

"How hard it is for the rich to enter the kingdom of God!" (Mark 10:23)

In Word Jesus has harsh things to say about wealth. "Woe to you who are rich," He says in Luke 6:24. "You cannot serve both God and Money," He says in Matthew 6:24. "A man's life does not consist in the abundance of his possessions," He says in Luke 12:15. He tells parables that cast a bad light on the wealthy (the rich man and Lazarus in Luke 16, for example). And here in Mark 10, He tells His disciples that "it is easier for a camel to go through the eye of a needle than for a rich man to enter the kingdom of God" (v. 25).

That to which your heart clings is your god." -Martin Luther

Many of us who read these verses are incredibly wealthy, by worldwide standards, and so we spiritualize them. Jesus is really talking about those who place their hope in riches, we determine. And because we know that salvation is a matter of the heart and not of the bank account, we are right to do so. But we miss an important lesson if we dismiss these warnings too quickly.

The lesson is this: There is false worship in every human heart, and Jesus knows that all of it has some component of wealth. We either seek wealth and materialism as an idol in itself, or we have other idols that we cannot support without more money (approval of others, achievement, education, lifestyles, hobbies, food, fashion, etc.). Almost any idol we can conceive of revolves around money as its object or for its sustenance. And when we harbor such idols, the kingdom of God is like the eye of a needle to us. We just can't fit.

In Deed What idols grip your heart? Whatever they are, cut off their supply. They are fed by wealth, and they consume the kingdom's resources, giving nothing of substance in return. If we are to live as kingdom citizens, we must turn our hearts toward kingdom purposes. Our wealth, our time, our abilities—all resources God has given us—must be invested in lasting goals. Our treasure will be where our heart is. And our hearts are in the kingdom.

Into the Deep

"Put out into deep water, and let down the nets for a catch."
(Luke 5:4

"God doesn't call people who are qualified. He calls people who are willing, and then He qualifies them."
—*Richard Parker*

In Word A lot of us have limited vision. We base most of our activities and plans on what we've learned from experience and the interests, talents, and abilities we know we have. We are reluctant to get in over our heads because of the discomfort we fe in such situations. We don't like having demands placed on us th are beyond our resources.

When Jesus calls us to follow Him, He always pushes us beyond our experience and beyond our abilities. Peter had been fishing all night with no results when Jesus' instruction came to put out into deep water. All of Peter's intuition told him that the exercise would be fruitless. But Jesus doesn't call us to do the same things we've always done in the same ways we've always done them. He calls us to launch out further and deeper, to place where we cannot depend on our own experience and abilities. H puts us in places where we must depend entirely on Him.

In Deed Next time you feel helpless in a situation and know you're in over your head, remember the sovereign Lord who placed you there. He has intimate knowledge of the deep. H is master over all the elements of His creation. He knows what awaits us there. He is Lord of the wind and the waves, the harvest, the loneliness, or whatever else might face us "in the deep."

The deep water can be a scary place to be. For Peter, it seeme like a pointless place to be. We are helpless there. But we cannot avoid it and be obedient to Jesus at the same time. This is the wa to bear fruit in His kingdom. This is where the catch is. The way of discipleship will eventually lead us there. Jesus knows what it takes to bear fruit—and it always involves going beyond our ow expertise, our limited vision, and our resources. He calls us to launch out into places where we have no choice but to depend o His instructions and His power.

Noisy Disciples

"If they keep quiet, the stones will cry out." (Luke 19:40)

In Word There is a tension in most of us between giving our all to God and maintaining our dignity in the eyes of the world. We are urged by Jesus and by the written Word to love God with everything that is in us—our minds, our hearts, our souls, everything. Sometimes this love will take the form of a loud voice (Psalm 33:3; 47:1), and sometimes it will take the form of an unpopular stand. Either way, we're often out of step with the world.

The crowd of disciples in this passage is praising God for all the things Jesus has done. These disciples are loud. They're perhaps inappropriate in this particular social setting. And, in the opinion of the Pharisees, they are theologically misguided, attributing the works of Jesus to the power of God. But Jesus doesn't seem concerned with their volume, their defiance of social expectations, or their controversial theology. They are doing what human beings were created to do—praise God. And, unlike the Pharisees, they recognize the work of God when they see it.

"The great thing, and the only thing, is to adore and praise God."

—Thomas Merton

In Deed The unbelieving world will expect us to keep our beliefs to ourselves, or, at the very least—if we must be Christians in public—be dignified about it. But we don't live according to the world's expectations. We live according to God's. And what are God's expectations for us? There may be many answers, but at least one—the main one—is our wholehearted worship. God *will* be praised. If we don't fulfill our purpose in worship, He'll raise up stones to do it. But He *will* be glorified by His creation.

From time to time, we need to ask ourselves who we're trying to please. Are we living to keep the world happy and ruffle as few feathers as possible? Or is God our only audience? Jesus and His disciples ruffled feathers because they pursued God with wholehearted devotion and single-minded purpose. So must we.

Painful Truth

"I am Jesus, whom you are persecuting." (Acts 9:5)

In Word Can you imagine the shame Saul must have felt when the risen and ascended Jesus met him on the road to Damascus? His whole life had been given to pursuing the God of Abraham, Isaac, and Jacob, and to understanding the Law of Moses. He had been a Pharisee *par excellence* by his own reckoning, confident in his righteous standing before God. Unfortunately, he had also zealously persecuted the very same God he sought to serve. In a moment, he went from thinking he was one of God's greatest friends to knowing that he had helped put God incarnate—and some of His followers—to death. The blow to the ego is staggering.

And yet it is the epitome of grace. The God Paul thought he knew would have stricken such a rebel down immediately. The God Paul came to know revealed his sin and showed him the way to salvation. What mercy! In the harshest, most emotionally painful moment of Paul's life, he received grace.

"It is often the offensive side of Jesus that we need most."
—John Piper

In Deed Grace begins with a crisis. It cannot be understood apart from a clear recognition that we need it desperately. Perhaps we have not sinned as grievously as Paul. But when we hear the truth about ourselves, we should be no less humbled. The revelation of our true nature and the fact that we were all once enemies of God (Romans 5:10) would be psychologically devastating if not for the grace that follows. Contrary to the popular image of Jesus as thoroughly benign and accommodating, He speaks the painful truth. And sometimes that truth is incredibly humbling.

God means for us to walk in this kind of humility. No redeemed person is spared from the knowledge of their offenses before God, because it is only in that knowledge that we can stand in His grace. It is harsh, yes, but behind the harshness is the love that brings us to Him. Is there any pride in the way we Christians relate to God or to one another? Let it be undone by the severity of truth and the comfort of grace.

A Lost Discipline

"When you fast . . ." (Matthew 6:16)

In Word Fasting is a lost discipline, for most. It certainly isn't a requirement of our faith—nowhere in the New Testament does Jesus or His apostles urge His followers to fast as a condition for spiritual blessing. And there are certainly many wrong reasons to fast: pagan ritualism, unspiritual worship of the physical, hypocritical righteousness, and political protest, to name a few. It can be done in prideful self-reliance and it can be done as an attempt to manipulate divine favor. But the abuses do not make the practice wrong. If they did, Jesus would have forbidden it. He clearly does not. He expects that His followers will have occasion to fast.

What better way is there to demonstrate a desire for eternal truth over temporal satisfaction? What better way is there to claim that our citizenship is in heaven, not in this world? Fasting plants our feet in an eternal kingdom and uproots them from the essence of this world. By denying one of the most basic desires of our flesh, we clearly cast our lot with the Spirit. We will return to food soon enough; but in the meantime, we declare an affinity for things greater than our bodily sustenance, as legitimate as it may be. We demonstrate a craving for the spiritual at the expense of physical. And there's something about that statement that inclines God toward us in an unusual way.

[F]asting is the [v]oluntary [d]enial of a [n]ormal [f]unction for [t]he sake of [i]ntense [s]piritual [a]ctivity."

-Richard Foster

In Deed There is no clearer way than fasting to say, "Lord, I need Your answer as though my whole life depends on it. I would rather die than not hear from You." By fasting, we define ourselves as spiritual beings—those who really understand that humans do not live by bread alone—when we abstain from food in order to talk with God.

And God hears. He does not honor false motives, but He honors true desperation. He answers those for whom hearing His voice is so obviously important. Fasting will do many things for you—point out your false loves and bring to the surface your character flaws, for example—but nothing is more important than this: hearing the voice of God.

Following Jesus

"Follow me." (Luke 5:27

"Christianity is Christ."

—H. A. Ironside

In Word What does it mean to follow Jesus?

• Not adherence to a system of belief. Systematizing the teachings of Jesus leads to frustration and fractious denominations. The "image of the invisible God" (Colossians 1:15) cannot be contained in a limited doctrine understandable by finite mind Doctrine is important, but it is not sufficient.

• Not membership in a personality cult. Fans are loyal to roc stars, athletes, and actors for a time, but feelings are fickle. Jesus' personality is winsome and worthy of praise, but there are times when He asks His followers to deny their feelings and obey Him

• Not spectating. Many came to Jesus to see the amazing things He would do. But when the teaching got difficult, "many of his disciples turned back and no longer followed him" (John 6:66).

• Not detached intellectual assent. Many will call Jesus "Lord" and agree with Him in principle, but not actually follow Him (Matthew 7:21).

No, to follow Jesus is not about living a religion, it's about knowing a living person. He didn't just leave us a legacy of teachings, He left us Himself. We don't get our marching orders from Him and then proceed to live the Christian life without Him. We don't observe and applaud His words and His works from a distance, without getting into the game ourselves. We don't base ou discipleship on our feelings, which come and go as often as the wind changes direction. We follow.

In Deed The promise of discipleship is that we are not alone in our obedience. We are following a person. We can talk with Him, cry with Him, listen to Him, and work with Him. Unlike many religions that teach their adherents a set of principl and then send them out to live those principles, the living Jesus i with us as He teaches us. We *should* have principles, feelings, curiosity, and reasons, but we do not base our lives on any of these alone. We follow *Him.*

Left Behind

"'Follow me,' Jesus said to him, and Levi got up, left everything and followed him." (Luke 5:27-28)

In Word Have you ever noticed that nearly every time someone follows Jesus, they leave something behind? Here, Levi leaves his tax booth. Peter and Andrew left their nets and James and John left the boat and their father (Matthew 4:18-22). The woman at the well left her water jar (John 4:28). The man who found the "treasure in a field" and the merchant looking for fine pearls sold all they had for the kingdom of heaven (Matthew 13:44-45). It is a subtle but consistent theme in the Gospels: To follow Jesus means to forsake something else.

"Salvation is free, but discipleship costs everything we have."
–Billy Graham

This points to at least two truths that we need to cling to. First, the value of following Jesus surpasses anything we possessed before we knew Him. Whether we are preoccupied with our livelihood, our relationships, our interests, or our duties, when we really see who Jesus is, everything else pales in comparison. The items left behind in these passages are almost reported as an afterthought. These people did not seem to agonize over their decision; they were just too focused on something better. They were completely preoccupied with Jesus.

Second, following Jesus implies a radical rearrangement of all of life. Nothing is the same after we meet Him. He redirects us from our previous path. No one in the Gospels became a follower of Jesus and squeezed their discipleship in around their current lifestyle. The encounter was too earth-shattering for that. Everything was new.

In Deed The greatest adventure a person can have is to follow Jesus without hindrances. When we try to pick up the trappings of our old life to carry with us, we soon find out that we follow at too great a distance. Jesus urges us onward, leaving all behind, with eyes focused entirely on Him. He calls us to a new way of life.

In Need of Shepherding

"I am the good shepherd." (John 10:1

In Word Anyone who has ever worked on a farm with sheep will attest to this fact: Sheep are stupid. They wander off without any sense of direction; having thoroughly consumed the foliage in one field, they must be driven to the next or they will not eat; they often do not recognize danger when it is present, an even when they do recognize it, they do nothing in defense; and they get lost easily. Of all God's creatures, they are some of the most vulnerable and simple. And this is exactly the image Jesus uses for us.

Anyone who has ever been a shepherd will attest to this fact: It is servile, thankless labor. It is a task that most would avoid doing, if they could (which is how David got stuck with the job a the youngest of eight brothers). It offers no rewards in the eyes o the world, and it is lonely work, offering a man no companionship outside of his flock. And this is exactly the image Jesus uses for Himself.

"God's investment in us is so great, He could not possibly abandon us."
—Erwin Lutzer

In Deed The sheep's relationship to the shepherd is one of absolute dependence. It is one of protection. It is one of long hours together in the same field. It is one of constantly being guided or rescued by the rod and the staff. When a sheep wande off and gets stuck in a ditch (which happens a lot), the shepherd must search for it, find it, pull it out, and compel it to come back. If he does not, it will die in its predicament. But a good shepherd always does.

This picture that Jesus chose to describe His relationship wit us may be foreign to most members of modern Western civilization, but it was a strong image for His hearers. It was a promise that regardless of their predicament, He would take the initiative to keep them in the fold; that regardless of their vulnerability, their welfare was entirely in His hands. The sheep-shepherd relationship is a humble picture, but it is a comforting and compellin illustration of us and our Savior. Think about it the next time you're stuck in a ditch.

Resurrection's Children

"They are God's children, since they are children of the resurrection." (Luke 20:36)

In Word God's people are given a marvelous name in this passage. We are a lot of things in Scripture, including sinners, children of wrath, sheep without a shepherd, blind, lost, and idolatrous. But none of that matters when someone meets Christ. We are in a new category of creation. We are "children of the resurrection."

All of a sudden, because of our encounter with Christ, everything is different. Our defining characteristic is no longer our past, with all of its rebellion and ignorance. It isn't the infection Adam and Eve passed to every succeeding generation. It isn't the idols we think we need for fulfillment. And it isn't a destiny of death. No, we are defined by something altogether different and far above our sinful world. Resurrection. It's not just a gift. It's who we are.

Jesus came to do "Genesis" all over again. "If anyone is in Christ, he is a new creation; the old has gone, the new has come" (2 Corinthians 5:17). We may feel like children of Adam and Eve, but we are not. We are children of God, and God is the author of resurrection, the fountain of life. We are fundamentally different than the fallen world, and we are fundamentally different than our old selves.

"Our old history ends with the Cross; our new history begins with the Resurrection."
—Watchman Nee

In Deed This means that when we're kicking ourselves for past failures, we need only look at the resurrection of Jesus and know that we are new children. When all the world surrounds us with its pettiness, bitterness, and rage, we can live in a transcendent way, with our hope and all of our values fixed firmly above the mess. When we are sitting at the deathbed of a loved one, or even lying in our own, we can remember the empty grave and know that no child of the Resurrection is contained by it.

Children of the Resurrection can stand out for their vitality, their hope, their faith, their way of life and love. We are members of a new creation. Remember that when you encounter the old one.

The Right Foundation

"Everyone who hears these words of mine and puts them into practice is like a wise man who built his hous on the rock." (Matthew 7:24

In Word Some unbelievers build beautiful mansions with their lives. Others build shacks. The same can be said of believers; there are both mansions and shacks among us, too. But nowhere i this passage does Jesus talk about the quality of the house. He speaks only about the foundation. If the foundation is not good, the quality of the rest of the house doesn't matter. It will wash away.

The world sees many non-Christians who have done wonderful works of benevolence, given much money to charities, demonstrated kindness, believed in various religions wholeheartedly, and come up with truly beneficial theories. And they wonder: How can the Bible say they do not have salvation apart from Christ? Jesus' answer: The foundation is wrong. Million-dollar mansions are worth nothing unless built on solid ground.

But there is also an application here for the Christian. We have, of course, chosen the proper foundation. But, astonishingly, some of us have a tendency to build elsewhere. We settle on the foundation of Christ mentally, but we wander from it as we build our lives. And whatever we've built on other sites will wash away when the storm comes. For many, very little is added to the foundation.

"Christ's words are of permanent value because of His person; they endure because He endures."

—W. H. Griffith Thomas

In Deed There are all types of houses in the world. Big and small, beautiful and plain, elaborate and simple, lavish and humble. Regardless of the style, the crucial question is the foundation underneath it. Yet it is a crucial question that we often answer casually.

Are Jesus' words the foundation for our work? For our attitudes? For our habits? For our use of time and money? For our relationships? If they are not, we build our houses in vain. If they are, whatever we build will be solid.

The Insanity of Sin

"The thief comes only to steal and kill and destroy; I have come that they may have life, and have it to the full." (John 10:10)

In Word Have you ever considered the insanity of sin? Sin, of course, is rebellion toward God, an enthronement of self in the human heart. We have all been guilty of it, and, in fact, continue to be guilty of it, sometimes habitually. Have you pondered the implications of that?

We know that God is the Creator of the universe, perfect in His goodness and love. He wants our ultimate happiness and knows exactly how we can get it. His wisdom is complete, His designs perfect. The promises of obedience to His will are extravagant, eternal, and incredibly exciting to think about.

"Sin is what you do when your heart is not satisfied with God." John Piper

And in spite of this knowledge, we often consciously reject the abundant life He offers in favor of a destructive fascination with sin. We are inexplicably attracted to the thief and apathetic toward the giver of life. The God of the universe invites us to have an intimate relationship with Him, and we consciously choose to offend Him. This is absurd. If we really believe the truths of the Gospel and promises of God, know the futility of disobedience, and still persist in our rebellion, isn't this by all standards considered irrational? And yet, every Christian can relate to Paul's confession: "The evil I do not want to do—this I keep on doing" (Romans 7:19).

In Deed Many Christians struggle with habitual sin. It has power—from the world, our own flesh, and the evil one. And that power is intense. We are to forsake it, but only Christ can break it (Romans 7:25). If this is your struggle, ask Him to break it now. Cry out to Him, don't stop asking until He does, and know that He will. He is stronger than the thief and His will is that we have life in all its fullness.

Productive Seeds

"Unless a kernel of wheat falls to the ground and dies, i remains only a single seed. But if it dies, it produces many seeds." (John 12:24

In Word To the eyes of casual onlookers who do not hol kingdom values, the Gospel is a waste. They see the life of Jesus as tragically "cut short." Just think of what He could have done had He lived longer! They believe the talents of many young people have been squandered on "religious service" rather than impressive secular-minded careers. Just think of the achievement that could have bettered mankind if they had focused on something "practical"! The fruit of the kingdom is hardly visible to those outside of it.

David Brainerd, an early missionary to the Indians of the American northeast, lived among them in a forest while his healt deteriorated. He died at 29, having seen only a handful of converts. But his diary prompted William Carey, Henry Martyn, and scores of others to go to mission fields. William Borden graduate from Yale before going to Egypt as a 25-year-old missionary. He died of cerebral meningitis within weeks. But thousands have been moved to action by the testimony of his eternal values. And, of course, Jesus spent only three precious years in public ministry before the appointed time of His sacrifice at the hands of a vision-impaired world. But His eternal kingdom is growing mightily.

"Sacrifice releases power. The greater the sacrifice, the greater the power released."

—John Richard Wimber

In Deed We serve in a kingdom of wheat kernels, mustard seeds, and hidden pearls—small things with huge impact. The world cannot see their value. In our more discouraging moments, neither can we. But history encourages us; the legacies of "wasted" lives have influenced the world in more dramatic ways than any of mankind's impressive achievements.

Do not be discouraged if your faithful service to God has imperceptible results. They are imperceptible only to the naked eye. They are highly valued in the eternal kingdom, where those who give away their lives find them again.

Refiner's Fire

"Those whom I love I rebuke and discipline."

(Revelation 3:19)

In Word Rarely do we view the difficult circumstances of life as statements of Jesus' love for us. We more likely interpret them as interruptions in our walk with God. In our best moments, we may interpret these interruptions as tools God will use to stretch our faith; in our worst moments, we may even see them as His disfavor. But we still tend to view them as distractions from the course He would have us pursue.

But God's hand is in even the most difficult circumstances, letting affliction have its deepest results. This *is* His chosen path for us, not a diversion from it. Whether He is letting hardship strengthen our faith, or disciplining us for some sin, as in this verse, He is always the Lord of our situation. The superficial source of our hardship may be easier to discern; we see Satan, other people, chance, our own sin, or a variety of other causes as the root of our affliction. But God is sovereign over all of them, and He is specific in His purposes. If we are in pain, He knows it and He allowed it to happen.

God tries our faith so that we may try His faithfulness."

— Anonymous

In Deed We can take comfort in the fact that God is behind our trials. He does not train those whom He does not intend to use in wonderful ways. Though we may suffer at times, we suffer with a purpose. He has a plan for us that only this type of hardship will prepare us for. He will develop our character to prepare us for His purposes, and His method is like a refiner's fire.

Many times we pray to know Christ better, to have deeper fellowship with Him, and to be more fruitful in His work. We must learn that this prayer will likely result in more of the refiner's fire, more time in the training camp of His kingdom. Should we stop praying it? Of course not. No one who has been used mightily by God has avoided the difficult developing of their character and faith. They have been through the fiery trials and would willingly go through them again.

Understanding Judgment

"Woe to you who are rich, . . . who are well fed now, . . who laugh, . . . when all men speak well of you."

(Luke 6:24-26

"Complacency is a deadly foe of all spiritual growth."

—A. W. Tozer

In Word These are indicting words. We can wholeheartedly agree when Jesus pronounces woe upon the self-righteous Pharisees. But the rich? That describes almost all Americans, by worldwide standards. The well fed? Ditto. Those who laugh? Anyone who is mentally sound does that. Those of whom others speak well? Most of us have a decent reputation. What exactly is Jesus trying to say here? And why do His descriptions sound an awful lot like us?

We should not dismiss these woes too quickly. We know from other Bible passages—which Jesus never contradicts—that there is nothing inherently wrong with wealth, food, laughing, and a good reputation. But these are sobering warnings. Those who take comfort in their wealth, food, pleasure, and reputation—and who ignore God because of them—will be tragically sorry. There is something inherently ungodly and dangerous in complacency, and all of these characteristics cultivate complacency. If you have them handle them with care; they are gifts from God, blessings given entirely by the grace of His goodness and not on your merit. They are no cause for pride, only for humble gratitude.

In Deed Regardless of how much money you have, know that you stand before God with absolutely nothing to offer in exchange for His blessing. You are entirely dependent on grace Regardless of how much food you eat, know that you stand before God wholly dependent on the bread of His Word; it alone sustains your life. Regardless of the quality of your positive outlook, let your rejoicing be primarily in the pleasure of His fellowship. And regardless of your prestige, know that you stand completely dependent on the reputation of God's Son for the Father's favor. Never lose sight of your poverty, and you will never experience these judgments.

Misguided Defense

"You have a fine way of setting aside the commands of God in order to observe your own traditions!"

(Mark 7:9)

In Word *What's wrong with tradition?* the Pharisees must have wondered. Jesus condemns it so easily, yet much of it was built on the Law, to which Jesus was never opposed. But that's the problem: Only *most* of the traditions of the Pharisees were biblical. The remainder was simply a historical fabrication. There's nothing wrong with tradition, but when it is mistaken for divine inspiration, it becomes idolatry. According to Jesus, it causes us to "nullify the word of God" (7:13).

We treasure many of our traditions. But do we realize how temporal they are compared to the Word of God? The Word was pre-existent—it has always existed and it always will. The Word became flesh and lived among us. It is a holy outpouring from the mind of God. By contrast, our longest traditions may have originated only thousands of years ago—a mere blink of the eye in the grand eternal scheme. They hold meaning for us because they have been handed down from generation to generation and they have been drilled into our psyches. But they are not sacred—most of them, anyway. Not when placed beside the incarnate or inscribed Word.

"Heaven forbid that we should go on playing religious games in one corner when the cloud and fire of God's presence have moved to another."

—David Watson

In Deed Human nature takes divine principle and uses it rather subjectively. We apply God's laws to benefit ourselves as much as possible—our interpretations always seem to work out to our advantage, for some reason. Like the Pharisees, we often major on the minors and minor on the majors. We stridently defend the minutiae of the kingdom and neglect its founding principles.

Jesus calls us to a kind of sharp discernment that can only come by the Spirit of God. Stake your life on His Word. Stake nothing at all on the rules of your own construction. Know the difference and live for what matters.

Until the Harvest

"Let both grow together until the harvest."

(Matthew 13:30)

In Word A common frustration for churches is the varying levels of commitment among their members. Some variation is normal, of course. But spend a long enough time in any congregation and you will find some participants with such a low level of commitment—or a high degree of ill-spirited commitment—that their citizenship in the kingdom of God is suspect.

As annoying as it is, God is not going to pull the weeds from His garden just yet. We'll have to get used to that. That sometimes makes His garden virtually indistinguishable from the surrounding uncultivated landscape—our kingdom citizenship is hard to decipher on social surveys, for example—but that's a necessary evil. Nascent wheat and nascent weeds look awfully similar sometimes. They'll just have to be separated later.

Notice that there isn't anything in this parable that gives believers permission to find and label unbelievers. That's a judgment call, but not ours—it belongs to God alone. We can certainly point out ungodly activity within the church, but we are not given authority to judge the saved from the unsaved. That requires 20/20 vision into the human heart, and we don't have it. Let God handle that.

"If you judge people, you have no time to love them."

—Mother Teresa

In Deed We will have to live with our frustration. The kingdom of God and the kingdom of this world are so intertwined that only the divine hand can sort the whole mess out.

Meanwhile, how do we respond to the weeds? The same way we respond to anyone: with the principles of the kingdom and the character of the King. Humility, forgiveness, grace, gentleness, purity, and love should mark our relationships with everyone, whether inside the church or out, whether a weed or a fruitful grain. That's God's way. It will be easier after the harvest time; it is critical now.

Genuine Fruit

"By their fruit you will recognize them."

(Matthew 7:20)

In Word How do we recognize an apple tree? Some knowledgeable people may be able to tell from the leaves or the bark, but most of us will rely on clearer evidence. If it bears apples, we have our answer. It's an apple tree. Peach trees don't bear apples, and apple trees don't bear peaches. We can tell the tree by its fruit.

False prophets abound. Jesus told us to guard against them and to expect to encounter many. He encountered many Himself. But how do we detect them? Jesus' answer is simple. It's all in the fruit.

When we hear a new teaching, we listen closely to the teacher's words to determine if they line up with our understanding of biblical doctrine. This is a good start. But a better indicator is the behavior of the teacher. If we really want to know what people believe, we will not focus on their words but on their actions. Words are easy to fake. Behavior is not. Jesus tells us we will recognize false teachers by what they produce. We won't find perfection in any human, but when someone comes with gentle words and ferocious actions, we know the truth about that person. We know that with bad trees, bad fruit will eventually be evident.

Our actions disclose what goes on within us, just as its fruit makes known a tree otherwise unknown to us."

—Thalassios the Libyan

In Deed We can apply Jesus' principle of fruit to ourselves as well. What do you really believe? What you do will indicate what's deep down inside. If we say we believe in the power of prayer but rarely pray, we don't really believe what we say. If we say we believe in the power of love to change lives, yet harbor critical and judgmental attitudes, once again we deceive ourselves. We may not be like the false prophets Jesus warns His disciples about by preying on people like ferocious wolves, but we are like them by exhibiting a contradiction between our words and our deeds.

What is the evidence of genuine belief? Learn to discern the truth. It's all in the fruit.

Be a Miracle

"This is a wicked generation. It asks for a miraculous sign."
(Luke 11:29

> *"God longs to make something supernatural of us."*
> —Andrew Murray

In Word This is a wicked generation, too, just as surely a was the one to whom Jesus spoke. Like that one, ours will hardly listen to any preaching that calls for repentance (as Jesus implies in verse 32 that true preaching will do). It is unable or unwilling to discern truth from error. A sign, however, would be convincing evidence, wouldn't it? Probably not. Secular mouths ridicule the signs of the church and the signs of the Bible as hoaxes or pre-modern myths. Still, we think, if there were clear evidence of a supernatural power behind the Gospel to which we testify, more people would be saved.

Perhaps so, but really the world has all it needs to accept the Gospel, especially if we are living it. That's the truest, most indisputable miracle—a changed life. If the world sees that the Gospel has recreated us from within, given us a new heart, and subdued our willful humanity, perhaps it will believe. People have been brought into the kingdom by such a sign. It's what everyone, dee down inside, really craves.

In Deed What kind of sign are you to this generation? Ar you a living testament to the power of the Gospel and the resurrection of Jesus? Can people look at you and say, "I'm not sure what's going on there, but the change is definite; something or Someone from above is in there"? Maybe on some days, maybe not on others. It's something we should be aware of. We are God's primary sign to any wicked generation.

We covet the ability to work miracles in the name of Jesus. By God's grace, that happens many times in the life of the church. Healings, deliverances, and clear answers to prayer are often given mercifully by His hand. But that can never be our focus. Our focus must be on the miracle that Jesus has wrought within, and whether we are demonstrating ourselves to be the miracle of God. There's a huge difference between doing a miracle and being one. Above all, make sure you are one.

Evidence of Love

"I love the Father and . . . do exactly what my Father has commanded me." (John 14:31)

In Word In John 8, Jesus had one of His many confrontations with the Pharisees. During the argument, these religious leaders appealed to their authority as Abraham's children. No, Jesus told them; they were Abraham's descendants, but not his children. Then the Pharisees appealed to their status as God's children. No again, Jesus told them; they would get along with Him well if they were God's children. They didn't get the point; He would have to spell it out for them. "You belong to your Father, the devil," He said (v. 44). It was the most offensive thing He could have said to them. Why was He so blunt? Because they were blind to this truth: Those who love God do what God says.

Jesus' statement in John 14:31 about doing exactly as the Father commands should not be foreign to us. Can we say the same thing? We're not sinless as He was, so we can't claim to have loved God perfectly. But we can make that our guiding principle, can't we? We absolutely *must* realize the connection between love and obedience. They were perfectly combined in Jesus; they can be increasingly combined in us.

> *"Obedience to God is the most infallible evidence of sincere and supreme love to Him."*
>
> *—Nathanael Emmons*

In Deed Many Christians get caught in an inconsistency between their words and their lives. It's quite common. We say we love God, but we fail repeatedly in our obedience, usually in one or two areas in particular. We have secret sins, nagging habits, persistent character flaws that we just do not want to let go of. We know this, and we know God's desire for us to leave those things behind. But we don't; it's too hard. That's when we need to ask ourselves a deep question: "Do I really love Him?" That's the issue, isn't it? If we loved Him more than that habit, sin, or character flaw, we would have victory. We pursue the things we love most. If we hang onto our hidden faults, don't we love them more?

Jesus often used "love" and "obey" in the same sentence. It isn't a coincidence. It's a challenge. Search your soul. Decide who you love, and obey Him with all your heart.

Trust and Rest

"Do you still have no faith?" (Mark 4:40

In Word The life of faith requires us to lean on an invisible source of strength and wisdom. We do not have an unfounde faith, but we learn quickly that it does not rest on our five senses. And as we trust God, we find that very real and visible storms war against our belief in the invisible God. Sooner or later, a greater test will come and we will have to choose: Trust God or trust ourselves. We cannot do both.

At some point in this walk of faith, we must learn to detach from the things that so greatly concern us and cast them wholly on God. This feels irresponsible at first, but it is actually irresponsible not to do so. We must stop thinking of ourselves as the source of deliverance in a difficult situation. It is not up to us to save. We may be useful tools of God, but not everything is riding on us. Usually, we approach crises as though God is depending o us to do the work while He supports us in the background. We need to turn that around. We must depend on God to do the wor while we are behind the scenes believing in Him. When He says to act, we must act. But most of us act far too quickly and believe much too slowly. We must be quick to believe and hesitant to interfere in God's work. By this we can keep our hearts from being so troubled, if we will really trust in Him.

"Nothing influences the quality of our life more than how we respond to trouble."
—Erwin Tieman

In Deed How do you react in a crisis? Do you feel responsible to step in and intervene? Perhaps God will require you to do so, but rarely until you have first trusted Him with a calm heart, sought His will diligently, made yourself fully available, and waited for His timing.

When we pray and ask for God's will to be done in a given situation, we must believe that His will is, in fact, very good, and that He is quite able to accomplish it. Any asking that maintains an internal sense of panic is not genuine trust. It reveals a hidden belief that we are perhaps more critical to the situation than God is. But to trust is to rest, and the heart that is calm has learned tha Jesus is above the storm.

Whose Approval?

"I will show you whom you should fear." (Luke 12:5)

In Word One enduring trait of most human beings is that we obsess about the approval of others. This obsession affects more decisions than we might realize; we might consider what others think about our job, or about the home we choose to live in, or the car we drive, or the clothes we wear. We are prone to act more spiritual than we really are when we are around other Christians, and we might act more worldly than we really are to make an impression on non-religious folks. We are, more often than we think, shaped by the opinions—real or assumed—of those around us.

And yet this is something completely absent in Jesus' considerations, and He expects His followers to be like Him in this regard. Jesus, in all of His teachings and His actions, shows no fear of men, whether they be hostile Pharisees or would-be disciples. His life and message are entirely God-directed, with no hint of compromise apparent. He fears no one.

"When you fear God, you fear nothing else . . . If you do not fear God, you fear everything else." —Oswald Chambers

In Deed Like our Master, our lives are also to be entirely God-directed. When we obsess about others' opinions, we have a distorted view of reality. We place more stock in something temporal and transient (and completely fickle) than we do in what is eternal and most worthy. We ignore the truly valuable (the will of God) to pursue an illusion (the approval of human beings). It is an incredibly costly exchange.

Jesus tells us emphatically not to fear men. He urges His followers to think only of God. In any decision we make, we are to consider His character and His plan and ignore the effect our decision might have on our standing in others' eyes. Do we fear for our self-esteem? His grace will be more than enough to compensate. We are—without compromise—to seek the esteem that comes from serving God rather than the esteem that comes from human approval. Only then will we be in touch with reality.

Just Believe

"Don't be afraid; just believe." (Mark 5:36)

In Word Jairus, the ruler of the synagogue, likely had a range of negative feelings toward Jesus when men from his house came and told him his daughter was dead. Jairus had risked a lot to plead with Jesus for his daughter's life. In a moment of desperation, he threw theology out the window in exchange for a miracle. He probably didn't care where the miracle came from, even if it was from Jesus; his daughter's life was at stake. Now, after Jesus had "wasted" precious minutes healing a bleeding woman in the crowd, the report meets them on the road. The girl is dead.

Jesus' response is strange to our ears. Throughout the episode, He completely ignores the circumstances. There is no acknowledgment here of the obstacles to His power. She's dead? No matter. Commotion and wailing? Not important. None of the hubbub is the truth of the situation. He is.

There are at least two things Jesus would have us learn from this verse: 1) Negative reports are not the final analysis of a horrible situation; and 2) fear is at war against our faith. When all hell breaks loose against us—and it quite literally does, sometimes—Jesus would have us ignore its ultimate weapon. Do *not* believe its reports. The enemy—and the death he wields against us—will devastate us if we let them. But we have a choice. We can fear, or we can believe. We can't do both. We have to pick one.

"Faith tells us of things we have never seen, and cannot come to know by our natural senses."

—St. John of the Cross

In Deed Does this mean that faith always brings about our desired outcome? Of course not; our desires are not the product of omniscience and are skewed sometimes. We don't always know God's will in a situation. But it does mean that faith always brings about *God's* desired outcome. If it's real trust, based on the real character of God, it prompts His perfect response in His perfect timing. But fear wars against our trust; it questions God's goodness and His power. Don't let it. Jesus' solution is simple—make a choice. "Don't be afraid; just believe."

Just Ignore Them

"Why all this commotion and wailing? The child is not dead but asleep." (Mark 5:39)

In Word Jesus, always the master of circumstances and never mastered by them, offers a seemingly ludicrous assessment of the situation. The girl isn't actually dead. She's just asleep. Perhaps it sounded well-intentioned but naive. Perhaps it was welcome evidence that this pesky, know-it-all miracle-worker was finally wrong about something. Perhaps it was considered a feeble, face-saving excuse from a guy who was late for an important appointment. Whatever the reason, the crowds laughed. They had been weeping and wailing, apparently inconsolably, but they stopped to laugh. The world always has time to interrupt its wailing in order to ridicule those who will not wallow with them in their distress. Simple solutions are always considered irrelevant and inconsequential—even when they're true.

This doesn't mean that pain is unimportant to Jesus. He weeps with us when we grieve (John 11:35). But He doesn't let the pain become bigger than the Comforter. He doesn't let our suffering overrule His provision. And He doesn't let death have victory over life. And when death laughs . . . well, He simply must prove a point.

"Humble yourself, and cease to care what men think."
—A. W. Tozer

In Deed Is your faith realistic? It shouldn't be—not by the world's standards, anyway. It should be completely in line with the will and the ways of God, but should not conform to the world's expectations, even when the laughing begins. Whatever conforms to the will and the ways of God is target practice for the skeptics—especially if miracles are involved. Don't be intimidated. The laughing has no impact on the truth of Jesus' power. Just as He ignored the report from Jairus' men (v. 36), He ignores the ridicule of an unbelieving crowd. We should, too. Faith knows things they don't know. God's reality is higher than human expectations—always. Raise your expectations to reflect His reality.

Just Get Up

"Talitha koum!" (Mark 5:41

In Word The first order of business for Jesus, once He arrives on the scene and tells the crowds the truth about the situa tion—that the little girl is not dead but asleep—is to get rid of all the naysayers. He "put them all out" (v. 40), allowing only the people who were desperate—her parents—and the people who were faithful—His disciples—to watch the miracle. Miracles mus be done in the presence of desperation and faith, when a need for God and a trust in Him can take center stage. Wailing? It distracts It acknowledges neither God's power nor His goodwill.

Once the wailers are gone, Jesus can do His work. And His miracle is astonishing in its simplicity. Like a father waking his child for breakfast, Jesus gently speaks the Aramaic equivalent of "It's time to get up, little one." Where the wailers proclaimed death, Jesus speaks life. Where they grieved loudly, He quietly takes her hand and tells her it's time to wake up. Where they laughed with contempt, He celebrates with joy. They were ready for her funeral; He told them to feed her breakfast.

"The miracles of Jesus were the ordinary works of His Father."

—George MacDonald

In Deed We face a lot of distractions in life. We hear the negative reports of those who think every situation is a hopeless one. With Jesus, no situation is hopeless. Even apparent disasters are entirely redeemable for a sovereign God who responds to faith. And where we encounter "impossible" situations, we are frequently fed complex, impotent approaches to them. Let Jesus walk into your situation and speak a soothing, simple word. Let Him enter into the distresses of your life and gently take your hand. Is it discouragement? Depression? Hopelessness? Dread? The ravages of death itself? No matter. Let Him come in, take your hand, and whisper the encouraging, life-giving words only a loving parent can whisper: "It's time to get up, little one." Let the wailers wallow in disaster, if they must. We need to tune them ou and listen to the gentle voice of our God.

Children of "All Authority"

"All authority in heaven and on earth has been given to me." (Matthew 28:18)

In Word There is no greater authority, not in this world or any other. Our universe is governed by the Son of God, the Ancient of Days incarnate, the Alpha and the Omega. If being in the presence of rulers and celebrities gives us a thrill, how much more wonderful to know Immanuel—God with us. Whatever impresses us, frightens us, threatens us, embitters us, or thrills us—all that we can imagine and more—is under His reign. He is the ultimate power.

That's great, we might think. But what does it have to do with us? The answer is glorious. This infinite power, ultimate authority, and King above all kings is the very same One who intercedes for us. He is on our side. And if the ultimate Authority intercedes for us, who will overturn His intercession? What request of His will be overruled? The greatest power in all the universe—*over* all the universe, in fact—is already inclined toward us, dedicated to working out our good, and available through our prayers. We might not notice such support if we are bent on our own agenda, but if we are bent on His, there is no obstacle that can obscure it.

Jesus Christ is God's everything for man's total needs."

-Richard Halverson

In Deed Sounds too good to be true? Yes, it does. And it often appears that way. While the ultimate Authority reigns benevolently over us, we have trials and tribulations. Our children may have life-threatening illnesses. Our finances may come to ruin. Our security might be in danger. Our relationships might suffer irreparable conflict. It doesn't always look like He's exercising His power.

But He is. The world He has placed us in is enemy territory, and we will not pass through it uncontested. When we focus on it, we will be discouraged and depressed. When we absorb its values and goals, we will be disappointed. And that's why Jesus comes to His disciples and says *all* authority is His. We need to know that—and to live like we know it.

Partners with "All Authority"

"All authority in heaven and on earth has been given to me." (Matthew 28:18

In Word Wartime stories of soldiers defecting to the victorious side are common. Why? No one likes to end up on the losing side. In any contest, if we can clearly see who will win ahead of time, that is likely whom we will support. If we already have a vested interest in the side we know will lose, we may decide not to even watch. Nobody wants to identify with the loser. No one wants to go down with the ship.

As Christians, we don't have that problem. We know who will win. We know who holds all authority in His hands. We know who is seated at the right hand of God and will judge the nations of the earth. We know that rebels against Him, persecutors of His people, and death itself do not win. The power structures and value systems of this world will fall.

"It is because of faith that we exchange the present for the future."

—Fidelis of Sigmaringen

But here is the dilemma the Christian faces: The world systems seem to be winning in the short term while the ultimate Authority often seems obscured in heaven, waiting for the final minutes of the game to reveal His victory. We are tempted in the meantime to play for the short term. Some might have lost sight of the scripted end, while some might knowingly plan to switch loyalties at the opportune time. But we cannot. We must choose sides now.

In Deed That's the essence of New Testament faith, the one salient feature of all of the members of the Faith Hall of Fame in Hebrews 11—they looked beyond the present to the kingdom of promise. None invested in this world. Abraham looked ahead to the city with foundations whose architect is God (Hebrews 11:10). Moses looked ahead to his reward (v. 26). All looked ahead to a resurrection (v. 35).

So must we. The Christian life is playing the game with a focus on its end. We cannot support both sides. Our involvement in the mission of Christ is based on its glorious result more than its humble present. Our actions today will acknowledge whom we regard as our ultimate Authority.

The Mission of "All Authority"

"All authority in heaven and on earth has been given to me." (Matthew 28:18)

In Word Our God is the God of the incomprehensibly huge. We can scarcely imagine the size of our solar system, and yet it is a tiny fraction of our galaxy. We can't begin to understand the size of our galaxy, and yet it is a tiny fraction of our known universe. If we sent our most powerful telescope to our most distant known planet and took a peek from there, we would still barely begin to see all that was created by His word.

Our God is also the God of the infinitesimally small. The intricacies of each cell are beyond our ability to replicate. The fullness of information in our DNA still exceeds the ability of our best computers to completely analyze. Yet every movement of every sub-atomic particle is sustained by His word. There is nothing so small that it escapes His attention.

"Christian mission is the only reason for our being on earth."
-Andrew Murray

In the vastness of creation, we begin to glimpse the height, depth, and breadth of the power of God, which, incredibly, is the same power that is working within us to conform us to His image. It is also the same power that sends us out to accomplish His agenda. And what is that agenda? He makes it plain: Make disciples of all peoples, baptizing them and teaching them (vv. 19-20). The highest goal of the God of the infinite and the infinitesimal is to be worshiped—*everywhere*. And though all creation testifies to His glory, there are places in this world where He is not even known.

In Deed What a sacred charge! If ever we wondered what God wanted us to be busy with, this is it. After Jesus' declaration that all authority in heaven and on earth is His—and that covers everything—He tells us where His authority is directed. It has one remaining goal: restoring the rebellious race back into the pure image of God.

Do we want meaning in our lives? *Here it is.* Do we want to know we are in God's plan? *This is it.* Do we want to know power? *This* is the mission that has "all authority" behind it.

The Work of God

"The work of God is this: to believe in the one he has sent." (John 6:2

In Word Have you ever wondered what it would take to do the works of God? Or why we seem so powerless in our Christian lives? Our prayers often lack effect. We are beaten and bruised by sins and attitudes that we can't overcome. We are battered by circumstances that seem to confine us. We know, beyond the shadow of a doubt sometimes, that we are not living the Christian life as portrayed in the book of Acts. Why not?

Jesus gives us the answer. Do we want to do the works of Go to live supernatural lives that are manifesting evidence of His Spirit's presence? Then we must believe Him. We want a formula for super-spirituality or an understanding of His power that only the most celebrated saints have experienced. But Jesus is almost mundane in telling us the key to spiritual success. It is belief in Him. Not only is this God's plan for our salvation when we first come to Him; it is a lifelong pattern.

This kind of belief implies trust. We often can accept God's will only insofar as we can understand it. But Jesus calls us further: Accept His will, even when we're confused by it. It's a matter of trust in His goodness.

This kind of belief implies obedience. To say we believe in Jesus while simultaneously ignoring His instructions, even the hard ones, is to attempt to bypass a relationship with Him. It is not true belief.

And this kind of belief implies faith in His power. He is the God who can move mountains, and He promises to do so in response to our faith. Do not doubt Jesus' power. He is always able.

"We are the wire, God is the current. Our only power is to let the current pass through us."

—Carlo Carretto

In Deed This is the work of God: to believe in Jesus. Trus obey, believe. We are simply branches on the vine. When we rely only on Him, we can expect God to work miraculously in us, an in fact, we come to understand that He already has.

Too Many Masters

"No one can serve two masters." (Matthew 6:24)

In Word Every human being is a temple. We who understand that the Spirit of God dwells in believers (John 14:17; 1 Corinthians 3:16) know this to be true of Christians. But in a sense it is true of everyone. We are either temples of the Holy Spirit, or temples of any number of idols. We are worshipers by nature, and the objects of our worship are placed on the altar of our affections.

We underestimate the power of our affections. We *will* pursue that which we love and value most highly. And when that happens to be something other than God—and it often is—then we are idolaters attempting to serve two masters.

Contrary to popular belief, we are not helpless captives of our hearts' desires. We choose them. We value relationships, riches, possessions, activities, and all other cravings by choice. We choose to dwell on certain desires, possibilities, and problems. When we dream about a venture, a purchase, a romance, or a game, we do so because we want to. We are not defenseless against those idols. We feed them. And while imaginations and dreams can be used for God's purposes, they can also fill us with substitutes for Him. When we let them, we find ourselves with too many masters.

"Every one of us is, even from his mother's womb, a master craftsman of idols."
-John Calvin

In Deed Jesus does not say no one *should* serve two masters. He says no one *can.* It is an impossibility. One will carry more weight than the other, in which case that one is the true master and the other is a weaker rival. And how easily we make God the weaker rival! We try to maintain our fellowship with Him while placing our greater affections on less worthy things.

Those who know the power of their affections are wise disciples. They have learned that we choose what we put in our hearts, and then we let ourselves be driven by them. We must remember: We are a house of worship, and there is only one rightful Master in that house. Anything else will pollute the temple.

Undoing Pride

Then he said to them all: "If anyone would come after me, he must deny himself and take up his cross daily and follow me." (Luke 9:2

In Word At the Fall, our first parents stepped out of a God-centered life and placed *themselves* at the center of their own lives. Every human being since, except one, has followed in their footsteps. We have all, at some point or another, said, "I will be my own Lord and follow my own authority." It is pride, the foundation of all sin; and it is cosmic treason, punishable by death.

When we meditate on the Cross and realize that we should have been the ones on it, our lordship of ourselves is undone. No one can gaze upon that ugly scene—the brutality and the blood—knowing that it was the punishment for our treason, not His, and still maintain a sense of pride. No one can walk away determined to remain on the throne of his or her heart, having seen the result of such a catastrophic decision. No one can willfully mishandle such mercy. Or can we?

"When Christ calls a man, He bids him come and die."
—Dietrich Bonhoeffer

Yes, the vestiges of our prideful treason remain, even after we have viewed the Cross and accepted the sacrificial Lamb as our own payment for sin. We trample upon the mercy of God, perhaps out of ignorance or habit, struggling with our self-will all the while. We don't want to, not if we've truly seen the Cross. But we do. We can all identify with Paul in Romans 7, doing the things we do not want to do, and not doing the things we want to do.

In Deed This is why Jesus tells His disciples: "Take up your cross *daily*." Not once at our first glimpse of Calvary. Not occasionally when we feel a particular need to repent. Daily. If we live by pride daily, as sons and daughters of Adam and Eve inevitably do, we must undo pride daily. And nothing undoes pride but the Cross. It reminds us that our remedy is not simply try and do better, but to die to ourselves and be resurrected with Christ. It was the ultimate expression of God-centeredness, and it is our model for living for Him.

Weak Vessels

"I praise you, Father, Lord of heaven and earth, because you have hidden these things from the wise and learned, and revealed them to little children. Yes, Father, for this was your good pleasure." (Matthew 11:25-26)

In Word God's ways are not our ways. If we were sending the Gospel into the world, we probably would have aimed at the most influential people, the ones most likely to impress others with their intellectual capabilities, oratory gifts, and social skills. But Jesus chose a rag-tag team of disciples, some uneducated, some marginalized by society. And throughout the ages, He has revealed Himself more readily to little children than to spiritual experts. Why?

God's purpose in the world is to reveal Himself—to be known and loved. When He works in the lives of the educated and skilled, observers often confuse the subtle power of God with the talents and gifts of human beings. When He works in the lives of the unlikely, there can be no mistake: The work is of God. Then He is recognized.

This is true not only in salvation. We who serve God in our churches and communities must also remember that God's preference is to demonstrate His own gifts, not impress others with ours. Battles are won in His strength, not ours. Wisdom comes from above, not within. His power is perfected in our weakness. We are simply vessels. Without Him we can do nothing (John 15:5).

't will do us ɡood to be ʻery empty, to ʻe very weak, ɑnd so to go ɑbout our Master's work."

-Charles Spurgeon

In Deed Our natural tendency is to work for God in the strength of the flesh. But the Christian life is not natural. It is supernatural. We must learn to recognize the persistent labor of the flesh and its interference in God's plan. All things that are accomplished for God—whether salvation itself or the life that follows—are accomplished by His initiative and power through our dependence and faith.

Casual Christianity

"When trouble or persecution comes because of the word, he quickly falls away." (Matthew 13:2

In Word Casual Christianity is an oxymoron. There is n such thing as a low-commitment version of our faith. It is impossible to say, "I'm a follower of Jesus, but I'm not prepared to lay down my life for the Gospel." Both of those assertions cannot be true. "When Jesus calls a man," to quote Dietrich Bonhoeffer, "H bids him come and die." Ours is a faith that demands our entire allegiance; it can be no half-hearted thing.

Church history is filled with martyrs. Missionary kids have seen their parents executed. Many Christians have lost a spouse child to persecution. Whole communities have been tortured or imprisoned. And many have given their own lives. Whether this is a tragedy or the glory of the church—and it is, in fact, both—is not the point. It is a given. It is assumed of Jesus' followers that they will follow Him wherever He goes. And He goes to places like the Cross.

"Jesus has many lovers of His heavenly kingdom, but few bearers of His cross."

—Thomas à Kempis

In Deed Martyrdom is not something that confronts most of us. Few of us are persecuted. Yet all of us can say with assurance that sometimes following our Savior is difficult. He as us to make sacrifices. He asks us to be obedient, even when obec ence is painful. And though He doesn't ask all of us to die for Him, He does ask all of us to live for Him. When we were bougl by His blood, we became His possession. Gloriously, joyfully Hi possession, but *His* nonetheless.

One of the great weaknesses of today's American church is our unwillingness to humble ourselves as our Savior did. We are often consumer Christians, shopping around for a faith that suit us well. But when we really encounter Christ, we face a choice: Stand firm in our faith, despite our many tests and troubles, or settle for a lukewarmness that can barely, if at all, be called "Christian." We must be prepared for the trials. They will come. And how we respond will tell us—and others—whether we are His disciples.

Life's Deceits

"The one who received the seed that fell among the thorns is the man who hears the word, but the worries of this life and the deceitfulness of wealth choke it, making it unfruitful." (Matthew 13:22)

In Word Many Christians begin with zeal in serving the Lord, but find only a few years later that their lives are consumed with possessions, debts, and busy schedules bent on maintaining a certain lifestyle. We must be wary of one of the enemy's primary weapons—clutter. His intent is not so much a disorganized home, as we often think of clutter, but a disorganized, encumbered life. The enemy wants to give us as much baggage as possible—materially and spiritually—in order to render us fruitless. We must not let him.

Have you ever found yourself considering a certain ministry or service, only to realize it's impractical because it would involve too much of a change in lifestyle? Or wanting to give more to ministries of the church, but realizing you can't; you owe too much to other people, or have too many plans about how to enhance your own environment? It's an uncomfortable position to be in, but it's an accurate reflection of today's verse. And many of us are there. The deceiver keeps us striving after an elusive contentment in status and things. He keeps us thinking that an adequate lifestyle is just around the corner. But it never comes.

"Our whole life is taken up with preparations for living, so that we never really live at all."

-Leo Tolstoy

In Deed Imagine standing before the Lord one day and explaining our fruitlessness. How defeated we will sound if we have to say, "Lord, I would have served You there, but I couldn't get by on that income. I would have given to that ministry, but I needed the money to insure my possessions. I would have shown others how to have peace in their hearts, but I was so worried about just surviving."

Be on guard against the worries of this life and the deceitfulness of wealth. We will have to answer for them. Better to weed them out before they choke God's Word in our hearts and the enemy uses them to render us unfruitful. Take up your pruning shears today.

Seasons of Fruitfulness

"The one who received the seed that fell on good soil is the man who hears the word and understands it. He produces a crop, yielding a hundred, sixty or thirty times what was sown." (Matthew 13:2

"Work designed for eternity can only be done by the eternal Spirit."
—A. W. Tozer

In Word No Christian is fruitful all of the time. There ar silent years of Paul, Peter—even Jesus—of which we know nothing about, years of pruning or preparation before a time of abundance. This is the scriptural pattern of God's work in our lives as laid out in Psalm 1: "He is like a tree planted by streams of water which yields its fruit *in season*" (v. 3, italics added). So we must not worry in our latent times.

But the other side of this coin is that every Christian is fruitf some of the time if the enemies of the seed are dealt with properl A persistent and consistent lack of fruit should prompt a believe to ask these questions: What is hindering God's fruitfulness in m life? Is there anything I'm tolerating that stands in the way of God's full work in me?

Jesus' parable of the sower in Matthew 13 (also Mark 4 and Luke 8) indicates three categories of enemies to the sower's wor the evil one (v. 19), trouble and persecution (v. 21), and the worri of life and the deceitfulness of wealth (v. 22). The Christian who does not actively stand firm in opposition to any of these will be the consequences of fruitlessness and miss out on the joy of God bounty.

In Deed Do you struggle with a discrepancy between the portrayal of the Christian life in Scripture—abundant life and rivers of living water—and your actual experience? You may be in a preparation phase, or there may be a hindrance. How can you know?

Fruitless periods in a Christian's life call for discernment— quality often lacking in such times. But God promises wisdom those who ask. So ask. If we seek His guidance and prepare to accept whatever He might say, He will show us what hinders His work in our lives.

Still the Light

"You are the light of the world." (Matthew 5:14)

In Word The age of secularization has pushed believers into the margins of life. We may maintain our beliefs as long as we do not carry them into public places, we are told. Yet there is a voice with higher authority and greater depth than our secular culture. It is the Lord of all creation who says: "You are the light of the world."

As much as the world may push us to the periphery of relevance, it has no answers. It usually doesn't even ask the right questions. But with certainty, it concludes that the Gospel is of little importance. The secular offense at the Gospel is astounding and absurd. But still we are told to be salt of the earth and lights in the world.

What a catastrophe for secular culture will the coming of the Son of Man be! It will be for our salvation, but unbelieving eyes will be amazed when He appears, having invested everything—all of their resources—in the fallacies of human institutions. Having spent centuries building earthly kingdoms, our fallen race will marvel—and gnash its teeth—at the only kingdom standing in the end.

We have the truth and we need not be afraid to say so."

—J.C. Ryle

In Deed Do not be intimidated by this world. It seeks answers but condemns anyone who claims to have them. It honors openness to all kinds of "truths" but scoffs when one accepts *the* truth. No, our Master will not let us be intimidated by this skepticism. He has given us neither a light to be hidden nor a spirit of fear. The world craves answers, and though it does not recognize Him, He is the answer. The world seeks wisdom and our God has given us the mind of Christ (1 Corinthians 2:16). We have no apologies to make for offering the light of salvation to a world in darkness. In fact, we owe apologies to the Lord if we do not. Be bold. "Let your light so shine before men."

Compassion of the Needy

"Which of these three do you think was a neighbor to the man who fell into the hands of robbers?" (Luke 10:3(

In Word The story of the Good Samaritan is one of Jesus' more familiar parables. It is an illustration of surprisingly good behavior (for a Samaritan) and of surprisingly bad behavior (for priests and Levites). We use it as a useful guide for ethical action—going above and beyond the call of duty in the ways of compassion.

When we read this as a moral instruction and decide which character we ought to emulate, we naturally avoid the portrayal of the indifferent priest and Levite and want to think we are mor like the Samaritan. We know in reality we have a little of both in us—some indifference tempered by compassion, or compassion tainted by indifference. We're an unfortunate mix of all who encounter this victim.

"Let all find compassion in you."

—St. John of the Cross

But eventually God makes us look deeper at this practical parable and see it as a striking picture of our world. In the big pi ture, our race has fallen into the hands of robbers; it has been stripped, beaten, and left for half dead. We have all been ravage by the wages of sin, and we suffer. This parable is not just a less on what to do, it is an illustration of what's been done for us. We stop asking which character we *ought* to be and God shows us which character we really *are*. The answer He reveals is humblin First and foremost, we are not the priest, the Levite, *or* the Samaritan. We are the victim.

In Deed Everyone who has ever really known Jesus by faith has first known helplessness. We once lay beside the road and hoped someone would stop. He did. He was our good neighbor. By God's design, this should have been the beginning of compassion for us—we don't just become merciful by thinkin of others in need, we become merciful by experiencing mercy. When Jesus spared us, He gave us a sobering command: "Go and do likewise" (v. 37).

The Samaritan in this story looks a lot like Jesus. So should w

Compassion for the Needy

"A priest happened to be going down the same road, and when he saw the man, he passed by on the other side."
(Luke 10:31)

In Word The priest and the Levite are easy targets. Their negligent behavior in this story is so apathetic, so self-centered, that we have no trouble knowing who to point our fingers at. But this is not a story about finger pointing. It is about becoming like Jesus. Just as we were helpless and He showed us mercy, others are helpless and we are to show them His mercy. This is our command regardless of interpersonal barriers. Labels like "Samaritan" are not relevant.

Jesus' point about the priest and the Levite, of course, is that they were not compassionate. But He also implies that we live in a world full of them. There are many of them travelling down the road. Nearly everyone in need will have been passed by several before a true neighbor comes along. Jesus isn't just condemning Levitical hypocrisy; He's casting His revealing light on the ugliness of human nature. When we see people in need, most of us would prefer not to get involved.

The parable of the Good Samaritan is an accurate picture of our world. Most people are missing the mark; few have found true meaning. There are many robbers who plunder, many priests and Levites who are negligent, and many innkeepers who will intervene if they're paid for it. And, in a sense, every one of these is as miserable as the helpless victims lying by the side of the road. The only person in this story who could possibly have a satisfying life is the Samaritan. The others, in pursuing their goals, miss the ultimate meaning of them all.

By compassion we make others' misery our own, and so, by relieving them, we relieve ourselves also."

-Sir Thomas Browne

In Deed Look at the story of the Good Samaritan as a parable of human nature. Do you want to be satisfied in life? Understand the robbers, priests and Levites, innkeepers, and victims; have compassion on them all for the misery they're in. Above all, be like the Samaritan who shows tangible mercy. Be like Jesus.

A Mustard-Seed Kingdom

"What shall we say the kingdom of God is like? . . . It i like a mustard seed, which is the smallest seed you plar in the ground. Yet when planted, it grows and becomes the largest of all garden plants." (Mark 4:30-3:

"He is invited to do great things who receives small things greatly."
—Cassiodorus

In Word Not only is this the rule of the kingdom; it is the rule of all kingdom things. The kingdom of God was almost unnoticeable when it began, in a sense, with a nomad named Abraham. Then a small nation of wanderers with the promise of a tiny tract c land. Then a Messiah of seemingly humble, obscure origins. Then a band of low-pedigree disciples. Then a fringe movement in the backwaters of an empire. Today, the kingdom of God has influenced the planet more than any earthly empire and any religious worldview. It is the largest and most fruitful of all the plants in thi ravaged garden. That's the historical implication of these verses.

But there's also a personal application of these verses. We tend to think that accomplishing something in God's kingdom means building large ministries with an extended reach. We are impressed by those who have done great things for God—defining "great things" as impacting lots of people in highly visible ways. And perhaps these are great things, in God's eyes. But the began small. God's kingdom is a mustard-seed kind of enterpris Huge ministries often begin with one small step of faith. Lives ar often changed by one kind word. Hearts are touched by one soft song, or one frightened witness, or a cup of cold water given in His name. Nothing in His kingdom is too small to count—or eve too small to grow into something huge.

In Deed Never despise the small things in your life. Never spend so much time reaching for the high-impact acts of ministry that you neglect the minute details of service. The massive doors of God's kingdom swing on tiny hinges of our faith and obedience. Focus on the hinges, and you'll see the doors ope wide.

Witnesses on Trial

"This will result in your being witnesses to them."
(Luke 21:13)

In Word We can become extremely self-absorbed in a trial. We see how it will impact us, we pray for deliverance from it, and we obsess about how to work ourselves out of it. But we often become blind to God's larger purpose. Our trials, though they seem like disasters to us, may be God's means for bringing honor to His name.

In this passage in Luke, Jesus tells His disciples they will be dragged through courts, prisons, and the world's halls of power. But He does not tell them to call their attorneys and clear their names. He tells them to be more concerned with His name—in other words, to be His witnesses. Their "disaster" is for His glory, He says, and He reminds them to go through trials with that purpose in mind.

God has called us to shine."
–D. L. Moody

Though few of us are hauled before the world's judges for our faith, we all go through difficulties. Rather than turning inward and focusing on our hardships and how to get out of them, Jesus would tell us by the implications of this passage to have a greater purpose in mind. We are to seek His glory in all circumstances, even the ones that pain us deeply. They are often His means of letting the world know who He is.

In Deed How does Jesus display Himself in our trials? That depends on our response. Are we in a situation where people are trying to take advantage of us, draw us into their controversies, or compel us to behave in conformity to the world's standards? Then Jesus is displayed in our refusal to be conformed. Our lack of contentiousness and competitiveness will indicate faith and hope in higher realities. Are we suffering in a way that would cause most people to despair or cry out in bitterness and anger? Then Jesus is displayed as we demonstrate that our treasure is above, and that this world's travails are swallowed up in our hope of eternal life. Whatever we go through, it can result in our being witnesses.

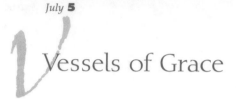

Vessels of Grace

"Freely you have received, freely give." (Matthew 10:8

"Nothing is really ours until we share it."
—C. S. Lewis

In Word This verse is often used in a financial stewardship situation, and certainly would apply to such contexts. But that is not the context in which Jesus spoke it; the next instructior that He gave the twelve disciples indicates that they will not be applying their finances to the kingdom's work on this trip (v. 9). No, the command is much more comprehensive than that.

We are first of all to recognize how much we have been given "Freely you have received," Jesus reminds the Twelve. They had been given forgiveness, a grace we often take for granted, forgetting not so much the magnitude of our sins but the magnitude of the One against whom we have sinned. They had been given words of wisdom from the universe's greatest teacher. They had seen His character modeled for them. They had seen healing of incurable diseases and rescues from impossible situations. They had seen, in short, the love and mercy of a God who had humble Himself and taken on the form of a man.

This—love and mercy with a humble spirit—is what we and the disciples are to freely give, whether it takes the form of time, money, a gospel witness, healing, comfort, or words of encouragement. All of the things God has given us in Christ are given not only for our own enjoyment and edification, but for us to pass on to others. We are often like hungry beggars who hoard the bread we've been given, not realizing that it comes from the hand of an unlimited supplier. We fear that His supply has a cap on it; that if we give away what He's given us, we lose out.

In Deed Those who freely give have found the opposite to be true. A consistent principle in Jesus' teaching is that those who give away God's gifts are given more to replace them. An irony of the kingdom is that hoarders never have enough and generous givers never lack. In giving, we become conduits of God's grace, vessels of His mercy.

The Test of Impossibilities

"Where shall we buy bread for these people to eat?"

(John 6:5)

In Word Jesus asks Philip this probing question. It seems innocent enough, but there is a test in it. Jesus gives Philip an impossibility to consider. And Philip's response indicates a mind-set with which we can all sympathize. We look at the situation, think of how to solve it in human terms, and lament about our lack of resources. There isn't enough money. There isn't enough time. There aren't enough people. We have insufficient means.

We, like Philip, forget whom we are dealing with. The situation is never too big for Jesus. He is not bound by our resources. In fact, if we had sufficient means, He probably would choose to work with someone else. His power cannot be demonstrated among people with self-sufficiency. He is waiting for the Andrews of the world to come to Him with a pitifully limited supply and ask, full of doubt, "But how far will [this] go" (v. 9)? Having brought His people to the point of knowing their own poverty and limitations, He is ready to work.

"We have a God who delights in impossibilities."

–Andrew Murray

In Deed When has Jesus confronted you with an impossibility? When has He said, "What are you going to do with this situation?" As we look at the world around us, we can relate to Philip. There are hundreds of millions of hungry people in the world. There are diseases running rampant with no known (or available) cure. There are relationships breaking under the strain of secular patterns of behavior. And worst of all, there are people dying and going to hell, many of them never having heard the Gospel. Like Philip, we might say we don't have enough resources. Like Andrew, we might show Jesus what we have, knowing it is paltry.

Whatever our response, we must acknowledge our insufficiency. Then, and only then, can we look to the sufficiency of Jesus. He already has in mind what He is going to do (v. 6). He already knows how He will meet the need. He is waiting for us to acknowledge our limitations and trust Him.

Where God's Heart Is

"If a man owns a hundred sheep, and one of them wanders away, will he not leave the ninety-nine on the hills and go to look for the one that wandered off?"

(Matthew 18:1

In Word David says that the Lord is his Shepherd. Jesus says that He is the Good Shepherd. And in Matthew 18, Jesus tel us that the Shepherd is zealously focused on restoring lost sheep.

The implications of this for our understanding of God are clear: He is a seeking God. If we want to know what His prioritie in the world are, we need look no further than here. He tells us. He is passionate about pursuing lost sheep. He will gladly leave behind the 99 in their comfort and safety in order to track down a single, misguided sheep. All heaven rejoices when that sheep is found (Luke 15:7, 10).

The implications of this are so clear for us: As co-laborers wit God, we are also to be seeking on His behalf. He is a missionary God, He sent a missionary Son into the world, and He calls us to have a missionary mind. If we are to be like Him, we too must have a consuming, searching passion for lost sheep.

"The salvation of one soul is worth more than the framing of a Magna Carta of a thousand worlds."

—John Keble

In Deed Do we want to align ourselves with God's plan Then we must single-mindedly pray for those who are lost. We must work to find them and to bring them into the Good Shepherd's fold. We must give our resources toward this end. We mus behave like a shepherd who is not content with a 99 percent success rate. God does not rest as long as there are lost sheep, and neither can we.

Today, there are more than four billion sheep outside the Shepherd's fold. Half of them live so far out of the fold that there are no representatives of the Shepherd nearby. If we want to be in tune with God's priorities, we must pray, give, train, tell, send, go—and never rest—as long as sheep are outside the fold.

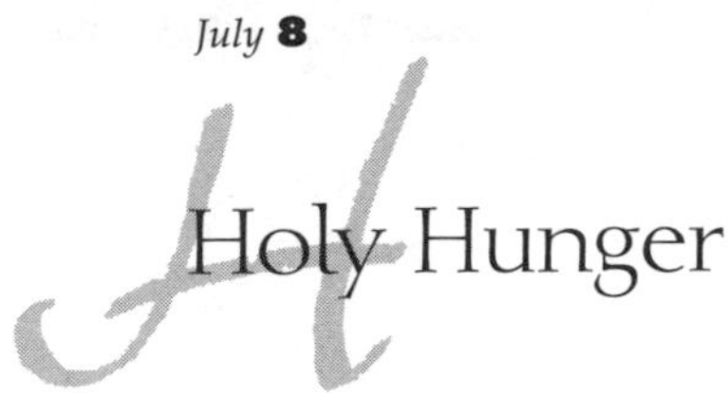

Holy Hunger

"Blessed are you who hunger now, for you will be satisfied." (Luke 6:21)

In Word Hunger doesn't feel very blessed. It feels like discontentment, and that makes us feel guilty. But there is a holy hunger that God blesses, and whether we know it or not, all of us have felt it acutely.

Deep in the soul of every man, woman, and child is a void that nags us for attention. We think it's a sign of dysfunction, and we try to heal it ourselves. Some of us fill it with food, but the sense of taste is only satisfied for a moment. Some of us try to fill it with moving from place to place or possession to possession, but the sense of adventure constantly craves a new direction. Some of us try to fill it with relationships, but that void can't be lastingly filled with another person. Some of us recognize that nothing has ever filled it and probably nothing ever will, so we get counseling to try to determine the psychological source of this persistent pathology. If we can't fill it, we try to deny it; if we can't deny it, we try to change it; if we can't change it, we try to fill it again. One day, if we're spiritually sensitive, we understand: It's a holy hunger, and only God can fix it.

There is a God-shaped vacuum in the heart of every man that cannot be filled by any created thing but only by the Creator." —Blaise Pascal

In Deed Jesus says the hungry are blessed. Why? Because the truly hungry have given up trying to satisfy themselves with the wrong things. They've found that gratifying the senses isn't ultimately gratifying, and that pursuing meaningful relationships isn't the ultimate in meaning. They've found that all of our raging appetites are really a sad reminder that we have a deeper hunger for the eternal. That God-shaped vacuum that Pascal spoke of can only be filled with God—not possessions, not people, not places. God may freely bless us with all these things in abundance, but only *after* we've found our contentment in Him alone. He is no enemy of the things He's created, but He opposes them becoming the focus of our lives. Those who have quenched their hunger with the things of this world have settled for empty calories; they're ultimately unsatisfied. The blessing of true hunger leads us to Jesus, the Bread of Life.

Meekness Wins

"Blessed are the meek, for they will inherit the earth."
(Matthew 5:

"Meekness is the mark of a man who has been mastered by God."
—Geoffrey B. Wilson

In Word There are many angles from which to look at th beatitude. Is it strictly for Jews and their promise of the land of Israel? Many commentators say so. Is it for all believers everywhere, a promise of millennial authority? Many commentators sa this, too. One thing is clear: It is consistent with the character of God to reward those who defer to Him. Whoever *the meek* are, and whatever *the land* or *the earth* is meant to be, God honors those wh are not always looking out for their own self-interests.

Our culture reviles meekness. It is considered by most to be weakness. But Jesus did not commend weakness. In fact, it takes great strength to be meek by Jesus' definition. Some experts in Greek say this word "meek" is the same word used for horses tha have been broken. They have submitted themselves to the master will. Considering the overwhelming evidence in the Bible that this is God's desire for us, we can safely assume that this kind of meekness is appropriate. God calls us to lay down our rebellion and know that He is at work and able to bring about His purposes in our lives. We do not need to strive so stridently for them.

Look at the biblical stories that confirm this dynamic. Abraham was meek in giving Lot his choice of the land; and Abraham inherited the land (Genesis 13:10-15). Jesus was meek a He rode into Jerusalem on a donkey; and He inherits the nations (Psalm 2:8). What about you?

In Deed This dynamic of meekness that results in inheritance is all through the Bible. It is explicit in Psalm 37:11 and in Jesus' beatitude, but it is implicit in many other places. How heavily dependent on it are you? Are you aggressively seeking your portion and establishing your rights? Or are you content to rely on the power of God to show up in His timing and in His way? Your "inheritance" depends on the answer. You can count on the promise: Meekness wins.

The Tyranny of the Tangible

"Stop doubting and believe." (John 20:27)

In Word We get onto Thomas for his doubting, but he, perhaps better than any other disciple, represents the modern mind well. We live in an "age of reason" in which many demand that if anything is true, it must be verifiable in a test tube. Unless we've seen it, touched it, tasted it, smelled it, or heard it—i.e., had some sort of sensory evidence—it's not worth our time. Need an example? The skeptics of our age, like Thomas, insist that the Resurrection is a religious fabrication. Why? Because they've never seen it happen.

Believers, too, can live under the tyranny of the tangible. We haven't seen the Resurrection, either, at least not in the visible sense that the first disciples did. While we aren't skeptical to the point of agnosticism, we have doubts when we pray. Why? We often have seen the power of the Resurrection only in our hearts. That should be enough, but for those who pray for God's direct intervention in their circumstances, the circumstances often seem much larger than the power of God. We are Thomases; unless we see, it's hard to believe.

"Never doubt in the dark what God told you in the light."

-Victor Raymond Edman

Jesus, as we know, tells us we usually won't see *until* we believe. Faith is the priority in the kingdom. And it is a choice. Like Thomas, we have the option of hearing the disciples' report and saying, "That sounds like my Savior; it must be true." But like Thomas, we often do not let ourselves believe the best about Him. Perhaps we don't want to set ourselves up for disappointment. Perhaps we just haven't seen enough miracles to convince us. Perhaps we let the concrete evidence of circumstances rule our minds.

In Deed The minds of those who follow Jesus *cannot* be limited by visual appearances. Jesus' command is both harsh and loving: "Stop doubting and believe." To what shall we apply this stern command? The Resurrection? Yes, and everything else that requires resurrection power—our prayers, our works, and our attitudes. Do not let discouraging circumstances define you. Stop doubting and believe.

Dealing With Doubt

"Stop doubting and believe." (John 20:27

In Word Every genuine Christian has struggled with doubts. At first, they are doubts about the big questions—does God really exist, is there life after death, etc. As we progress in th life of faith, we settle these major questions, but we continue to struggle with the more subtle ones. When God says He is my Refuge, does He really mean it? When I pray, has He really heard me? When He promises me my daily bread, can I really depend on it? A world of unfulfilled need and despair nags us into thinking God is not always reliable, or that He is too obscure for His reliability to mean anything to us practically. When we see peopl go hungry or suffer harm, can we realistically expect God's prom ises to be true for us? Doubts—very real ones, often based on oth ers' experiences or even our own—creep in and try to convince u that God isn't all He says He is. They wage war against our faith. Sometimes they seem to win.

"Turn from your doubts with horror, as you would from blasphemy; for they are blasphemy."

—Hannah Whitall Smith

Jesus' remedy is not to argue them away. He does not tell Thomas to reason with his doubts. He just tells Thomas to stop doubting. Thomas already has enough evidence—he has now seen the Resurrection, if the whole of Scripture had not been enough already—and must simply stop doubting. The questions are not legitimate in the face of a God with a proven track record.

In Deed We will find ourselves in one of two cycles: a downward cycle, in which doubt undermines faith, which undermines experience, which in turn further undermines faith; or an upward cycle, in which faith births the experience of God's intervention, which in turn supports greater faith. Elsewhere, Jesus ha said it will be to us according to our faith—God will respond to our trust. The converse is also true; God will not always respond to our doubt. He will not constantly prove Himself to a closed an doubting mind. The evidence is already there. Thomas saw it. We must believe it. The doubts must simply be forsaken and faith embraced.

Responding With Faith

"Blessed are those who have not seen and yet have believed." (John 20:29)

In Word Not only does this blessedness apply to the initial faith we have in our Savior; it is the sum of the Christian life. We are constantly asked to stake our lives on an invisible God and a risen Savior whom we do not see. His footprints are all over history, so it isn't a baseless faith. There is nothing naive or blind about it. It is entirely rational and rooted in experience—ours and others'. But it is still often hidden to our five senses, and when we let those senses rule, we find the life of faith difficult.

Thomas found the life of faith difficult, at least at first, in those early days when resurrection seemed like such an impossibility. Would he have been a Christian in these days, when the Savior's ascension is considered ancient history? Though He lives to make intercession for us, He is hidden to our eyes. Those who depend too heavily on their eyes will miss the blessings that come only by faith. They will be suspicious of the many promises of God, as though there is a fine-print legal loophole to all of them. They will wonder whether Scripture is a reliable revelation of His character. They will more and more find the invisible God "unknowable," while those with the eyes of faith find Him more and more real.

All unbelief is the belief of a lie."

–Horatio Bonar

In Deed How much of your walk with God is based on your five senses? Do you invest your heart in Him only when He is demonstrating His favor? Or do you trust that His love is real even when you don't see it? When the Bible says that God is a Refuge, a Help in trouble, a Deliverer, a Healer—and all the wonderful things it says about Him—that revelation is a greater reality than the paper and ink you hold in your hand or anything else your eyes can see and fingers can touch. There is a profound blessedness in believing that. God manifests His presence to those who believed Him before having seen Him. He readily intervenes on behalf of those who know He will. Believe, and be blessed.

Careful Listening

"Consider carefully how you listen." (Luke 8:18

In Word Many times, we think that by hearing the Word of God and understanding its meaning, we have integrated it into our lives. We read numerous Bible passages and listen to countless sermons, thinking that if we have intellectually comprehended the message and agreed with it, it is ours. But Jesus' parable of the soils says there is more to the story than hearing and believing His Word. Some hear and believe and then fall away in times of testing. Others hear and believe and then do not mature because of life's worries. Hearing and believing is not enough.

Those who bear fruit for God and fulfill His purpose for their lives are those who first hear the Word, then believe it, then retain it, and then persevere in it (v. 15). They let it sink into their hearts. They meditate on it. They build their lives around it. It becomes a part of them, and they abide by it because it has reshaped them. It defines their identity—and their behavior.

"All true knowledge of God is born out of obedience."
—John Calvin

In Deed Recent surveys and demographic studies have indicated that Christians and non-Christians in the United States have remarkably similar behavior patterns. Why? Because many of us stop at hearing and believing. We are not careful about how we listen. We are like those of whom James speaks: "Anyone who listens to the word but does not do what it says is like a man who looks at his face in a mirror and, after looking at himself, goes away and immediately forgets what he looks like" (James 1:23-24 This is a type of self-deceit (1:22). It gives us the impression that we are growing in the Word, but we are growing in knowledge only. Real growth comes from real application—diligence in integrating the Word into our hearts and then living it. Careful listening brings radical change and lasting fruit.

God's purpose for His Word is that it be unhindered by testing, worries, riches, and pleasures. It is to be a seed that lands on our fertile soil, takes deep root, and grows steadily. Be careful. Listen in a way that will fulfill His purpose.

Lasting Fruit

"I chose you and appointed you to go and bear fruit—fruit that will last." (John 15:16)

In Word It seems like an awesome responsibility and an impossible task. Jesus tells His disciples—and us—to go and bear lasting fruit. But how? The disciples fished, collected taxes, or pursued some other such profession, but that was all momentary sustenance, not permanent achievement. Even while following Jesus, they mostly observed His work, only occasionally participating in it. Nothing they did themselves was lasting. Likewise, the best of our works have proven futile over time. Nothing we've done endures, no matter how well intentioned or diligently carried out. The best we've been able to muster is temporary and flawed.

"You have nothing to do in life except to live in union with Christ."
—Rufus Mosely

How, then, can Jesus reasonably leave us with this mission—to bear fruit that lasts? Doesn't He know what we're made of? It's a ridiculously impossible assignment. We're created from dust and corrupted in sin. How can we contribute to an eternal kingdom?

Jesus knows the impossibility of His command. In fact, our obedience to it depends on our understanding that it's impossible. It's one of His many counterintuitive messages. Just as we must die to live and serve to be great, we must know our own futility to finally be productive. We must get to the end of ourselves. He spells it out for us in verses 4 and 5: "No branch can bear fruit by itself; it must remain in the vine. Neither can you bear fruit unless you remain in me. . . . If a man remains in me and I in him, he will bear much fruit; apart from me you can do nothing."

In Deed We're often tempted to try to work for God. Nothing we do with that approach will last. The strength of the flesh cannot produce the fruit of the Spirit. Only Jesus can do that. There is no way we can follow His commandments without letting Him live through us. As branches, our only task is to remain attached to the vine. It's the vine that bears the fruit. Are you abiding in Him?

Master of the Storms

"You of little faith, why are you so afraid?"

(Matthew 8:26

In Word Why does Jesus have to ask His disciples this? He knows why they are afraid. They are weak, vulnerable humar beings. They are no match for the violent forces of nature. What normal human being wouldn't be afraid? And what Savior wouldn't understand this human tendency?

Jesus asks this question because these normal, fearful people in the boat with Him have missed the key element in the situation. It isn't the storm that matters. It isn't the size of the waves or the structural integrity of the boat. It's the company they are in. They are accompanied by the image of the invisible God, the One by whom all things were created (Colossians 1:15-16). As His disciples, wherever we are, no matter how fierce the winds are, we are with Him. That changes *everything*.

"There is never a fear that has not a corresponding 'Fear not.'"
—Amy Carmichael

We need to hear this convicting question on numerous occasions in our lives. Storms swell, sometimes gradually on the horizon, and sometimes, as in this story, suddenly and furiously, without warning. Either way, fear is usually our first reaction. It isn't that we overestimate the storms. They really can be damaging. We've seen them destroy the lives of other people. No, our problem isn't having an inaccurate view of the storm. It's in having an inaccurate view of Jesus. As long as we're preoccupied with the storm and Jesus seems to us to be asleep in the back of the boat, we will fear. It is a natural—and inevitable—human response.

In Deed But Jesus asks us to do the unnatural and avoid the inevitabilities of our human frailties. He asks us to have faith in Him. Yes, the storm is dangerous. Yes, we are weak and vulnerable. Left with those two facts alone, we are overcome. But Jesus gives us another fact to throw into the equation—Himself. He is the King of all creation, God with us. With our eyes fixed on Him, we can say "What storm? What danger? What weakness?" The storms *must* obey Him. What do we have to fear?

Master in the Storms

"You of little faith, why are you so afraid?"

(Matthew 8:26)

In Word One of the hindrances to a faithful response to Jesus in the storms of our lives is our acute awareness that He let us get into the storm to begin with. We would rather have a Savior who didn't sleep in the back of the boat. We would prefer that He navigate us around the storms rather than deliver us from the middle of them. But our God has never guarded His people from storms. He even lets us suffer in them sometimes. Why?

Jesus could have navigated His company around that storm. It blew up without warning, but the Lord of creation isn't surprised by anything. He knew about the Cross ahead of time, and He knew about this storm. But if He had let the disciples avoid it, they would never have known Him as the Master of the winds and the waves. They would not have asked the question: "What kind of man is this?" (v. 27). They would not have known Jesus as their Deliverer that day.

As sure as ever God puts His children in the furnace, He will be in the furnace with them."

—Charles Spurgeon

In Deed Jesus lets us get into the middle of storms so we will know Him. When we avoid the dangerous waters, we avoid the Deliverer. When all is well, our faith only needs a Jesus who is asleep in the boat. While that may be more comfortable to us, it subverts the purpose for which we were created. We were made to know Him, and whether we like it or not, some of His characteristics can only be discovered in the deep, treacherous waters.

When we think we prefer our comfort to the storms of life—a universal tendency for us humans, by the way—we are actually choosing stagnancy over fulfillment. We must realize that we can't really know the Deliverer unless we need deliverance. We can't know our Redeemer unless we need redemption. We can't know our Refuge unless we experience danger. Do we *really* seek comfort and ease? No. Deep down, we want real faith. We want to know the One who accompanies us—even in the storms.

Quiet Places

"Come with me by yourselves to a quiet place and get some rest."
(Mark 6:31

"Jesus knows we must come apart and rest awhile, or else we may just plain come apart."
—Vance Havner

In Word The person who does not get alone with Jesus i sure to have difficulty as a disciple. This getting away is essential there can be no growth or genuine service without it.

It is in the quiet places that Jesus refreshes us. Burnout is a common problem in whatever field we work, and the world has no lasting solution for it. Secular advice tells us to get away for a change of pace. If we follow that advice, we can postpone burnou for a time; but we will quickly get tired again if all we've done is relax. Jesus did not tell His disciples to go away to relax. He told them to come with Him. His presence is the difference between a temporary rest and a lasting refreshment.

In the quiet places, Jesus does give us rest, but He also teache us how to depend on Him more fully, how to serve Him more effectively, and how to trust Him more implicitly. The quiet place are places of growth. We deepen our fellowship with Him, and instead of a temporary rest, we have a relationship that will continue to sustain us when the pressures of life are on us again. The things we learn in the calm with Him today are the things that will help us survive in the storms ahead.

In Deed Quiet times with Jesus—even extended ones—are to be frequent occurrences. Jesus often went to a solitary place to pray. The times He had alone with His Father strengthened Him and guided Him for His mission in this world. In the same way, we generally cannot experience the presence of Christ in the busyness of life unless we have first experienced His presence in the quiet moments. We cannot get to know Him better when the shrill voices of our duties compete with His gentle leading. If we want to serve Him well, we need His sane, calm voice to speak clearly to us. And the only way to cultivate our hearing is in quiet places.

Bridging the Distance

"The tax collector stood at a distance." (Luke 18:13)

In Word It's a familiar story. Two men went to the temple to pray, and only one of them went away with an answer—an ashamed tax collector who couldn't even look in heaven's direction.

Why would Jesus tell His disciples a parable that commends standing at a distance from God? Doesn't He want to draw us near to God? Doesn't He encourage prodigals to come home? Doesn't He tell us to call God "Father"? God's welcoming arms and His invitation to intimacy are solid, biblical themes. Yet in this parable, Jesus condemns the Pharisee's familiarity with God and applauds the tax collector's distance. Why?

The difference is the attitude bringing us to God. Are we entitled to be there? Do we come to Him expecting approval for our good behavior? Or do we see Him as a Captain who welcomes mutineers back with open arms, a King who opens His palace to former coup instigators?

The moment we start to feel worthy of being God's children, we're in trouble. It isn't wrong to be comfortable with our Father. *But on whose merit does He accept us?* Ours? No, we are welcome in God's presence because Jesus is good, not because we're good. And we never really understand His goodness unless our soul has first felt the loneliness of spiritual exile. Grace is for rebels who have known their offense.

"I remember two things; that I am a great sinner, and that Christ is a great Savior."
—John Newton

In Deed We probably don't applaud ourselves for the things that the Pharisee believed made him acceptable—avoiding the really bad sins and appearing better than others. But we can become awfully casual about being in God's presence. We can act like entitled children who demand the Father's attention rather than privileged children who are overwhelmed by the Father's mercies. We don't remember the depth of the chasm that Jesus bridged.

In this parable, Jesus doesn't mean to teach us to stand at a distance from God. He means to remind us how great a distance was there. May we never forget.

Radical Love

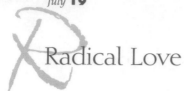

"If you love those who love you, what credit is that to you?"
(Luke 6:32)

In Word The culture of the kingdom of heaven is not at all like the culture you grew up in. It doesn't matter whether your culture of origin is North or South American, African, Asian, or European; and it doesn't matter whether your language of origin is English, Spanish, Lao, or Farsi. You are called to a radically different life and language the moment you ask the Son of God to recreate you by His Spirit.

The first area Jesus deals with in this passage is the area of our loves. Most of us are conditioned to love those who will return the sentiment. But in the kingdom, love is not a sentiment; it's a choice. We would hope that eventually the choice will be followed by sincere feelings and genuine compassion, but it starts with a choice. The *agape* kind of love that Jesus compels us to have for others cannot be answered with an "I don't feel like it." Feeling isn't the issue. The issue is whether we will live according to our citizenship in this kingdom of God.

"Love means loving the unlovable—or it is no virtue at all."
—Anonymous

The culture of the kingdom is shaped by its King. If He loved us while we were yet sinners, we must love others while they are yet sinners. If He forgave people who nailed Him to the cross, we must forgive those who nail us to a cross. The King makes the rules, and the rules are different than everything you grew up with and everything your culture tells you is standard.

In Deed Do you have a standard sort of love? Jesus' calling is much higher than that. He never asked any of His disciples to fit in with the crowd. He never told His followers to just do what others expect of them. No, His calling means for us a radical departure from all the norms we once knew. It means divorcing the ways of this world and embracing a purer love. It means not many people will travel with us on this road we've taken. But how it is worth it! Jesus promises "credit" to us if we do things His way—His wildly radical way. We must stand out from the crowd.

Radical Behavior

"If you do good to those who are good to you, what credit is that to you?" (Luke 6:33)

In Word It's hard learning this new kingdom culture, especially for those of us who would prefer to blend in with the crowd. But with Jesus, there is conformity to His character and His kingdom, but there is no blending in with this world. Jesus was uncompromising in His behavior, whether He was tempted in the wilderness, proclaiming truth at the temple, preaching from a mountain, or pointing out the hypocrisy of His adversaries. Truth never took a back seat to protocol in Jesus' ministry. Neither did good works ever take a back seat to crowd preferences and political agendas. Jesus did *only* what He heard the Father tell Him. No other voice really mattered.

Can we say the same thing about our behavior? Do we follow only the voice of the Father to the exclusion of all other voices? Are we uncompromising in our stance on right and wrong and good and evil? More than that, are we kind and looking out for the welfare of those who are bitter and wicked toward us? That's our high calling, you know. God expects us to stand out from the crowd with our display of good works, and the only way to stand out is to do them for people who don't deserve them. *Everyone* can do them for those who are good to them in return. Only a God-filled person can uncompromisingly benefit an ill-spirited person.

We are to do acts of kindness to those that least of all deserve it."
– William Law

In Deed Yes, this is unnatural. But where in Scripture does God ask us to act naturally? Our nature is fallen; we inherited it from Eden's disaster. No, we are to act according to a different nature. It may feel strange to us at first, but it is offered freely nonetheless. We must accept the radical promptings of the Spirit of God and be clothed in the character of Jesus. Then we must move out into this world with a different agenda than we ever thought we'd have. We must be radical in our behavior and display the radical nature of our God.

Radical Generosity

"If you lend to those from whom you expect repayment, what credit is that to you?" (Luke 6:34

In Word We give our love and change our behavior much more easily than we let go of our things. Have you noticed that? The least valuable commodity we have—material possessions—is that which we grip the tightest. Our feelings will change as often a the direction of the wind, and our love with it. Our behavior can b adjusted whenever the situation demands. But let go of our things That's just asking too much.

God's call to a radical change of lifestyle includes a radical change of our emotional investment in our money and our things. We are to use the currency of this world—materials and money—t strengthen the currency of the kingdom—faith. This often means that we will have to give away our holdings to those who ask for them or who need them and are afraid to ask. We must hold everything with a loose grip.

"The test of generosity is not how much you give, but how much you have left." —Anonymous

"But I have little to give," we might complain. We probably have little because in the past we have not been generous with what we have. God's principles cannot be violated; He has promised that those who are good stewards with what they've been given will be given more. If we lack, we may lack for a reason: a history of bad stewardship. Even if this is not the case, the "I have little to give" excuse does not hold up. If we have little, we must give little. Jesus commended the woman who dropped two small coins into the coffer. Why did she give all she had? Because it was all she could give.

In Deed We least want to be radical in the area of our possessions. We don't mind being noticed for our love and our kindness nearly as much as we mind being noticed for our sacrifice of things. Yes, there are many donors of large amounts in this world, but they usually also retain large amounts. This isn't bad, but it isn't radical either. Jesus calls us to be radical. Sacrificially radical and sacrificially generous.

An Undeserved Kindness

"He is kind to the ungrateful and wicked." (Luke 6:35)

In Word The Bible is clear in its assessment of the human heart: It is wicked. It seeks its own good above all else, it tries to hide its secrets from God, it harbors evil attitudes against others, and it cultivates bitterness when wronged. Most of all, it does not worship God unless His Spirit enables it. Our upbringing helps us cover up our natural inclinations, but we know how we were before we met Christ. Salvation reversed the tide for us, but the seeds of corruption are always available for cultivation.

While we all have evil in our hearts by our nature as sinful human beings, there are those in this world who do an exceptional job of displaying it. Most of us want to do good and to behave respectfully and kindly toward others. But we invariably encounter those who seem to have no conscience about themselves, and even seem to enjoy their selfish wills. When we are wronged by them, we are left standing with nothing but the Gospel to guide our response. Will we let it?

"Kindness has converted more sinners than zeal, eloquence, and learning."
—Frederick Faber

Of all the people in this world, Jesus was treated most unjustly. Perfect innocence was ravaged by the utterly corrupt. What was His response? He stood for truth and suffered the consequences. But He never retaliated or fought. Never. And He calls us to be like Him.

In Deed How do we respond when we are wronged? Are we appalled at the evil in others' hearts? We can't afford to be; the same seeds are within us. Do we retaliate in like manner? We violate the command of Jesus if we do, and we sink to their level. Do we seethe with resentment toward them? Again, we disobey Jesus if we do, and our attitude harms only ourselves.

What, then, is the appropriate response? Jesus tells us to love our enemies, even to do good to them and lend to them. How this grates on our old nature and attacks our pride! But this is exactly what He did with us, and His heart's desire is for us to be like Him. Will we? See your injustices as a chance to prove His Gospel. Be kind to the ungrateful and wicked.

House of Prayer

" 'My house will be called a house of prayer.' "
(Matthew 21:1

"None can believe how powerful prayer is, and what it is able to effect, but those who have learned it by experience."
—Martin Luther

In Word As Jesus is overturning the money-changing tables in the temple, He quotes Isaiah 56:7, a verse from a passage about Sabbath-keeping and God's worldwide mission—"a house of prayer *for all nations,*" Isaiah reads. It is a striking irony: The moneychangers had a limiting effect on who could worship God by their monetary controls and exploitation, while Jesus speaks o the global inclusiveness of the true worship of God. They had missed the whole point about worship—it is to be freely and joyfully given. God's house is about prayer. Nothing else. Not profit, not expedience, just pure, undefiled communion with Him.

The New Testament application of this is not what we might think. We often apply Jesus' indictment of the moneychangers at the temple to our own church buildings. They, too, are to be houses of prayer, of course. But Jesus never calls a church buildin "God's house." Neither do any of the New Testament writers. God's house, after the gift of the Spirit, is the heart of the believer He dwells in us—individually and corporately. And as His house *we* are the house of prayer.

In Deed Do you consider yourself—your own heart—a house of prayer? It is where God dwells, according to post-Pentecost Scripture (1 Corinthians 3:16 and 6:19; 2 Corinthians 6:16; Ephesians 2:21-22). There is to be pure, undefiled communion there. And it is global—a house of prayer *for all nations.* God's dwelling place is a worldwide body doing a worldwide ministry, lifting up the whole world's needs to its Head.

John 2:17 tells us that Jesus is consumed by His zeal for His Father's house. Knowing that *we* are His Father's house makes that verse profound indeed. Jesus will zealously pursue commun ion in you, even if it means overturning some tables. There are to be prayers and holy fellowship in that sacred place.

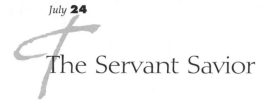

The Servant Savior

"You do not realize now what I am doing, but later you will understand." (John 13:7)

In Word Many commentators see a parallel between the foot-washing Jesus gives His disciples and the Incarnation as described in Philippians 2:5-11. In that passage, Jesus is said to have been in His very nature God, but made Himself nothing, taking the nature of a servant instead. His obedience even to the point of death is the ultimate expression of that servanthood.

Here in John 13, Jesus gives us a visual illustration of the divine descent to our needy planet. He removes His normal clothing and wraps Himself with the garment a slave would wear (v. 4), just as He left the radiance of God to put on a human body. He performs the most selfless of tasks—a menial service that shocked those who called Him "Lord"—for the sake of His beloved disciples. And when He was done, "he put on his clothes and returned to his place" (v. 12), just as the Son of God put on His resurrected body and returned to His place of exaltation.

"Love and humility are the highest attainments in the school of Christ."

- John Newton

No, of course the disciples did not understand what He was doing. Though He had predicted His own death and resurrection several times, they kept trying to figure out the symbolic language they were sure He was using. It had still not registered with them that His execution would be a literal event. They had not yet considered that the Lord, the Messiah, was—at the very heart of His mission—a servant.

In Deed It's hard for us to grasp, too, isn't it? The Lord of all creation at our feet? We treat Him that way in a casual sense sometimes; our prayers often seem to imply that He exists for our glory, that He ought to do what we ask Him to if He really loves us like He says. But that is a servanthood we mistakenly feel entitled to, not a real recognition of the incredible condescension God undertook in order to meet our most profound needs. Jesus left the glories of heaven in order to wash our feet. We *still* don't realize entirely the magnitude of what He did. But later we will understand.

The Savior's Servants

"I have set you an example that you should do as I hav done for you." (John 13:15

In Word A genuine appreciation of what Jesus did for u in His incarnation, death, and resurrection is just the beginning. His ministry is not just a beautiful event that we can admire for i wisdom and for the salvation it brings us. It also has practical implications for us. Looking back at that divine descent from glory to corruptible flesh, from self-existing life to a humiliating death, the disciples were to be struck with a personal realization: We are to do as He did.

Jesus took off His respectable clothes and wrapped Himself i a servant's towel. He washed the dirtiest part of the human body in a semi-arid climate and a pedestrian culture. There is nothing glorious about cleaning feet. There is no recognition to be had there, no accolades for a great accomplishment. The disciples hac surely had their feet washed before—by "real" servants—and ha likely never even thanked them. Why should they? They were only doing what servants are obligated to do. Jesus spotted the dirtiest, most thankless area of physical need for the disciples an met it as an illustration of His mission. Then He got up and told the disciples that they should behave in exactly the same way.

"We can do no great things; only small things with great love."

—Mother Teresa

In Deed How often do we consciously do acts of servic that others consider meaningless and unworthy of their talents? How often do we approach the needs of this world with a self-emptying attitude that will stoop as low as those needs demand? It goes against our human nature, doesn't it? We're always striv-ing to work our way up, not work our way down. We think if w can attain to a higher status we can impact more people for the kingdom of God. Perhaps so, sometimes. But Jesus' example might lead us in another direction—farther down. Lower. Towar less glory. With less recognition. According to the Savior, that's th way to greatness in God's kingdom. As strange as this behavior seems, it's how He saved us. And it's how others will be saved. Jesus calls us to do as He has done for us.

Lord of the Harvest

"Ask the Lord of the harvest . . . to send out workers into his harvest field." (Luke 10:2)

In Word Anytime the Bible gives a name for God, we can know that the name is descriptive of His character. When Jesus calls God "the Lord of the harvest," He is not describing something peripheral to God's nature. The harvest is at the very core of God's heart; it is who He is by nature.

We often struggle with how to pray in accordance with God's will. The prayer in this verse is a sure thing; if we pray that the Lord of the harvest will send out workers into His field, we know we are praying the intent of His heart. We do not have to weaken our request, as we so often do, with the disclaimer "if it's Your will" at the end of our prayer. No, it *is* God's will—without a doubt. We can be sure of it.

We often want to spend a little time with God but have very little to do with His harvest. That is a concept as absurd as a farmer's family wanting very little to do with the crops. A farmer's life revolves around his fields; so will the life of his family. God's work revolves around His harvest; so will the work of His family.

The church exists by mission as a fire exists by burning."

–Emil Brunner

In Deed Have you struggled with God's will for your life? Have you questioned where He would have you invest your energy? Whatever He has you do, you can be sure of this: The harvest will be an integral part of your relationship with Him. It is impossible to know the Lord of the harvest well without getting involved at some point with the harvest itself.

Perhaps your involvement begins where this verse does—with the asking. The first step in God's work is prayer. And rather than telling His disciples to pray for converts, Jesus' instruction is first to pray for workers. He would be foolish to bring new sheep into the fold without a prior increase in shepherds. There must be more workers.

This is one of Jesus' most direct commands. You cannot follow Him well without obeying it.

Go

"Go and make disciples of all nations." (Matthew 28:19)

In Word Perhaps we've heard this so often that it's lost its impact. Perhaps stories of missionaries and martyrs throughout the centuries have deadened us to the utterly astonishing nature of this command. Perhaps we just don't care as much as we ought. We've lost the urgency. We've diverged from the plan.

The fact is that roughly four millennia after God promised to bless all the nations of the earth through Abraham's descendants, and nearly two millennia after the ascension of Jesus, huge pockets of people—massive populations, in fact—have *never* heard that there is a Savior from the awful devastation of sin and death. We are uncomfortable that thousands of children on other continents starve to death, but we are numb to the eternal hunger of billions. We grieve over the ravages of disease in impoverished places, especially when the diseases could have been easily treatable; but we casually hold the antidote for the sin epidemic in our hands and let the pathogen with eternal consequences consume its many victims unhindered. Isn't God more urgent than this? Is His passion to save really this sluggish?

"We ought not to ask, 'Can I prove that I ought to go?' but, 'Can I prove that I ought not to go?'"

—Charles Spurgeon

In Deed The God who pursues has issued a directive. The disciples of the High Commander are ordered to pray for pursuers to rush into His harvest, and even to go. It's an urgent appeal, and it's comprehensive as well. We are called to do more than spread the Word verbally; we are called to live it everywhere. Like light that floods a dark room, salt that influences a whole meal, or leaven that raises an entire loaf, we are urged to follow in the footsteps of the One who came to save. Those footsteps take us to a self-denying Cross for the benefit of others. It's the kingdom way.

Jesus' command is comprehensive, compelling, and urgent. Give. Pray. Go. Die, if necessary. Fill the world with His glory.

Powerfully Unburdened

"Take nothing for the journey—no staff, no bag, no bread, no money, no extra tunic." (Luke 9:3)

In Word Jesus is commissioning His disciples for their first mission—to blanket the area with the good news of His kingdom. He gives them power and authority over demons and diseases, a considerable wealth to carry with them (v. 1). But He prohibits their carrying any materials. They are loaded with power but light as a feather. They can go in His strength and not in their own.

In a sense, this is how Jesus commissions all of us to go through this life. He gives us the incredible riches of being united with Him in faith, co-laboring with the Father and being fellow heirs of the Son's kingdom. Jesus' treasures are ours, from right standing with God to useful spiritual gifts. But He promises us no earthly status—no staff, no bag, no money, no second set of clothes. He is our provision, and we will not succeed on this mission until we are stripped of everything that might distract us from that fact. We only function correctly when we come face to face with our insufficiency. And we only accomplish our mission—living and communicating the kingdom of God—when we're unencumbered by false props.

"Be simple; take our Lord's hand and walk through things."
–Brother Andrew

In Deed How are you living out your mission? Are you drawing your strength from his power and authority? Or are you depending on the props? Those who go through life carrying sacks of provisions find themselves powerless; they have unwittingly confessed a mistrust in His providence. Those who go through life unencumbered find that His strength accompanies them in abundance.

What encumbers you? You will need to get rid of it, or at least change your attitude toward it. Know the difference between living in His power and on your self-reliance. They cannot co-exist. Carry out your mission full of His strength and unburdened by your own.

An Uncommon Mission

"As the Father has sent me, I am sending you."

(John 20:21

In Word A cursory reading of this verse might give us the impression that Jesus is saying, "The Father first sent me; now it's your turn." But there is more to this verse than that. He is also saying, *"In the very same way* that the Father sent me, that's how I'm sending you." The crucial question then becomes: How did God send Jesus?

Philippians 2 gives us a good understanding of the nature of Jesus' mission. He humbled Himself, He took the form of a servant, and He became obedient to the point of death (Philippians 2:6-11). Jesus went from heavenly riches to earthly rags; from exaltation to humiliation; from authority to obedience; from ultimate significance to ultimate rejection; from comfort to hardship; from safety to danger; from glory to sacrifice; and from life to death. And He calls us to go into the world *in exactly the same way*

Read that list again. Every one of those humbling transitions goes against our grain. We're trying to work our way up, not empty ourselves. We want more significance, more safety, more authority, more attention, more comfort. But Jesus calls us to die to ourselves, to take up our cross and follow Him. He sends us out as He was sent.

"The service that counts is the service that costs."

—Howard Hendricks

In Deed Does your attitude match that of Jesus? Do you take your mission seriously enough to go into the depths of this world—whether those depths are in another country, your own city, or even your own family—and live the gospel of humility for others to see? Jesus' mission is to redeem this world, and He intends to shine the light in every vile, dark corner of it—through us. He calls His followers into prisons and concentration camps, into opium dens and brothels, and into leper colonies and psychiatric wards. He also calls them into night clubs, corporate conference rooms, university classrooms, and sports arenas. There is no place too uncomfortable, dangerous or unlikely. Are you willing? As the Father sent Him, so He sends us.

Wake Up!

"Wake up! Strengthen what remains and is about to die, for I have not found your deeds complete in the sight of my God." (Revelation 3:2)

In Word God seems to work with us in seasons. We may go through periods of feeling particularly close to Him, followed by periods of apparent distance. We may have times of plenty followed by times of scarcity. We can see God using our labor and blessing it, and then we see His pruning process and wonder where His blessing has gone. Or we even may willfully distance ourselves from God's work through apathy, sin, or a plan to "retire." Our temptation in any of these times is to think that God is done with us. But we must resist that temptation. If we're alive, He isn't.

For those who have long been Christians, we can easily become discouraged when we try to measure our present with our past. Just as a marriage may not always have the intensity of the honeymoon, so will our discipleship rarely contain the newfound excitement that we felt when we first came to know Jesus. While there is certainly deep joy in discipleship, there is also cross-bearing, hard work, commitment, and perseverance through trials. We also find that we commit sins that we once, early in our discipleship, thought we were done with. Our discouragement about the present, especially when it doesn't measure up to our fond memories, may lead us to wonder: "What have I lost that I once had? Have I become unfruitful for God? Has His blessing left me?"

"The experience of revival is nothing more than a new beginning of obedience to God."

—Charles Finney

In Deed The answer, of course, is that God is still at work in us. Our job is to be alert, to cultivate the gifts He has given us, and to persevere in the good works He has prepared for us in advance (Ephesians 2:10). Unless He has already taken us to heaven, He has not found our deeds complete. There is no "falling away" too substantial for Him to restore. There is no weakness greater than His strength. There is no retirement in His service. Wherever we are in our walk, there is revival to be sought and work to be done.

The Burden-Bearer

"Come to me, all you who are weary and burdened, an
I will give you rest." (Matthew 11:2

In Word Life can be a huge burden. We often refer to it a "rat race"—an ever-busy condition that never really accomplishes anything of significance. We may feel caught in a trap of meaningless activity that helps us survive for the moment but does not lift us to any higher meaning. For that, mankind looks religion.

Religion, too, can be a huge burden. It places demands on us that are clearly higher than our ability to accomplish. It places ideals before us that our earth-bound souls long to embrace but cannot ever really reach. It keeps us striving, in the strength of o flesh, to attain to the depths and the promises of the spiritual realm.

This is why Jesus came promising the provision of the Fathe for all of our needs and the gift of the Spirit to give us direction and the ability to accomplish God's will. This is why the One wh demands that we take up our cross and follow Him and who upholds every tiny stroke of the Law can come to us and say: "M yoke is easy and my burden is light" (v. 30). Our Source of existence and the Light of the World never told us to get wrapped u in our anxieties, to eke out an existence, or to strive in the streng of the flesh. He only told us to come to Him with everything, an He would fill us with Himself. What He has demanded of us, H Himself will fulfill.

"He rides at ease whom the grace of God carries."

—Thomas à Kempis

In Deed We get caught up in the folly of self-effort. We think our provision is up to us, so we struggle. We think our righteousness is up to us, so we strain. We think our spirituality a work of human willpower, so we press on even harder. All the while, Jesus says to us: "Come to *Me.*" He will give us rest.

Faith and complete dependence on Jesus are to precede obe ence. When we strive for obedience first, we are overwhelmed with our inabilities. Remember that the frail body with which y try to bear your burdens is filled with the incarnate God. Take H yoke and let Him lead.

The Gentle Teacher

"Take my yoke upon you and learn from me, for I am gentle and humble in heart, and you will find rest for your souls." (Matthew 11:29)

In Word The demands of our faith often overwhelm us. Perhaps that's because we see them as demands. When Jesus tells us to follow Him, when He insists on complete obedience and undying allegiance, when He reminds us that we have not lived up to the laws of God, we frail creatures feel as though He is pointing out our obligations and telling us to do better. He is not. He is offering us a better way.

Rather than placing demands on us, Jesus offers us new life. What we perceive as His requirements are actually compelling pieces of evidence that we need not try to do better but to give up trying to do it ourselves. We're supposed to see how impossible His standards are. That's the point.

Quit sweating, quit wrestling. It is not try but trust."
-John G. Lake

When Jesus tells us to take His yoke—the piece that binds and guides a beast of burden—upon us, He is not telling us to leave a state of freedom for His captivity. We're already captive. We already have a yoke on us—our own. We are already slaves to our sense of independence and self-management—and it is a horribly burdensome yoke. No, when He offers us His yoke, He is offering us a way out of this self-effort we've insisted on for years. He is offering us life-giving direction and purpose. He is generously giving us His own life.

In Deed Dependence on Jesus is a prerequisite for obedience. We cannot reverse the order without being crushed beneath the obligations of life and our attempts at self-righteousness. We must be taught dependence first.

There is a huge difference between a taskmaster and a teacher. Which way do you most often relate to Jesus? Have you been reverting to the self-management to which we were all once enslaved? Learn to see His yoke as a life-giving promise. Though He insists on everything we have in the transaction, He demands it for our freedom, not our captivity. Remember the gentleness of your Teacher, and know that His yoke *never* adds to your burden.

Lighten Up

"My yoke is easy and my burden is light."

(Matthew 11:3(

In Word This can be a comforting verse. It can also be a diagnostic tool. We can measure our lives by it and know whethe we are enjoying the relationship with Jesus that He intended.

Most of us frequently find ourselves stressed, burdened, ove whelmed, and frustrated. When this is the case, especially for lor periods of time, we can know that something is wrong. Jesus doe not intend for us to walk through this life alone. He does not mean for us to take assignments from Him, or from "fate," and carry them out in our own strength and by our own plans of action. His purpose is to be intimately involved and acutely pres ent in the details of our lives. In fact, our lives become His.

> *"If He bids us carry a burden, He carries it also."*
>
> —*Charles Spurgeon*

What is the reason for our being overly burdened? Are we resisting His guidance and living with the consequences of rebel lion? Then we will be overwhelmed with our own independence Or is it more subtle than that? Whenever we obsess about problems, we deny Scripture's command to cast our anxiety upon the Lord (1 Peter 5:7, Philippians 4:6). Whenever we dread the impending future, we are not exercising faith in the sovereign Lord of our circumstances. Or, more pointedly in the context of this verse, whenever we try to live up to His holiness in the strength of our sinful flesh, trying to achieve our own righteousness, we deny the life-giving Spirit and full identity in Him that He offers us.

In Deed Trying to do too much, whether in the chores c life or the righteousness of the law, is actually a form of pride. It' a subtle form; it seems to be dutiful and humble, but it actually stakes a claim that we are sufficient in ourselves to accomplish God's purposes. We aren't, not by a long shot. Only He is sufficient. There is something profoundly restful about knowing that Accept the offer of His yoke and His burden. It's a liberating sub mission.

Grateful for Grace

"Were not all ten cleansed? Where are the other nine? Was no one found to return and give praise to God except this foreigner?" (Luke 17:17-18)

In Word Nine lepers accepted the generous gift of Jesus and walked away without saying "Thanks." What were they thinking? Were they resentful that God had allowed them to get leprosy to begin with? Perhaps so. They were possibly brought up to believe that their salvation from God was a birthright, an inherent part of their genetic relationship to Abraham. If so, leprosy would have been an unwelcome intrusion on their rightful status in the kingdom. Rather than being humbled by it, they were perhaps even angry with God over it. They would have seen Jesus as only giving them their due. Thankfulness is difficult to express when one starts with an attitude of entitlement.

"Gratitude is born in hearts that take time to count up past mercies."
-Charles Jefferson

But the Samaritan gave thanks. He likely had been brought up to believe that Samaritans are outcasts, rejected by God's people and alien to His kingdom. Perhaps his leprosy was an outward evidence of the sinfulness that he knew to infect his heart. He would have understood his cleansing to be an amazing gift of grace. He shamelessly—and appropriately—expressed his gratitude by throwing himself at Jesus' feet and praising God with a loud voice.

In Deed How have we responded to our healing? When God cleansed us of sin, did we accept it politely, as though we were entitled to it? Many of us who were raised in the church think of salvation this way. We see it as an obligatory gift—like children who expect, or even demand, a certain level of Christmas generosity from their parents. Gratitude for something we take for granted is difficult.

Those who have truly known their diseased condition are often shameless and persistent—even embarrassing—in their gratitude. And this is exactly the attitude Jesus commends. He welcomes exuberance. More than anything, it reflects a genuine understanding of His grace.

Harvest Eyes

"Open your eyes and look at the fields! They are ripe f harvest." (John 4:3

"People matter so much to God that every one warrants an all-out search."

—Bill Hybels

In Word The contrast between Jesus and His disciples i this passage is stark. Jesus is busy telling a sinful woman of eternal truths. The disciples are focused on their physical needs. Jes sets off a spark and sees a whole town ablaze with spiritual hunger. The disciples are obsessed about their daily bread. Jesus was ready to minister to people. The disciples were ready for lunchtime.

Don't we see a similar contrast in our own lives? Sometimes we can be outward-focused, seeing people's needs and trying to meet them. More often, we are just trying to get through the day feeding ourselves and our families, and trying to earn enough to pay the bills. We get caught up in our own agenda and neglect t more urgent needs of a hurting world—perhaps not in principle but certainly in practice.

Jesus urges His disciples to look beyond themselves. He tells them to thrive on a different kind of food—the will of God and His passion for people who need the Gospel. They are to be outward-focused, filled with vision. Their ambition should be to see the gathering of the kingdom of God, not just to get through the daily grind.

In Deed We tend to neglect the eternal purposes of God and hone in on the peripherals of life. But life isn't about going into town to shop (John 4:8), or about lunchtime (v. 31). Those ar necessities of sustaining life, not its substance. The substance of life is eternal, and we can invest it in either the kingdom or in th world. Jesus points us to His kingdom.

Are your eyes filled with visions of harvest? Do you understand why we are here? Do not be distracted by the daily routine or by the needs of the hour. Learn to recognize moments for reaping. Jesus has given us a mission and told us to have a vision for what's going on around us. Focus outward, not inward. Lift up your eyes and look at the fields. It's harvest time.

Internal Affairs

"What comes out of a man is what makes him 'unclean.' " (Mark 7:20)

In Word Jesus confronts the Pharisees with a startling truth: The problem of human corruption can't be cleaned up from the outside. It is an inward problem. It is entirely possible for the Pharisees—and us—to discipline ourselves in our prayer habits, eating and drinking patterns, sexual behavior, social graces, and generous giving to the extent that we come across as righteous in the eyes of God and men—all the while struggling with monsters of corruption in our thought life.

This is the misunderstanding of the Pharisees' religion and of any religion that takes sin seriously. They all attempt to reform the visible result of sin without treating the internal condition. Jesus is the only remedy that cleans a person from the inside out, if we will let Him.

No one overcomes the corruptions of his heart except by the enabling strength of the Spirit of God."

—Jerry Bridges

In Deed The problem many of us have faced (or continue to face) is that we can restrain our outward behavior while retaining all of the evil thoughts within us. What we've changed is our appearance, not our heart. This is the condition of the Pharisee, and it's not Jesus' solution for sin.

If the problem of sin is an inward problem, it must be treated with an inward solution. Jesus' audience in Mark 7 had outward solutions to the problem. Yet their unclean thoughts remained. What is the inward solution? The habitation of Christ Himself in our hearts by faith, and our constant, conscious reliance on Him (and cooperation with Him) to change us from within.

If this is your struggle—and you are not alone, if it is—resist the way of the flesh. Do not be content with covering the outward manifestation of an unclean heart. Invite Jesus to do an inward work, conforming your heart into His pure image—not just once, but constantly. Believe that He will, and see what happens.

Pursuing Calm

"Who of you by worrying can add a single hour to his life? Since you cannot do this very little thing, why do you worry about the rest?" (Luke 12:25-26

"Never try to carry tomorrow's burdens with today's grace."
—Anonymous

In Word Worry is a plague. We encounter difficult situations and think about the ways we want them to turn out. Or worse, we think about all the ways we don't want them to turn out, obsessing about everything that can go wrong in them. We play a mind game called "What if?" We ask ourselves, "What if something goes wrong? What if I get sick? What if I don't have enough money to eat? What if my work fails? What if . . .?" The possibilities are limitless. And they grow larger the more we think about them. In our minds, the potential disasters swell and overwhelm us. When they do, our Protector and Provider seems to grow small and faith disappears. What is the solution? We know there is a place of rest for the believer—Jesus has promised it to us. But how do we get there?

Jesus tells us in verse 31 to set our minds on the kingdom. This is hard to do. In a crisis, we are prone to set our minds on the desired outcome. We fix our gaze on the preferred result and ask God to accomplish it. That outcome may be good and holy, but as long as it is our hope, we are not focused on Jesus and His kingdom. Jesus asks us to set our minds on God and accept what He accomplishes. The outcome may be exactly the same in both cases but calm in our hearts will only be a reality in the latter approach. We cannot experience the peace of faith when our eyes see God as a tool to accomplish our purposes. Our eyes can be either on God or on outcomes. Not both.

In Deed Jesus is constantly telling us to think in a way contrary to our fallen nature. It's difficult; we need frequent reminding. But it's the only way to internal rest. Pry your hopes off of your circumstances and put them on the Person who promises peace. Desire only Him, and you will never be disappointed. Or worried.

Resting Calmly

"Who of you by worrying can add a single hour to his life? Since you cannot do this very little thing, why do you worry about the rest?" (Luke 12:25-26)

In Word Not only are we not honoring God when we let our minds run wild with worry about outcomes, we also are not being very practical. There is really very little we can do to effect real change in a situation. We can do our part, certainly—God expects to be active and obedient to His promptings—but we are never the master of circumstances. He is. The more we try to control them, the more we unwittingly wrestle control from Him. At the bottom of this wrestling is a mistrust that He actually does work all things together for the good of those who love Him and who are called according to His purposes (Romans 8:28). Whenever we try to exercise control, we reveal our suspicion that God's sovereignty might not be reliable. We are saying, in effect, that we trust our own intervention over His.

"Pray, and let God worry."
–Martin Luther

Jesus certainly never condemns our attempts to work in His kingdom and be obedient to His purposes. He expects our active participation in His plan. But when we worry, we indicate that we are striving for more than obedient participation. We are aiming for the role of mastermind behind the circumstance. Faith has no part in this worry. And where there is no faith, there is no rest.

In Deed Worry is such a difficult state of mind to maintain, but we accept it so often. We let it affect our moods, relationships, and health. It becomes larger than life.

Jesus essentially tells His disciples to let God take care of the things He has promised to take care of, and to fulfill the role only of a disciple—to act in faith and obedience. It's an easy place to be, if we'll stay there. It's an acknowledgment that He, in all His sovereignty, is supremely trustworthy—that He desires no bad thing for those who love Him. The responsibility for change is left to Him, and the only responsibility we assume is to faithfully follow His lead. Wherever He leads, we can calmly, restfully go.

Opposed to God

"Whoever exalts himself will be humbled, and whoever humbles himself will be exalted." (Matthew 23:1

"Pride makes us artificial and humility makes us real."

—Thomas Merton

In Word Jesus has just launched into a discussion of the sin of the teachers of the Law and the Pharisees. And what was their great sin? Misinterpretation of the Law? Too much zeal? Ba theology? No, it was the double-edged sin of hypocrisy and prid The two go hand in hand, and, in fact, are one. They were hypocrites because they recognized the unrighteousness of others bu not of themselves. They were proud because, in order to hide the own unrighteousness from themselves, they had to constantly build themselves up. They would make their religiosity very visible with wide phylacteries, long tassels, seats of honor, and impressive titles. They loved to be loved.

Don't we all? What's wrong with seeking to accomplish grea things and earning the respect of others? Nothing, if it's done wit the right attitude. But defining your righteousness by your outward appearance is not the right attitude.

Don't think we're immune to the sins of the Pharisees. We jockey for position in our clubs and committees. We hijack conve sations to reveal impressive things about ourselves so that others will respect us. We earn grand titles because, to be honest, we lik them. Are we building ourselves up in order to cover something else up? Is there really a naked, unrighteous humanity within us that we're desperate to hide?

In Deed Absolutely. From the fig leaf to the Pharisees to the fashions of the day, we've been doing the same thing: coverin up. We don't want others to know how human, how weak, and how needy we are. But the only way for God to exalt us—to save us and make us one with Christ—is for us to go ahead and dispense with the coverings we've used for self-esteem. We can't exalt ourselves and let Him exalt us at the same time. The opposing methods cannot operate simultaneously.

Embrace humility. It's the only way up.

Living in the Light

"Whoever lives by the truth comes into the light, so that it may be seen plainly that what he has done has been done through God." (John 3:21)

In Word Much has been made of the possibility of people in the church bringing discredit to the Gospel. The line of reasoning is this: The Gospel cleanses us from sin; therefore, when one of us falls into sin, the cleansing power of the Gospel is discredited. But is this true? Does a sinning saint damage the Gospel's reputation?

That depends. Someone who claims to be right with God, but who clearly is not, may weaken the witness of the message. But someone who falls, confesses, and repents—no matter how great the fall—only confirms the power of the truth. That person has demonstrated the meaning of grace.

Look at it this way: It's easy to discredit a gospel of legalism; all you have to do is break its laws. But the only way to discredit a gospel of grace is to be perfect. Grace assumes that the laws have been broken by everyone already. Why would we be outraged when we see someone fall into sin? Our message of mercy presupposes that we will. It accounts for the depravity of the human condition. How can our sin contradict our assertion that God forgives sin? When we see sin and repentance, we don't see a discredit to the Gospel; we see the Gospel in action.

"For him who confesses, shams are over and realities have begun."

—William James

In Deed Jesus said that those who live by the truth will come into the light and their confession will be evidence that God is at work. He does not mean that those who live by the truth are those who never sin. He means that those who live by the truth will deal with their sin. They will bring it into the light and accept God's forgiveness. That does no harm to the Gospel; it affirms it.

Are you hiding your sin? The church often unwittingly encourages its members to do so. But *that* denies the Gospel. Bringing it openly to the Cross exposes the sinner as sinful, but also exposes the Gospel as powerful. May we always know the freedom to live in the light.

Liberating Surrender

"If anyone would come after me, he must deny himself and take up his cross and follow me." (Matthew 16:24

In Word There are two attitudes with which we can approach this verse. The more typical attitude is dread; we look at self-denial and cross-bearing as burdensome responsibilities, demands that we are ill-prepared to fulfill. We see this principle of Jesus' teaching as an imperative for deep sacrifice—walking the way He walked. It looks like a difficult road.

But if we can get past the pain of this verse, there is a profound liberation to be experienced. We realize that this verse is no just about sacrifice, it is about surrender. And the benefits of surrender are well worth the pain of sacrifice.

Think about it: Our biggest burden is us. We cannot manage our own lives, but we are exhausted trying to do just that. We can not determine our own futures, and it is mind-boggling to try. We cannot handle our own problems—eventually we are in over our heads far more often than we'd like to be. And when Jesus says any follower of His "must deny himself," it is not just a denial of satisfying things or of attempts at self-fulfillment; it is a denial of all the self-management that weighs us down. It is a call not only to surrender what is pleasing to the senses, but to surrender everything that rivals our dependence on God—including the burden of our willful independence and the awful responsibility of becoming "successful" in the way we define success. We should be eager to make such a denial.

"Carry the cross patiently and with perfect submission, and in the end it shall carry you."

—Thomas à Kempis

In Deed We see the pain of self-denial and cross-carrying when we read of Jesus' crucifixion. But we forget—the Cross was the path to ultimate fulfillment and glory. It was so for Jesus, and it is so for us. The initial cost looks remarkably overwhelming at first glance, but there is ultimate liberation beyond it. It's the liberation of surrender to a wiser, gentler, more powerful Lord than the one we're accustomed to—ourselves. We can find freedom by embracing this Cross.

Full Submission

"Now they have seen these miracles, and yet they have hated both me and my Father." (John 15:24)

In Word Our standard approach to the strange story of pharisaical unbelief is to attribute their rejection of Jesus to spiritual blindness and hardheartedness. And though they certainly were blind and hardhearted—these are Jesus' terms—there are some alarming hints in Scripture that many actually knew Jesus to be the Messiah and rejected Him anyway. Nicodemus' statement in John 3:2 is revealing: "We know you are a teacher who has come from God." In John 15:24, Jesus affirms that their guilt comes from their rejection in spite of their knowledge of who He is. They couldn't let Him disrupt their hold on spiritual authority.

"It is so hard to believe because it is so hard to obey."
–Søren Kierkegaard

We tend to think of unbelief as the result of intellectual stumbling blocks to the Gospel, or philosophical objections, or a lack of evidence and authentic miracles. But these things are usually cited by unbelievers simply as a covering for deeper issues. The real issue of unbelief is the inclination of the human heart. It wants to remain enthroned. It *cannot* accept a savior without denying its own ability to save.

The human rebellion is well disguised with convincing excuses. "We didn't know. We didn't have enough proof. Jesus' teaching didn't make sense to us. We did the best we could. Love and tolerance are the key, not dogma." Underneath the mask, the heart's contempt for its Creator runs deep. We hide it well, even from ourselves. But it's there.

In Deed Watch for this tendency in your own heart. Often we assent to Jesus mentally but resist Him deep within. Have you known this struggle? It's subtle, but human nature often is. We come across as enthusiastic believers, but the unbelief deep inside wants to put up a good fight. It wants to retain the right to a little bit of sin, to maintain a little autonomy. We often really want only a partial submission to our Creator. Let the Holy Spirit search—and transform—the deep places of your heart. Let Jesus complete His miracle in you.

Shining Lights

"Your eye is the lamp of your body." (Luke 11:3

In Word Many commentators see a Hebrew idiom in thi verse: "a good eye" refers to generosity, and "a bad eye" refers to stinginess. Others broaden the image to include truth and purity on the positive side, covetousness and lust on the negative. No matter how one takes the symbolism, Jesus is clear: What our eye see—what we strive for and what we take in—is important. The conduct of our eyes, literally and figuratively, with regard to money and other human passions, determines to a large degree the amount of light we receive from God.

Just as light allows us to see into once-dark places, our eyes allow us to understand who we really are in the depths of our souls. If our eyes take in the true light that comes from God—His Word and the glory of His Gospel in Christ—we see well. There i clarity and wisdom that can only come from seeing things as Go sees them. But if our eyes consume garbage—the cravings of sinful man and the pride of self-indulgence—then we see ourselves in the dark, obscurely and distortedly, if at all. What we choose to see has a lot to do with whether we are walking in God's light and whether we are shining His light for others to see.

"The body has two eyes, but the soul must have but one."

—William Secker

In Deed Joyful generosity is a clear indication that one i walking in the light. So are purity and God-directed desires. Stinginess, self-indulgence, and impure vision are likewise clear indications that one is not walking in the light. And all of these are cultivated by what we choose—and refuse—to see.

With what do you feed your soul? Can you set it on a stand for others to see? One of a Christian's greatest struggles is trying to see it all—we become confused and divided. Do we gaze on light, darkness, or both? If you really want to know, do an inventory of things that fill your eyes, metaphorically speaking. Is you vision occupied with money? Lustfulness? Selfish extravagance? so, be careful for what you see. Purify your sight, and let your light shine.

All About Attitude

"This poor widow has put more into the treasury than all the others." (Mark 12:43)

In Word With service in the kingdom of God, attitude is everything. What attitudes are behind our gifts? What attitudes are pleasing to God?

We often think we have fulfilled God's requirements in our service for Him. We may read the Bible for half an hour each day, feel like we've eaten our spiritual vegetables, and then move on to more interesting things. Or we may give our 10 percent when the offering plate passes by, glad to have our monthly obligation out of the way before spending the rest on the things we really want. And we may teach a Sunday school class or help out in a soup kitchen as a means of putting in time for the kingdom, savoring our remaining hours as time to pursue our own desires. We can easily be satisfied with fulfilling our duties.

You can give without loving, but you cannot love without giving."
—Amy Carmichael

But God much prefers acts of love to acts of duty. The widow in this story didn't have to give as much as she gave. There is no law of God that demanded at least those two coins. Even one of those coins would have been a high percentage of her income. Why did she give more? Her heart was filled with love for God's work. Jesus' comments were not necessarily about giving more, but about giving rightly. It wasn't an issue of quantity. It was in issue of motive.

In Deed Even if we gave 90 percent of our income, our time, and our effort for the kingdom of God, it would not be enough for Jesus if there were no love in it. It may be better to ful fill our responsibilities as Christians than not to fulfill them at all; but the kingdom of God is not primarily about fulfilling responsibilities. It is more about expressing gratitude and about being passionate for His glory. When we bring God our offerings—whatever they are—we must come with a genuine desire to give them. We must offer them because we love God and we desire to see His kingdom come. And we must give them in thankfulness that He, by example, knows a lot about lovingly giving it all.

Love and Obedience

"If you love me, you will obey what I command."

(John 14:1

In Word We fool ourselves if we think our love for God and our obedience to Him are separate issues. They are two sides of the same coin. Observe how often in this passage love and obedience are linked: "If you love me, you will obey what I command" (v. 15). "Whoever has my commands and obeys them, he is the one who loves me" (v. 21). "If anyone loves me, he will obey my teaching" (v. 23). "He who does not love me will not obey my teaching" (v. 24). And later in the chapter: "The world must learn that I love the Father and that I do exactly what my Father has commanded me" (v. 31).

"Love is the root; obedience is the fruit."
—Matthew Henry

The belief that love and obedience are not related is epidemic among Christians. Would we say in our human relationships, "I love my wife/husband but ignore most of what she/he says to me"? The incongruity is clear in such a context. Why is it muddled in our relationship with God?

We have become so paranoid of having a theology of "righteousness = works" that we have ignored obedience altogether, as though it did not matter to God. Jesus is clear that it does. Obedience is not our means to righteousness; it is the clearest expression of our devotion to Jesus. It is meaningful worship. When we are disobedient, we are saying that God's Word does not matter to us. That isn't love.

In Deed As Christians, we need to recover a desire for obedience as an expression of love for our Savior. If we truly love Him, as we say we do, what He says will matter to us profoundly. We will not follow the acceptable parts of His teachings and ignore the objectionable parts. We will not approach our relationship with Him as though we are trying to get by with the bare minimum behavioral change. We will devour His teachings, turning them over in our hearts, meditating on their applications, and living them as clearly as we can. This, according to Jesus, is what loving Him is all about. This is genuine worship.

Complete Joy

"I have told you this so that my joy may be in you and that your joy may be complete." (John 15:11)

In Word Jesus' intent is for every Christian to have joy. Why then do so many of us struggle to have it? What circumstances or thoughts are we allowing to steal the joy we're supposed to have?

We allow the worries of life to consume us and rob us of joy. We allow broken relationships to deprive us of that contentment of spirit that comes with genuine joy. We stress over possibilities and obsess about those who have wronged us. We get absorbed in the past and preoccupied with the future, and we miss the present joy He offers us. What is His remedy? What is the "this" that He told His disciples in verse 11 that would result in their joy?

When Jesus speaks to His disciples about joy, He has just told them to remain in His love—through obedience (vv. 9-10). And He goes on to tell them to love each other as He has loved them (v. 12). It isn't a suggestion; it's a command. And He even defines love for them. It's the kind of attitude toward another that would cause someone to lay down his life (v. 13). That's love. And Jesus orders His disciples to have it. The result will be joyful lives. It isn't a difficult formula in principle—just in practice.

"Joy is the experience of knowing you are unconditionally loved."
—Henri Nouwen

In Deed When we do not have joy in our lives, it is because we have left something out of the formula. We have not remembered the wealth of Jesus' love; or we have not loved others as extravagantly as He has loved us.

It seems like it should be more difficult than this. We think that to have joy, something must happen to change our circumstances. Or something must heal our past wounds. So we focus on the circumstances, the wounds, or some other source of discontent. All the while, Jesus asks us to look past the surface of our joylessness and major on love. The circumstances, the wounds, and all other sources of discontent will soon be changed or become irrelevant. Joy will overcome them. And our joy will be complete.

A Matter of Motives

"Let your light so shine before men, that they may see your good deeds and praise your Father in heaven."

(Matthew 5:1

"Be careful not to do your 'acts of righteousness' before men, to be seen by them."

(Matthew 6:

In Word How are we to reconcile these two commands? On the one hand, Jesus tells us to let others see our good works. A few verses later, He tells us not to do our good works for others t see. What's the difference?

Motive is the key. Many people do their acts of righteousness in order to bring praise to themselves. It's a hollow righteousness that may earn compliments and status, but it's nothing that God will honor. It comes not from a love for God or from genuine faith, but from a need to be accepted by others. Such acts imply that these folks are not convinced of God's acceptance of them in Christ—they must try to earn love elsewhere.

But truly righteous acts come from hearts that seek God's glory—and God's glory should never be hidden. Those who do good works with a right heart never point to themselves. They point to God, and are glad to do so. Their works cause others to marvel at God's grace and power, not a human being's goodness.

"Do you attract attention toward or away from God?"

—Anonymous

In Deed It's a constant temptation to cross that line and begin doing things for our own glory. We must examine our motives for the good things we do, and we must also examine the stage on which we do them. Do we seek God's glory? Are we real istic enough to know that anything good coming out of our lives comes from His grace and mercy and not from our own purity or ingenuity? Are we concerned that the "important" people see? The rewards of heaven are reserved for those who are backgroun players to the glory of God. We must magnify others' view of Hir without drawing attention to ourselves.

Surrendering Worry

"Who of you by worrying can add a single hour to his life?" (Luke 12:25)

In Word "Do not worry." It is one of Jesus' most frequently repeated commands. It is also one of the hardest to obey. Worry comes naturally. We say we just can't help it. (We can.) We say it's just part of who we are. (It is part of who we *were* naturally, before faith in Christ—not now.) We justify it by saying that Jesus wants us to think responsibly about the future. (There's a huge difference between being responsible and being worried.) And as much as we think we admire people who do not worry, we may criticize them as being "too laid back," or lacking a serious outlook on life.

"Worry is an intrusion into God's providence."
–John Haggai

Our problem with worry is a heart issue. It's all about whether we are surrendered to God. Do we really trust Him to take care of us? Do we believe He will lead us in His will, and that His will is always good? Do we really value His plan, even when His plan leads us through difficult circumstances? If the answer is "yes" to all of these, then we have perhaps recognized Jesus as Lord in the way that He desires. But for most people the answer to these questions is "no"— at least occasionally, if not frequently.

Think about what's really in your heart when you worry. If we are worried and anxious, we don't really accept His lordship, do we? If we have really submitted to Him, we trust Him to handle our lives. They are in His hands, and *whatever* He chooses to do with them is alright with us, even if His will is difficult. The path is His, the means to live it are His, and the outcomes are His. This is what surrender is all about. And if we're really surrendered, we're not worried about it.

In Deed Are you in a difficult place? You have a choice: You can trust that it's either *God's* difficult place (or a place from which He will soon provide deliverance); or you can wonder if He's lost His grip on your life and let you wander too far out of His will. The only issue is what your heart chooses to believe about God.

Close to His Heart

"If anyone wants to be first, he must be the very last, and the servant of all." (Mark 9:3

In Word Could our human nature come up with any les appealing prospect than service as a means to greatness? Probabl not. We see what servants put up with. We want no such menial responsibility. We want to be important. We want our lives to count for more than that.

What our human nature does not comprehend is that the kingdom of God is not built with stature and prestige. It is not made from human wisdom and creativity. It is built by the Spirit, and only the things the Spirit inspires will last. If we have invested much in our own importance, we will be devastated when God's kingdom is the last one standing. It is not built on ou importance, but on God's. It is raised on the foundation of God's character, and whatever of His character we have will remain. Prestige won't. Service will. The yardstick is turned upside down

Humble service lasts because it matches the nature of God. It is fully in line with His character when it is done in His name. Even though we know this, we more easily follow our baser instincts—we, like the people of Babel, want to make a name for ourselves. We, like Cain, are overly concerned with our own repu tation. We, like Nebuchadnezzar, are fascinated with the cult of self. We aren't convinced that Jesus' path to greatness is the right one.

"Christ is with the humble, not with those who set themselves up over His flock."

—Clement of Rome

In Deed Why not? Has anything He has said led us astray? He who is faithful will not point us in the wrong directior His kingdom is a place of service because it is a place of love, and love cannot help but serve.

How badly do you want to fit into God's kingdom culture? How much do you want fellowship with Him? The level of your service will give you the answer. To know Him and to be like Him is to serve for Him and with Him. You can't get any closer to His heart than that.

Persistence Remembered

"Everyone who asks receives; he who seeks finds; and to him who knocks, the door will be opened." (Matthew 7:8)

In Word The verb tenses of the asking, seeking, and knocking in this verse (and v. 7) imply continuous, persistent action. Jesus could have told His disciples to ask once, seek briefly, and give a single knock when they pray to their Father. But the fact that He didn't leads us to one of the most perplexing set of questions about prayer that confronts believers regularly: Why is there a delay? Isn't God willing to answer us? If so, why is persistence important?

Since God already has provision for all of our needs and every aspect of His mission even before we ask, He could give His answer immediately. But He usually doesn't. He has far greater purposes in our prayers than just the asking and receiving. He wants us to learn more about who He is.

"Importunate praying never faints or grows weary. It declines to rise from its knees till an answer is received."
—E. M. Bounds

A lot happens between the time we present a request to God and the time He provides the answer. If we grow more intense in our request, we create a situation that will stick in our memories—and that of others, if we've drawn them into our petition—long after God has resolved it for us. When His answer finally comes, we have a memorable testimony of His goodness to us. But if we forget about the request soon after asking it, we were not very serious about it and never would have turned the answer into a testimony about Him anyway. An unfortunate side of human nature is that we are forgetful recipients of good things. Immediate answers to casual requests would reinforce our forgetfulness. It would not establish God's name in our lives.

In Deed How many prayers have you dropped because God seemed not to be hearing? If He did not give a definite "no," He may have wanted the delay to draw you closer to Him and establish a better sense of His provision in your need. Don't just ask, seek, and knock; keep asking, seeking and knocking. Such times of persistence lead to a greater, more memorable experience of His goodness.

Persistence Refined

"Everyone who asks receives; he who seeks finds; and to him who knocks, the door will be opened." (Matthew 7:8)

In Word Imagine a parent who responds positively to every request that a child gives, no matter how fleeting. Before long, the child would have far too much to be able to enjoy, and certainly more than his level of responsibility could handle. A parent's solution to this unwise asking might be to answer only those requests that were appropriate for the child. But if the child asked everything that entered his mind and knew no rationale for the answers, he would learn little about himself and little about his parent. There's a more instructive way. He could first learn which type of request the parent is inclined to answer; and he could learn more about himself as to which desires were genuine and lasting, and which were frivolous and temporary. His understanding of the relationship between him and his parent would blossom, and he would mature.

Imagine, then, the perspective of our heavenly Father who hears constant requests from His children. Should He just grant the ones He knows to be best, even if we never discern a pattern in the answers? Perhaps so, but there is a better way. Delaying the answers will cause us to reflect more on Him and His will; and it will allow us to determine which desires were abiding and which were transient. A relationship will develop where we once sought a mail-order service.

"The Lord seems constantly to use waiting as a tool for bringing us the very best of His gifts."

—Catherine Marshall

In Deed The frustration we feel when we ask God for something and His answer tarries is definitely not the product of an unwilling God. And it is not necessarily the product of improper requests on our part. It is the product of our own frivolity. We toss up petitions casually, hoping He will answer one of the many we present. His preference is for us to learn which ones He will favor, and then to offer them up persistently and faithfully, learning about Him in the process. God designed us for a deep relationship with Him. Let your delays cultivate it.

Persistence Rewarded

"Everyone who asks receives; he who seeks finds; and to him who knocks, the door will be opened." (Matthew 7:8)

In Word As much as we hate to admit it, we are never more attuned to God's voice than when we are in desperate need. We search our hearts for obstructive sins; we examine our relationships for hindrances of conflict or bitterness; we diligently dig into God's Word for His promises and assurances; and we hang onto any little word of His faithful and unfailing character. We grow during these times more than any other. Most people looking back on their lives will readily admit that the times of need were the times of flourishing in their relationship with God. And God built us exclusively for relationship.

Given this, why would God possibly want to rush us through that process? Why would He hasten to answer our prayers and subvert the purpose of this experience? We often think His delay is due to some divine indifference, a lack of caring on His part for those He says He loves. But it is just the opposite. His delays are granted us precisely because He cares so much. Immediate answers to fleeting prayers would never bring us this close to Him, no matter how much we try to assure Him that they would. He knows how we work. He knows we can learn from Him and be conformed to His image in no other way.

It is when the answer to prayer does not come . . . that the trial of faith, more precious than gold, takes place."

–Andrew Murray

In Deed We see our need as a desperate situation. God designs it for an opportunity to know Him more intimately. When we are truly needy, we learn of Him as Provider. When we are really sick, we learn of Him either as Healer or as Comforter—whichever role He wants to reveal to us. We might think we are being punished by His silence. We are not. We are being rewarded. He is drawing us closer to Him, saying, "Come nearer, learn from Me, know Me as your Strength, your Defender, your Refuge." Keep praying. This is a far greater blessing than an immediate answer.

Keep Watch

"Stay here and keep watch." (Mark 14:34

"The Christian life is not a playground; it is a battle-ground."
—Warren Wiersbe

In Word Peter, James, and John had surely noticed Jesus distress on their walk to the Garden of Gethsemane, but they seem blissfully unaware of the nature of the battle that is raging around them. They see only with their eyes. But Jesus is nearing the conclusion of a long warfare with the enemy, and the unseen war is most intense in this garden. Whether the cross of Christ will or will not occur hangs in the balance between the bitterness of Jesus' assignment and His submission to the Father. We know the outcome, of course, and all the suspense is lost on us. But the three disciples in the Garden didn't even know suspense was in the air. They slept.

Life can give us the same illusion. We know it has its struggles, and we are distressed on occasion. But we are often blissfull unaware that there is a cosmic warfare going on around us, and i is always intense. We have been told to stay awake and keep watch, but we keep falling asleep. Like the disciples, we may be thinking only about tomorrow's issues while our enemy is wagin a war over eternal issues. We think we're taking a midnight stroll in the garden; but our Commander has led us into a high-stakes battle. Regardless of our apathy or exhaustion, this is not a time for sleep.

In Deed Whether we like it or not, when we put our faith in Christ we left civilian life. We try to revert to a peacetime lifestyle whenever we can, but the attacks of the enemy have a way of reminding us where we are. We are on the battlefield, and though we know the outcome already, our opponent, Satan, forestalls his final defeat as long and as vengefully as he can.

That's why the New Testament emphasizes faith and prayer as much as it does. Faith is our weapon against the enemy, and prayer is our communication with the headquarters from which come all our resources. And until we have been called home to Jesus, His orders for us remain the same—stay here and keep watch.

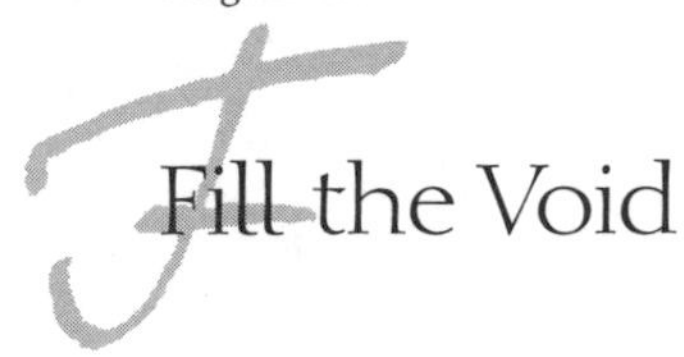

Fill the Void

"I saw Satan fall like lightning from heaven."

(Luke 10:18)

In Word Yes, Jesus was there. Before dust was made man, before the serpent was in the garden, before there even was a garden, Jesus saw. From what we can tell, this high angel wanted to be higher, and he was aggressive about it. But there is only one ultimate throne, and it belongs to God. There wasn't room in heaven for two sovereigns. Lucifer had to go. Jesus and the whole Godhead watched him fall.

Who was this sick creature? Michael is the warrior archangel, and Gabriel is the messenger archangel; was Lucifer the worshiper archangel? Did he sing songs of praise before he yearned to be the object of them? He certainly has his hand in music now; is he perverting his background as a once-sacred artist? Did his familiarity with God's glory breed the contempt he now has for it? What did he see in the Most High God that made him think he could occupy that position? Did he mistake God's gentleness for vulnerability? What could he possibly have experienced in heaven that would inspire such lunacy? Perhaps we'll never know the answers to these questions. Or perhaps one day we will. For now, Scripture only gives us hints.

"In prayer we act like men; in praise we act like angels."
—Thomas Watson

In Deed There are some things we can know for sure: Satan hates God. He also hates the fact that God can take such weak, ignoble, sin-struck creatures as ourselves and make us one with Christ, bringing us into blissful, worshipful fellowship with the Trinity. That's where he wanted to be! He thought his high position qualified him. How is it that our low position qualifies us? What an unexpected replacement we are. It grates on him with undying annoyance.

We have learned something that Lucifer forgot: We can only fulfill the purpose for which God created us. Lucifer was made to praise God's image. We were made in it. The void of praise that his exit left behind is to be filled with us. Never forget that; never let the evil one convince you otherwise. He wants to distort what God has done in you. You are obligated and privileged—to the praise of God's glory—to fulfill it daily.

The Evil Personality

"I know where you live—where Satan has his throne."

(Revelation 2:1

In Word Jesus' words to the Pergamum church may hav referred to this city as Satan's central power base. Even so, we know that the words also apply to us. Satan is not omnipresent like God, so we don't know exactly where that finite creature is a the moment. But we *do* know that we live where he has his throne. He runs rampant on this planet. John confirmed it in one of his letters: "The whole world is under the control of the evil one" (1 John 5:19).

If you have been a child of God for long, if your home has been the body of Christ for any time at all, you know: Evil is not force to explain; it is far more personal than that. Let the philosophers and theologians wrestle with the "problem of evil." We wrestle with the evil one. We are not harassed by a concept. "Ou struggle is . . . against the rulers, against the authorities, against the powers of this dark world and against the spiritual forces of evil in the heavenly realms" (Ephesians 6:12). We don't engage in a philosophy of evil; we fight against evil personalities.

"The enemy will not see you vanish into God's company without an effort to reclaim you."

—C. S. Lewis

In Deed This is a frightening task, but it's our only way to victory: Forsake all thought of evil simply as a force in this world. Never depersonalize it. Recognize that there is a relentless malicious intelligence behind all the pain you see. Some of Satan' minions know you by name. Jesus' ministry made that clear. He never cast out a problem; He cast out spirits. He held conversations with them and called them by name. You can't do that with an abstract principle.

How does that help us in our daily struggles? It brings us face to face with reality. When the Bible tells us to overcome evil with good, it is not speaking about abstracts. It means we are to overcome the evil one with the Good One. We have a Warrior, a Victor, a conquering King. Read Revelation and see. And when a hell breaks loose against you, rely completely on Him.

Faith, Then Sight

"Did I not tell you that if you believed, you would see the glory of God?" (John 11:40)

In Word One of the foundational dynamics of the kingdom of God is this principle: faith, then sight. How often we try to reverse the order! Our natural inclination—and probably that of Martha in this passage, as she mourns the death of her brother Lazarus—is to say we'll believe when we see the glory of God. But throughout Jesus' ministry, He is emphatic that we have it backwards. We'll see the glory of God when we believe.

It's the way of the flesh that says, "I'll believe it when I see it." Jesus says, "You'll see it when you believe it." It's one of the hardest principles for Christians to grasp. The work of almighty, sovereign God is often actually dependent on the level of our faith. It isn't that we limit Him; it's that He has limited Himself. His *modus operandi* in this world is to act in response to faith: the prayers of faith, the obedience of faith, the attitude of faith. As incredible as it seems, the biblical witness is that our belief prompts His intervention. And without belief, He often does not intervene.

Faith expects from God what 's beyond all expectation."
-Andrew Murray

In Deed Do you find yourself in a difficult situation? Believe God, and you will see His glory. That doesn't mean that we lay out a plan of action for Him and then complain when He meets our needs another way. Faith does not dictate God's method of intervention. But it certainly invites His act of intervention—in His way and in His time.

This will mean believing that God has specifically allowed your crisis in the first place. Jesus let Lazarus die—on purpose! He said His friend's sickness was for the glory of God to be revealed (v. 4), and He intentionally stayed where He was for two days after hearing of Lazarus' illness (v. 6). When a crisis comes, do we complain that God was not watching over us, or do we watch for His glory? Our inward response might have more impact than we think. Jesus is clear: "If you believed, you would see the glory of God."

Prayer's Agenda

"Father, hallowed be your name." (Luke 11:2

In Word We fly by the words with little recognition of what they mean. We know they are about the glory of God, but they are a formality, a ritual part of a ritual prayer. Once we've said them—or the whole prayer, for that matter—we can get on with the *real* prayer, the whole reason we are coming to God in th first place. We need something. The "hallowed" part acknowledges who He is before we acknowledge what we need. It's the proper protocol.

But wait. Why did Jesus start with this? Why is it the first lir of His model prayer after that beautiful, comforting address to "Father"? And why, after starting with such intimate familiarity, does He go straight to this holy, formal language we have come t expect and ignore? "Father" is a good start to the prayer, but we lose Him soon after. We pray "hallowed be your name" much more often than we mean it.

> *"You are not drawn to God primarily for your own benefit but for His."*
> —Gonville Ffrench-Beytagh

So what does it mean? Obviously, it's about high and holy things, like the glory of God and bringing honor to His name. But what is Jesus trying to tell us with this ultra-formal lead sentence? Could it be that this is somehow to be an emphasis in our praying?

Yes, Jesus is setting the agenda for us. When we pray, we are to begin with a clear statement that what we seek above all else i God's honor and His kingdom. We're not here in this prayer con versation primarily for us, though we will surely benefit; we're here primarily for Him. We're setting our agenda by explicitly stating that we desire His. We bend our knees and bow our head because there is something higher at stake here than our desires *du jour*. We must confess that our interests—as legitimate as they may be—are consistent with the highest value in the universe: God's glory.

In Deed Is that where your prayers begin? Not with tha particular statement, necessarily, but with that attitude? It's an essential key to unlocking the mystery of prayer. God's glory is the point of all creation. It should be the point of our prayers as well.

Prayers for Glory

"I will do whatever you ask in my name, so that the Son may bring glory to the Father." (John 14:13)

In Word We often read Jesus' sweeping promises about prayer suspicious of what's really in the fine print. If we're looking for a catch, here's one in this verse: The point of our prayers is to bring glory to the Father. We just knew the promise was too good to be true, right? We knew that Jesus would never promise us *carte blanche* to ask what we want in prayer, no strings attached. This surely excludes all prayers for those "unspiritual" aspects of our lives, doesn't it? Does this mean that we can only pray the really holy prayers, or that we must become so absorbed in heavenly things that earthly things just don't matter anymore? In other words, do we have to walk on water first before God honors His promise?

The chief purpose of prayer is that God may be glorified in the answer." –R. A. Torrey

No. This "glory clause" is not a burdensome condition on our prayers, and here's why: Once we've been adopted into God's family, He is glorified by His provision for even our very basic needs. Why? *Because He links His glory on earth to our welfare* (see Exodus 4:31; Deuteronomy 4:35; Psalm 79:9; John 11:4). We should, in fact, seek to tie every prayer request to some aspect of His glory and always pray with a view toward honoring Him. But if we think this means He only answers the spiritually impressive prayers of spiritually impressive saints and missionaries, we have not understood Jesus at all. His promise, as unimaginable as it is, really does apply to all of us who sometimes ask Him to intervene in our mundane affairs. It is for both the grand vision of the kingdom and for the nuts and bolts of everyday life.

In Deed Do you want to see this promise realized as a pattern in your prayer life? Here's the condition: When He answers, give Him glory. That's it. That's what answered prayer is all about—God receiving glory and honor. That's why He promises. Yes, our prayers must be in line with His purposes, but His purposes are broad and our benefit is integral to His glory on earth. Don't be afraid to ask. Then, when He answers, give Him the glory.

Fulfilling His Mission

"I have brought you glory on earth by completing the work you gave me to do." (John 17:

"The will of God is the measure of things."
—St. Ambrose

In Word Mission statements abound in this world. Few institutions or people that have them, however, really live up to them. They are ideals to strive for. But Jesus' declaration is that His mission statement has become reality. He has lived up to it. All that the Father has given Him to do, He has done.

Jesus did not preach to everyone in the world. He did not he everyone, and He did not go everywhere. He didn't try to do more than He was assigned. In fact, many times He left the scene in search of solitude, even while needy people were clamoring fc His attention. He didn't respond positively to every request that came to Him. He didn't stay busy for the sake of busyness. Wher He ascended into heaven, there was still—and there remains today—much work to be done. But Jesus focused on the work that God had given Him to do, and He accomplished it. He didn stray from His mission.

In Deed One day we will approach the end of our lives We will stand before the Father—figuratively on this side of death, literally afterward. Will we also be able to say, "I have brought you glory on earth by completing the work you gave me to do"? Is Jesus our model as we seek the will of God and minister in this world?

Blessed are the people who will be able to echo these words a their life ends. It will not mean that we were everything everyon else expected of us. It will not mean that we worked so hard that we're sure we managed to accomplish God's will sometime during all our activity, although we're not sure when. It will not mea that we addressed every situation for which we felt sympathy, or gave to every organization or missionary that said they needed our financial support. It will simply mean that we discerned God's will for our lives and devoted ourselves to accomplishing by the power of His Spirit. May we be single-minded for that goal.

Fulfilling His Prayers

"I am not praying for the world, but for those you have given me, for they are yours." (John 17:9)

In Word Just as Jesus' work was not scattershot, hoping to hit God's target, neither are His prayers. There is a plan in action here. It isn't that Jesus doesn't care for the world—His familiar statement in John 3:16 would rule that out, as would v. 21 of this same prayer. Rather, He knows that the fate of the world is dependent on the faith of those who have followed Him. His sovereignty will accomplish His purposes, but in His sovereignty He designated simple human beings as His means for reaching the world. If they fail, the message He has entrusted to them is lost. If they falter, the spread of the Gospel is limited or corrupted. The gospel mission of the Son of God is now dependent on the disciples He has called.

"If I could hear Christ praying for me . . . I would not fear a million enemies."

-Robert Murray M'Cheyne

The situation has not changed. The gospel mission of the Son of God is still dependent on the disciples He has called. His kingdom is being built by His ministry through those who can envision it and who rely on Him. We are active participants in the mission of God.

For that reason, we can apply Jesus' high priestly prayer to us. Just as He prayed specifically for the eleven who were with Him that final night, His strategic prayers are still targeted on us. The exalted Savior still makes intercession on our behalf at the throne of the Father (Hebrews 7:25). Our High Priest has not left us in this world alone with a message to tell and no support for telling it. He is not just a heavenly observer. He is an active participant in the work He initiated.

In Deed If ever we feel weak or alone in the work to which God has called us, we can turn to John 17 and read Jesus' prayer. It is a prayer for us, and the Son of God does not have unanswered prayers. His will is one with the Father's, and His prayers are accomplished. Dwell on this encouraging thought: If you belong to the Father through faith in the Son, the Son is praying for you even now.

Fulfilling His Fellowship

"Holy Father, protect them by the power of your name—the name you gave me—so that they may be on as we are one." (John 17:11

> *"The soul that is united with God is feared by the devil as though it were God Himself."*
> —St. John of the Cross

In Word "The Name" of God is the holiest and most sacred of all words, especially in the Jewish context of Jesus' ministry. There is an inexpressible reverence for His name that we often fail to appreciate in a culture that incorporates the Deity intc common slang. This inherent reverence exists because of the awesome power of the Person it invokes. There is nothing more myste rious, more feared, more awe-inspiring than "The Name" of the living, eternal God.

Jesus' request for the unity of His disciples is backed by the power of "The Name." This is no casual request. Just as our prayers that end with "in Jesus' name" carry a force we can scarcely comprehend, Jesus' desire for our union with one anothe invokes a power that is unmatched. The name of God solemnly seals this unity. It is done.

This is no common unity, either. We are united as one *just as the Father and Son are one!* The level of our spiritual bond compare to that of the Trinity!

No wonder, then, that the enemy of God has spent centuries trying to spoil the unity of the church! He cannot succeed, of course. But He can create the illusion that there is no real fellowship in the body of Christ, and he can provoke arguments among the body's members. That we allow him to do so indicates our lac of understanding of the Lord's intercession in John 17. We permit the appearance of divisions where we cannot in fact be divided. The body of Christ is an organic whole. It cannot be truly separated.

In Deed The unity of true believers has never really been at stake in all of church history. What has been at stake is whether we behave like we are united. We *are* one in Christ—that is reality. Do we *act* as one in Christ? Pray that our churche would reflect the spiritual reality of the body of believers. And then live with that oneness in mind.

Fulfilling His Joy

"I say these things while I am still in the world, so that they may have the full measure of my joy within them. I have given them your word and the world has hated them." (John 17:13-14)

In Word At least two things are clear from these verses: Jesus intends for His disciples to have "the full measure" of His joy; and He intends for them to have it even while the world hates them.

Both of these themes are common in Scripture. The Christian life is to be an exceedingly joyful life. There are abundant blessings in the household of God—His mercy, His protection, His provision, His purposes, and more. He has blessed us with *every* spiritual blessing in the heavenly places (Ephesians 1:3). For this we can be thankful and rejoice in *everything*, for this is *always* God's will for us (1 Thessalonians 5:18; Philippians 4:4). There is no doubt in God's revealed Word that tremendous joy is on His agenda for us.

'he opposite ·f joy is not orrow. It is ·nbelief." Leslie Weatherhead

And yet how many of us fail to experience that joy! Is it the trials that come to us? Awareness that the world does, in fact, hate us, just as Jesus predicted? Do our own failures convince us that we are outside of the gospel of Joy? Jesus' last words to the disciples before this prayer give us both sides of this coin, as well as the answer to how we can experience joy in our trials: "In this world you will have trouble. But take heart! I have overcome the world" (John 16:33).

In Deed Does joy elude you today? If so, though you are not alone by any means, you are not setting your gaze on the Christ who has overcome the world. The Savior who lives within you is the same Savior who went through ultimate hardship and gave us a firm hope above and beyond it. His promises are abundant, and they are real. He does not offer us joy without a concrete basis for it. Count on it, rest in Him, and experience His joy in "full measure."

Fulfilling His Glory

"Father, I want those you have given me to be with me where I am, and to see my glory, the glory you have given me because you loved me before the creation of th world."
(John 17:2-

"Our great honor lies in being just what Jesus was and is. What greater glory could come to any man?"
—A. W. Tozer

In Word The glory of God is to be shared. That is the point of creation. We exist to appreciate God's glory—there is no higher purpose for us. It is no wonder, then, at the end of Jesus' earthly ministry, that this is His prayer. He wants us to be with Him, to see His glory, and to understand the love between the Father and the Son, which—through Him—extends to us. This world is not about us and our welfare. It is about Him and His glory. "All things were created by him and for him" (Colossians 1:16). We are onlookers at the divine spectacle and glad participants in the heavenly celebration.

But the amazing thing about Jesus' prayer is that He not only wants us to share His glory by letting us see it, He also wants us share His glory by *having* some of it (v. 22). Unworthy as we are, He has given us the glory that the Father gave Him—we are calle by His name and filled with His Spirit—as a further display of who He is for the sake of all creation to see. In beholding His glo we are able to reflect it (2 Corinthians 3:18; Romans 8:18). What a privilege!

In Deed We often feel trapped in mundane lives—just existing rather than actually living with purpose. Jesus' prayer reminds us that our purpose far exceeds our ability to even begin to comprehend. We are partakers in the glory of God. We were created to see it. We were created to enjoy it. And we wer created to share it with Him. We are inextricably bound to Christ, who is in perfect unity with God the Father and the Ho Spirit. No other created being has such unity with God! No angel or spirit can know such fellowship as that which we will experience—and can already begin to experience—with the ete nal Father! Trapped in a meaningless existence? Never. We are children of God. Share His glory.

Temptation's Adversary

"Lead us not into temptation." (Luke 11:4)

In Word Temptation is a struggle for all who have ever tried to live a godly life. Godliness doesn't come naturally to us, and we are constantly tempted with what does: ambitions, lusts, bad habits, self-interest, conflict, and more. The natural self is much harder to live with once we've decided not to follow it any more. It just won't go away. Most of us will go through stretches when we can successfully subdue it. But those stretches don't last. We give out, and the sinful nature is still there. All we have to do is let down our guard and relax for a minute, and it quickly reminds us of the old things it offers us.

Much of "Christian living" literature tries to address this problem. We are encouraged to starve the sinful nature, ignore it, talk back to the devil who feeds it, beat it into submission, and more. These can all be helpful and effective techniques. But there is another that should come before all of them: We should ask God to lead us away from tempting situations. We often determine to subdue the flesh and then live in a climate that cultivates it. We decide to forsake materialism, but look through catalogs that entice us with all sorts of offers. We decide to abandon lust, but watch programs that provoke it. We decide to break a habit of food or drink or other substance, but we don't rid our environment of the substance. We want to starve the flesh, but we don't really *want* to.

"To realize God's presence is the one sovereign remedy against temptation." —François Fénelon

In Deed Jesus gives us an acceptable—even commanded—model prayer. Ask God to lead you away from temptation. Cooperate with Him. Ask yourself why you can be so embracing of temptation and so hesitant in faith, when it really should be the other way around. The deceitfulness of the sinful nature is subtle. The only effective counter-attack is a firm "no" and an appeal for divine assistance. It's OK to ask for that; Jesus tells us to. Don't hide your temptations from the One who is glad to oppose them. Point them out and let Him steer you away.

A Wounded Community

"I have compassion for these people." (Matthew 15:3

In Word Many of us became Christians, expecting to fin holy people in God's kingdom. We may have envisioned the church as a collection of folks who have gotten it right, who kno what life is about and live it well. We may have thought our relationship troubles were over, if we related only to the redeemed.

But if we've been there long enough, we realize that while th people are holy in Christ, they (and we) are still deeply flawed ir themselves. When we go to church we are surrounded by addict dysfunctional families, people with broken relationships, physica and emotional cripples, distorted perspectives, and every kind o problem known to mankind. The crowds that came to Jesus repre sented in their physical infirmities the whole range of handicaps that plague our sinful natures. In our churches, the physical hanc icaps are unmistakable, but the emotional, psychological, and spiritual ones are usually hidden well. Eventually they show themselves. How will we react?

Jesus looked out upon the lame, the blind, the crippled, and the mute (v. 30), and had compassion. He healed them and He fe them. What do we see when we look out upon the crowds that are coming to Jesus? Do we expect to find cleaner, healthier people? We will not. We will see similar crowds with similar problems—a world of infirmities laying all before His feet.

"The best exercise for strengthening the heart is reaching down and lifting people up."
—Ernest Blevins

In Deed Perhaps we were disappointed when we foun out how deeply flawed Christians can be. We are holy in Him, o course; all sins are washed away in His sacrifice. But the sinful nature often rears its ugly head. How do we respond when we s the nature of the world within the walls of the church?

Jesus' followers are the walking wounded, those who have risen from death and are still removing their grave clothes. We bring our flaws to Him and He is compassionate. We must be also.

Choosing Your Road

"Small is the gate and narrow the road that leads to life, and only a few find it." (Matthew 7:14)

In Word Centuries of legalism have given us an unfortunate interpretation of "the straight and narrow." Heaven, we are led to believe, is only for those who can live up to the demands of the Gospel, and there are precious few who can. But history tells us that attempts to "live up to" the requirements of God are many. Every religion places demands on its adherents, and while no one lives up to those demands perfectly, many do an awfully good job. Their good job, however, will not fit through Jesus' narrow gate.

If "straight and narrow" living—doing right and avoiding sin, as most would define it—were the key to life in God's kingdom, the Pharisees would have had it made. Yet Jesus had more conflicts with these good-works gurus than anyone else. And His encounters with tax collectors and prostitutes were certainly not reflective of a gospel of good works. His mercies indicated a far different approach to the kingdom.

The small gate and narrow road of which Jesus speaks is Himself. And the *only* people who find Him are those who give up walking the road themselves. When we make ourselves the gate—and we do, whenever we think our efforts are the key—we miss the true gate. "I tell you the truth, I am the gate for the sheep," Jesus said (John 10:7).

esus Christ s God's •verything or man's otal needs."

-Richard Halvorson

In Deed As much as we may think we have found this small, narrow gate of trust in Jesus, we lapse into self-effort frequently. Once saved by grace through faith in Him, we try to live by effort through faith in ourselves. We try to work for God, rather than letting Him work through us. We try to obey Him with a belief that we actually can, rather than submitting in our weakness to the Spirit who works out obedience in us. We aim to be righteous, rather than trusting Him as our righteousness. But the narrow road *always* leads away from ourselves. *Everything* in the Gospel is about Him. It's never our burden, and always of grace.

More Than a Miracle

When Jesus saw their faith, he said to the paralytic, "Take heart, son; your sins are forgiven." (Matthew 9:

In Word A broken man was brought before Jesus by his friends. They were seeking his healing from the miracle worker they had heard so much about. There was probably little theolog in their actions. They had a friend who was paralyzed, and they had heard of someone who could help. That was all they needed to know. So they thought.

But they encountered more than a wonder worker. They heard the voice of God. "Take heart, son; your sins are forgiven." Those who say that Jesus never claimed to be God have never wrestled with this verse. Only God can forgive sins. And Jesus said He had that authority. The paralytic and his friends were co fronted with Deity—the Source of all life and the Master of all di eases. Even spiritual ones.

"The healing acts of Jesus were themselves a message that He had come to set men free."
—Francis MacNutt

In Deed When we come to Jesus, we often come with only our perceived needs on our minds—our circumstances, our health, our direction, etc. Just like the paralytic, we receive no rebuke from Him when we do. His words are gentle and comfor ing. But He also takes the opportunity to teach us about Himself In fact, He may allow deep needs to surface in our lives specifically so we will come to Him for help and learn about Him in th process.

What did the paralytic learn? That God's first purpose for hi was spiritual wholeness—healing from the crippling disease of sin. That faith in Jesus is the key to receiving healing from God. That the work of the group on behalf of the individual is valuabl in the eyes of God. And that the Son of Man has authority over everything that afflicts us.

We come to the wonder worker for a miracle. We leave know ing God. He is not content just helping us get by in this world ar meeting only the needs we think we have. He who offers us Himself will not rest until we get up and go home knowing Him and His authority.

More Than One Man

When Jesus saw their faith, he said to the paralytic, "Take heart, son; your sins are forgiven." (Matthew 9:2)

In Word Here, hidden in a brief story of Jesus' healing power, we have a model of the church. A paralyzed man cannot make it to the Healer on his own. He needs his friends. Did he ask them to take him? Or did they decide on their own what their friend needed? Either way, it was *their* faith that moved Jesus. Not just the faith of the cripple, but the faith of the group as a whole. It was a community effort. A group of guys acting on behalf of the one in need.

Rarely in Scripture is God's work between Him and only one person. He works through community. His plans are too great to be appreciated in isolation. Jesus promises to be where two or more are gathered in His name. He tells us not to forsake the assembling of ourselves together. He defines us as His body—many parts working together as one whole. He has revealed Himself through the nation of Israel, and He works through the church to reach a needy world. Though God will work with us as individuals, He does it for others to see. God is a group experience.

"The Bible knows nothing of solitary religion."
-John Wesley

In Deed What does the church do with our needy ones? Sometimes we criticize them for being needy. Sometimes we tell them to go to Jesus themselves. Sometimes we even tell them to get help first, and then they'll be suitable for meeting Jesus. We miss the whole point.

God's purpose in this world is to display His glory. Sometimes that is for one or two people to see, but usually not. Usually, He wants as many people as possible to observe His answers to prayer. Usually, He wants as many as possible to hear His stories of deliverance. Usually, He wants people who come to Him to be brought by others who believe in Him. This is our work—carrying our wounded to Jesus in faith, so that we all may be "filled with awe" (v. 8) and give praise to God.

Driven by the Wind

"The wind blows wherever it pleases. You hear its sound, but you cannot tell where it comes from or whe[r]e it is going. So it is with everyone born of the Spirit."

(John 3:

In Word The wind and the Spirit of God are a lot alike. Both Greek and Hebrew use one word for both meanings. Jesus, too, emphasizes the similarity. But what does this mean for the believer? What is it like to be blown by the wind of God?

Undiscerning eyes do not understand the way of the Spirit. The unspiritual mind does not see the reasons for God's movements in the lives of His people. The world stresses human wisdom, common sense, "risk management," and setting oneself up for success. It understands principles of ambition in careers, retal ation in relationships, pride in achievements, and *carpe diem*—sei ing the pleasure of the day—as a way of life. It holds in contemp those who do not value worldly treasures. And it cannot comprehend the motivations and decisions of citizens of God's kingdom who are propelled by the eternal Spirit. Kingdom values are a mystery to those who have fixed their gaze on this world.

"All the Holy Spirit's influences are heaven begun, glory in the seed and bud."

—Matthew Henry

In Deed Is your life driven by the Spirit? Not if it is predictable and reasonable. Not if the unbelieving world can explai[n] it. There is considerable contrast between the ways of the flesh and the ways of the Spirit. Read of the believers in Acts or of the faithful in Hebrews 11. There is an eternal wisdom behind the va ues Jesus preached. There is a heavenly city being built for those who shed their earthly ambitions.

Beware of a way of life that is acceptable to conventional, human reasoning. The mind of sinful humanity neglects the eternal for the temporal and the holy for the profane. Its followers, therefore, give tainted advice. Do not follow it. Live supernatural lives under supernatural guidance. Be blown by God's Spirit. He blows wherever He pleases and takes us where the world cannot go.

Don't Worry

"Quiet! Be still!" (Mark 4:39)

In Word There is something profoundly comforting about the fact that Jesus can immediately quiet the winds and waves that besiege us. It doesn't matter whether they are forces of nature, forces of the underworld (see the next passage, Mark 5:1-20, for an example), forces of the circumstances that surround us, or forces of our own creation. Whatever is out of control, He can control it.

The unsettling part of this is that He often doesn't. We, like the disciples on the boat, have fretted over threatening forces and said to Him: "Don't you care if we drown?" (v. 38). And while we can certainly assume that He cares, we cannot assume that the winds will die down right away. Sometimes He lets them rage. Perhaps it is to prolong the question of verse 40—"Do you still have no faith?"—or to cultivate in us the right answer to that question. Whatever the reason, it is alarming, and we cannot calm down until we are able to join in the affirmation of verse 41—"Even the wind and the waves obey him!" Only when we are there can we rest.

There is no need for two to care, for God to care and the creature too."

—Charles Spurgeon

The assurance we have is that He *will* bring us there. It is a certainty, just as certain as the disciples' safety in the boat that day. He was not going to let them drown, no matter how afraid they became. Even when it seemed all else was completely out of control, He wasn't. There was purpose in His silence, and there was good timing in His rebuke of the elements. He doesn't miss a thing.

In Deed What threatens you? Are you feeling out of control? Perhaps the elements have frightened you out of your wits. Don't worry. He is the absolute authority over *everything* in your life, if you will trust Him with it. There is perfect timing in His commands, and your storm will not linger a moment too long. Recognize who He is—even join in His rest in the back of the boat. Learn that when you are with Him, every threat is a false one.

Peacemakers

"If you, even you, had only known on this day what would bring you peace—but now it is hidden from your eyes."

(Luke 19:42

In Word Jesus wept over Jerusalem. He probably weeps over it even now. Its inhabitants did not know the things that make for peace. Neither does our world today.

What makes for peace? The world thinks it is political agreements, diplomacy, military threats, law enforcement, good psychology, cultural exchanges, education, economic prosperity, and more. And all of these can be good. They can create a superficial absence of conflict. But that absence of conflict can be interrupted by one suicide bomber, one lone gunman, one contentious lawsuit, one harsh word, or one bitter spirit. Even if all the world were to agree that conflict is undesirable in a given situation, one dissenter could set off waves of violence with one small act. No, the key to peace is not political, economic, social, or psychologica It is spiritual. And the Prince of Peace is the One who holds the key.

"All men desire peace, but very few desire the things that make for peace."

—Thomas à Kempis

Real peace involves a change of heart. Contracts can't do tha Treaties can't either. Neither can armies, judges, or security guards. The only thing that can change a human heart—really change it—is the Gospel of Jesus. It's the only thing that reconcile a heart to God, and it's the only thing that fundamentally alters the fallen nature we're born with.

In Deed What can you do to create peace on this violent planet? You can try to encourage it, enforce it, legislate it, financially support it, and socially or psychologically orchestrate it. Bu unless your efforts reach the human heart, you've only inhibited conflict, not created peace. To be a real peacemaker, you must introduce people to the only power on the planet that can change a heart from within—Jesus. His Spirit reconciles a person to God and transforms human relationships. Let His Spirit work through you. Be a peacemaker. And you—and your world—will be blessed.

Sovereign . . . and Good

"Take courage! It is I. Don't be afraid." (Matthew 14:27)

In Word How often we need to hear these words from Jesus! We grow weak when the troubles of life threaten us. Difficult trials come, and we grow suspicious of God, wondering if His will for us might be too hard this time. We let fear invade us and paralyze us. All the while, we forget two unalterable facts that the Bible emphasizes again and again—God is sovereign, and He is good.

There is nothing beyond God's control. Old Testament stories of the Red Sea, Jericho, Goliath, captivities, fiery furnaces, lions' dens, and the like should have convinced the disciples that even when perilous threats arise, God *always* uses them purposely to further establish His people. Jesus affirms the sovereignty of God; He numbers the hairs of our heads and watches over sparrows. When this Jesus walks across life-threatening waters and says, "It is I," fear should vanish. God is sovereign.

"The center of God's will is our only safety."

-Betsie ten Boom

But God's sovereignty often means nothing to us unless we also know that He is good. An evil or dispassionate god could be sovereign, and we would not trust him. But the disciples should also have known from the Old Testament that the sovereign God is kindly disposed toward His people. He shepherds them, shelters them, nourishes them, and delivers them. Jesus has also made this clear: The Father gives good things to His children and blesses them. When His Son walks across life-threatening waters and says "It is I," it is not for further danger. It is for relief. God is good.

In Deed The wind and waves of this world are harsh. When we obsess about them, we grow suspicious of God's power and goodwill. Our courage fails us. But anyone who has a hard time making it through the storms of this life needs to clutch these truths like a lifeline that will pull them to safety. God's sovereign power supervises *everything* that comes into our lives, no matter how threatening it appears. And He is—in His unchanging nature—very, very good.

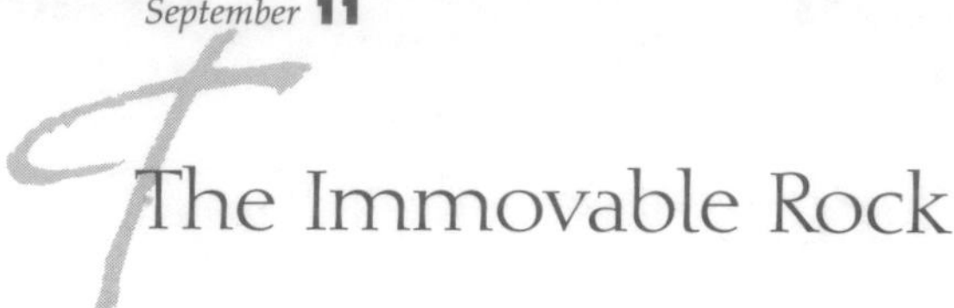

The Immovable Rock

"Do not let your hearts be troubled." (John 14:1

In Word Jesus is preparing His disciples for the most cat astrophic experience they will ever face—His execution. Their Messiah, their Liberator, their political Savior, is about to die a shameful death. Their hopes for revolution against Rome will be sealed in a guarded tomb. They will suffer despair and disillusionment. Their world will be rocked.

We know the end of the story; we do not despair when we read of Jesus' preparation for death. Our hearts are not troubled, because we know of the Resurrection and the power of the Gospel. No, our hearts are troubled about other things. We see what is going on in the world around us and wonder if the end is near. We hear of wars and rumors of wars. We are panicked by falling towers and biological pathogens. We notice that the site of the Crucifixion is once again the most controversial plot of land on the planet. And we worry.

> *"Rock of Ages, cleft for me, let me hide myself in Thee."*
>
> *—Augustus Toplady*

Jesus says "don't." Our hearts should not be troubled. Even i all hell breaks loose around us—and for the disciples, it quite lite ally did—there is a place of supreme safety beneath the surface o those turbulent waters. Jesus dwells there, and He allows us to dwell with Him even now. The world cannot touch the one who rests in Jesus' care, however brutal it becomes. It may threaten all that is corruptible—our possessions and our bodies—but it can never harm our lives.

In Deed Worry occurs when we've overvalued something that is corruptible. We know that possessions, opportunities health, relationships, jobs, and all else we need for day-to-day existence are important. But they are not essential to our life in Christ. We often overvalue them—they become our idols—and w overestimate our role in preserving them. When they are threatened, we worry. Our hearts are troubled. But if we fix our hearts exclusively on Jesus, our hearts find rest. Our Refuge, our Shield, and our Provider tells us not to worry. And He can be trusted. Th Rock of Ages does not move.

A Matter of Trust

"Not as I will, but as you will." (Matthew 26:39)

In Word Jesus taught us to pray like this, resigning our will to that of the Father (Matthew 6:10). And then He went out and followed His own teaching. It is a mystery to us that there might be some discrepancy between the Father's will and the Son's, though we can certainly understand the impulses of human flesh resisting the torture of the Cross. But with us, there is no mystery. There is frequently a divergence between the divine will and ours; we face constant tension between our impulses and His direction.

In our prayer life, this is especially troublesome. We know how to pray for our desires, but we wonder whether our desires are consistent with His. We are told to pray specifically, but taught to pray according to His will. And when we don't know the specifics of His will, this is a problem. How do we overcome it?

Trust involves letting go and knowing God will catch you." –James Dobson

George Müller, the 19th-century believer who ran orphanages entirely on faith, said that in every prayer he sought to begin with no will of his own. His first words in each request were a disavowal of his own preferences. After self-will was removed, God's will would become clear. Many believers testify to the same principle: God's will becomes evident when ours becomes subdued. Then we can pray—and act—as specifically as He directs.

In Deed The issue this usually raises for us is trust. It's a hard thing to resign self-will in a situation and cast ourselves with unreserved abandonment on the Savior. It feels careless, like jumping off a cliff and hoping He'll catch us. As trustworthy as He is, we remain suspicious that He might not act in our best interests—that there might be some conflict between what is best for His kingdom and what is best for us.

But there never is. There's no difference between His will and what we would want for ourselves if only we knew all the details. We can say "not as I will" and *always* trust Him to step in with His best. With His character, He could do no less.

A Powerful Touch

"Someone touched me; I know that power has gone out from me." (Luke 8:46

In Word Jesus' words to the masses crowding around Him sound accusing, but in fact they are inviting. The result of th trembling woman's confession that she was, in fact, the one who touched Him is not punished with, "How dare you?", as she might have expected, but with the ultimate reassurance: "Your faith has healed you. Go in peace."

What does this passage say about us? It says that we need n approach Him with trembling, as though we have no right to be in His presence. We don't, of course—like this woman, we are rit ually unclean—but He has given us the privilege of His presence by grace, and we can take full advantage of it. He welcomes us t touch Him.

What does this passage say about Jesus? It says that He is touchable—a Savior who is accessible, not hidden in obscurity, demanding our qualification, but waiting only for us to acknowledge our need. It also says that His power flows to those who are bold enough to touch Him.

> *"Faith is extending an empty hand to God to receive His gift of grace."*
>
> —A. W. Pink

In Deed There is an unusual combination of attitudes i the approach of the bleeding, trembling woman. We rarely find it in ourselves. When we have desperate need, we often lack faith. When we find ourselves strong in faith, it's usually before we're at the end of our rope, when we see plenty of plausible opportunities for Jesus to intervene. But the woman came in des peration *and* in faith. The two are often mutually exclusive in ou experience, but when we have both, we have what it takes to touch Jesus. Only despair drives us into His presence, even through a dense, crushing crowd. And only faith is bold enough to grab His garment against all protocol, knowing that He is the source of all mercy and help.

Do you have what it takes to touch Him? The desperation t bring your impurity into His holy presence? Enough boldness t press through the crowds and grab Him? Then come, and watc His power flow.

Close, but Not Quite

"You are not far from the kingdom of God." (Mark 12:34)

In Word The teacher of the Law, having come to probe Jesus' theology, is probed himself. He commends Jesus' insight into true devotion, and thinks the matter is settled with His endorsement. Jesus steps over the endorsement with authority and commends the teacher's belief that the love of God and neighbor are the substance of God's heart more than burnt offerings.

We are satisfied with the teacher's position, too, and are glad that, at least for once, a legal expert got it right. But Jesus stops short of declaring him right with God. He's got the right idea, but he isn't there yet. To be "not far from the kingdom of God" is still to be outside of it. Something more is needed.

Christ came to save all through His own person." –Irenaeus

This should alarm us. Don't we know many who profess love of God and neighbor and consider it salvation? Don't many of us describe that as the essence of our faith as well? Why isn't this enough for Jesus? What's the problem?

We need to learn two lessons from the teacher of the Law. (1) Knowing doctrine is *not* the same as knowing God. Plenty of people know the right words and agree with the right things. That's not enough. We cannot enter the kingdom of heaven unless we're born of God's Spirit. We cannot get there without knowing Him. (2) Knowing God is *not* possible without knowing Him through Jesus. The exact representation of God on earth, the body in whom God met a sinful race, cannot be bypassed without rejecting the One who sent Him. Though many try to identify other ways, it just isn't possible.

In Deed Jesus' semi-compliment to the teacher is a slap in the face of our culture. Modern religionists have so watered down God that He is alleged to be known on their own terms. Jesus would tell all who believe in a generic god and do good works in his name: "You aren't far from the kingdom. But you are not yet there."

Consider Your King

"You do not have in mind the things of God, but the things of men." (Mark 8:3

In Word Peter surely should have known better. Other Gospels tell us that he had just confessed Jesus as the Messiah. And in a moment of horribly incongruous thinking, he took Jesus aside and rebuked Him for predicting His own death and resurrection. Did he really believe Jesus to be the Christ? And he still felt it appropriate to rebuke Him?

We're astounded at Peter's lack of logic, but we repeat it in our own lives frequently. We also claim Jesus as our Messiah, and unlike Peter, we see the death and Resurrection in hindsight. We have no problem with it; we even celebrate it every Easter. But do we live it? Do we see it as our guiding principle? Do we really understand the difference between the things of God and the things of men?

"The cross of Christ is the most revolutionary thing ever to appear among men."

—A. W. Tozer

We avoid the way of the Cross at all costs. Intellectually, we know that Jesus calls us to follow Him on that way, but our natural human instincts pull us in the opposite direction. They pull us strongly, and more often than we like to think, we let them. We are guided by "the things of men" whenever we live without an eternal perspective. When we see ourselves as citizens of the world, rather than citizens of the kingdom of God, we are led to make bad choices. We are too easily governed by the limited perspectives of secular man, when the wealth of God's wisdom is available to us—and compelling us to see all things with an eternal view.

In Deed What lasts forever? God, His kingdom, His Word, and the souls of people. Nothing else. Yet when God calls us to invest ourselves entirely in these things, we are sometimes like Peter. We mentally take Him aside and try to persuade Him that He isn't realistic. We try to tell Him the best way out of our predicaments or the best course for our future. Is Jesus naive about the ways of the world? No, we're naive about the ways of the kingdom. We're the ones who need to be reminded to consider the things of God.

Consider Your Investments

"What good is it for a man to gain the whole world, yet forfeit his soul?" (Mark 8:36)

In Word If someone has a sum of money to invest, he or she will have to make some choices. The money can be put in full into one investment, or it can be divided among more than one. Many people choose this latter option in order to hedge their bets. But when one option is considered far superior to all the others, diversification takes a back seat to opportunism. Attractive investment opportunities draw all of our attention and all of our money for the possibilities they entail. We want to capitalize.

In the economy of God, one investment is clearly superior to all others. It's a sure thing. And Jesus calls us to place all of our resources, time, and talents there—exclusively. Why? Because He knows the return it will yield, and He knows we will not be disappointed. But there is often a part of us that wants to diversify. We want to invest some in God's kingdom, certainly, but also some in this world. We're afraid to put our resources only in one place. Whether we put a lot or a little into the temporal, Jesus says, it's a bad deal. The world will end in bankruptcy, and the kingdom of God will inherit all wealth. And its wealth will be everlasting.

There are no crown-wearers in heaven who were not cross-bearers here below."

– Charles Spurgeon

In Deed Human beings pursue comfort and pleasure with an alarming passion. It isn't that comfort and pleasure are wrong; God created both for us to enjoy. But He never called us to pursue them. He never asked us to focus our attention on our earthly life span in order to make it as easy or profitable as possible. To the contrary, He constantly calls His disciples to take everything they have now and invest it in everything they know about God's eternal kingdom. "Whoever wants to save his life [i.e., live for the "now"] will lose it, but whoever loses his life for me and for the gospel [i.e., lives for the kingdom] will save it" (v. 35). Consider your investments well, and avoid the pursuits of this world. Whatever you do, do it for the glory of God.

A Loss of "Life"

"Whoever wants to save his life will lose it, but whoeve loses his life for me will save it." (Luke 9:24

"A man's god is that for which he lives."

—Martyn Lloyd-Jones

In Word Jesus' words are frightening. Who doesn't want to save his own life? The emotionally disturbed, perhaps, but the rest of us hang on to it with a passion. We try to build it up and establish it with our reputations, our careers, our enjoyments, our families, our friends, our accomplishments—anything we can think of, really. We begin life with an emptiness that needs to be filled—or, more accurately, that *demands* to be filled. From childhood forward, we seek fulfillment in whatever will temporarily satisfy that emptiness. And that's the problem; we seek fulfillmen with unworthy things. Sometimes those things are good and noble, other times not. Either way, they are not the eternal fulfillment God wants us to have. They will eventually destroy us.

Jesus condemns what is for us a very natural tendency, this urge to establish our lives with whatever makes us feel alive. But simply feeling alive isn't the same as having life. In His love, Goc will strip us of all of these false props. They are our idols. If you don't think you're that attached to them, measure your reaction when God pulls them away. We clutch them with desperate hands; they are sometimes the only life we've known.

In Deed Jesus tells us to go ahead and let go. We must lose those things we call "life," those earthly fulfillments we thought we needed. We have deeper cravings than those, and Jesus knows how to satisfy them. When we cease clinging to thos things, people, or ideas that we've used to define our lives, we ca cling to that which God has given for true life. When He exposes our idols, we can know true worship. But that's the catch: He must first take them away, and we must let go of them. That hurts. It genuinely feels like losing your life. In the end, it's the only way to save it.

Getting Personal

"Follow me." (Matthew 9:9)

In Word One of the greatest temptations Christians face is to avert our eyes from the person of Jesus and place them on the things of Jesus—His doctrine, His people, His word, or His mission. This is a great temptation because there is absolutely nothing wrong with any of these things. In fact, without serious attention to them we could not be His disciples. They are essential.

The fallacy that trips us up is our focus on these things as objective entities apart from living fellowship with the person of Jesus. When we focus on the things of Jesus, such as His teaching, it can turn into a sterile, academic pursuit or a legalistic enterprise, sort of like following the Law of Moses. It's an objective standard outside of ourselves, but from the mouth of Jesus rather than another lawgiver. Or, if we focus on the mission of Jesus, it can become a personal venture with our own strategic planning. We end up with zeal for a cause, but no fellowship with the Spirit behind the cause.

This is why Jesus doesn't call His disciples by saying "Follow My teachings," or "Follow My example," or "Follow My reasoning." It is always personal. "Follow Me." Too many believers have a sterile faith that emphasizes the impersonal aspects of Jesus. But He will not let us be content with that. He confronts us with Himself, and we do not progress far in our discipleship unless we're focused on a relationship rather than religious pursuits.

Jesus does not give recipes that show the way to God. He Himself is the way."

—Karl Barth

In Deed As good and instructive as theology and doctrine can be, we must not turn to them as the substance of our faith. They are descriptions of the relationship we have with the living Lord. Jesus is not a system of belief. Daily study and application are not enough. These must be built on daily communication—two-way communication between the disciple and Jesus Himself. If this were not essential, Jesus would not have given us His Spirit to live with us and in us. Wherever your discipleship is today, make sure it remains intensely personal.

Fit for Following

Another said, "I will follow you, Lord; but first let me go back and say good-by to my family." Jesus replied, "No one who puts his hand to the plow and looks back is fit for service in the kingdom of God." (Luke 9:61-6

In Word The request from Jesus' would-be follower doesn't seem out of line. Everyone, when setting out on an adventure, says goodbye to their family. We seldom go anywhere of significant distance without letting someone else know. So why does Jesus have a problem with this request from a potential disciple?

Jesus does not want us looking back. The issue isn't a casual goodbye. The issue is where the heart is focused. Jesus' call is always immediate and thorough. The timing of His call is never an accident. When He calls, it is the appropriate time to turn our hearts solely toward Him.

The illustration of someone putting a hand to the plow and looking back is powerful. It is the ancient-world equivalent of saying, "Whoever tries to drive forward while looking out the rear window is not fit for the road." Jesus isn't saying that this disciple isn't worthy. No one is—that's a given. He is saying that this disciple will not do well in a kingdom that requires unrivaled allegiance to the King as a condition for citizenship. Our path toward Jesus must be straight and unhindered. Those who look behind do not make straight paths.

> *"Christ is my Savior. He is my life. He is everything to me in heaven and earth."*
>
> —Sadhu Sundar Singh

In Deed What hinders your service in the kingdom? Is anything constantly drawing your attention in another direction than Jesus? If so, it must be dealt with. We often let the preoccupations of life—relationships, careers, possessions, interests—distract our gaze. But we serve a jealous God (Exodus 34:14) who is intent on winning our hearts.

Jesus welcomes any disciple who fixes his or her gaze on Him and is prepared to follow whole-heartedly. But our world is filled with distractions. Let your eyes fall on Jesus alone.

Behaving like Children

"Which of the two did what his father wanted?"

(Matthew 21:31)

In Word In this brief parable, one son says he will do what the father asks and then changes his mind later. The other son says he will not work for the father, but changes his mind and actually goes to the vineyard later. Both act in contradiction to their stated intentions. And Jesus gives them absolutely no credits or criticisms for their words; what they do is all that matters to Him. It is the surest evidence of their true beliefs.

The parable is a pointed statement to the Pharisees that it is possible to identify ourselves so much by our stated allegiances that we miss the whole point of faithful obedience to God. While we should trust and celebrate the fact that we are irrevocably God's children, we should not take our children's status for granted as our natural right. True children of the Father act like they really are His children and He really is their Father. Our service in the vineyard really does matter. It's an accurate indication of where our heart lies.

The problem with our discipleship may be that we are content to be God's children in name only, while avoiding real participation in our new family. Like the son who was overtly willing but inwardly apathetic, we want the benefits of the kingdom of God without ever really getting our hearts attached and our hands dirty.

"A man's real belief is that which he lives by."
—George MacDonald

In Deed Those of us who were raised as church-goers should beware of this problem. It is possible to be so comfortable with our standing before God that we miss Him when He speaks. We may believe that because we once said we were headed out to His vineyard, we are by nature obedient and faithful. We can be lulled to sleep in our own false sense of security. Meanwhile, the conspicuous sinners of our day find true security by coming when they're called. They understand the call as a demand for repentant faith, not an option for presumptuous children. We must remember that God measures our hearts by the fruit they actually bear.

An Unlikely Ambition

"He who is least among you all—he is the greatest."

(Luke 9:48)

In Word Jesus is always using unexpected examples. Tiny mustard seeds illustrate the potential of His kingdom. Despised Samaritans illustrate what it means to be a true neighbor. And when Jesus speaks of being great, He illustrates the concept with the lowliest people of all. In some passages, servants are the example. In this passage, it's children—not just children, in fact, but *little* children. The least self-conscious among us. The most naive about the world's understanding of "greatness." The last in line when it comes to "getting ahead."

This object lesson for the disciples, like so many others, is yet another indication that God's whole value system contradicts our own. Ever since the Fall, we human beings have been caught in a misguided ambition—toward self-fulfillment, toward achievement, toward impressive accomplishments, and toward status. The problem with our ambition is that it strives toward unworthy goals. It misses what is truly valuable. It exalts self to the exclusion of God. We can even twist our ambition to make it appear godly, striving for influence and status allegedly for the sake of God's kingdom. But if it's not by God's means, it will never accomplish His purposes. And His means run contrary to our instincts.

"Jesus' life began in a borrowed stable and ended in a borrowed tomb."

—Alfred Plummer

God's means for greatness are not climbing up the ladder, but going down. Why? Because when our ambition accomplishes much, we get glory and we compete with God. When our ambition rests in what God can do, He gets glory. That's why God chose a wandering Aramean for a patriarch and a shepherd for a king. And it's why He came as an infant in an obscure little town. He is more clearly the author of greatness when the great get such lowly starts.

In Deed Do you desire greatness in God's kingdom? It's not a bad desire—Jesus encourages it even in this verse. But the means may not be what you'd expect. Measure greatness not by status but by dependence on the One who is greater than all others.

Discernment, Not Judgment

"In the same way you judge others, you will be judged, and with the measure you use, it will be measured to you." (Matthew 7:2)

In Word The first verse of this passage is one of the most familiar in the New Testament—"Do not judge, or you too will be judged." Even many in the secular world quote it as a mantra for tolerance, using it as an excuse to avoid moral standards. And, to an extent, there is some truth in their interpretation—God has not called us to be judgmental or to set ourselves up as arbiters of eternal rewards. We are not in a position to look down on anyone. But are we to have no moral discernment at all?

How rarely we weigh our neighbor in the same balance in which we weigh ourselves."

—Thomas à Kempis

No, verse two clarifies for us what Jesus means. There is a type of human judgment that points out others' faults without recognizing our own. The double standard is an indication that we've never really accepted God's mercy. Our view of others reflects our understanding of the Gospel. If we first recognize that we were guilty before God and that His grace has showered us with forgiveness in Christ, we'll see others compassionately. He bridged a huge gap between Him and us, and we must always be aware that our position in Him is all of grace. Then, and only then, can we stand up for what's right. We begin to see others as we see ourselves—candidates for mercy rather than candidates for wrath.

In Deed Our society has many moral ills, and nowhere does Jesus tell us to be quiet about them. When we take a stand on the moral issues of our day, we are adhering to biblical principles. But we can do that without being judgmental. We must take a stand from a position of identification with sinful humanity, not from a position of superiority over it. We have been, and often still are, part of the problem. Those who lecture others about immorality as if they are above it believe deep down that they have earned God's favor, and no one listens. But when we speak as sinners saved by grace, many will hear with open minds.

Our Highest Value

"What is highly valued among men is detestable in God's sight." (Luke 16:15

In Word What is highly valued among men? In the context of this passage, it is money. It was true in the Pharisees' day and it is true in ours. But there are also other things highly valued among us: prestige, comfort, accolades, pleasure, accomplishments, property, and more. We even highly value some very good things: love, faithfulness, honesty, and a host of other virtues that both Christian and secular culture hold as ideals. Can Jesus really mean that all of these things are detestable in God's sight?

"That to which your heart clings is your god."
—Martin Luther

It is a consistent principle of the Bible in general, and also of the Gospel Jesus taught, that *anything* that motivates us other than a love for God Himself is detestable in God's eyes. *Anything* we treasure more than Him is an object of idolatry and a violation of the first of the Ten Commandments: "You shall have no other gods before me" (Exodus 20:3).

It is true that most of our values are inherently opposed to a loving pursuit of God, but even the values He endorses are detestable when they become an end in themselves. The "love" that our secular culture pursues is not pleasing to God if it is not in the context of His love. If the virtues for which we honor other are not the work of God's Spirit in their lives, they are products o self-effort and monuments to the "goodness" of independent humanity. They are by nature dishonoring to God if they are not testimonies to His grace.

In Deed Yes, God detests the things we highly value if they are valued apart from Him. And we must constantly ask our selves: "Is there anything in my heart that did not originate from His Spirit? Is there anything I treasure as an entity in itself rather than as a gift from Him?" If we can answer yes to these—and at times we all can—then we must redirect our passions and our ideals to the character of God Himself. He is our highest value.

Fear God Alone

"Do not be afraid of those who kill the body and after that can do no more." (Luke 12:4)

In Word The context of this verse in Luke 12 is persecution from those who would silence the gospel message. But Jesus' message here can apply to our daily lives, whether we face life-threatening persecution or not. For, in fact, we often do fear others more than we fear God. We let people intimidate us and we let circumstances restrict us, and in the process we end up conforming to others' expectations, cultural constraints, and a host of other ungodly influences.

Do you ever feel pushed around? Jesus tells us to fear only God. His will is to be the overwhelming influence in our lives. We must realize that neglecting His will is drastically more costly than facing the consequences others may impose on us when we do His will. Carrying out God's purposes and living according to His character must be our highest priority, despite any opposition or criticism we might face from those who do not understand.

"I need nothing but God, and to lose myself in the heart of Jesus."

-Margaret Mary Alacoque

In Deed Whose opinion is largest in your eyes? Are there people in this world who have disproportionate influence on you? Many of us frequently try to please everyone else and then fit God's will in around our obligations. But nowhere in the Bible does God say we are obligated to make everyone else happy. Nowhere does He say we should sacrifice His purposes in order to keep peace with others.

God will put all of us in situations from time to time that test our allegiance. He will allow people and events into our lives that will seem huge and powerfully influential over us. And their influence will run contrary to God's will for us. What is our response? Whether we are facing persecution for the sake of the Gospel or just making daily decisions in the trials of life, we are to be preoccupied with God. Jesus urges us to remember that God is more powerful than our trials and our intimidators, and our allegiance is only to Him.

Transforming Words

"Fill the jars with water." (John 2:

In Word The hosts have done their best, but it isn't enough. The wine has run out at the wedding feast. They are about to be embarrassed. Everyone is about to go home. The big celebration is about to fizzle. As diligent as the hosts probably were in planning for the feast, they didn't accurately estimate the refreshment needed. Or perhaps they bought all they could afford and hoped it would be enough. It wasn't.

The wedding feast at Cana is a lot like life. It's a good attempt at a celebration, but it doesn't quite satisfy. It requires lots of planning and preparation, but there are inevitably unexpected crises. Always visible are the laughter and dancing, but behind the scenes there is stress over whether it will all work out. And everyone knows it will eventually end.

But when Jesus steps into the situation, everything changes. His word is enough to take our stone jars and fill them with satisfying substance. At His word, these ritual cleansing jars—the utensils of legalism—become the vessels of abundant life. The shadow gives way to reality.

"I never have difficulty believing in miracles, since I experienced the miracle of a change in my own heart."

—St. Augustine

In Deed Jesus is the life of the party—literally. He steps into our world and changes futility into fulfillment, blandness into flavor, obligation into celebration, law into life. And, like the servants at the party, *we never see it happen!* We don't know *how* He does it, just that He does. We see the problem, we invite Him to be the solution, we hear Him give the command to prepare for a miracle, and we do so. We fill the pots with the water of our faith and obedience, but we don't understand the miracle that is taking place inside. He turns water to wine without our understanding either how or exactly when. The dancing can continue, the guests can keep laughing, and we can relax and enjoy the celebration.

In John's writings, the ministry of Jesus begins with a wedding feast. It also ends with one (Revelation 19:7). The kingdom of God is all about celebration. And it begins when Jesus speaks transforming word and provides new wine.

One of a Kind

"I will also give him a white stone with a new name written on it, known only to him who receives it."

(Revelation 2:17)

In Word In our age, it is easier than ever to get lost in the crowd. We are counted as statistics in each census and survey. We are targeted as anonymous consumers by mass marketers. On nearly any city street or crowded interstate, we can feel like an insignificant minnow in the sea of humanity.

When we read Revelation, John's vision of heaven may offer us no more sense of uniqueness. Great multitudes of angels and humans—more than can be counted—surround God's throne (Revelation 5:11; 7:9). In our search for significance, we may grow disheartened when we think of heaven's myriad worshipers.

Why else were individuals created, but that God, loving all infinitely, should love each differently."
-C. S. Lewis

But Jesus has an encouraging word for us in His message to the church at Pergamum. He will give us a white stone with a new name written on it. Many interpretations of this stone have been proposed, but one thing is clear: If your name is given by Him, it will be unique and special. It will signify your adoption into the family of Jesus, and it will be appropriate to the person you really are. It will indicate what God knows to be true of you, from your strengths and gifts to the problems you've overcome. The earthly names our parents gave us may or may not reflect our character; but there will be no inaccuracies in the name He gives us.

In Deed C. S. Lewis believed our new name may indicate the unique ability we have to worship some particular aspect of God.* Why not? He is certainly large enough and His glory manifold enough for every one of His billions of creatures to worship a different aspect of His character. We may each worship God for eternity in a way in which no other one of His children can worship Him.

Are you feeling lost in the shuffle of humanity today? Know that God created you uniquely. There will be no long lists of Joneses and Smiths in the kingdom's phone book. Your white stone will be one of a kind—for His glory.

*C. S. Lewis, *The Problem of Pain,* HarperCollins, 1996, p. 154.

Pleasure in Trust

Jesus, full of joy through the Holy Spirit, said, "I praise you, Father, Lord of heaven and earth, because you have hidden these things from the wise and learned, and revealed them to little children. Yes, Father, for this was your good pleasure." (Luke 10:21

"God has His reasons, based on His infinite wisdom, which He does not always choose to reveal to us."

—Spiros Zodhiates

In Word So much of our lives is counterintuitive; it doesn't make sense on the surface. Trials go against our natural understanding, defying the human reasoning that we rely on so heavily. The road God put us on may take a sudden turn. Circumstances that were comfortable may be radically stripped from us in a moment. Or, we may just question why He made us the way He did. And we wonder how to make sense of it all. We want understanding, but live in confusion.

Jesus gives us a model of how to respond to God when things don't fit our own wisdom. He is facing no crisis in this text, just acknowledging that the ways of God contradict the ways of man. If we were God, we would not have hidden eternal mysteries from the wise and learned and revealed them to little children. And we certainly are not inclined to praise God for doing so. We are dumbfounded at the obscurity of His logic. But Jesus affirms God's counterintuitive ways. He simply attributes them to "the good pleasure" of the divine will.

In Deed Our mouths should be so filled with praise. It's easy for us to honor the ways of God when they coincide with our logic. It's difficult when they seem obscure. But an implicit trust God's will, curious as it may be to us, is the key to being "full of joy through the Holy Spirit." It's also a product of that fullness. They feed each other. Trust in God results in mouths full of praise while praising God results in hearts full of trust. Are you disturbed by the mysteries of God's will? Aim to participate in this blessed cycle. Then His good pleasure will be yours.

Born of the Spirit

"I tell you the truth, no one can see the kingdom of God unless he is born again." (John 3:3)

In Word This saying was strange to Nicodemus, but for us it needs no explanation. We have already come to grips with the necessity of a spiritual birth in order to be in God's kingdom. The relevant question for us is this: Are we living according to that birthright?

Those of us who have genuinely accepted Christ by faith know what it means to be born again. We have believed that God's life has entered into us and have begun to see the world as a child of a different kingdom. His words have come alive to us, and we walk in newness of life. But we don't always act like natural citizens of a new kingdom. We don't always feel that life is new, or that our Father is God Himself. Why not?

The soul, like the body, lives by what it feeds on."

-Josiah Gilbert Holland

There are two options for the believer—the way of the flesh and the way of the Spirit. It is entirely possible for us to be born of the Spirit and to walk according to the flesh. Paul's pointed question to the Galatians is relevant to us: "After beginning with the Spirit, are you now trying to attain your goal by human effort?" (Galatians 3:3).

In Deed God did not birth us by His Spirit in order for us to live in the strength of our flesh. There is a supernatural source readily available to us for our decisions, our purity, our gifts and talents, our ministry to others, the unity of our relationships, our worship of God, and more. It must astonish Him that so many of us neglect that source and revert to the insufficiency of human ingenuity and resourcefulness. But we do. Frequently. We are so accustomed to our old nature—it is comfortable in spite of its weakness—that we forget to invite the power of God to live in us. We must learn the customs of the kingdom of God in order to see it. There, the all-sufficient Savior chooses to *be* our life rather than watch us struggle in our own strength. He inhabits His devotees, and, if they will allow it, He'll demonstrate His presence. Let Him. You were born for this.

The Gift of Insufficiency

"Remain in me, and I will remain in you. No branch can bear fruit by itself; it must remain in the vine. Neither can you bear fruit unless you remain in me."

(John 15:4

In Word Jesus declares with emphasis that He is the source of our life. This should be a huge relief to us, but sometimes it is an affront. The human ego balks at the declaration in verse 5: "Apart from me you can do nothing." But once we let it sink in, we realize this is really the only way to accomplish anything lasting. It stands to reason that eternal fruit can only come from an eternal source.

Human pride gets in our way. Self-effort and self-sufficiency may be admirable qualities to unspiritual eyes, but nowhere in th Bible is anyone rebuked for being too dependent on God. The Bible *does* contain numerous rebukes for being too self-reliant. Th glory of God is the centerpiece of the universe, and everything that points to it is blessed. Self-reliance doesn't point to it. God-reliance does. Lasting fruit can only come from Jesus Himself.

"The more we depend on God, the more dependable we find He is."
—Cliff Richard

In Deed Every one of our days should begin with a "de laration of dependence." We should start every morning with an emphatic acknowledgment: "Lord, I am insufficient in everythin I will encounter today. I have insufficient wisdom to make the decisions I'll be required to make. I have insufficient strength to resist the temptations I'll face. I have insufficient skills to manage the conflict that may arise. I have insufficient resources to ministe to the people I'll encounter. I am entirely dependent on You."

The blessing of the Gospel is that in our insufficiency, Jesus i sufficient. Salvation began when we recognized that our righteousness was insufficient to co-exist peacefully and eternally wit a holy God, and it has continued ever since into every arena of our lives. We are deficient in every meaningful way. Embrace tha deficiency, and let the eternal Vine be your life.

Priceless Treasure

"Blessed are the eyes that see what you see." (Luke 10:23)

In Word The love of God is so abundant and available that we easily forget how precious it is. Everything else that so saturates our markets is worth little. But when we apply capitalist theories of supply and demand to God's love, we end up taking Him for granted. We forget the treasure of the Gospel.

Jesus told His disciples that they were blessed beyond measure by knowing Him. They were in a privileged place. Prophets and kings throughout history would have sacrificed anything to see Him and to hear His words (v. 24).

We can make the same observation. We're aware that the philosophical quest for knowledge has persisted for thousands of years. We've known of kings and generals in our day and throughout history who have sacrificed everything for some sense of real power. We're acquainted with both grand religions and fringe cults that thirst for wisdom from above. We've seen people live and die in their search for meaning. All the while, we have access to the Spirit of God who has come to reside in our hearts through our faith in Jesus. The Treasure the world has always hungered for is ours—in intricate, intimate detail.

"The man who has God for his treasure has all things in one."
—A. W. Tozer

In Deed Are we casual about our knowledge of Jesus and His Word? Have we been so saturated with the message of the Gospel that we take it for granted? Are we really aware that taking up God's Word to read it is to taste the riches that finite minds have sought for all history? Like farm animals with access to life's priceless pearls, we have the revelation of the all-wise God on our bookshelves and His Spirit in our hearts. Our eyes have been blessed.

This calls for a celebration. A constant celebration. A party so unequalled in sheer delight that the emotional high lingers forever. Is this the condition of your heart? Remember your Treasure. Give Him thanks today.

All About Him

"If I testify about myself, my testimony is not valid. There is another who testifies in my favor, and I know that his testimony about me is valid." (John 5:31-3

In Word Neither in Jesus' culture nor in ours is someon well accepted who claims his own authority. Self-proclamation is not an admirable trait, unless it is solidly backed up by truth and humbly presented. Jesus tells His hearers that His own testimon is not valid enough to meet the standards of the Law, so He offe others: John the Baptist, the works and miracles Jesus has done, the Father Himself, the Scriptures in general, and Moses in particular.

Jesus' assertion is staggering. All that the Jews held to be reliable, He says, points to Him as the Messiah. Prophets and prophecies of Scripture, miracles of God, the story of the nation, the Mosaic Law, everything—it is all about Him. We can add other witnesses, too. Paul says that even nature and history poin to Jesus, and the gospel writers tell us that the voice from heave declared Jesus' authority at His baptism and the Transfiguration He is the centerpiece of the universe. The answers to the great philosophical questions—Why are we here? What is the meanin of life? Where are we going?—are all wrapped up in Jesus.

In Deed We who have expressed faith in Jesus as our Savior have little trouble accepting this. We believe Him to be G incarnate, the key to all understanding and the giver of life. By Him we interpret the world.

But if the entire universe, all history, all humanity, and every true revelation are about Jesus, what does that say about the dire tion of our lives? Shouldn't *we* be entirely about Jesus as well? If we are not, we are swimming against the tide of all creation. We don't fit the direction of history and the reality of transcendent truth. Test yourself: Does *everything* about you point to Him?

> ***"Of all the great sages and prophets throughout world history, Jesus alone claimed to be God-become-man."***
>
> ***—Luis Palau***

Sifted

"Simon, Simon, Satan has asked to sift you as wheat."
(Luke 22:31)

In Word We wonder why we have trials sometimes. Jesus gives us a glimpse of one reason right here. Satan has asked it of Simon Peter. It is quite possible that he asks it of us as well. And this is no polite request; some translations of this verse capture it more strongly: "Satan demanded to have you, that he might sift you like wheat" (RSV). The enemy of our souls boldly asserts his right to fight to retain what he has long held. We are targeted for sifting by the one we want to leave behind. And Jesus lets him do it.

This verse is rich with implications for us. For example, isn't it interesting that Jesus gives no indication of having put up a fight for us? Certainly He prayed for Peter, but He apparently did not resist the demand in the first place. Jesus does not say that He prayed for Peter to be spared from the sifting. In fact, He seems quite willing to let it happen, as though Satan is actually doing the bidding of the Lord. What the enemy means for evil, God means for good. He lets the evil one have his way with us—for a time.

"The gem cannot be polished without friction."
-Anonymous

In Deed Nowhere in the Bible does God promise to spare us from temptation. Our faith will be assaulted in numerous ways, and while God is not the author of this, He specifically allows it. The enemy of our souls, the evil one who has held this world in his grip from the early days of creation until now, fights against our trust in God. Like he did with Job, he may insist to God that our faith is not genuine because it is not tested. If he can prove that it is not, he can slander the Almighty with his skepticism. God takes him up on the challenge.

Do you ever feel as if all hell is sifting your faith to see what remains? Hang on. You are in a process that God has allowed, and that He has also strictly limited. Your sifting will not last. Your faith will, and there will be no chaff to it. Trust God's sovereignty over the enemy.

Supported

"I have prayed for you, Simon, that your faith may not fail." (Luke 22:3

In Word We know that the prayers of the Son of God do not go unanswered. There is no conflict, no separation between the persons of the Trinity. When the incarnate God asks, the enthroned God hears. If Jesus prayed for Simon Peter, Simon Pet is secure. His faith will not fail.

What do we make, then, of Peter's famous denial? Three times he swore that he did not know Jesus. Three times he lied about the One to whom he had sworn undying allegiance. Wasn this a disaster, by any standard of religious affiliation? Didn't he prove that he was not *really* devoted to Jesus? Didn't his faith fail?

No. When Jesus sees our faith, He sees the lifelong process. He sees whether our faith will be proven false by our testing or refined by it. His covenant to strengthen us does not waver with the ups and downs of our circumstances or our moods. When we fall, He knows whether we will get up. He sees the big picture, and in the big picture our momentary faltering does not determine the final outcome. He doesn't dwell on the toddler who stumbles; He knows us as the mature adult who walks.

"The devil tempts that he may ruin; God tests that He may crown."
—St. Ambrose

In Deed We tend to dwell on our faltering efforts at fait remembering well the stumbles and falls we've taken along the way to maturity. We should not take them lightly; Jesus did not expect Peter to casually dismiss his denial. But we should not se them as the condition that defines us. Jesus saw Peter's failure in advance, yet He prayed with confidence and assurance that his faith would not fail. In the final analysis, it did not. And that's what counts with Jesus.

Do not let your failures define you. They are not how God measures you. In fact, they are how the enemy wants to measure you; that's why he asks to sift you. Don't trust his measurement. Trust Jesus. He has prayed for you.

Strengthened

"When you have turned back, strengthen your brothers." (Luke 22:32)

In Word Jesus assumes failure on Peter's part. He doesn't say, "If you need to turn back . . ." He says "when." It's a given. Peter will fall.

But also notice that Jesus assumes Peter's repentance. It, too, is a given. There is no question here of whether Peter will turn back. It will happen. And there is an instruction for after his return that probably could not have been given before his fall: "Strengthen your brothers." In denying Jesus, grieving over his own treachery and fickleness, and coming back to Jesus with repentance, there is something different about him. Peter, literally "the rock," is in no position to strengthen his brothers before his failure; he is the epitome of instability. But afterward? These are his orders from Jesus. Peter has grown into his name.

Why? What is different between the pre-denial Peter and the post-repentance Peter? Perhaps it is that the one who is honest about his failures is the one who can be strongest in his faith. It was Peter who ran to the tomb three days later when the other disciples did not believe the report of the women who had just been there (Luke 24:11-12). It was Peter whom Jesus told to feed His sheep (John 21:15-19). It was Peter whose Holy Spirit anointing made him the preacher of Pentecost (Acts 2:14). And it was Peter who, so we're told, hung on his own cross—upside down. Knowing his weakness, God gave him the strength to strengthen others.

We forget that God is a specialist; He is well able to work our failures into His plans."

Erwin Lutzer

In Deed We are apt to think that failure disqualifies us from serving God well. To the contrary, sometimes it is the only thing that *does* qualify us. It removes any pretense of self-reliance. Like a phoenix rising, we ascend from the ashes of our own undoing, testifying to the resurrecting power of God. From failure to forgiveness, weakness to strength, death to life—it's God's way. Remember that the next time you despair over your failures.

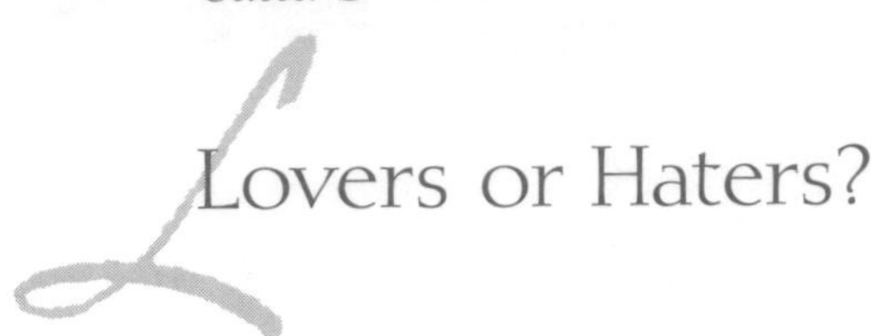

Lovers or Haters?

"The man who loves his life will lose it, while the man who hates his life in this world will keep it for eternal life." (John 12:25

In Word Human nature wants it all. We want to live for-ever in God's presence, but we're reluctant to sacrifice anything i the meantime. We want heaven on earth as well as heaven in heaven. The fact that this is a spiritual impossibility doesn't faze us. We want it anyway.

Jesus doesn't offer His disciples an impossibility. He speaks harsh realities. We must make a choice: Invest ourselves in this life—which is passing and subject to decay—or invest in the king-dom of God—which is eternal. There is no "all of the above" in Jesus' gospel presentation. It's either one or the other.

This is hard on us, especially those of us who have been trained to believe only what we see. We see this life; we want to be comfortable in it. We strive to regain Eden, creating our insu-lated lifestyles and filling them with conveniences and pleasures It just isn't within our human nature to forsake all that the world offers us for a kingdom we can't even see. But Jesus never calls u to live according to our human nature; He calls us to die. The Or who likens Himself to a grain of wheat that falls into the ground and dies, only to produce more wheat in the long run, tells His disciples to do the same. He is the prototype; we are the follower Just as He makes His choice between the Cross and this passing world, so must we. There is no middle ground. We have to pick sides.

In Deed Can you honestly say that you hate your life ir this world? Or at least that your hope in eternal life pales your here-and-now plans by comparison? If not, Jesus calls you to rac cally change your perspective. You cannot hang on to your visib life and your eternal life at the same time. One must be forsaken Which will it be?

> *"A man's greatest care should be for that place where he dwelleth longest; eternity should be his scope."*
>
> *—Thomas Manton*

Believers or Followers?

"Whoever serves me must follow me." (John 12:26)

In Word Much of the emphasis of modern evangelism is to create believers in Jesus. Faith is the overriding concern. Considering the overwhelming emphasis on faith in the Bible, this is an appropriate focus. But what kind of faith do we promote? What kind of faith does Jesus expect?

Jesus makes it clear that faith in Him does not mean simply an intellectual agreement with His claims. No, to believe in Jesus is to serve Him and follow Him. It is absolutely meaningless to claim faith in Jesus and then live contrary to His teachings with no apparent interest in aligning ourselves with them. Faith means hanging the entire balance of our lives on His claims and His commands. It means not only accepting Him as our Savior, but following Him as our Lord. To separate these two roles of Jesus is to make Him into something He is not, and it is to make our beliefs almost meaningless. Whoever believes Him, loves Him, serves Him—that person *will* follow Him. Whoever does not follow Him does not serve Him, love Him, or really even believe in Him.

"You must be willing to follow if you want God to lead."

-Anonymous

So what does it mean to follow Jesus? It means that wherever He is, that's where we'll be. Is He at the right hand of the Father? Then we who follow are seated there with Him (Ephesians 2:6). Is He on the Cross? Then we who follow Him are there also (Galatians 2:20). Is He in prisons and slums? Then we will be there too. Wherever God is reconciling this vile world in Christ, that's where Jesus' true followers will be.

In Deed Ask yourself the hard questions about your discipleship. Are you a believer or a follower? In modern English, there's a difference. But in Jesus' vocabulary, each of those words implies the other. To believe in Him means to serve Him, as He commanded; and to serve means to follow.

Where are you willing to follow Jesus? Many will follow Him as long as He does not rearrange their lives. But this isn't true following; it's self-deception. Jesus will often take us where we are reluctant to go. If we serve Him, we will go anyway.

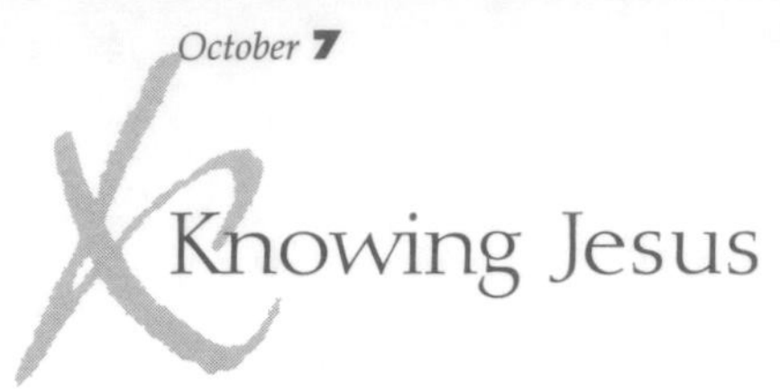

Knowing Jesus

"I tell you that one greater than the temple is here."

(Matthew 12:

In Word One of the most mind-boggling tendencies of human beings is to zero in on the trappings of our faith at the expense of its substance. This applies to all faiths of all times, bu never is the error so grievous as when we do this with the Son o God. In this story in Matthew 12, the Pharisees are more concerned with the Sabbath and the temple than they are with the Lord of the Sabbath and the One who inhabits the temple. They major on the details but miss the big picture.

We also have peripherals that we obsess about. On Sunday mornings, we often experience worship services without experiencing worship. We sometimes conduct Bible studies without fellowshiping with the Author. We do works of ministry without relying on the One who would minister through us, if we'd let Him. We pray our prayers without conversing with the Spirit wh inhabits them and hears them. We are so prone to digress from a relationship with Jesus Himself to the religion that makes Him it object, that we must guard ourselves daily. Someone greater thar all of our activities and beliefs is here.

> ***"There is but one thing in the world really worth pursuing—the knowledge of God."***
>
> **—Robert Hugh Benson**

In Deed Which elements of your faith are religious activity? Which are part of a genuine relationship with the Savior? Ca you still distinguish between the two? We easily criticize the Pharisees for their blindness to the God who walked among ther but we can be just as blind. It doesn't take long to digress from knowing Christ to practicing Christianity. And we are far too easily diverted to the latter.

It is sadly common for Jesus to become Someone we talk *about*—the historical Founder of our faith—rather than Someone we talk *to*—the Keeper of our hearts. Daily redirect your attentio from the outward signs of our faith to the Person who gives us our faith. Know the One who walks with you.

For Such a Reply

"For such a reply, you may go; the demon has left your daughter." (Mark 7:29)

In Word Jesus has just told a woman exactly what she didn't want to hear. She came to Him in desperate need, falling at His feet, crying out on behalf of her demon-possessed daughter. Jesus' response seems callous and brutal: "You're a dog, a Gentile, a foreigner with no claim to the Jewish Messiah." Was this tongue-in-cheek? An inside joke? Was there a twinkle in His eye that softened the cruelty of its content? We don't know. What we do know is that she persisted, and Jesus responded positively. Her persistence was no affront. It honored Him.

Let not our prayers die while our Intercessor lives." -Anonymous

Often God's initial answer to us after a prayer is not His final word; it is a test. It is given to see how we will respond. Is it a response of faith and trust? Or a response of complaint? The nature of the reply may determine the result we see. We will either honor Him with a confident declaration of His merciful nature that gives to "dogs" like us; or we will dishonor Him with resentment and resignation. In either case, He may or may not give us the answer we expected or hoped for. But when we respond in faith, He *will* answer, one way or another. It is inconceivable that He would ignore those who fall at His feet and pray to Him in faith and on His terms.

In Deed We have many responses to unanswered prayer. We may try to assert our "rights" and demand God's intervention on our terms. We may grow critical, forgetful of His unwavering love for us. Or we may just get discouraged and resign ourselves to His apparent lack of concern.

How do you respond when Jesus answers "not a word"? Do you turn away in bitterness? That's certainly not what He wanted. His desire is to see us profess our knowledge of who He is, even when the superficial evidence we see seems to contradict His true nature. He welcomes persistence, He expects faith, and He sympathizes with those who know their desperate need.

Authority for Life

"I have given you authority to trample on snakes and scorpions and to overcome all the power of the enemy; nothing will harm you." (Luke 10:19

"No soldiers of Christ are ever lost, missing, or left dead on the battlefield."
—J. C. Ryle

In Word The Christian life presents difficulties that we would never have encountered before our faith in Jesus. We struggle with sin as never before; we have entered into a warfare that harasses us with crippling or distracting circumstances daily, or even hourly; and we are called to a ministry that requires great persistence and endurance. It's easy in the midst of this battle we call "life" to feel downtrodden, overwhelmed, burdened, and even trapped. We grow tired and may feel that there is no way out of our situation.

But there is a way through it. God has given us the privilege of worship, which elevates our perspective to see God as all-encompassing and our problems and battles as incredibly small. And, as this text indicates, He has given us authority. Snakes, scorpions, and the power of the enemy are under our rule in Christ, not rulers over us. The burdens of life, the threats of temptation, the urge to give up, the circumstances that harass us—all are found to be insubstantial when we realize our authority and the size of the God who gave it to us. Jesus is Lord over everything the enemy can throw at us.

In Deed It is not God's will for us to be bound by circumstances or to be crippled in battle. It is not His will that we live discouraged lives or just function day-to-day. It is His will for us to have abundant life—a consistent, joyful celebration of the triumph we now have and will fully realize in our eternal position in Christ.

How do we get there? A big hint is given in verse 20. While the enemy would have us focus on his scorpions and snakes, overwhelmed with his power, Jesus would have us looking elsewhere: on the eternal prize. Rejoicing that our names are written in heaven is the key to the burdens of life getting smaller and God getting bigger in our eyes. Our pictures are in the King's family album. *That's* authority.

Extraordinary Love

"My command is this: Love each other as I have loved you." (John 15:12)

In Word Admiration for Jesus' message of love is almost universal. In spite of all our admiration, though, it is rarely followed. We have no trouble with the idea that we are to love each other—by our definition of love. But Jesus raises the bar on love—*His* definition is the substance of this command. We are to love each other *just as He has loved us.*

What does this mean for us? In order to know, we must find out how He loves us. How does He define love? By serving His disciples—washing their feet, to be exact—He "showed them the full extent of his love" (John 13:1). It was a highly symbolic demonstration of the ultimately sacrificial love that Jesus refers to in verse 13: "Greater love has no one than this, that he lay down his life for his friends."

This is an extraordinary love. It isn't natural for us. In fact, it's virtually impossible. We want to love others this way, but we don't. We hold it as an ideal, but we hardly ever live up to it. Was Jesus being unrealistic? Does He really expect fallen, corrupted human beings to behave like the divine Son of God?

He loved us not because we were lovable, but because He is love."
—C. S. Lewis

In Deed Jesus knows our feeble efforts at love. It is no coincidence that this verse comes immediately after His teaching on the branch's relationship to the vine. Love is a form of bearing fruit, and Jesus is emphatic that we can bear no fruit on our own (v. 5). It is by our abiding in Him, and by His abiding in us, that fruit happens. It is by the same union that love happens.

If we attempt to love others as Jesus loves us, we will fail. We can try to muster up feelings, but they will fall short. We can try to love independently of our feelings, but it will be a hollow, lifeless love. No, there is no remedy for our lovelessness other than the living Vine bearing fruit through His branches. He is the source. Do you want greater love for others? Bask in His love, and see what happens next.

Divided Souls

"Do you want to get well?" (John 5:6

In Word It's an obvious question, isn't it? The man has been an invalid for 38 years and was hanging out at a pool allege to have mystical healing powers. The Son of God, with all of His insight into peoples' hearts, comes to him with a no-brainer of a question. "Do you want to get well?" Everyone at the pool could have anticipated the answer. All the signs were right there on the surface.

But Jesus always goes beneath the surface. He understands well the divided minds we fallen people have. He knows that sometimes, as much as we think we want change, we're comfortable with the status quo. Did this invalid *really* want to get well? He doesn't even give an answer, just an excuse: When the water stirs, no one helps him in the pool (v. 7). No one to help? *For 38 years?* Mixed motives make for slow responses. Surely tired of being an invalid, he probably also feared the dramatic change in his life that healing would bring (v. 14 may indicate why). Jesus had to confront him with a pointed question, as if to say, "Are yo ready for what will happen to you when you've really encountered Me?"

"Change is not made without inconvenience, even from worse to better."

—Richard Hooker

In Deed Aren't we like the invalid? We say we want to be delivered of our sins, but we still look for ways to be tempted by them. We say we're done with some bad attitude, but we continue to think the thoughts that cultivate it. We want to have our prayers answered, but wonder if people will still give us attentio or sympathy when they are. We ask to be filled with His Spirit, but are scared to death of what He'll have us do. We'd love freedom, but are comfortable captives. We want to change, but we don't want to change. We're divided souls.

Jesus comes to us with the same pointed question: "Do you want to get well?" It's not as obvious as it seems. We must be pre pared for radical change if we want a real encounter with Him. We must be willing to leave old ways behind. If we really want to know Him, we must first know that nothing will ever be the sam again.

Facing Hostility

"It is enough for the student to be like his teacher, and the servant like his master. If the head of the house has been called Beelzebub, how much more the members of his household!" (Matthew 10:25)

In Word Perhaps Jesus' disciples thought that following Him was the way to victory, by earthly definitions. Perhaps they thought Jesus might usher in a new culture of harmony and peace. Perhaps His followers today think the same thing. If so, His words are more than a little discomforting. He prepares them for hostility, persecution, and even death. His kingdom will clash with all others.

The hostility that was present in the leaders of Jesus' day is present in our day as well. Our society claims to seek wisdom and respect spirituality, but it turns vicious at the mention of an exclusive path to God. We see a strange phenomenon in our culture: Jesus is almost universally respected as a "good teacher," yet His actual teachings—many of them, anyway—are almost universally reviled. This wise, holy teacher spoke not only of love, peace, and devotion to God, but also of sin, hell, and the evil heart of man. Even worse, He asserted that He was the only way to God. When His followers assert the same, respect proves as illusory as it did for Him; we are reviled as He was. That's the way of the world, and if we follow Him long enough, we will have to face it.

The servant of Christ must never be surprised if he has to drink of the same cup with his Lord." –J. C. Ryle

In Deed Much of the Christian life is tension between two impulses: the desire to be liked and respected by the world, and the desire to know God and be like Jesus. These two impulses cannot thrive together; one must be subdued. Unfortunately, many have chosen the former, compromising their faith in the uncompromising Christ. Jesus urges His disciples to make a better choice. Though hostility and persecution are not enjoyable, they are the last gasps of a dying kingdom—the kingdom of human pride. They are temporary attacks on an eternal reign. We must walk the way of the Teacher, no matter the cost.

Obeying God's Heart

"Which is lawful on the Sabbath: to do good or to do evil, to save life or to kill?" (Mark 3:4

In Word This verse is about the Sabbath, a critical issue for the Pharisees and, if we're honest, a critical aspect of God's revelation for humanity. We cannot dismiss the importance of the Sabbath if we hold any value in Old Testament teaching; it is central to one of the Ten Commandments and a consistent scriptural gauge of devotion to God. But, according to Jesus, it isn't to be deified. Neither is any other element of law. God's dictates are vitally important; but our interpretation of them is never meant to conflict with His character.

We may not get as riled up about Sabbath-breaking as the Pharisees did, but we have the same tendency to get the letter of the law confused with the substance of God's heart. It may not be Old Testament law that restricts us; we all have church traditions and Christian methodology that give us the rules we crave. But whatever is done in legalism at the expense of spiritual vitality and true worship irks Jesus profoundly. His reaction to the synagogue leaders is unsettling: "He looked around at them in anger" and was "deeply distressed at their stubborn hearts" (v. 5).

None of us wants Jesus to be deeply distressed at our stubbornness. But we may assume that this is how He reacts to us when we value form over substance.

"If the Spirit of grace is absent, the Law is present only to convict and kill."

—St. Augustine

In Deed God is holy, and we must conform to His holiness. This means restrictions on our behavior, because our behavior was once governed by fallen human nature and well-trained in following its godless impulses. But when the restraints become the essence of our faith, we are far from the heart of God. According to the Word, this distresses Jesus deeply. Faith in Him is not primarily about restrictions; those are just useful tools. Faith is about following His character. That's the whole point of obedience. It's an issue of our heart—and His.

Returning to God's Heart

"Which is lawful on the Sabbath: to do good or to do evil, to save life or to kill?" (Mark 3:4)

"God is not deceived by externals."
–C. S. Lewis

In Word Why is Jesus so emotional in this passage? He does not simply condemn the Pharisees' misunderstanding of the Law; He glares at them in anger and is "deeply distressed" (v. 5). Throughout the Gospels He encounters overtly immoral prostitutes and dishonest tax collectors without expressing any such revulsion. But the deception of the religious leaders is different. And this isn't the only time they have evoked such a reaction from Him. On other occasions, He calls them things like "whitewashed tombs," "snakes," and "blind fools" (Matthew 23, among other texts). What makes their sin so much worse? Why is He so hard on them? They're just trying to obey God, aren't they?

The sin of the hypocritically religious is not necessarily more offensive to God than other sins. All sin falls short of His glory and exchanges the eternal for the corruptible. He is offended and grieved by it all. But unlike other, more obvious sins, religious hypocrisy is hard to return from. Once you are there, it's incredibly difficult to find your way out. The sins of the flesh are easily recognizable, and those who commit them know their corruption. All they must do is acknowledge their sin and repent. But the sins of hypocrisy are subtle and deceptive. They are a matter of motives, which are hidden deep in our hearts, often even out of our own view. In order to repent of them, we must see them. And seeing them is the hard part.

In Deed The most loving thing Jesus can do for the self-deceived is to verbally rake them over the coals. We think He is being unloving when He rebukes fools and vipers. But He is actually being compassionate, trying to jolt them out of their illusion. We must let Him do the same for us—at times, we are all hypocritical. Sometimes His Word will wound us. He is brutally, lovingly honest. Suffer those wounds, if necessary. It's the way back to His heart.

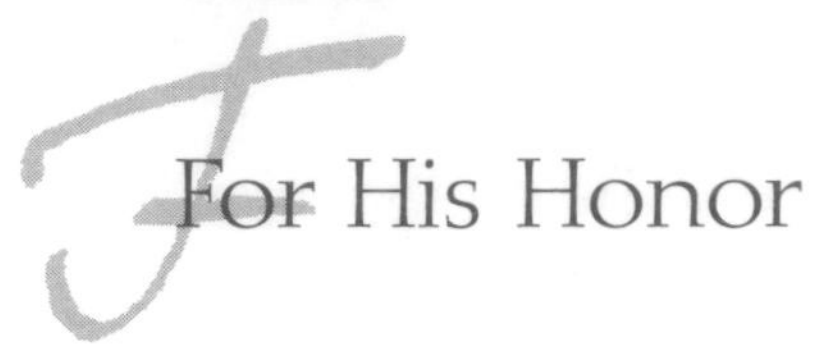

For His Honor

"Father, glorify your name!" (John 12:28

In Word One of the ways we can determine whether we are becoming Christlike is to see how we act in a crisis. When the pressure is on, what will we do? Or, even deeper, when the pressure is on, what motives will direct us?

Jesus came to the hour that He had long predicted. He was clear about His purpose in coming to Jerusalem; He would die there. The disciples couldn't understand it, but He had foretold the Cross and Resurrection numerous times. And now the hour had come.

It wasn't a pleasant hour. Nothing in human flesh—even tha of the divine Son of God—enjoys suffering. Jesus does not ask God to save Him from this hour in John 12 (v. 27), but when He gets to the Garden of Gethsemane, He wants to know if it's possi ble for the cup of suffering to pass Him by (Matthew 26, Mark 14 Luke 22). Human nature is often so ambivalent; the spirit is willing, but the flesh is very, very weak. Even God, when clothed in human flesh, wanted the less painful way. But—and here's the measure for us—in the middle of His crisis, one motive still guided Him: He preferred the glory of God's name over His owr self-preservation. God's reputation weighed heavier on His heart than His own comfort and life.

"Man's chief work is the praise of God."

—St. Augustine

In Deed Are you becoming Christlike? It is God's plan for you to be conformed to the image of His Son. But how can yc know if you're growing toward that goal? Examine your motives especially in the midst of a crisis. What is your agenda? Do you prefer the glory of God to your own escape? When it really come down to it, what would you sacrifice for His glory?

Jesus sacrificed a huge following, His school of disciples, His comfort and health, His current reputation, and even His life in order that God's name might be honored. Would you?

Healing Power

"Daughter, your faith has healed you. Go in peace."
(Luke 8:48)

In Word This is what we all desperately want to hear. We have a very limited and physical understanding of it; we want it to apply to all of our infirmities, especially the ills of our body. Jesus certainly doesn't rule that out; He frequently heals physical diseases. But when He doesn't heal ours, we tend to go to the opposite extreme, claiming that He doesn't mean this physically at all. That's wrong; the God of the Old Testament said He heals His people (Exodus 15:26), and He means it very concretely. This Jesus is the God of the Old Testament incarnate; He means it no less concretely.

In spite of this blessed awareness of the power of God to heal, we still know that it does not apply at all times and in all circumstances. Every human being since Jesus has gotten sick and died, without exception. Even those cultists who claim that their interpretation of Scripture precludes illness eventually get sick and die. It's part of our fallenness in this world, and no matter how thoroughly Jesus has saved us, He never promises to perfect the body. He will resurrect it. That implies that it first must fall victim to the wages of sin.

What does His healing power mean to us, then? It does not mean that we forever avoid the decay that has befallen all mankind. It means that there is an ultimate answer to this problem. Sometimes we are given signs of it now—amazing, glorious signs of physical healing. Sometimes we die with the promise on our lips. Either way, the answer is sure. Jesus will heal.

"The same power that brought Christ back from the dead is operative in those who are Christ's."
– Leon Morris

In Deed Yes, we are the walking wounded, it's true. Sooner or later, all of us can relate. But there's a Healer who walks with us. He means for us to depend on Him with everything that's in us. He does not push us through this world simply to survive. He leads us that we might overcome. Hang on to that hope. Whether you see it today or not, His power does not fail. It cannot. Your faith has healed you, and it will always heal you. Live with His peace.

True Worship

"God is spirit, and his worshipers must worship in spirit and in truth." (John 4:24

"This is adoration; not a difficult religious exercise, but an attitude of the soul."

—Evelyn Underhill

In Word The greatest pleasure of the Christian life is worship, though we scarcely realize it until we've dived in wholeheartedly. We approach it at first as an obligation. We're fairly self-focused, and it's hard to turn our hearts toward God. But if we do, in spirit and in truth (i.e., with zealous inspiration and according to who God really is), we find inexpressible delights. Jesus seeks to turn us, like the woman at the well, into worshipers with substance rather than worshipers of ritual. How do we make that change?

Many of us ask God this question: "What is my responsibility toward You?" While not a bad question, there is a better, more heart-warming question: "What can I offer You to show my devotion?"

Do you see the difference? The first question presupposes a requirement we must meet. It almost assumes that there will be a minimum standard, and after having met it, we will cease our God-ward activity and resume our self-ward obsession. The second question presupposes a desire to express love and devotion. It assumes that there can never be enough we can offer Him, but whatever we can find to offer, we will. There is no self-focus in it at all; it is entirely enamored with God.

In Deed Jesus would have us not ask which requirements we are to fulfill, but what more of ourselves we can offer Him. When we look for our required obligation, we do not worship in spirit, because the Spirit of God would not inspire us to fulfill quotas of devotion. And we do not worship in truth, because we underestimate God's worth. He is worth all we are, and more.

Blessed is the worshiper who can truthfully—and with pleasure—say to the Lord: "What can I do for You? You name it, it's Yours. Whatever I can offer You, please let me." This is the kind of worshiper the Father seeks.

First on His Agenda

"The Spirit will take from what is mine and make it known to you." (John 16:15)

In Word The things we often crave the most from the Holy Spirit are His direction and His power. We want Him as our guide and our enabler. We want to know which relationships He wants us to focus on, which career direction to take, and which area of service to perform. Then we want Him to empower us to perform these things. And this is well within the ability and the assigned role of the Spirit to give us. Jesus has promised it to us. Everything that He would be for us if He were physically present, as He was for the disciples, is ours in the gift of His Spirit. The Spirit makes Jesus known to us in every way.

But the Holy Spirit has higher priorities for us than the ones for which we usually beseech Him. First and foremost He wants to give us the guidance and power to be holy—to be sanctified. He wants to bring to life the cleansing words of Jesus and make the kingdom of God the treasure of our heart. The guidance about careers, relationships, and service—and the power to perform them well—are primary in our mind, but secondary in His. In order to receive them, they must be secondary in ours as well. We want works, then character. He insists on reversing the order.

'Be ye holy' is the great and fundamental law of our faith."

–Matthew Henry

In Deed Have you sought special guidance from the Holy Spirit? Have you pleaded with Him for His power? Is there some act of service, area of ministry, or life decision that occupies your thoughts? Perhaps the Holy Spirit wants to meet you there, but has a prior item on His agenda. Perhaps He is waiting to fulfill His primary purpose for you before moving on to His secondary purpose. If He were to follow our agenda, we would move from one area of service to another without ever being made into His likeness. But He wants first things first. Let Him have His way. Let Him saturate you with Jesus' words and ways. Make His holiness your first pursuit. Then God will be glorified in everything you do.

Coming to Him

"Many will say to me on that day, 'Lord, Lord, did we not prophesy in your name, and in your name drive ou demons and perform many miracles?' Then I will tell them plainly, 'I never knew you. Away from me, you evildoers!' "

(Matthew 7:22-2

"Whoever comes to me I will never drive away."

(John 6:3

"Christianity is not a religion but a relationship of love expressed toward God and men."

—Sherwood Eliot Wirt

In Word Clearly, many people come to Jesus with a false security that they are His servants. His words to them in Matthew 7 are sobering and chilling, especially for those of us who know that, in spite of our intentions, we can often be insincere in our faith.

On the other hand, some of the most comforting words Jesus ever spoke are found in John 6. He will never drive away those who come to Him, and it is the Father's will that "everyone who looks to the Son and believes in Him shall have eternal life" (v. 40). What is the difference?

The difference is that those who are cast away from Him wer performers. They came to Him on the basis of their deeds—that's all they appeal to, isn't it?—and not on the basis of faith in His deeds. Perhaps they came to the Christian religion or to the church; but they didn't come to *Him.*

In Deed Those who are genuinely His are those who came to *Him.* They invested all of their hopes in His work, His faithfulness, His teaching, His fellowship, and His death and resurrection. There is an intimacy implied here that the "Lord, Lord' people do not have. There has been a true partaking of the Bread of Life—a willingness to ingest His very person and nature so tha it becomes the life of the believer. Impressive works can never do that.

Are you subconsciously trying to impress Jesus? Don't. Eat o His bread and be nourished by His presence. It's the substance of genuine life.

Foreigners

"If you belonged to the world, it would love you as its own." (John 15:19)

In Word Christians must make their relationship with Christ their foremost preoccupation. But we must also be aware of our relationship with the world. From time to time, we must ask ourselves whether we are living as citizens of heaven in a foreign land or as citizens of this world looking forward to a foreign kingdom. If we find ourselves with the latter point of view, it's time to rearrange some priorities.

Having been born as descendants of Adam, thoroughly indoctrinated in the ways of this world, it is often difficult to remember just how alien our life in Christ is to this fallen planet. But we have been born of something entirely different than corruptible human flesh. We have been born "not of natural descent . . . but born of God" (John 1:13). We have radically different origins than we might have thought.

"If you keep in step with God, you'll be out of step with the world."
–Anonymous

This is why Jesus speaks often of the persecution His disciples will face. "I have chosen you out of the world. That is why the world hates you," He tells them (v. 19). There is no softening of this blow, no encouragement to get along as well as they can with the culture they live in. It is an ominous warning, one that many of us will never realize in the same way the disciples did. But we will experience the tension it foretells nonetheless.

In Deed Have you felt discouraged when there is friction between you and this world because of your identity in Christ? The clash of cultures between the kingdom of God and the kingdom of this world can be frustrating. But let it encourage you. Remember that it is a sign of your foreign citizenship. It is evidence of your relationship with the eternal Son of God, who also did not receive a king's welcome here. It would be much more troubling if all was well between you and your culture. Know that becoming like the Master is the greatest thing a servant can do, and rejoice that your relationship with Him is taking precedence over your relationship with the world.

Snakes and Doves

"Be as shrewd as snakes and as innocent as doves."

(Matthew 10:1

In Word Jesus could not have given us an instruction more laden with meaningful imagery than this. We read it and know exactly what comes to mind when we think of snakes and doves. Where have we heard of these before in Scripture? The ser pent of old "was more crafty than any of the wild animals the LORD God had made" (Genesis 3:1). And the Holy Spirit descend like a dove (Matthew 3:16). We are to be as shrewd as the serpent knowing his tactics. And we are to be as innocent as a dove, indwelt by the Holy Spirit of God. This is the prescription for any Christian who wants to be useful in God's service—always aware of evil, yet powerfully uncorrupted by it.

"Conquer evil men by your gentle kindness."

—Isaac of Syria

There is a profound implication to Jesus' words—a foreshadowing of the battles we face as His disciples. He has just commissioned His disciples to go and preach, heal, and give. Those whom He has sent will face a shrewd, malevolent resistance. And the safeguard against that evil is purity.

In Deed The world is full of snakes. There are crafty rep tiles under the command of the master serpent who have laid traps all over this world of need. They use an array of weapons—physical, emotional, philosophical, psychological, and, above all, spiritual. We are told by Jesus to be very aware of his strategies, as was Paul, who said: "We are not unaware of his schemes" (2 Corinthians 2:11). If we are too casual about the danger, we are apt to fall into it.

Interestingly, Jesus does not tell us to be shrewd and then act shrewdly. He tells us to be shrewd and then act innocently. While our awareness is to measure up to the most devious plans the enemy has, our actions are to measure up to the pure, gentle char acter of God. Our attitudes are at war with a conniving enemy; our behavior refuses to engage him. Is this where you struggle? Remember when you encounter snakelike attacks not to respond in kind. Be a dove.

Big Mountains

"I tell you the truth, if you have faith as small as a mustard seed, you can say to this mountain, 'Move from here to there' and it will move. Nothing will be impossible for you." (Matthew 17:20)

In Word The key to having mountain-moving faith is not the size of our faith. A mustard seed's worth is enough. The key to this faith is the size of our God. And there is no shortfall there. Jesus is clear: Nothing will be impossible.

Why, then, don't we experience dramatic answers to our prayers as often as we'd like? If our faith isn't too small—and it's hard to get smaller than a mustard seed, so that can't be the problem—and our God is so big, what's the problem? It's a matter of perception. Though God is big, our expectations for Him are not. Or they are misplaced. One way or another, they do not accurately reflect His power *and* His goodness *and* His wisdom. We misunderstand one of these three attributes. The answer to the immobility of our mountains is within us: It all depends on how we see God.

Our inclination is to pray that God will move our mountains—according to our wisdom—so that we can see Him as able and willing. In His mercy, He sometimes answers. But God's inclination is to reverse the order. He wants us to see Him as able and willing before we pray. Then we will see mountains move—according to His wisdom.

"Faith, mighty faith, the promise sees, and looks to that alone; laughs at all impossibilities and cries: It shall be done."

—Charles Wesley

In Deed Are there issues that overwhelm you? Relax and rejoice! God is teaching you an invaluable lesson about Himself. If you are crushed under the burden, He has you in a good place. He will drive us to this place whenever our problems are large and He is small in our eyes. He will let us be defeated so that we'll have no choice but to turn our eyes toward Him. He will let us come to the end of our own abilities in order to accomplish His desire. What is this desire? For us to see Him as so large that everything else becomes small. But the mountains will usually remain until we see Him this way. Faith precedes experience.

Big Prayers

" 'If you can'?" (Mark 9:23)

In Word Many times when we are confronted with an "impossible" situation, we tend to ask God to help alleviate the symptoms rather than to intervene in a mighty way. It's as though we are afraid of asking too much. We just don't see miracles that often, so we assume God isn't interested in doing them. But to the contrary, according to the Bible, He is intensely interested in intervening in our situations. He is waiting for simple, believing, worshipful hearts.

Such was the case with the father whose son was possessed by a destructive spirit that "robbed him of speech" (v. 17). Everyone, including Jesus' disciples, tried to help. No one could. What was Jesus' response? Did He rebuke them for assuming too much from Him? No, He rebuked them for their unbelief (v. 19). When the father appealed to Jesus—"if you can do anything . . . "—Jesus finds the hint of uncertainty ludicrous. " 'If you can'?" He repeats incredulously. Of course He can. He's God incarnate, the One by whom the father and the mute boy and the surrounding crowds were created. He is not limited by the situation itself in any way.

"Large asking and large expectation on our part honor God."

—A. L. Stone

In Deed Do our prayers also undermine Jesus' mastery of a situation in our own minds? Do we also hint that He might not be able to do what we ask? That the circumstances might just be too overwhelming even for Him? Jesus would lovingly mock us as well with the same response: "If you can?" Of course He can. His adequacy is not the question. And because no situation is bigger than He, neither is any prayer. Our requests should be huge. The issue for us is not whether He can, but knowing His will and His ways—and assuming the best of them.

Jesus really may answer our prayers exactly the way we expect Him to—or He may not. But He *always* stands ready to intervene in response to our belief. *Never* does He refuse a persistent, patient, trusting plea for His involvement. He is always willing. And He always can.

Big God

"I tell you the truth, if you have faith as small as a mustard seed, you can say to this mountain, 'Move from here to there' and it will move. Nothing will be impossible for you." (Matthew 17:20)

In Word Many times we put our faith in faith. We take Jesus' teaching about mustard seeds and mountains to mean that faith is the object we are to desire most. But we must be careful. Though Jesus is consistent and frequent in His praise of faith, He never says that faith is the end of the matter. It is not faith in our own ability to have faith that is the key to answered prayer. It is faith in *Him.*

A bleeding woman came to Jesus for help in Matthew 9:20-22. She never said to herself, "If only I can muster up enough faith, I will be healed." Rather, she says: "If I only touch his cloak, I will be healed." Jesus is the object of her faith. He commends her unbridled pursuit of Him and His power, not the self-cultivation of spiritual development. In her mind, there is nothing of herself in this pursuit—no strain to believe more, no determination to be better or to grow in knowledge. It's simply Jesus. He is the variable that matters.

Jesus' commendation of faith is a far cry from some modern ministries' emphasis on the faith of the believer. In fact, if we stressed the power of Jesus and never considered the quantity of our faith, we would be in a league with those whom Jesus rewards with words of approval. The substance of faith is never what matters; it's the object of faith. How much we have isn't the issue. It's the One in whom we trust.

You might as well shut your eyes and look inside to see whether you have sight, as to look inside and discover if you have faith."

–Hannah Whitall Smith

In Deed Have you struggled to have more faith? Take your eyes off your faith and put them on God. Your understanding of God *is* your faith. Your belief will never grow larger; your view of God will. Meditate on His grandeur and you'll find yourself trusting Him more. And you'll also find that nothing is impossible.

Big Answers

"Rise and go; your faith has made you well." (Luke 17:19

In Word We know that all blessings come from God. He is the author of all that is good, and all we receive comes from His grace, not our merits. Knowing this, we might ask why Jesus says it is the faith of this leper that has made him well. Why doesn't He say: "Rise and go; *I* have made you well"? Or "the Father has made you well"? Why does everything seem to depend on the faith of the recipient?

Perhaps faith is the currency of heaven like dollars are the currency of the American economy. Perhaps God's own ground rules for this planet limit Him to intervening in the affairs of man only when asked with a right understanding of who He is. Perhaps faith is a mystery we will never comprehend this side of heaven. Regardless of the reason, it is solidly biblical. God responds to faith in Him, and He often withholds His blessing when faith is absent. When faith is gone, God seems distant. And when faith is great, God reveals Himself as greater still.

An awful lot depends on how we see God. If we see God as hard and begrudging, we will find Him to be so, both to His and our own disappointment. When we see Him as able, willing, loving, magnificent, and awesome, we will find Him to be so, to His and our own delight. This is not just a matter of psychology, in which the faithful and the faithless receive the same blessings but value them differently. It is a matter of a living relationship with an available God. When we open our mouths wide, He fills them (Psalm 81:10). When we don't, He doesn't.

"Praying without faith is like trying to cut with a blunt knife—much labor expended to little purpose."
—James O. Fraser

In Deed Does God seem absent? Unavailable? Slow to act and as overwhelmed by your problems as you are? There are times when He may test our faith in this way. But it is more likely that He is acting in exactly the way your faith expects Him to. You want big answers to your prayers? Pray big prayers, and *know* the size of the God you seek.

Big Faith

"According to your faith will it be done to you."
(Matthew 9:29)

"Faith is the bird that sings while it is yet dark."
—*Max Lucado*

In Word This is both discomforting and liberating. It is discomforting because we don't want so much to depend on us. We want God to intervene on our behalf regardless of how much faith we have, because we know how weak our faith is. But it can be liberating when we realize that sometimes the *only* hindrance to our prayers is our faith. All we must do is grow in faith, and then God will act.

The problem we face with this is the order. We say we will have greater faith when we see more of God. God says we will see more of Him when we have greater faith. The belief comes first. This causes us great trouble. We wish we could have more faith; we really want to, and we try to muster it up. But we need something to base that faith on, and when our own experience is lacking in the miraculous, our faith finds no footing. We know there is a level of the faith life that is satisfying, if only we can get there. We've heard others tell of it, and we believe them. We just don't think we have the means to get there.

In Deed Our two-fold solution is simple. First, we must ask God to increase our faith. This is how a father appealed to Jesus when his son was suffering (Mark 9:24), and Jesus honored his request. Second, we must base our faith in God on something other than our own experience, at least until our mind's beliefs become our heart's realities. The Bible is the answer. Meditate on the psalms and praises of the Word. Worship Him for His goodness, His love, His power, His protection, and more. Saturate your life in His praise, and God will grow huge in your own eyes. And when He is huge, huge things happen—according to your faith.

Jesus first made the blind men acknowledge His ability (v. 28). Only then did He answer. Faith is nothing in itself. It's the object of our faith that matters. You want big faith? Worship a big God. The rest comes naturally.

Great Expectations

"According to your faith will it be done to you."

(Matthew 9:2

In Word Jesus speaks frequently of "great" faith. In one place, He could do no miracles because there was no faith there. He did not rebuke people who asked to have greater faith. Faith apparently a very measurable thing.

But just because faith is measurable does not mean it is just a matter of quantity. It is also a matter of quality. Faith is qualified not only by its object, but by its appropriateness. The object of ou faith is God—He is large enough to accomplish anything on behalf of those who believe in Him. But the appropriateness of our faith is another matter. We can trust in God's ability without knowing anything of His ways. We can believe that He *might* me our need without any understanding of whether He wants to. And our suspicion of Him at this point is often the flaw in our belief.

Expectant faith is not assuming that whatever we name we can claim. But neither is it simply a trust in His ability without any knowledge of His willingness. We *know* God can do great things on our behalf; we seldom believe that He will. Before Jesu ever asked the blind men in this story whether they believed He was able to heal them, they had already appealed to His willingness: "Have mercy on us," they cried out (v. 27). They already knew what He was like, and they counted on His grace to be applied to them.

"The reason why we obtain no more in prayer is because we expect no more."

—Richard Alleine

In Deed We often tacitly acknowledge God's omnipotence, His ability to intervene in our lives, even in very specific ways. But this is only half of faith. It has nothing to do with our expectations as long as it remains only a theological proposition. The other half of faith is understanding the mercy of God and H great willingness to intervene. This is what brings His glory from the realm of theology into the practicum of our lives. You want mercy and power? Expect mercy and power. And it will be done to you.

His Mission and Ours

"The Son of Man came to seek and to save what was lost." (Luke 19:10)

In Word Think of the odd assortment of people to whom Jesus was drawn. In this passage, it's a dishonest tax collector. Elsewhere, it's a prostitute, a raging, demon-possessed lunatic, an adulteress, beggars, lepers, and just about everyone else who had no legitimate case to make about their own righteousness and well-being. His harshest words were reserved for the self-righteous, those who thought they needed nothing more than what they already had. They were just as lost, but could not know it unless they were directly confronted. The overt sinners, though, knew it already. They needed help.

If Christ was so drawn to sinners, why isn't the body of Christ equally drawn? Many of us can hardly say we live to seek and save what is lost. We often act as if we live to affirm and support what is superior. We tend to avoid the unseemly and cultivate the faithful. Cultivating the faithful is good, as Jesus spent three years doing so with His disciples. But His search for that which was lost and broken was zealous and relentless. Is ours?

"When the Spirit of God comes into a man, He gives him a world-wide outlook."
—Oswald Chambers

In Deed If our identity is in Jesus, and His Spirit is living in us, we will be drawn to others as He was. We will be brokenhearted about those who suffer in sinful, diseased conditions just as He was—and is—brokenhearted. The zeal of our search to bring His redemption into a captive world will in some way reflect His zeal. It will be a diagnostic measure of the reality of our union with Him.

Is this alarming? Perhaps for many of us it is. The knee-jerk reaction to the imperative of seeking and saving the lost is to try to cultivate a desire to do so. Resist the urge. Be aware of the need, but respond by cultivating your union with Jesus. You cannot muster up the appropriate zeal, but fellowship with His Spirit will make His agenda contagious to you and those around you. Let His mission become yours.

Hard Teachings

"You do not want to leave too, do you?" (John 6:67

In Word A huge controversy is brewing on the lakeshor Jesus has begun to talk about the necessity of eating His flesh anc drinking His blood, mentioning also that He came straight out of heaven to this planet. There are people there who cannot handle it. Not just observers, but "disciples"—people who have followec Him devotedly. They leave. And Jesus asks the Twelve if they plan to do the same.

The benefits of following Jesus are incredible. There are mira cles to be seen, lives to be changed, hearts to be softened, and deep, deep teachings to be absorbed. But it is a difficult path to follow. It involves recognizing who He really is, a theological stumbling block for many. It also involves not just following Hir as a separate individual, but consuming His flesh and drinking His blood—absorbing all that He is and taking on His own character and nature. And it inevitably involves moving in the direction of the Cross. (The Resurrection, too, of course, but the Cross comes first and often looms larger to human eyes.) The benefits c discipleship are great, but they come in a package with hard faitł and a rejection of our own nature. It's a difficult package to carry

"Discipleship is more than getting to know what the teacher knows. It is getting to be what He is."

—Juan Carlos Ortiz

In Deed Do you know people who are into Jesus for th benefits but shun the difficulties of discipleship? At all costs, avoid their example. They are like the disciples of John 6:66 and the seeds of Matthew 13:20-22. They follow Jesus in their minds but are far from Him in their hearts. They seem to have it made, enjoying the benefits of Christ and His body, but they probably c not really know Him—not with any depth, anyway. Jesus offers you a better way.

His way is more difficult. It means wrestling with His word just as the twelve disciples did. It means partaking in His flesh and His blood, with all its blows to the human ego and its abandonment of worldly goals. We cannot just observe Him; we mus become His flesh and blood. But there is truth and resurrection i His way. It is the way to life.

Our Significance

"I will not leave you as orphans; I will come to you."
(John 14:18)

In Word We crave significance. In our seemingly never-ending search for it, we look to those who love us, the opinions of others, the satisfaction of our own accomplishments, our positions and promotions, our pleasures, and many other false measures. Millions of dollars are spent every year on counselors who will help us find this sense of importance. People have ended their lives when it seems forever elusive. We want to know that we matter.

Anything we can find significance in will eventually prove empty. The trophies, the promotions, our work, our popularity, the love we crave—none of it lasts. Well, almost none. There's one source of significance that counts for *everything*: the fact that we are children of the Most High God.

"Best of all, God is with us."
-John Wesley

Jesus told His disciples—and through them, He tells us—that we are not orphans. We have a Father. We may think that children of presidents, kings, and the rich and famous are in a privileged position. Inwardly we are often jealous of them. But their privilege doesn't match ours, because their parents do not match ours. *Our* Father is the author of all that is—even of their parents' fame and power. Jesus tells us to pray to the Almighty God as "Father," John tells us that God gave to those who believe in Jesus the right to become His children (John 1:12), and Paul says the Spirit of God's Son is in our hearts crying out "Abba, Father" (Galatians 4:6).

In Deed Isn't it ridiculous that we search for significance in anything else? That's like trying to find beauty in graffiti when we're offered the works of Michelangelo. Why would we persist in such an absurdity?

Are you feeling unimportant? Lonely? Discouraged? Empty? Directionless? You are *not* an orphan. Meditate on your role as a child of the Most High. Let it really sink in. Let it consume you. It's incredibly significant.

The Dwelling Place

"Not one stone here will be left on another; every one will be thrown down." (Mark 13:2

In Word Throughout God's revelatory history, He has had a chosen dwelling place. In the wilderness and the early yea in the Promised Land, it was the tabernacle. After the reign of David, it was the Jerusalem temple. That temple had been rebuilt after Israel's captivity, and was being remodeled as Jesus spoke. I was an honor to God. Why, then, does Jesus herald—and apparently approve of—its destruction?

When Jesus walked this land, He Himself was God's chosen dwelling place. With the advent of the Holy Spirit into the hearts of those who believe, God's habitation is now those who are in Christ. We constitute a mobile, global body in which God lives and moves. No longer do people come from all nations to worship and pray to God in the building in which He dwells. The building in which He dwells goes into all nations.

"The worship of God is not a rule of safety—it is an adventure of the spirit."
—Alfred North Whitehead

The temple—the one composed of stones—was temporary and inadequate. It was an illustration of the temple to come, one made of living stones (1 Peter 2:5). As living stones, we have moved beyond superficial appearances and formal structures. Th worship of God is not contained in well-constructed walls, either literally or figuratively. As Jesus announced the downfall of the Jerusalem temple, so He stands before the worship of our lives and insists on the collapse of all that is superficial. We may no longer confine Him to one segment of our heart and say we'll meet Him there one day a week. Our walls cannot restrain Him.

In Deed What is your worship like? Is it like an archaic building, or is it fresh? Does the Spirit of God want to break out your rituals like a butterfly breaking out of a cocoon? You are no the dwelling place of the living God; you do not have the option of defining your parameters for worship or service. He will mov beyond your walls and take you wherever He wills—to new heights and new depths. And it will be glorious. Let the old ston fall.

God the Blesser

"If you, then, though you are evil, know how to give good gifts to your children, how much more will your Father in heaven give good gifts to those who ask him!"

(Matthew 7:11)

In Word Crying out to God in a situation of need is a normal—and universal—human experience. But when we cry out, what do we expect? Don't we often ask from a heart filled with despair, as though our prayer is only a shot in the dark? "I have no doubt He'll hear it," we think, "but He probably won't answer. I'll plead as a last resort, but I'm not holding my breath." In other words, we pray with high hopes but low expectations. We make false assumptions about our Father's willingness to give.

God's gifts put man's best dreams to shame."

Elizabeth Barrett Browning

God is a blesser by nature. He gave us life. He gave us a beautiful creation. He sustains our every moment of existence. We've rebelled and corrupted it all. And His response is merciful. Through miracle after miracle, He brought His people into a saving relationship with Him, and He has demonstrated His commitment throughout the millennia to continue saving. He gave us unequivocal, mind-boggling promises about the power of prayer. And yet we still think He might be reluctant to hear us in our hour of need.

In Deed This is what sin does to people. It corrupts our understanding of God. We come to see Him as a distant Sovereign who only rarely grants us His favor. We think He is reluctant to grace us with His gifts when, in fact, He constantly gives us His grace. With pretty strong language, Jesus attacks this distorted concept of the Father. It is an abominable view that assumes God's generosity is comparable to man's. No, Jesus says. God blesses. Lavishly. Far beyond our comprehension. It's who He is.

Every petition must begin here. We pray without faith—and therefore without much result—when we start with a lesser view of God. The one who comes to God with the assumption that He blesses will find that He actually does.

Servant Hearts

"You also, when you have done everything you were told to do, should say, 'We are unworthy servants; we have only done our duty.' " (Luke 17:1

In Word Jesus frequently points out that the attitude of the servant is perhaps as critical as the service itself. In the kingdom of God, the heart counts. Our actions are certainly importan but the God who sees the intricacies of our motives knows that right actions will naturally flow from right attitudes. He aims Hi Word straight at our hearts, where He most desires to shape us.

Jesus' teaching in Luke 17 is a little unsettling to our egos. W want to hear a "Well done!" in response to our good work for th Master. And elsewhere Jesus indicates that we might receive one But that is not the attitude with which we come to Him. He rids us of any assumption that God may employ a system of *quid pro quo*. Everything we receive from Him is a gift. Though we often try to negotiate favors from God—"I'll witness to my neighbor i You'll answer my prayers for a raise," or some similar barter—w are never in a position to do so. We serve Him because that's wh servants do. Period.

"If you take little account of yourself, you will have peace, wherever you live."
—*Abba Poemen*

In Deed God is gracious and He blesses us with innumerable and invaluable blessings. Jesus is clear about that. But H is also clear that we can never come to God with a sense of entit ment to those blessings. We can never say, "God, I've behaved well, why are You treating me this way?" To do so indicates that at some level, conscious or subconscious, we still think our stand ing with God is dependent on our performance. It isn't. Our standing with God is dependent on Christ's performance, and w are forever indebted.

God is intensely interested in our works. Our performance does matter to Him, but only as a response of faith, not as an act of merit. Our attitude of service indicates the degree in which th Gospel has penetrated our hearts. And if it has truly penetrated our hearts, it will be humble service indeed.

The Kingdom Mission

"As you go, preach this message: 'The kingdom of heaven is near.' Heal the sick, raise the dead, cleanse those who have leprosy, drive out demons. Freely you have received, freely give." (Matthew 10:7-8)

In Word Has Jesus sent us on an impossible mission? There are sides of this kingdom we've never seen, and few of us have much experience in miraculous healings, resurrections, cleansings, and exorcisms. Has Jesus called us to declare what we have not seen?

No, even if there is much we do not know about His kingdom, we are called to declare what we do know. This is exactly what the King of heaven is telling His subjects. They have been in on His miracles, liberating the captives of sickness and sin. They are to do what He has shown them. Their mission comes straight from experience.

This is our calling, too. Have you seen Jesus heal? Then declare His healing. Have you seen Him deliver? Then declare His deliverance. Have you seen Him release captives? Then declare His freedom. Whatever He has done for you, you are to do for others. It's that simple.

Christianity is one beggar telling another beggar where he found bread."

-D. T. Niles

In Deed We often hoard the gifts God has given us as our own possessions. They are not; they were given for a broader reason. He intends not only to care for us, but to care for us in such a way that we become like Him in His care. Those who have been forgiven are to forgive. Those who have had debts cancelled are to cancel others' debts. Those who have been given ample resources are to give them away.

Christian service is easily summed up. We are to minister to others as Jesus has ministered to us. His blessing is the means for us to bless others. However we have experienced the kingdom of heaven, that's how we are to share it. Then, as we become His channels, we experience the nearness of the kingdom—and the King.

The Kingdom's Costly Ways

"You don't know what you are asking." (Mark 10:3

In Word James and John asked Jesus for a favor—a hug favor. They wanted to sit next to His throne in the kingdom. Were they envisioning a heavenly kingdom? Or reigning from Jerusalem independently of Rome? Either way, they were out of line. They were ready for the benefits of the kingdom but had no yet counted the cost. And they had miscalculated the type of rule this King would have.

Jesus clarified things for them. His is a kingdom that begins with death, and the way up the kingdom's ladder is the humility of service. James and John had somehow missed Jesus' three earlier attempts to warn them of His impending execution (one each in Mark 8, 9, and 10). They had not fully understood that following Jesus implies a cross—literal or figurative—that all disciples must carry. No wonder they didn't know what they were asking. They knew neither the events on which this kingdom would be founded nor the principles on which it would be run. We can loo on their request in hindsight and chuckle; but it would not have been beyond us to have asked the very same thing.

"He who seeks not the Cross of Christ seeks not the glory of Christ."

—St. John of the Cross

In Deed In truth, it is still not beyond us to ask Jesus inappropriate things. It isn't that we don't understand His message or His authority. Like James and John, we prefer to focus on the fullness of the finished kingdom rather than the processes th usher it in. We forget the warfare being waged and try to implement the spoils of victory now. We bypass the nature of servants on our way to the privilege of sons.

When we pray, Jesus must sometimes tell us, too: "You don't know what you are asking." We have a distorted picture of the kingdom. It does, in fact, include reigning with Jesus in authority power, and victory. But the foundation being laid includes humb service and crosses. Let your prayers reflect this reality. Love the benefits, but know the costs. Ask with the awareness that God may lead you in costly ways.

Circumstantial Deceit

"Lazarus is dead, and for your sake I am glad I was not there, so that you may believe." (John 11:14-15)

In Word Circumstances don't get much worse than this. The loved one Mary and Martha had been praying for had died. Jesus was four days late and under fire from those who had come to expect miracles. Mary's pointed words are sadly resentful: "Lord, if you had been here, my brother would not have died" (v. 32). Defeat apparently reigned.

But circumstances don't tell the whole story. How often in the Gospels were appearances deceiving? Wind and waves threatened to capsize a boat; thousands hungered; disease ravaged its helpless victims; demons held hopeless captives. And, don't forget, God was executed by men. In all of these situations, those who stared at the problems despaired. Those who stared at the Truth found hope. And hope was fulfilled.

An acquaintance of George Müller once told a story of going from England to Quebec for an important engagement. The ship was stuck in the North Atlantic fog and Müller was told by the captain he would by no means make it to his meeting on schedule. Müller's response? "My eye is not on the density of the fog, but on the living God who controls every circumstance of my life." The fog cleared.*

Real trust in God is above circumstances and appearances."

-George Müller

In Deed Our human tendency is to feel trapped by visible situations. But circumstantial evidence is not the truth of a matter. It is deceptive. God's assessment is always the truth of every situation. And it doesn't include our being trapped by superficial appearances.

Are circumstances threatening what you know to be God's plan? They lie. As surely as the North Atlantic fog lifted, and as surely as Lazarus was raised, circumstances are unreliable measures of reality. God's plan, when believed, is immovable. Those who focused on their problems in the Gospels found those problems to be overwhelming. Those who focused on Jesus found their problems to be illusory. Focus on Jesus. There is no deceit in Him. Just ask Lazarus.

*From *Streams in the Desert*, Mrs. Charles E. Cowman, Zondervan, 1965, pp. 256-257.

No Negotiations

"The thief comes only to steal and kill and destroy; I have come that they may have life, and have it to the full."
(John 10:1

In Word Satan is a terrorist. He will try to hijack us fron the path God has us on or hold us hostage for an unacceptable ransom that flies in the face of God's will for us. His mission is tc steal our joy, terminate our lives, and degrade our relationship with God, and he's very aggressive about it. If there's anything h can do to interrupt our abundant life, he will attempt it.

The believer must resolutely fix his or her gaze on God and His Word and remain unswerving in devotion to Jesus. When w abide in His fellowship, we will be tempted by the enemy to resort to human wisdom rather than godly guidance. For example, a bill may scream to us that we cannot remain in the calling God has given us—it isn't financially feasible. A relationship ma drain us of the energy God gave us to serve Him. Or we may be accused of weaknesses that urge us to deny our usefulness to God. The enemy's tactics are limitless, but his intention is plain: Get the Christian off track. He wants us to mistrust Jesus and sta making decisions based on fear and anxiety.

> *"The devil does not sleep, but seeks our ruin in a thousand ways."*
>
> —Angela Merici

In Deed We must always remember Jesus' mission— giving us abundant life. It may not always be easy or comfortab but it will be good and founded on His joy. When we are confident in God's will, and circumstances arise that seem to contradi His will, we must know where they come from and cling to God If we let circumstances constrain us, Satan will manipulate them indefinitely, stringing us along our whole lives in uncertain, fear induced steps.

Our faith must fix its gaze on Jesus and not waver. Do not negotiate with the terrorist when he threatens. His tactics will ro us, kill us, and leave us devastated. God's voice must be the onl one we hear. It's the key to abundant life.

Sibling Rivalry

"I tell you that anyone who is angry with his brother will be subject to judgment." (Matthew 5:22)

In Word These are hard words. They address every one of us. Most of us can claim not to have murdered someone else, but none of us can realistically claim to have avoided anger—even sinful, unjustified anger. Deep down inside, we know it's probably wrong to harbor our own sense of vengeance, as though God gave anyone the privilege of sharing in His omniscient judgments. But we're only human, right? It's a small sin, and everyone does it. Surely it's not equal to murder, is it?

You may know the familiar commentary on this verse: Murder begins in the heart; the anger we feel is the source of the crime. But still, isn't there a difference between thinking the thoughts and acting on them? Why is Jesus so harsh toward this very natural response to injustice?

Jesus condemns our anger and judgment for at least two reasons: (1) *It dishonors Him as the judge of creation;* it usurps His standards and places our own above them. And, (2) *it slanders a being created in His image!* It is mental murder of a divine image-bearer, perhaps without physical consequence, but with character assassination and spiritual condemnation instead. Anger accomplishes in the spirit what murder does in the flesh. It further degrades God's fallen creation.

"No matter how just your words may be, you ruin everything when you speak in anger."

—John Chrysostom

In Deed Parents of more than one child can imagine God's perspective on human anger. Like God, we are generally sympathetic toward all of our children. We may be angry over their actions at times, but it is a measured, sympathetic anger, motivated by a desire to redeem. Siblings, however, want their offending brother or sister to pay! Jesus warns us that God's children are siblings, not parents, and our perspective is grossly distorted. The Father's judgment is thorough and accurate, and it can be trusted. Leaving our anger to Him acknowledges that, worships Him for it, and respects His ability to redeem His image-bearers.

The Test of Forgiveness

"If you forgive men when they sin against you, your heavenly Father will also forgive you. But if you do no forgive men their sins, your Father will not forgive yo sins."

(Matthew 6:14-1

"It is idle for us to say that we know God has forgiven us if we are not loving and forgiving ourselves."

—Martyn Lloyd-Jones

In Word We're steeped in the belief that our salvation is accomplished by His grace through our faith in His blood sacrifice—nothing else. When we come upon a verse like this, we bal It's conditional. It tells us that our forgiveness is dependent on a action of ours, as though we might earn salvation. Is that what Jesus is really saying? Do we earn our forgiveness by forgiving others? Or is Jesus making another point?

If someone has really taken the Cross personally—understood the reality of its message and applied it to his or her life— that person will understand forgiveness in a way that prevents judgmental attitudes toward others. It is not possible to simulta ously appreciate the magnitude of God's forgiveness while with holding forgiveness from others.

Jesus told a parable that illustrates this truth. In Matthew 18:23-35, a king forgives his servant a huge sum of debt. The ser vant, in turn, goes out and demands payment from a minor debtor. The servant had not really learned from the king's generosity. He had not taken it to heart. Likewise, our attitude towa others is a litmus test of our acceptance of God's forgiveness. If we've accepted His, we demonstrate it to others.

In Deed Take the test. Use these verses in Matthew 6 as your measure. Have you really seen the Cross as yours? To answer that question, you must ask yourself how you view others. Do you forgive easily, as one who has been forgiven much? Or do you hold grudges? If the latter is true, re-examine your understanding of what Jesus did for you. Know the depths from which you came to God. Then sympathize with others where th are.

Keep On Asking

"Ask and it will be given to you." (Luke 11:9)

In Word Jesus has just finished a curious parable about a man banging persistently at his neighbor's door in the middle of the night, asking for an inordinate amount of bread. This is prayer, Jesus says. It doesn't matter if the hour is inappropriate, the request is large, and the initial answer is "no." True prayer means desperation outweighs protocol.

Some translations capture the continuous nature of this verse. Jesus implied to His disciples that they are to keep on asking, keep on seeking, and keep on knocking; then they will receive. We don't know why persistence is required; Jesus doesn't tell us that. But the fact that it is required is clear. Prayer calls for boldness and relentlessness.

"Pray as if everything depended on your prayer." -William Booth

If you are like most people, you pray about a matter for a while. Then, having not heard from God, you give up, assuming it wasn't His will to answer. But nowhere in the Bible are we told that God's silence means "no." In fact, Jesus demonstrates to a Canaanite woman that His silence means "keep on asking" (Matthew 15:22-28). Scripture never gives us permission to drop a request because we got no immediate answer. We are to have a no-ceasing attitude to our prayers (1 Thessalonians 5:17). If God wants to show us our prayers are unscriptural or out of line with His will, He will show us. If He wants to say "no," He will actually *say* it. Silence is not "no."

In Deed Often our prayers are characterized by tentativeness and transience. They are not confident declarations of His will in a situation and expectant invitations for Him to RSVP in power. While we should always be open for Him to redirect our prayers, or even to say "no," we should never assume that a slow answer, by our standards, is a non-answer. Jesus never gives us a hint that God is rejecting us in His silence. Like the farmer who waits for his harvest, we are to wait for His answers. Jesus is clear: Keep on asking!

Undivided Love

"Love the Lord your God with all your heart and with all your soul and with all your strength and with all your mind."

(Luke 10:27

"Man is most truly himself . . . not when he toils but when he adores."

—Vida Scudder

In Word Most Christians walk a fuzzy line between devotion to God and devotion to other things. We believe in our hearts, of course, that we *should* be wholly committed to God and love Him fully, and we desire to do so. But at war against our undivided love for Him are other attractions—things we might call minor flaws or distracting habits; attitudes we might know are pushing the limits of Christian character, but are hard to resist; pleasures we might entertain without wanting to ask God whether or not they are within His parameters. We can live with a little bit of impurity.

But Jesus doesn't ask for low levels of tolerance for impurities and indiscretions. He implies no tolerance for them. What He specifically asks for is wholehearted, undying, all-out, passionate love for the Creator. According to the Law of Moses and the Gospel of Jesus, God desires *everything* that is in us. Every corner of our heart, every ounce of our strength, every impulse of our mind, every breath of our soul. He wants it all. Everything.

The grand deception of the enemy is that this type of passion for God would rob us of pleasures and privileges. Satan wars against that kind of love, and so does our self-centered flesh. We are divided in our hearts, and are miserable. Paul felt it, too: "What a wretched man I am! Who will rescue me from this body of death?" (Romans 7:24). But he didn't have to tell us. We have experienced it ourselves.

In Deed When it finally dawns on us that an all-out passion for God—regardless of whatever petty sacrifices it may involve—is incredibly fulfilling, we're amazed that we were ever divided in the first place. Missing out by obeying and loving God? That's ludicrous. Jesus was right. This *is* the greatest commandment. Be obsessed with it.

A Bold Approach

"Go in peace and be freed from your suffering."
(Mark 5:34)

In Word Of all of the petitions we offer up to God, most of them are centered around one of these two desired provisions: His peace and freedom from suffering. When life is tumultuous and confusing, when doubts run rampant, and when circumstances threaten us, we want His peace. When life hurts, we want relief. We would almost always consider these very words of Jesus the specific answer to our prayers. And we wonder: Why don't we hear them more often? If we really want to know, we would benefit from examining why this woman heard them spoken to her.

Prayer is an effort to lay hold of God Himself, the author of life."

–Sundar Singh

The bleeding woman had not only suffered physical pain, weakness, and the anxiety of knowing something was dreadfully wrong with her for 12 years; she also had to live with the knowledge that for 12 years, she was ritually impure. According to Old Testament Law, she could not enter the temple courts, and she could not offer sacrifices (Leviticus 15:25-30). She could not know normal fellowship with God's people. She could not approach the holy.

This woman obviously knew who Jesus was, at least to some degree. She would not have sought Him if she didn't. Her human solutions had failed (v. 26), so she sought the divine. It was an act of ultimate desperation, but also an act of great faith. What drives someone deeply washed in the idea that she is unholy to Someone who is holy? A bold belief that there is mercy to be found there. A brash expectation that within the holiness of God is His abiding grace.

In Deed What drives you to the Holy One for your petitions? Is it a belief that there is some right to be there, that something within you will compel Him to answer? If so, the answer probably will not come. Or is it a bold assurance of His merciful character that takes you where you really—by all natural means—have no right to be? Jesus responds to such boldness. It knows exactly who He is.

Adapting to Truth

"Everyone on the side of truth listens to me." (John 18:37

In Word Pilate responds to this statement of Jesus with a question that has characterized human thinking for centuries: "What is truth?" (v. 38). Our typical approach to this question has us trying to figure out what we believe to be truth and then measuring all things and people by that self-developed standard. This is exactly what Pilate is doing at Jesus' trial.

But Jesus refuses to be measured by external standards. He Himself is the definition of truth. Those who listen to Him have accepted truth. Those who do not listen to Him have not. It is not a matter of reconciling His words with our concept of reality. It is a matter of reconciling our concept of reality with His words. There is a world of difference.

It must be amusing, in a sense, for Jesus to hear philosophers and skeptics analyze His teachings in relation to their theoretical constructs. That's like trying to test the veracity of a reliable yardstick by lining it up next to an unmeasured tree branch. The process is backward. The branch must be measured by the measuring stick, not vice versa. The philosophical arguments must be tested according to Jesus' teachings, not the other way around.

In Deed Isn't this backward way of thinking often our approach to truth, too? We sometimes try to reconcile Jesus word with what we assume to be true of our culture, our sense of morality, our relationships, some standard of value like "the American dream" or "life, liberty, and the pursuit of happiness." But our faithfulness to truth is measured only by how we relate to Him, not by how we fit into other standards. We don't define truth and then figure out if Jesus fits into our framework. We are constantly to adapt to Him—always. He *is* the Truth (John 14:6). Everyone who listens to Him is on the side of Truth. And everyone on the side of truth listens to Him.

"Everyone may be entitled to his own opinion, but everyone is not entitled to his own truth."

—Doug Groothuis

The Spoken Word

"Simon, I have something to tell you." (Luke 7:40)

In Word The King of the universe, the One by whom all things were created, has singled out a man—a simple, somewhat pretentious man—to whom to impart some eternal truth. What a privilege! A spoken word, straight from the mouth of God incarnate and into the ear of a lowly, corrupt human. What will Simon do with such a treasure? How will the divine revelation—in his own home, nonetheless—forever change his life?

Scripture doesn't tell us the rest of Simon's story, unfortunately. As with so many others Jesus encountered, we're left to wonder what happened in the end. What did Simon do with this eternal word?

The question points us to another aspect of revelation. Not only is it an awesome privilege to receive it; it is also an awesome responsibility. Woe to the one who hears divine counsel and does not respond appropriately. Did Simon? We don't know. The issue is left hanging—just as it is with us.

The words of God which you receive by your ear, hold fast in your heart. For the Word of God is the food of the soul."

–St. Gregory I

In Deed Have we also heard the eternal voice of our Savior? Has the divine counsel come down to us as well? Of course it has. It has been put on printed pages and been more widely distributed than any other collection of words in the history of the world. For those who believe, it is also accompanied by the witness of the Holy Spirit. But we may nevertheless read this revelation as casually as Simon might have heard it.

We must constantly remind ourselves: What a privilege! We must also remind ourselves: What a responsibility! An eternal treasure has been given to us. The Alpha and Omega, the Beginning and the End, has pulled us aside, as He did Simon, and whispered: "I have something to tell you." Only one response is appropriate: grateful, worshipful obedience.

Jesus has a word for us. He has spoken. Has that really sunk in? Let it! Whatever He has said, He has trusted you with it. Worship and obey.

More to Learn

"I have much more to say to you, more than you can now bear."
(John 16:12

In Word Jesus made it clear to His disciples that His teaching would continue long after His death and resurrection. Their instruction in His ways would not be confined to His earthly ministry. He never said: "Close the book on my teaching. His clear purpose was, through His Spirit, to continue training them, speaking to them, guiding them, and revealing to them divine mysteries.

We must be careful of such a claim. Many have taken Jesus' words of future teaching and gone off on unbiblical tangents. Tha is emphatically *not* what Jesus has in mind. He does not give license to us or to cult-founders to come up with new strains of pseudo-Christian theology. But neither does He tell His disciples that His presence will now consist entirely of words on a printed page. He is much more alive than that. The Resurrection was not from the grave to the printing press, it was from death to life. We know He lives not because He once spoke, but because He continues to speak to us.

Many believers are uncomfortable with the reality of the Ho Spirit, but Jesus made His presence foundational to the life of discipleship. We can only become disciples when the Holy Spirit behind the biblical words writes them on our hearts and lives them through us. He spoke to Paul, John, Peter, and others, and He still speaks. Do we have ears to hear?

"There is hardly ever a complete silence in our soul. God is whispering to us well nigh incessantly."

—Frederick William Faber

In Deed Never let your discipleship become simply a set of principles. The Bible is the backbone of our faith, but we tend to read it historically, as though Jesus is only an ancient teacher and not a living Lord. He will *never* contradict His Word, but the Word is not just a memory preserved. Jesus is alive. He continues to teach. He still disciples us. We still follow wherever He leads because He hasn't stopped leading yet. When you read the Bible, do you read the words of history or hear the words of a risen Savior?

Guarding the Truth

"False Christs and false prophets will appear and perform signs and miracles to deceive the elect—if that were possible." (Mark 13:22)

In Word Jesus warns of false Christs and prophets—deceivers who are subtle and impressive enough to lead true believers away, at least for a time. It's a sobering thought. We like to think we are so devoted to Jesus that we're immune to the deceptive spirits of this age. Not so, says Jesus. Even His well-trained disciples, who saw Him in the flesh and learned straight from the words of His mouth, are given strong warning. The false saviors are coming, armed with miracles and signs. And we are their prey.

In fact, many of them have already come. Jesus' prediction is frighteningly accurate. There are those who have already said, "Look, there he is!" (v. 21), and many have believed them. There are cults all over this planet, many of which have begun by someone speaking lies in the name of Jesus. Their membership consists primarily of those who have once sat in the pews of our respected, faithful congregations. If these have been led astray, so can others. How can we protect ourselves against deception?

The best protection against Satan's lies is to know God's truth."

-Anonymous

In Deed Jesus gives us the answer in verse 23: "Be on your guard." Deception usually comes to those who were not wary of their vulnerability. Perhaps they started adding a little unbiblical philosophy to their biblical faith. Perhaps they saw quick results that their patient discipleship would not match. Perhaps they assumed they knew enough of God's Word to put it on the shelf and safely entertain competing worldviews, never noticing their foundation eroding beneath them. Whatever the case, they thought they were safe. But they weren't.

What are you doing to be on guard? Deception can have eternal consequences for you and those you influence. Pray earnestly for discernment. Cling to Jesus' Word like your life depends on it. In many ways, it does.

Eternal Words

"Heaven and earth will pass away, but my words will never pass away." (Mark 13:3

In Word Once again, Jesus points us to the priority of H Word. It is what will keep us from deception (13:22-23), and it is what we can cling to when heaven and earth seem uncertain and the end of the age seems near. There is nothing transitory about Jesus' words. If we fasten ourselves to what He says, we are bound to Jesus Himself. And if we are bound to Him, we have nothing to worry about when the heavens and the earth seem unstable.

Jesus' hearers would have been struck with a profound reality in this statement. It echoes the words of Isaiah 40:8: "The gras withers and the flowers fall, but the word of our God stands forever." Once again, Jesus implicitly claims to be God—He has forgiven sin, He has allowed Himself to be worshiped, and now He has asserted the eternal nature of His words in a manner parallel to God's declaration through Isaiah. These are outrageous claims if Jesus is only a good teacher. But He is so much more. No one wants to place all hope in the words of a good teacher when the very foundations of earth are being shaken. They want more. They want an eternal assurance. Jesus offers it without apology.

"Some read the Bible to learn, and some read the Bible to hear from heaven."
—Andrew Murray

In Deed There is a deep sense of security that comes from knowing that the words of Jesus are a permanent reality. They are not confined to the world as we know it; even if time itself were to come to an end, His words would not. They do not fail us. The sun may grow dark, the stars may fall from the sky, and everything we see can be shaken (vv. 24-25). But those who have hung their hopes on His words cannot. We are on solid ground, regardless of the earthquakes that may rumble around u

If you invest your whole self into Jesus' teaching, letting it saturate your mind and sink to the depths of your heart, you wil have a profound knowledge of your security in an uncertain age. Do you want that? It's His open invitation.

Always on Watch

"If he comes suddenly, do not let him find you sleeping." (Mark 13:36)

In Word Jesus has placed His followers on the walls of this world, the earthly city. We are keeping watch. It is a fearful thing for the inhabitants within those walls if the owner returns for His reckoning and no one warns them. It is a disgraceful thing if the warning doesn't come because the watchmen are asleep.

Jesus is protecting His followers from embarrassment. His warning is emphatic. "Watch out" (13:5). "You must be on your guard" (13:9). "Be on your guard" (13:23). "Be on guard! Be alert!" (v. 33). "Keep watch" (v. 35). "What I say to you, I say to everyone: 'Watch!' " (v. 37). He does not repeat Himself because He is forgetful; He repeats Himself because it is extremely important, in an age of deception and persecution, to prepare oneself—and others—for His coming. Jesus could not be speaking any more strongly. His disciples absolutely *must* be alert.

Why is He so emphatic? Do true believers need to be worried about His return? Is He trying to strike fear into those to whom He has already promised safety and rest? No, Jesus does not want His followers to be anxious and worried. But He knows how easy it is to develop a passive spirit. There may be times when God has us sit very still and patiently, but He *never* wants our hearts to be passive observers of kingdom events. He wants our constant attention and a readiness to gird ourselves for action.

[Jesus' return] is not a reason for star-gazing, but for working in the power of the Holy Ghost."

—Charles Spurgeon

In Deed The watchmen on the walls must always be alert. We must always be prepared to be pressed into service. We must pray diligently and zealously that His will would be done—in our own lives and in our world. We must see His kingdom as an imminent reality. We must live as those in a war zone—we may have times of respite but we can never retire. And we can never be too comfortable in our sleep.

A Test of First Pursuits

"Seek first his kingdom and his righteousness, and all these things will be given to you as well." (Matthew 6:33

"I will place no value on anything I have unless it is in relationship to the kingdom of God."

—David Livingstone

In Word The call of God is all about seeking. Jesus constantly calls His disciples to set their hearts on Him, denying the supremacy of any other loves and declaring His alone. Self must die, possessions must be left, kingdoms must be chosen. It's not about becoming ascetic or fanatical, it's about the direction of the heart. Which way does it point?

History's landscape is littered with the empty relics of those who wholeheartedly pursued some this-worldly or false-worldly goal, only to come to an agonizing dead end. Many of their goals are easily recognizable to us—like money, power, and pleasure. Many are more subtle—like legalism, insincere worship, and luke warm living. In any case, failure lies in wrong choices. And wron choices are the result of hearts pointed in the wrong direction.

Most of us who believe in Jesus are intent on seeking first the kingdom of God. At the same time, we find ourselves awfully pre occupied with other things. We want our hearts to be directed rightly, but there are competing interests involved. Some of them are good; none of them are worth elevating higher than Jesus. But in the confusion of competing calls, how can we be sure His kingdom is our first pursuit?

In Deed Try this diagnostic test: Make a mental note of what occupies your thoughts. Your checkbook and your schedule may indicate your priorities well, but a better indication is what you think about. What fills your mind when you lie down to slee at night? When you wake up in the morning? When you find yourself daydreaming in the middle of the day? If you detect a dominant pattern or a theme, know that this is where your heart lies.

Do this test and determine to make God pre-eminent in your affections. Be careful for what you seek first.

Misplaced Thanks

"The Pharisee stood up and prayed about himself: 'God, I thank you that I am not like other men—robbers, evildoers, adulterers—or even like this tax collector.'"

(Luke 18:11)

In Word Be careful what you thank God for. Not that we shouldn't be thankful for everything He has given us, and for every circumstance of our lives, or even for life itself; of course we should have grateful hearts. But often we thank God for privilege, not realizing that our awareness of it was meant to prompt our sensitivity to others. Thankfulness for what God has blessed us with is not enough; knowledge of the blessing is granted us that we might extend the blessing to others.

"Some people always sigh in thanking God."
–Elizabeth Barrett Browning

The Pharisee's assumption of his place of privilege, in this parable, caused him to be insensitive to others. He thought God's blessing on his life—if being a Pharisee can be considered a blessing—meant that God favored him and had passed over others. Nothing could have been further from the truth. God's favor comes to those who know their need. Abundance and status are deceitful, often blinding us to the very need God wants us to acknowledge.

Our gratitude often contains a tragic irony. We think we are being spiritual by thanking Him for things, but we may end up thanking Him for our own idols. Are we *really* grateful to God for material blessings? Or are we just thankful to have them, regardless of how we got them? The difference is subtle. How can we tell?

In Deed Ask yourself this question: If God took the blessings away, would I still love Him? If so, you were truly thanking God. If not, you only saw Him as the means to another end.

This Thanksgiving, thank God for all He has blessed you with. But be aware of spiritual pitfalls in the blessings He has given. Do not let them mask your deeper needs.

Another Love

"The Father himself loves you because you have loved me and have believed that I came from God." (John 16:2

In Word This verse usually doesn't surprise us at all, because we know, according to Scripture, that God *is* love (1 John 4:8). We would expect Him to love His disciples—and us. But if we read it carefully, it may surprise us that there seems to be a condition attached to God's love. Jesus tells us that the Fathe loves us "because." Doesn't unconditional love mean God loves us, *period?* Why is our having loved Jesus first given as a condition of the Father loving us? Why is there this frightening "because" in the text?

In Jesus' long discourse of John 14–16, He has been speaking up to this point mostly of *agape* love, that unconditional, noblest form of love by which God defines Himself and the community c His believers. But here, Jesus switches terms. This is the *phileo* kind of love, the brotherly affection that characterizes true friendship. God loves (*agape*) everyone in the world; but He has a genuine, enthusiastic intimacy (*phileo*) with those who have affection for Jesus. It is not unconditional. It is a very human kind of love, and God took on a very human form to have it with us. Amazing isn't it?

"This is adoration; not a difficult religious exercise, but an attitude of the soul."

—Evelyn Underhill

In Deed We often love Jesus because we ought to, not because we just can't help ourselves. And we *should* love Him thi way. *Agape* is the only kind of love that stands firm when circumstances shift. But we should love Him with pleasure, too. God means to be enjoyed.

What kind of love do we have for Jesus? Is it only the *agape* love—noble and purposeful, but sometimes lacking in the warmt of friendship? Or is it the *phileo* kind of love as well—an irrepressible affection for One whose presence we actually enjoy? If we believe in Jesus—lovingly and enthusiastically—we experience the kind of love that comes from the heart of God not only because it is *right*, but also because it is *enjoyable*. Cultivate both kinds of love. Enjoy the blessing of God's affection.

All About Him

"The Father himself loves you because you have loved me and have believed that I came from God." (John 16:27)

In Word One of the keys to our understanding the love of God—whether it's *agape* or *phileo*—is that it's all about Him. We have a hard time accepting His love because we know that we're often unlovable. And we have a hard time loving Him, because we're often unloving. It's not our nature to love unconditionally, or to accept unconditional love. It's not even in our nature to love and be loved *conditionally* with any real consistency. Whenever we think that love is about us, we are easily confused.

Love is about God. He doesn't love us because we're lovable—too often, we aren't. He loves us because He is love. It's His nature. On the other hand, we don't love Him because we're loving—too often, we aren't. We love Him because He is lovable. That's also His nature. There's nothing unlovable about Him. Whether God is on the giving or receiving end of love, the source of that love is Him. It's His nature to give it, and it's His nature to receive it. We actually have the easy end of the deal.

God loves us not because of who we are, but because of who He is." –Anonymous

In Deed Is the love of God lost on you? Are you one of the many who find it hard to believe God's love for you is unconditional? Do you find it hard to love Him back? The burden of love is not on your shoulders, either in giving it or receiving it. It's all about Him.

When you find it difficult to accept God's amazing, unconditional love, meditate on His loving nature, not on whether you are worthy of it. Consider how Someone who defines Himself as "love" could think of you in any other way—regardless of what you've done. And when you find it difficult to love God with the type of worship and adoration He expects, meditate on His worthiness, not on your ability to love in return. Love isn't mustered up, it's completely absorbed in its object. Let Him occupy your thoughts, and love will flourish. Where He's involved, it always does.

Forgiven Much

"He who has been forgiven little loves little." (Luke 7:47

In Word The greatest commandment of all, said Jesus, is to love God with everything we are and everything we have. We are to have passion for the Almighty that exceeds all our other passions. It's what we were created for. But here, in the context of fallen humanity, Jesus lays down a principle about our love. It is contingent on the mercy we have experienced. The fallen human heart does not love the holy heart of the divine unless mercy paves the way. And where love is faint, mercy has been missed.

Simon the Pharisee demonstrated little love for Jesus. Curiosity, perhaps. Some level of hospitality, of course. But little love, if any. What does this say about his understanding of God's mercy? According to Jesus, it means he has missed it. He doesn't have a clue. He probably sees himself right with God already. An he sees Jesus as a prophet, a teacher, a troublemaker who needs a good lecture, or something other than the One who takes away the sins of the world. He does not know Jesus' forgiveness, and h doesn't know his own need. And his love for Jesus—and for God—is miniscule.

"The more we meditate on the Cross, the deeper our companionship and knowledge gets of Christ the Lord."

—Pishoy Kamel

In Deed What about your love for God? Does it overflow with gratitude? Does it weep at His feet? If not, go back to the Cross. Get a good understanding of what happened there. Contemplate the huge chasm that once lay between the deadness of your spirit and the life of your God. Remember the cold rebellion—that chilling apathy toward our Creator—that we've all started out with. Understand that we were separated from any deserving claim on His goodness. Everything that brought us back to Him was all grace—nothing else. Pure, unbridled mercy. A love that knows no restraint and accepts no resistance.

Few people really understand God's mercy. Become one of them. Know the magnitude of His grace. And let your love for Him reflect it.

Forgiving Much

"He who has been forgiven little loves little." (Luke 7:47)

In Word Not only does Simon the Pharisee not understand God's mercy toward him, he doesn't understand God's mercy toward the sinful woman. And if he doesn't understand that, he certainly can't demonstrate it. He is woefully unequipped to be a minister of God's grace.

We fall into the same trap. We accept God's mercy, but when it leads us to righteousness, we complacently forget our constant need for the mercy we once accepted. And we forget that whenever God lets us experience His character, we are to assume that character and demonstrate it to others. God doesn't just show Himself to unbelievers in the Bible and in sermons. He shows Himself through the church. But if the church doesn't act like Him, how will unbelievers see Him? We become as unequipped as Simon.

"Nothing in this world bears the impress of the Son of God so surely as forgiveness."
—Alice Cary

The person who has encountered God's grace—really, deeply experienced it—will show it. It is a traumatic event when our need for mercy is revealed. It changes our whole perception of everything. We suddenly find that we who have been judged and forgiven have no basis for judging anyone. We discover that while the world operated on principles of pettiness and payback, the ground of God's kingdom is mercy. Everything turns upside down. Or right-side up.

In Deed Has God's mercy made you more merciful? Are you like the woman weeping at His feet? It is difficult to imagine her getting up and rebuking someone else for their sin. Or are you more like Simon the Pharisee? It is difficult to imagine him forgiving a transgressor of the Law. One of them shows clear signs of understanding God's grace. The other does not. One's life is revolutionized. The other's is pretty much the same as it always has been.

Jesus says the merciful will be "blessed" (Matthew 5:7). They are to be envied and admired. Why? They get it. They understand. They have tasted the sweetness of mercy, and they invite others to the banquet where it is served.

Eternal Food

"Do not work for food that spoils, but for food that endures to eternal life, which the Son of Man will give you. On him God the Father has placed his seal of approval." (John 6:27)

In Word Thanksgiving is usually celebrated with lavish spreads of delicious food. We know it as a day of abundance. We eat and are satisfied—beyond satisfied, sometimes. We enjoy the bounty God has given in full measure.

We should always be so grateful. But we should also realize the greater blessing. Knowing God is an infinitely worthwhile treasure. Men and women throughout history have sought to fill their aching hearts with something lasting and truly satisfying—some have found it in the favor of God in Christ, but many have not found it at all. One of the saddest scenes in all humanity is the person who has tried to fill his internal void with all sorts of false pleasures—riches, relationships, beauty, power, and prestige. These things can give pleasure, but they cannot satisfy, and in the end they are gone. None of them lasts forever.

"A life in thankfulness releases the glory of God."
—Bengt Sundberg

The food that Jesus provides lasts forever. Though scorned by many, it is of infinite worth. It is unimpressive to the material mind, but in the end it will be seen by all for what it is—priceless beauty and awesome privilege. Everyone—believer and unbeliever—will gaze at the gift of salvation and say, "That's what my heart really desired all along."

In Deed The best Thanksgiving satisfies for a day, at most—or a week, if leftovers are included—but it doesn't endure. It's the gratitude that lasts, not the material gifts. And it's the eternal gift that prompts eternal gratitude. If we really saw the value of each—food that spoils and food that endures—we'd never get the two confused. Remind yourself this Thanksgiving to really see the difference.

Near Hearts

" 'These people honor me with their lips, but their hearts are far from me.' " (Mark 7:6)

In Word Throughout Scripture, God says He takes pleasure in the praises of His people. Regardless of whether those praises come from the mouths of babes, the songs of the assembly, or the stones crying out, God enjoys worship. But there is a prerequisite. It's not every form of praise that He enjoys. It's every form of *genuine* praise. It must be heartfelt. If it doesn't spring forth from an overflowing heart—or at least a heart repentant for its lack of overflow—it shouldn't spring forth at all. Lip service has no place in His kingdom.

In spite of this verse—it is, after all, a quote from Isaiah, not a new piece of information for Jesus' hearers—the Pharisees and teachers of the Law didn't get it. We often don't either. We frequently sing our songs of worship with no real passion, read our responsive readings with no real sense of appreciation for them, and hear our pastors with no real retention of their words. It isn't that we're non-worshipers; we just slip easily into lukewarm worship.

It's a short step from the warmth of interior fellowship with God to the coldness of outward expressions, even when the warmth was once vibrant and genuine. At those times, the outward expressions were the delight of God. But they easily become empty shells. Our hearts wander far from Him, while our actions remain in place. And when our hearts are far from Him, He seems far from us.

"The great thing, and the only thing, is to adore and praise God."
—Thomas Merton

In Deed Do you want the presence of God to be revealed in your life in a powerful way? Worship Him from your heart. Read your Bible with a passion for His fellowship. Sing your congregational songs while meditating on each word. Fellowship with other believers with a thankfulness for the Spirit that works in and through them. As Paul instructs, "sing psalms, hymns and spiritual songs with gratitude in your hearts to God" (Colossians 3:16). The warm, welcoming presence of God will be as real as the praises of your heart.

A Place of Insufficiency

"What is impossible with men is possible with God."
(Luke 18:27

In Word We almost get the impression sometimes that when something is impossible for us but necessary or fruitful for God's kingdom, He'll step in and help us out, perhaps a little reluctantly. He becomes our "God of the gaps"—He makes up the difference when we just don't have the strength. But in the back o our minds, we think He'd prefer that we have the strength.

Nothing could be further from the truth. God is not reluctant about our impossibilities. He relishes them. He sometimes even waits until we arrive at them before He acts. Just as it was Paul's weakness that allowed God to show His strength (2 Corinthians 12:9), it is our powerlessness that demonstrates His power. If we were self-sufficient in everything, no one would ever see God.

In today's verse, the disciples are astounded when Jesus says it is difficult for the rich to inherit salvation. They wonder who, then, can be saved. But why is it so difficult for the rich to be saved? Since we're all saved the same way, through faith in Jesus, what makes it harder for the rich? A sense of self-sufficiency. It is an obstacle to God's work in anyone's life. In laying down this principle of salvation, Jesus is giving us a principle of *any* spiritua work—it must be all from God and not at all from us.

"Complete weakness and dependence will always be the occasion for the Spirit of God to manifest His power."
—Oswald Chambers

In Deed Are you in a place of insufficiency? Don't despair. It may feel as if God wasn't watching or caring for you when you arrived there. But not only was He watching; *He planned it!* He brought you there because it is the only place wher He can step in and work and be acknowledged as the power behind your victories. If you were not completely unable to meet your own needs, you would receive credit for fulfilling them. He had to bring you face to face with your inabilities in order to brin you face to face with His abilities. You are exactly where He want you to be.

A Place of One Last Hope

"What is impossible with men is possible with God."
(Luke 18:27)

In Word When God leads us to the place of insufficiency, we are compelled to cry out to Him. It is the cry of desperation. We have no hope but Him, and we know it. We are deeply, excruciatingly aware of it. We had hoped to have our stressful situation resolved by now, but we are at the end of our rope. Only God can fix things now. Or, as is often said, "All we can do now is pray."

The Israelites fleeing from Egypt found themselves in a similar situation. They stood at a precarious position at the edge of the Red Sea. There was no way out. Deep waters lay ahead, a hostile army behind. It was impossible. And that's exactly what God had planned all along—their impossibility.

Over and over again, the Bible stresses the importance of faith. It's a strange commodity, isn't it? Why didn't God choose works as the currency of His kingdom? Why didn't He choose our flawless understanding as His condition for acting on our behalf? Because those things don't set Him up to display His glory. They would display ours, such as it is. Only faith is the helpless place that sets the stage for His greatness. Only trust declares our own futility, creates a vacuum He can fill, and acknowledges Him afterward.

We need more Christians for whom prayer is the first resort, not the last."

–John Blanchard

In Deed Our place of one last hope was the place where God would have had us all along. Everything else we tried before we arrived there wasn't a legitimate hope anyway. We should have said at the start, "All we can do now is pray." It was God's preference all along to be our only hope, our only source of strength, our all-sufficient Savior. While we were trying everything we could before we got to the end of our rope, we were dreading the day we would reach it. But God was excitedly anticipating it. He stands ready to be the strength in our weakness, the wealth in our poverty, the health in our sickness, the deliverance out of our captivity, and the comfort in our despair. From beginning to end, He is our hope.

Unassuming Children

"Whoever humbles himself like this child is the greatest in the kingdom of heaven." (Matthew 18:4

In Word Most cultures love their children. Few give the any respect or honor. We look down on them. It's a loving condescension, of course, but it's a condescension nonetheless. Adults don't aspire to have the status of a little child or strive for their accomplishments. We spend most of our childhood hoping to grow up so we can do more and be more. We aspire to adulthoo

This may be normal human growth, but it runs contrary to the kingdom of God, at least in terms of spiritual development. Our bodies grow, our intellects accumulate knowledge, our talen are developed, and everything about us matures upward. But to mature spiritually, we must go in the opposite direction. We mus intentionally avoid seeking status. We must not try to earn spiritual respect. True spiritual maturity and respect in the kingdom God are issues of humility. And in order to have them, we must become like society's least impressive contributors—children.

"For those who would learn God's ways, humility is the first thing, humility is the second, humility is the third."

—St. Augustine

In Deed Human beings can be quite ambitious. We admire that drive when it comes to athletics, art, business, and every other area of human achievement. We like the prestige and the honor that accomplishments bring us. But when we transfer such ambition to our spiritual life, it misses God's purpose for us He did not make us to be spiritually independent. We are entirel dependent creatures, who must learn that the way to grow up is to go down.

Have you learned that status in the kingdom of God is an inverted version of status in the world? The first will be last and the last first (Matthew 20:16). Those who wish to rule must serve (Matthew 20:26). And the greatest in the kingdom of heaven has aspired to the humility of . . . well, just a child. It's a hard lesson learn, but it's a solid principle. Aspire to greatness—the greatnes of being discounted like a child. It's the way up in the kingdom.

Unburdened Children

"Whoever humbles himself like this child is the greatest in the kingdom of heaven." (Matthew 18:4)

In Word When we were children, most of us were comfortable with life. Some childhoods are difficult (increasingly so as our culture deteriorates) but most are free from worry. We didn't obsess about family finances, our health, our security, or any other "adult" concern. As we grew older, reality set in. After all, we would one day be adults and have to concern ourselves with these things. But there was a time, however brief, when we could simply live life and trust all the details to older and wiser people.

Though we grew out of our human childhood, we are always God's children. We grow up spiritually, but we never grow to be independent of our heavenly Father. The carefree attitude that many children have can be ours. Why? The details are being taken care of by Someone older and wiser. He has not asked us to stay up late to worry about how to make ends meet. He has not burdened us with resolving the family crises. He has let us see some of the family stress, of course, and He even asks us to play a role in handling it. But bearing the burden? Never. That's the Father's task, not ours.

A child lives by faith, and his chief characteristic is freedom from care."

—Hannah Whitall Smith

In Deed We tend to think that ignoring the burdens of life is irresponsible. And we are not to ignore them; we are to cast them into His arms. But there is nothing irresponsible about that. In fact, it honors God when we refuse to worry about something He has promised to do. He has never betrayed our trust. Sometimes the most faithful thing we can do is to sleep calmly, or to run freely, or to rest without anxiety. Such a posture indicates that we are trusting His ability to parent His children. We know whose hands guard our family, and we know how secure His house is. The more we act like unburdened children, the more we prove our faith. And that always pleases our Father.

Convinced of Sin

"When he comes, he will convict the world of guilt in regard to sin and righteousness and judgment: in regar to sin, because men do not believe in me." (John 16:8-9

In Word The Holy Spirit is the consummate convincer. I is His area of expertise: Where we are ignorant, He reveals. And we are perhaps nowhere more ignorant than with regard to our own sin. It is our biggest blind spot, at least before He shines His light into our darkness.

Why must the Holy Spirit convict us of sin? Because we do not at first believe in Jesus. If we did, there would be no need. He is the Lamb of God who takes away the sins of the world. We would be forgiven and cleansed already through our faith. But because we did not believe, and many remain who do not, He must come and convince. We are only driven to a Savior when w know we need saving. The Holy Spirit must convict us of sin so that we will know we need saving. We must know so we will believe.

"Before God saves a man, He convicts him of his 'sin-nership.' "

—A. W. Pink

This is the struggle between the human race and faith. We resist being told we are sinners. After all, we've spent quite a bit of effort to present ourselves otherwise. We've put our best foot forward to make the right impression—on God and on others. Why would we willingly hear the witness of a Spirit that says we're corrupt to the core? Why would resourceful people such as ourselves readily present ourselves to Someone who came to sav us? Save us from what?

In Deed This is not just an evangelism issue. It is also a discipleship issue. Having been saved by grace, we still seek to be perfected by works. The Spirit will not let us. He will not only remind us that we came to the Savior one day years ago; He will compel us to come to Him today. And tomorrow. And the next da As long as sin is present, so the Spirit will convict. And as long as He convicts, we must not resist. Drop the pose of self-righteousne and remember your need of grace. Let your belief in Jesus' salvation be as real as it was on day one.

Convinced of Righteousness

"He will convict the world . . . in regard to righteousness, because I am going to the Father, where you can see me no longer." (John 16:8, 10)

In Word The Holy Spirit not only convinces us of sin; He convinces us of righteousness. Is there a difference? Doesn't an awareness of our sin imply that there is an awareness of a righteous alternative? Yes, but it tells us nothing of what that righteousness will look like. We know it will preclude the sins we regularly commit; but other than avoiding the bad things, we don't know the good things righteousness will lead us to do. That's where the Spirit comes in. He shows us Jesus.

While Jesus was in front of His disciples, they knew what righteousness looked like. They went where He went, they watched what He did, they responded to His instructions. Now, He tells them, He is going away and the Spirit is coming. We have the Bible, of course, so we see Jesus through the eyes of its writers. We, too, know what righteousness looks like. But we have no idea what it demands of us today other than by example. And Jesus did not simply leave us with an example. He left us with Himself. The Spirit is His presence; He shows us what He is doing. He convinces us what righteous living is all about.

"God works immediately by His Spirit in and on the wills of His saints."
—John Owen

In Deed A popular catch phrase asks us "What would Jesus do?" It isn't a bad question, but there's a better one: "What is Jesus doing?" The first question makes Jesus a dead example. The second recognizes His living presence.

Jesus isn't dead, you know. He's very much alive, and His Spirit is very much living with us and in us. He is here to show us how to live—not just in principle or by example, but today in our actual circumstances and relationships. His Spirit convicts us regarding righteousness because we need His righteousness to live in us and through us. We need Him to act in our lives. And our world needs to see Him desperately. Let them see Him through you.

Convinced of Judgment

"The prince of this world now stands condemned."

(John 16:1

In Word Jesus does not pull any punches. All throughou His ministry He has called a spade a spade. So when He calls Satan the prince of this world, we know He is precise in what He says.

Did you really wonder who was governing the world systems? Surely we have seen enough headlines to know. There is a malicious, personal evil unleashed in this world through the foolishness of our Fall in the garden. He has ravaged this planet with vengeance and hate. He has distorted all that is good and corrupted all that is God's. He's in this mess up to his ears: the economic systems, the political systems, the religious idolatries, and in the very heart of man. Yes, at both a macro and a micro level, the adversary has exerted his illegitimate authority.

"God reigns in the hearts of His servants; there is His kingdom."

—Jeremy Taylor

The Holy Spirit of whom Jesus speaks comes into this world for a threefold purpose: to convince of sin, of righteousness, and of judgment. He can do so because judgment has been rendered. The prince has been passed over in favor of the Son. The usurper has been usurped. The regent gives way to the heir. The mutinee has been stripped of his power.

In Deed There is a very practical side to the advent of the Holy Spirit in your heart. He is there to convince you that the authority that Jesus has regained—remember that all authority ir heaven and earth has been given to Him (Matthew 28:18)—mean that as His co-laborer and joint-heir, you are no longer under Satan's thumb; he is under yours. You represent the One with all authority; you must learn how to represent Him to the enemy.

Do you feel defeated? Then the Holy Spirit wants more of your heart. You must fellowship more deeply with Him. There is no defeat there. God has rendered judgment, and the Spirit will convince you of it. He will also help you enforce the victory. The malicious prince is forever condemned.

Fruitful Gifts

"Whoever has will be given more; whoever does not have, even what he has will be taken from him."

(Mark 4:25)

In Word This is one of the fundamental principles of the Gospel: God's gifts are not given to level the playing field for us; they are given to bear the most fruit. Whoever is found to be faithful with what God has given has demonstrated a trustworthiness that allows for greater blessing. Whoever squanders God's gifts has proven to be an investment with bad returns. If God's gifts were primarily about us, this would be grossly unfair. But God's gifts are primarily about building His kingdom; profitable returns attract greater investments. Fruitful servants attract more resources from the Giver of all good things.

"Use your gifts faithfully, and they shall be enlarged."

-Matthew Arnold

Jesus does not specify what is being given in this verse. Is it material resources? Understanding and the light of the Gospel? Talents and spiritual gifts? Spiritual or temporal responsibility? Yes, it can be any or all of these. In the gospel of Matthew, this verse comes at the end of the parable of the talents (Matthew 25:29). In that parable, it is clear that the gifts of God are intended to grow His kingdom. But the specific gift is not the issue. Where it is directed is the issue. What we do with whatever God has given us matters.

In Deed What do you do with what God gives you? Many people assume that 10 percent of all of God's blessings—money, time, and even talents—is like a God-tax, with everything else available to squander on personal consumption. Jesus is no enemy of the pleasures of life, but He never gives blanket permission to use God's resources frivolously. All He gives is for one primary purpose—building the eternal kingdom. Wherever we prove faithful in building that kingdom, we will be given ample resources, increasing with our measure of generosity. Wherever we prove unfaithful, we'll find ourselves empty—perhaps not now, but eventually. Examine your investments, direct them toward eternity, and expect God to make them fruitful.

Cost and Blessing

"If anyone would come after me, he must deny himself and take up his cross and follow me." (Mark 8:34

"The only life that counts is the life that costs."

—Frederick P. Wood

In Word There are two extremes we often take in our obedience to God: We can try to follow Him without any cost involved at all; or we can assume that God's will always contradicts ours and is a heavy, dreadful price to pay. These are unbalanced views—neither is accurate. Sometimes our will coincides with God's; sometimes it doesn't. The walk of discipleship—the self-denial Jesus calls for in this verse—is a matter of discerning th difference and seeking His will in all things. It does not mean the will be no cost; and it does not mean there will be no joy. Following Jesus involves both.

When we are pursuing God's will, we must know that it inevitably involves sacrifice. We may want to be obedient and fo low Him without price, but that is not God's way. May we never offer Him anything that costs us nothing. If we do, it's not a gen uine offering. It's low-value surplus.

No, following him means making the hard choices that we know to be His will, even when they conflict with our own plans But it does not mean there is no blessing or joy in the sacrifices. God's way always brings blessing—perhaps not by our definitio of blessing, but His is the only true definition anyway. God has never asked of us more than He gives.

In Deed If you believe you are walking as a disciple, ar there seems to be no sacrifice in your discipleship, check again. Somewhere, you are missing His voice. Don't go to the other extreme, however, and expect all of discipleship to be drudgery and pain, and for there to be no joy in it. Quite the contrary. The is incredible joy in it, and very little is drudgery. But there is still some element of cost—always. God accepts only the best of our flocks and the first of our fruits. That means that, as living sacrifices (Romans 12:1), our offerings will cost us dearly—the very best of who we are. They also bring us blessing—the very best o who He is.

Always Enough

"How many loaves do you have?" (Mark 6:38)

In Word It is a common human tendency to focus on what we lack. Whether we are looking at possessions or problems, we usually zero in on the down side and try to figure out what to do about it. We may have most of what we need toward a certain expense or be mostly pleased with a project. But that's not what we usually see. We ignore the "most" and focus on the little bit that still needs fixing. Our dissatisfaction and want loom larger to us than all that God has already provided. We grow quite discontent with just a small element of imperfection. The glass, for most of us, is always half—or even only 10 percent—empty.

Jesus did not look at His circumstances this way, and He did not teach His disciples to do so either. He knew what He had already been given, and He knew the God who promised to supply all our needs. When 5,000 men and their families needed feeding, Jesus counted a small handful of fish and loaves—and gave thanks! He took what they had in hand and looked to heaven (v. 41). And instead of focusing on the 5,000 men and their families for whom there was no available food, Jesus gave thanks for what they had. It wasn't much, but it was what God had provided. And God never falls short in meeting a need.

He who can give thanks for a little will always find he has enough."

-Anonymous

In Deed Could it be that we often miss out on God's supply because we focus so much on the need and so little on what He has already given? Has Jesus given us a lesson here in praying for provision? There is no pleading, no reminding God of how many people are hungry or how little food there is, no prayers of anguish for the provision Jesus hoped would come but suspected might not. Jesus went through none of the rituals we go through when we see a great need and a lack of resources. Resources are *never* insufficient when God is involved. So Jesus gave thanks. And the text is succinct and understated as it tells the result in verse 42: "They all ate and were satisfied."

Hospitable Hearts

"Here I am! I stand at the door and knock. If anyone hears my voice and opens the door, I will come in and eat with him, and he with me." (Revelation 3:20)

In Word This verse is often used to pose Jesus' invitatio of salvation to the unbeliever. But Jesus is speaking to those who already know Him, and there are profound implications for us. Jesus is clear that He is interested in more than your initial salvation experience. He does not want only to be followed and obeyed. He wants to be savored and enjoyed. In the dining room of our life, He wants the lengthy, personal fellowship of the common meal, not the brief acknowledgment before it. When Jesus enters in, it is for intimate union.

Jesus invites Himself into our churches and our hearts, and most of us have probably given a formal RSVP, allowing Him in. But perhaps we have not thought much deeper than that. When visitor is coming to our home, we hope to make it as warm and inviting as possible, if, in fact, we want him to stay. We'll go to great lengths to give another person the pleasure of our hospitality. Will we do so for Jesus? When He stands at the door and knocks, waiting for us to hear His voice and open the door, will He find that the atmosphere within has been prepared for His coming? Will He feel welcome there?

"A Christian has a union with Jesus Christ more intimate than the members of a human body have with their head."
—St. John Eudes

In Deed Jesus is not someone we need to clean up entirely for before He comes in—He'll do a lot of that when He comes. But we do need to be prepared—and willing—for a thorough cleaning. And He's not just at our door for a visit; He's mo ing in. He puts all His touches on the place and fixes it up just as He likes. Do we regularly make it clear to Him that He is welcon to do that? If not, the formal RSVP doesn't mean very much.

But Jesus is mostly here for the fellowship. The clean-up is important, but sitting around the table and enjoying the compan is vital. That's the whole point of His invitation. If you want that tell Him how welcome He is.

Hunger and Thirst

"Blessed are those who hunger and thirst for righteousness, for they will be filled." (Matthew 5:6)

In Word Everyone hungers and thirsts. The difference between people is what they hunger and thirst for. Some hunger and thirst for accomplishment, others for recognition, and others for material or physical desires. For those who set their minds on such attainments, Jesus has no promise of fulfillment. But for those who set their minds on true righteousness, He gives His word: They will be satisfied.

Much of our anguish in this world results from unfulfilled desires. Our hunger and thirst may remain unfulfilled because they are misplaced. They were designed for eternal satisfaction, but we try to fill them with temporal things. Substitutes always fall short. We were created to enjoy the pleasures of life and the gifts of God, but we were not created to be filled by them. We were created to be filled by God Himself. His righteousness—Himself, in other words—is the ultimate prize we crave. We just have a hard time seeing that, so we run after lesser things.

How to be pure? By steadfast longing for the one good, that is, God."

-Meister Eckhart

In Deed Where are your hunger and thirst directed? If you have a sense of obligation to be righteous, that obligation may never be realized. If you want to impress people with your righteousness, that will never fill you either. If you strive to achieve a level of righteousness that God can accept, you will never arrive. But if you know your own inadequacy and starve for a fulfillment that comes from outside of yourself—far beyond the ability of your own efforts—then let your hunger and thirst point you to the Bread of Life and the River of living water.

We hesitate to get our hopes up for such a promise. We have been awfully disappointed by human failures—ours and others'—much too often to think our deep-down hunger for purity can be satisfied. We're afraid of such idealism. But Jesus never fails on a promise. We can be fulfilled. Let your hopes—and your hunger—run wild.

An Odd Celebration

"Rejoice in that day and leap for joy, because great is your reward in heaven." (Luke 6:2

"Hope can see heaven through the thickest clouds."
—Thomas Brooks

In Word This is Jesus' instruction for those who are hated, insulted, and rejected because of Him. It's hard to understand. It runs so counter to our natural emotions in such situatio that we can hardly believe He is serious about it. Rejoice? *No one* enjoys being rejected. Leap for joy? That isn't a normal reaction t pain. How can Jesus possibly say something so apparently absurd?

Jesus probably doesn't expect His disciples actually to enjoy being insulted and hated—it isn't a pleasant feeling, even when we're sure our principles are worth it. He knows that. He does, however, expect His disciples to see the bigger picture. He wants us to view the entire landscape and know that the rejections that come with wholeheartedly following Jesus are simply low-lying hills in the foreground. How they appear is a matter of where we stand.

Those who suffer willingly are standing in an eternal perspe tive. They have put away their misguided ambition of creating their heaven on earth and have embraced the coming kingdom. They can be content with temporary trials because their eyes are open to the eternal panorama.

Those who rebel against their suffering, however, are still hoping in the here and now. Somewhere deep inside they had expected a better deal in this life and not yet invested their hope in God's kingdom. They had an agenda for this life that didn't fi with His.

In Deed This is not just a verse for those who are being persecuted now. Its instruction prepares us for any trial by point ing us to eternal realities. Is God's kingdom where we've place our hopes? If so, we will not only tolerate our rejection by this world, but we'll see it as happy confirmation that we are, in fact, in union with Jesus. In a very real sense, it will be an occasion to jump for joy.

Grief and Joy

"I tell you the truth, you will weep and mourn while the world rejoices." (John 16:20)

In Word The disciples had come with Jesus into Jerusalem with great expectations. The Messiah's moment of victory had come. But how painful the moment and obscure the victory! They had no idea. They would later recall these words of Jesus—while the world rejoiced at the downfall of a "trouble-maker," the disciples grieved the death of a dream. Later, He tells them, the moods will be reversed; their grief will be turned to joy (v. 22) when they realize the dream was greater than they had imagined.

Jesus could just as easily say these words to us. We know His victory came through the Cross; it's not His death we grieve today. But His Cross also belongs to us as His disciples; we're called to take it upon ourselves. Meanwhile, the world rejoices. It pities those who have fallen "victim" to the constraints of the Christian faith. It can't imagine that we find fulfillment without following their unbridled pursuit of physical and emotional pleasure.

Griefs exalt us, and troubles lift us."

—Charles Spurgeon

But in our grief, there is joy. And in our joy, there is grief. We know both simultaneously. The Cross is painful, and the world's rejection hurts. We live in a broken world, partly of our own doing, and we suffer because of it. But we rejoice that the suffering does not compare to the glory to be revealed (Romans 8:18). We look forward to a coming celebration, and we can begin celebrating even now.

In Deed Many Christians have not found the balance between grief and joy. We can either wallow in the former, forgetting the joy of knowing Jesus and the promises He gives us, or dwell on the latter as escapists, unmindful of the needs of our generation. Our joy is to be a sober-minded joy, and our grief is to be a hopeful grief. Heartfelt ministry and joyful expectation—both are the inheritance of Jesus' disciples.

Evil on a Leash

"You would have no power over me if it were not given to you from above." (John 19:11

"God is so powerful that He can direct any evil to a good end."
—Thomas Aquinas

In Word The situation is bleak. As He stands before Pilate, all Jerusalem, it seems, is arrayed against Jesus, the disappointing "deliverer." The Jewish leadership is screaming for His execution, and the Roman authorities are compliant and compromising enough to let it happen. Evil rules the day.

One of the amazing ironies about the crucifixion of Jesus is that while evil is winning the battle—rather handily, in fact—Go is winning the war. God and Satan have exactly the same goal in this situation—the death of Jesus—but for entirely different reasons. The enemy's purposes reflect his evil nature; but his vision limited. He doesn't realize that God hasn't lost His grip on his leash; he thinks he has finally broken free enough to do some rea damage. All the while, he is accomplishing God's greater purposes.

Do you ever wish you could have the assurance that Jesus has? Do you want to *know* that the enemy—and his instruments this world—would have no power over you if it were not given them from above? Do you want the peace of knowing that whatever weapons he wields, they will end up furthering God's purposes for you, rather than harming you as he intends? Such assurance, such peace can be ours. We can quote Jesus' line with confidence: Any power that comes against us is allowed by God above—for a reason.

In Deed When your situation is critical, remember the calm of Jesus in the midst of His greatest storm. Remember Joseph's insight: "You intended to harm me, but God intended it for good" (Genesis 50:20). Remember the principle Paul lays down for us later: "In *all things* God works for the good of those who love him, who have been called according to his purpose" (Romans 8:28, italics added). Are you in a difficult place? It has been allowed from above. It always is. God is accomplishing His purpose through it.

The Overcomer

"To him who overcomes . . ." (Revelation 2:7)

In Word Jesus says this phrase, or something very much like it, seven times in His words to the seven churches in the second and third chapters of Revelation. It can be a terrible burden for a believer to read such an imperative and to know the odds against fulfilling it. Apparently, there is an awful lot of overcoming to do. We just don't have the resources, the strength, or the wisdom. Yet Jesus' command remains. Each member of each church is promised glorious privileges if he or she overcomes, but the implication is that all privileges will be lost if we lack the ability to do so.

Shall we despair over this? Not ultimately. The answer comes much later in the book. Revelation 17:14 says: "The Lamb will overcome them because he is Lord of lords and King of kings—and with him will be his called, chosen and faithful followers." We are not overcomers. He is. We can only be victorious—whatever the obstacle or threat happens to be—insofar as we are related to the Overcomer, the Lamb of the living God.

"God never gives us a responsibility, a load, or a burden without also giving us the ability to be victorious."
–Bill Bright

In Deed We face intense struggles in our Christian life. Circumstances rise up against us, often orchestrated by a malicious enemy; our devotion to God is threatened by temptation, also orchestrated by that enemy in full cooperation with our frail flesh; and persecution is inevitable for those who stand faithful in Christ. How can we, in all of our weakness, overcome such massive obstacles? Our own track record certainly isn't compelling evidence of a victorious nature within us. When we look at our natural capabilities, we will despair at the supernatural battle that comes against us.

Despair leads us to the right place. The answer cannot come from ourselves—we are too weak. Only those who are His "called, chosen and faithful followers" can survive. When Jesus says "To Him who overcomes," He is telling us to rest faithfully in Him.

Amazing Grace

"My God, my God, why have you forsaken me?"

(Mark 15:3

In Word Are you aware that every crack of the whip on Jesus' back, every thorn piercing His scalp, every stroke of the hammer and thrust of the spear is what God thought about our sin? Have you considered that every time Jesus struggled to breathe, cried out in thirst, tried to heave His body up against th pull of gravity, it was punishment deserved. Not by Him, of course. By us.

Does that sound harsh? Surely we aren't all that bad, are we We're human, of course, and therefore imperfect; but do we reall deserve such punishment?

According to the Bible, we do. And if we really think about it, as well intentioned as we assume we are, we can all recall times that we have shunned the personality of the Holy for something that utterly violated it. On purpose. What cosmic treachery! We're foolish if we think it was just an innocent mistake and that God w overlook it. Look at the Cross to see what God thought about it.

Jesus knew the answer to His question in verse 34, even as He asked it. He wasn't seeking the divine reason behind His suffering; He was pointing us to it. The quoted psalm that begins with this cry of anguish (Psalm 22) speaks of God's deliverance c all His people. That's the answer. He was forsaken so we wouldn't be.

"By the Cross we know the gravity of sin and the greatness of God's love toward us."

—John Chrysostom

In Deed "God made him who had no sin to be sin for us" (2 Corinthians 5:21). Whenever your faith grows apathetic, whenever your sense of His grace grows dim, whenever your mercy toward others finds its limits, think of that. Contemplate the staggering absurdity of the infinitely Holy suffering the consequences for those who rejected His holiness. Let your cry become "My God, my God, why haven't You forsaken me?" and be grateful. Let His grace amaze you and prompt your zealous, passiona worship.

An Important Invitation

"A certain man was preparing a great banquet and invited many guests." (Luke 14:16)

In Word God is preparing a great banquet. It will be the most extravagant celebration ever. And we're invited.

According to Jesus, many who are invited never show up. Why not? If the celebration is so great, why isn't it more appealing to more people? Perhaps it's because the invitation is often so plain—it comes from a poor Galilean with a motley assortment of "groupies." Perhaps it's because the prelude to the party has often been disguised as a joyless, austere gathering of misfits who are still trying to figure out exactly why they were honored with such an invitation. Or perhaps it's because many recipients of the invitation think they have more important things to do.

That was the case in Jesus' parable of the kingdom. A home, a possession, and a relationship were the hindrances mentioned by those who couldn't squeeze the banquet into their schedule. They assumed that news of the really important banquets would be spread through fancy marketing and the grapevine of the elite. Or maybe they just got so busy that they didn't have time for banquets at all. Perhaps the intentions were good, but the ability to fulfill them was limited by too many commitments—commitments of infinitely lesser importance.

"Give me a person who says, 'This one thing I do,' and not, 'These fifty things I dabble in.'"

—D. L. Moody

In Deed Isn't that our situation sometimes? We've accepted God's invitation, of course—at least in principle. But we've filled our lives with so many other "musts" that we may not have time to dress for the ball. We're too busy, too committed, too preoccupied with other things. We forget one of the fundamental essentials of discipleship: A person cannot follow Jesus when his or her affections are anchored elsewhere. Our commitment to Him cannot be diluted; when it is, it isn't a commitment at all.

God's preparing for a banquet. Make sure you're preparing for the banquet, too.

Enslaved

"I tell you the truth, everyone who sins is a slave to sin."

(John 8:3‑

In Word We live in a rights-obsessed culture. Our courts are flooded with cases, from the reasonable to the absurd, in which people feel their rights have been violated. As "politically correct" speech becomes codified in our laws and slight offenses become major litigations, people are intensely aware of their sens of freedom—from government, from discrimination, from social restrictions, and more. All the while, the real battle is fought at another level. We aren't just people struggling with slight infringements on our freedoms. We're slaves.

The Jewish religious leaders defined freedom much as our culture does: in terms of political oppression. They may have bee dominated by Rome, but technically they were living in a free ter ritory. They, like us, missed the real issue. Life isn't about the physical ability to do what we want to do. It's about being released from spiritual bondage. The frustration that most people feel when they encounter limitations is not usually about the visi ble situation. Deep down, we are frustrated with an ominous real ity: God created us to soar, but our sinful human nature clipped our wings. We were crafted for glory but wallow in captivity.

In our optimistic moments, we console ourselves with the mantra of self-acceptance—"I'm only human." But we know there's more to life than the humanity we settle for. We long for the glory of God's riches. Far too often, though, we misdiagnose the problem.

"Jesus Christ is the key which unlocks the door of the prison cell of our own making."

—Kenneth Pillar

In Deed The problem is sin. It's a part of us and we can' escape it, not by ourselves. We think we need to try harder, do better, know more, think clearer, etc. No. We need Jesus. We need to realize the gravity of the problem—the sin that plagues us—and beg for freedom. It comes from outside of ourselves, not fron within. It comes from Jesus.

Set Free

"If the Son sets you free, you will be free indeed."
(John 8:36)

In Word Even as believers we fall for the lie: "I'm only human." We *are* only human, of course, but humanity means such a different thing to Jesus than it does to sinners. We define our humanity as a cage from which we cannot escape. Jesus defines it as the image of the invisible God. To us it is corruption incarnate. To Jesus it is the holy pinnacle of creation. Jesus would never be caught saying, "I'm *only* human." He left the glories of heaven in order to put on human flesh for a lifetime. It was a condescension, to be sure, but a divine one. We must not degrade it by appealing to our personal frailties in our moments of weakness. Only human? Jesus went to the cross for humans.

The only perfect freedom is serving God."
–Malcolm Muggeridge

At the root of our "only human" disclaimer is a tendency to settle for spiritual mediocrity. We're comfortable saying we're free in Christ—in theory—without experiencing freedom from sin—in practice. We like the status of being free while settling into the ease of our slavery. We're abused by that slavery, but abused people often prefer what's comfortable and predictable rather than handle the responsibilities of liberation. We need a harsh reminder: When the Son sets us free, He expects us to be free. Completely free.

In Deed Do you settle for mediocrity? Are you comfortable with certain sinful aspects of your life? Perhaps they are areas you once struggled with but finally gave up trying. Perhaps you fell for the lie that some sins are just permanent parts of our character. Perhaps you forgot that nothing—no sin, no deception, no habit—is too big for Jesus to handle.

And that's the problem. You gave up because you found that you couldn't handle it; you couldn't overcome your sin. You thought Jesus meant that He gave us the ability to set ourselves free. No, it's the *Son* who sets us free. Abandon mediocrity, rest in His strength, and *never* settle for anything less than complete purity. He calls you to be free indeed.

Gnats and Camels

"You strain out a gnat but swallow a camel."

(Matthew 23:2

In Word It's easy to criticize the Pharisees and the teachers of the Law. Jesus gives us so much material in Matthew 23; th woes pronounced against them are harsh and pointed. Six times in this chapter He calls them hypocrites; five times He says they are blind. He labels them whitewashed tombs and a brood of vipers. All of this is directed at people who thought they were pleasing God. All of this condemnation comes upon those who sought to be righteous. What did they miss?

Jesus accuses them of majoring on the peripheral trappings c holiness while rejecting the very character of God. They've given to God everything the Law demanded they give. They've sacrificed according to its minutest details. They've upheld the moral judgments of the Torah and have avoided wrong behavior. They tithe even their spices! But they couldn't see the heart of God. They missed the Personality behind the Law. They performed act of righteousness with no connection to the Spirit of righteousness They paid attention to the gnats and ignored the camels.

"There is no true holiness without humility."

—Thomas Fuller

In Deed Yes, these hypocrites are easy targets. They are so outwardly focused that they're inwardly bankrupt. But don't we have similar tendencies? Test yourself: Do you ever go through the rituals of a worship service without an attitude of worship? Do you sing the words of the hymns without even thinking of their meaning? Do you consume the wafers and the wine without consuming the Spirit behind them? Are you so focused on law that you condemn the lawless? Do you miss the heart of God?

God's character is the source of justice, mercy, and faithfulness (v. 23). It is full of love, compassion, and truth. Whatever we do in His name should be saturated with such attributes. If it isn' we've swallowed the camel. We've missed the heart of God.

In Search of Pure Motives

"Your Father, who sees what is done in secret, will reward you." (Matthew 6:4, 6, 18)

In Word Three times Jesus says that the Father will reward what is done for Him in secret: once each with respect to our giving, our praying, and our fasting. By implication, we can apply this to other acts of devotion as well. God does not want us showing off for other people, especially when He is the audience. It cheapens the gift, nullifies the sense of sacrifice, and calls into question the devotion. It substitutes the reward of knowing Him with cheaper prizes. It undoes everything our obedience to Him is supposed to accomplish.

"Man sees your actions, but God, your motives."
–Thomas à Kempis

Why is this so hard for us? Because we are a tangled mess of fears and insecurities. We have issues of pride and ego. We seek temporal comfort, status, and approval. With all of these variables at work, our motives are rarely pure. When we do something for God, are we doing it for public affirmation? Because we want to bargain with Him? From insecurity or fear? It's hard to know.

One way God uses to clarify our intentions—for our sake, of course, since He knows them already—is to require us to relate to Him in private. There is a public side to our relationship with God—we share our faith, pray together, and demonstrate love, for example—but it must always begin in private. If we follow this rule and find that there is no joy in it, we have discovered exactly what God knew all along: We were doing it for reasons other than love for Him. Private devotion is His primary method for exposing an impure heart. It removes all pretense and asks us if anything is left.

In Deed Do you ever wonder about your real motives for serving God? Do you relate to Him well in private? Take away the audience and see. Get behind closed doors and examine what's left in your relationship with Him. It can be a humbling experience, but it's a necessary one. And, according to Jesus, it never goes unrewarded.

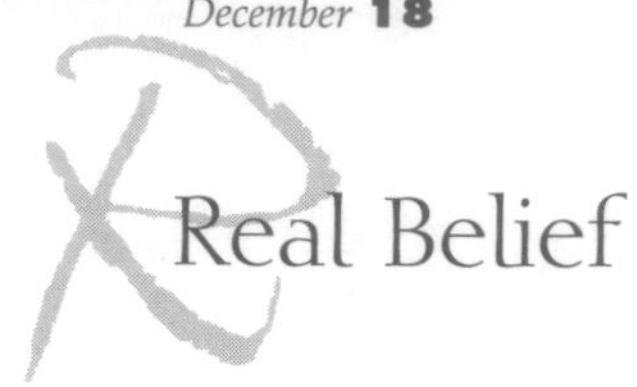

Real Belief

"For God so loved the world that he gave his one and only Son, that whoever believes in him shall not perish but have eternal life." (John 3:1

In Word What does it really mean to "believe" in Jesus? Is it simply an acknowledgment that He is Lord and Savior? Doe it just pertain to eternal life—the sweet by-and-by? Or is it more comprehensive than that?

Jesus said that the work of God is for us to believe in the On He has sent (John 6:29). But what does it say of our belief when we:

- ask for His forgiveness and then work for His favor and wonder if His grace is enough to cover all we've done?
- ask Him to take care of our burdens and then fret about them incessantly and wallow in insecurity?
- ask Him to intervene in our circumstances and then manipulat them ourselves in order to get a better outcome?
- ask that His kingdom come and then panic about current even and prophecies of the end times?
- ask that His will be done and then tell Him specifically what our will is and why He ought to accomplish it?

These are all inner contradictions we'll find in our faith from time to time. We say we believe in Jesus—not just for salvation, but all it entails—but we might do well to ask ourselves occasion ally if we *really* do. For people who have been promised provisio protection, comfort, guidance, forgiveness, salvation, and more, we spend an awful lot of time concerned with just those things. I we say we believe, but act like we don't, which is a truer reflectio of our real beliefs? Words or the attitudes of our hearts?

> ***"The issue of faith is not so much whether we believe in God, but whether we believe the God we believe in."***
>
> ***—R. C. Sproul***

In Deed Paul strongly warned the Corinthian believers: "Examine yourselves to see whether you are in the faith; test yourselves" (2 Corinthians 13:5). It is good advice, no matter how long we've been Christians. Our human tendency is to walk by sight, not by faith. But genuine belief is God's only accepted currency. Check yours frequently.

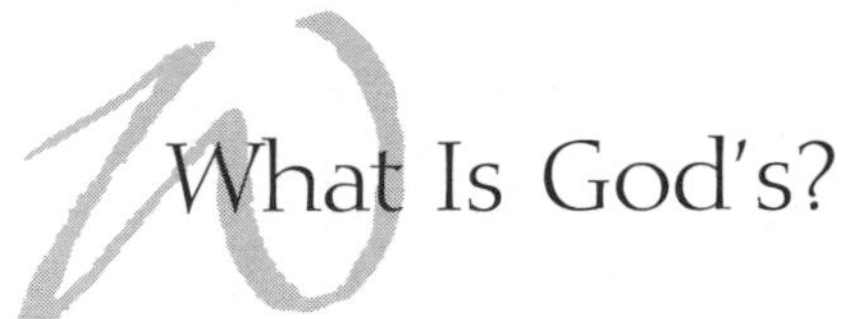

What Is God's?

"Give to Caesar what is Caesar's and to God what is God's." (Mark 12:17)

In Word This is one of Jesus' most memorable (and quotable) statements. We are amazed at His sharp answer and His ability to elude the traps set for Him by the Pharisees and Herodians, just as His listeners are noted for being amazed at the end of the verse. We often apply this text to distinguish between our secular responsibilities and our devotion to God. Jesus clearly upholds our obligation to pay taxes and support our government. We are to give to Caesar what is Caesar's without the guilt we might otherwise feel for investing in an earthly kingdom. But the second half of His statement begs a question we rarely answer. We are to give to God what is God's. But what exactly is that? What, by Jesus' definition, is God's?

Everything. It is clear from the whole of Scripture and from the specifics of Jesus' teaching that everything belongs to God. Even our taxes, which He tells us to give to "Caesar," are His—we give it with His permission and blessing. But even Caesar's treasury is under God's sovereign domain. So is our home, our family, our career, our possessions, our interests and hobbies, our ministry, our relationships, and anything else we can think of. So when Jesus tells His disciples what He expects of them, He has every right to ask it.

I feel that if I could live a thousand lives, I would like to live them all for Christ."

—Charles Spurgeon

We would do well to notice what Jesus, our authority, asks of His disciples. He insists on (1) their love of God and each other—those are the greatest commandments, He says; and (2) their allegiance—to the point of leaving all behind and following Him even to death. He expects all who claim Him to be zealously, passionately His.

In Deed Far too frequently, we focus on the first half of Jesus' wise retort in verse 17 and miss the second half. But it is the all-important emphasis. Give to God what is God's—your heart. Your life. Your everything. Keep no corner of your soul to yourself. It's all His.

First Love

"You have forsaken your first love." (Revelation 2:4)

In Word The beginning of a romantic relationship is usually its most exciting stage. All things are new, the future is full of possibilities, and love flourishes. New lovers are apt to do anything for one another and are often embarrassing in their affection for each other. They don't embarrass themselves, of course—just everyone around them. To them, it's a perfectly natural thing to lavish praises and passionate words on each other.

But after a while, love can grow comfortable and sometimes even boring. The excesses of courtship are forsaken for less extravagant displays of affection. In fact, affection itself may become more obscure. Why doesn't the passion last for most couples? Perhaps it is that we are finite beings who find the interesting things to explore in our beloved somewhat limited. Perhaps though we enjoy the excitement of passion, we enjoy the comfort of predictability more. But where there is true love, passion can *always* be rekindled. Always.

"We should find no pleasure or delight in anything except in our Creator, Redeemer, and Savior."

—St. Francis of Assisi

The Ephesian church had forsaken its first love. Perhaps it had rejected its Lover outright. More likely, it had just let its love grow stale. Predictable. Boring. Comfortable, but not too exciting. Like saying "I love you" as a ritual rather than as an overflow of affection. Like mouthing the words of worship without meaning them or even thinking about them.

Jesus calls them back to Himself. He isn't satisfied with the predictable and stale. He has *never* told anyone that his or her praises were too lavish. And with Him, there is no limit to the stage of fascinating discovery. There is always something new to learn—and celebrate—about God.

In Deed Would Jesus say such a thing to you? Have you lost your first love? You follow Him, but do you enjoy Him? Is your relationship with God stale and cold, or passionate and exhilarating? God loves the stage of embarrassing affection. It's His permanent desire. Is He enjoying your relationship with Him? Are you? The fire of first love can be rekindled. Ask Him to ignite its flame in you.

Jesus, Our Righteousness

"Do not think that I have come to abolish the Law or the Prophets; I have not come to abolish them but to fulfill them." (Matthew 5:17)

In Word When we think of the Christmas story, we usually think of the birth narratives in Matthew and Luke. These explain how Jesus came into this world. But why did Jesus come? He answers that Himself in many of His teachings. One of the answers is given in Matthew 5:17.

We don't often think of this verse in terms of the Advent. To us, it is more often a confusing statement about legalism and the role of the Law in a Christian's life. But there is much more to it than that. The Law and the Prophets are the Word of God—immutable and inviolable. The Law that Moses received at Sinai cannot be broken without catastrophic consequences. The prophets cannot be ignored without the same results. Yet the Law was broken and the prophets ignored repeatedly. Only by man fulfilling them can man be saved. How could God accomplish our salvation in light of our numerous and willful violations? He sent a Man.

O come, O come, Emmanuel, and ransom captive Israel."
–Latin hymn

Jesus fulfilled all righteousness. When He went to John to be baptized, it was not for His own need. It was a baptism on Israel's behalf—and, by extension, ours. "It is proper for us to do this to fulfill all righteousness," He said (Matthew 3:15). He accomplished what we could not: true obedience and true repentance on our behalf.

In Deed Jesus did not come to tell us "never mind" about the Law. That's not a basis for God's forgiveness, though we often presume that it is. God has never just ignored our offenses. Humanity could not be saved without a Law fulfiller. That's why Jesus came. He paid attention not only to every small letter and stroke of the pen, but also to the Spirit behind them. In so doing, He accomplished what we could not—righteousness. And then He gave it to us.

That's the reason for Christmas. The baby in the manger was our only hope to fulfill God's Law. Thank God He did.

Jesus, Our Peace

"Do not suppose that I have come to bring peace to the earth. I did not come to bring peace, but a sword."

(Matthew 10:3-

In Word Isaiah prophesied about the coming "Prince of Peace" (9:6). The angels declared peace on earth in Luke 2:14 as they announced the coming Lord. But Jesus had a different declaration. He will be the source of division on earth. People will figh about the truth of His words. They will draw swords against eac other in heated conflict over His claims. The fact of His cross and resurrection would become history's greatest scandal. When persecution comes, friends and family members will turn each other in. And when judgment comes, He will be the dividing line by which families and nations are split.

Was His prophecy true? History bears it out. There is no mor controversial figure in the entire human race than Jesus. He has been blessed as God incarnate and cursed as a man-made delusion. He has changed countless lives even while "scholars" have disputed whether He ever existed.

No, the kind of peace the world seeks is harmony on this planet. Jesus made it clear that His peace is of a different order. It reconciles God with His traitorous creatures and humanity with its holy God. It puts a new Spirit in a once-conflicted heart. It is a peace within and a peace from above, but it is not universal peace among our race. Many hate Him. It will always be so. Such is the rebellion of man.

"O hush the noise, ye men of strife, and hear the angels sing."
—Edmund Sears

In Deed Who would have thought that the infant in Bethlehem would be so scandalous? But the enemy knew it in the garden, Herod saw it in the star, and Pilate heard it from the mobs. No one could make such kingly claims without controversy, even when demonstrating their truth. The pride of the human heart will bow to no Lord, especially One who reveals its sin. The Prince of Peace? Absolutely. But not the kind the world expects. Our peace is deeper and better—and it lasts forever.

Jesus, Our Love

"I have come down from heaven not to do my will but to do the will of him who sent me." (John 6:38)

In Word Why did Jesus come? Why did the Creator decide to clothe Himself in creation and enter this world through a young girl late one night in the company of livestock? We know the answer, of course. The Bible is very clear: Jesus came to save us. But His incisive declaration in John 6:38 should tell us something about the will of God: It is good. Jesus defines it for us: "This is the will of him who sent me, that I shall lose none of all that he has given me, but raise them up at the last day" (v. 39).

For everyone who has ever wondered how God sees him or her; for everyone who has ever doubted God's love when a prayer has gone unanswered or a life has become broken; for everyone who has cried out to God, "Are You there?" or "Do You care?", Jesus has this answer: He has come to do God's will, and His will is very, very good.

"Love came down at Christmas."

—Christina G. Rossetti

The goodwill of God is a natural, theological belief for those who hold to 1 John 4:8—"God is love." But as a practical belief, we often fall far short of affirming this. Causing us to doubt God's love is one of the enemy's most frequent points of attack and one of the flesh's most devastating points of corruption. In fact, everything but the Bible itself sometimes seems arrayed against this belief: circumstances, moods, relationships, and the harsh words and deeds of other people. Nevertheless, it is true. Hold out for it. The Bible promises that if we will only believe, God's will toward us is a cause for celebration, not despair.

In Deed Jesus came into this world as an act of divine love, not vengeance. When we're suspicious of His agenda, we need to remember: There is nothing of judgment in His work until He comes again. So relax. We need no clearer illustration. He is here by God's will, and it is God's will and great pleasure to love us.

Jesus, Our Truth

"You are right in saying I am a king. In fact, for this reason I was born, and for this I came into the world, to testify to the truth." (John 18:37

In Word Jesus was an enigma. He came into this world as the child of a working-class family from a notably un-noteworthy region of the country. He amazed people with His teaching and His miracles, but He always defied their expectations. When they expected Him to act like an average Galilean, He wouldn't. When they expected Him to act like a king, He wouldn't. No one could get a handle on exactly who He was.

The same is true for us today. The God-man, the Creator incarnate, defies our expectations as well. We pray to Him as our King, but He often leads us in the way of true humanity. Then we follow Him as a human example, but He often insists on His kingly authority in our lives. He is not just our teacher, but our Lord. And He is not just our God, but our friend. The enigma of Galilee remains enigmatic today, even as we pray to Him. But what an enigma! He simultaneously fulfills our deepest needs for human fulfillment and for intimacy with the holy. He is exactly the answer to everything we didn't know we wanted.

"The hopes and fears of all the years are met in Thee tonight."

—Phillips Brooks

In Deed Jesus said He came into the world to testify to the truth. This is what Christmas is all about. Think about it—infinite truth in a finite body! It is an answer to all of those questions the philosophers have asked for centuries: Why are we here? Who made us? Where are we going? In Jesus, God pulled back the curtain on divine mysteries and made them visible. Not completely understood, of course, but tangible at least. He opened the window on all that has been going on behind the scenes in this drama we call life. We can see the divine in something as mundane as human history. An enigma? Yes. But a blessed revelation, too. The Incarnation gave us truth—in person.

Jesus, Our Teacher

"Let us go somewhere else—to the nearby villages— so I can preach there also. That is why I have come."

(Mark 1:38)

In Word We like the idea of our own private Jesus. We celebrate the Bethlehem miracle as our own personal advent—not just Immanuel, God with us, but "God with me, personally." It is not wrong to understand Jesus this way; He is the Savior not only of the world but of us as individuals. But it is wrong to understand Jesus *only* this way. And while we would readily admit that Jesus is for everyone who believes, we often act as if He is strictly a personal matter—relevant to ourselves, marginal to others. Jesus reminds us that He is not in an "us against them" relationship. He is always reaching out.

Jesus *is* the Gospel. And the Gospel did not remain in Bethlehem. He did not remain in Galilee, and He did not remain in Israel, even during Jesus' earthly lifetime. Over time, He did not remain within the Roman Empire. Today, He continues to spread into the far reaches of the world. The Gospel does not sit still. There are always other villages, and Jesus always seeks them out. That is why He came.

". . . dear desire of every nation, joy of every longing heart."

—Charles Wesley

In Deed Do you see the teaching of Jesus as universal property? We certainly accept its universal application as a theological tenet. But is that global focus part of our own outlook? It needs to be. The Jesus who dwells in our hearts does not sit still, and if we are sensitive to Him, He will not let us sit still either. Whether He takes us to the other villages is not the point; the question is whether we are responsive to Him when He says that's where He wants to go. Like the disciples, we are probably aware that "everyone is looking" for Him (v. 37). Like them, are we willing to accept His reply? It may surprise us that He did not respond by welcoming those who were looking for Him. But Jesus is always aware of the many, many sheep in this world who have no shepherd. Are you?

Offering Prayers

"Your will be done on earth as it is in heaven."

(Matthew 6:10)

In Word When we pray, we are often quite focused on our own preferences. We want God to act on our behalf and to accomplish what concerns us, as His Word has promised He will do. Jesus nowhere condemns this type of prayer, contrary to some pseudo-biblical teaching. He is intensely interested in our concerns, and He encourages us to ask what we will. But there is a better way, and a prior focus that must precede all such prayers. It is a preoccupation with His kingdom and the glory of His name. It is a greater appreciation for His will than for our own.

God is the owner of this world, but He created it with mankind as its stewards. His verbal contract with earth's managers stipulates that generally He will intervene not arbitrarily, but when asked. In His sovereignty, He has often limited His earth-ward actions to depend on the invitation of man. Even when He required an Intercessor, He came Himself in the form of a man. It is His *modus operandi* in this world.

Therefore, when we pray, we must understand our requests to be the medium through which He acts. First and foremost, our prayers are the holy offerings by which He moves. We must ask not only, "Will You accomplish this for me," but, "Take my prayer and use it as You wish." Our requests are His treasured currency, not simply our pleas.

"God does nothing on earth except in answer to believing prayer."

—John Wesley

In Deed Prayer is not so much an act of persuasion as it is a gift for Him, a rolling out of the red carpet for God to intervene in the world He created and owns. Our requests are the vehicles by which the Landlord may politely—and without violating His original agreement—step in to help us property managers.

Do you ask with a spirit of offering? Do you see your prayers as gifts to Him that He may use as He wills? Try praying with this mind, and watch Him meet you there.

Blessed Obedience

"Blessed . . . are those who hear the word of God and obey it." (Luke 11:28)

In Word A woman in the crowd recognized the depth of Jesus' teaching and thought He was a fine example. His mother was surely proud, and she was overwhelmed enough with His family's honor to shout it out to the listening crowd (v. 27). Jewish mothers long for sons such as this.

Jesus, however, took this common concept of "blessedness" and pointed it in the right direction. True blessedness, He says, is not about family honor. It's a matter of obeying the Word of God. He has just finished a discourse on the various entities that can possess a human heart, and the woman's shout, rather than being a distraction, was an opportunity to affirm His point. The human heart demonstrates its owner by its obedience. And the heart whose owner is God is blessed.

"Obedience is the key to every door."
—George MacDonald

Obedience is an elusive issue for us. We are obedient to the Word up to a point, which, in effect, means we are not obedient at all. Obedience "up to a point" is ultimately disobedience; it demonstrates that we hold some masters to be higher than the Lord. We can create the illusion of obedience by doing everything right until doing right conflicts with our convenience. But when convenience supercedes obedience, we have found our true idols. We discover what rules us.

In Deed We must be careful of our own capacity for deceiving ourselves. We like to think we are obedient to God. But once in a while, He puts His finger on something that conflicts with our discipleship. Perhaps we commit to give to the kingdom of God, but a more urgent financial obligation arises. Perhaps we're fasting, but an important dinner invitation comes our way. The possibilities are limitless, but the dilemma is always the same: We must choose between the inconvenience of obedience and the expedience of moral laxity. We must decide who our real master is. Jesus tells us we will be blessed—utterly happy and favored—if we adhere to the Word of God in such times. Then we, like Jesus, will be children who honor Him.

Loving Obedience

"If anyone loves me, he will obey my teaching."

(John 14:23)

In Word How reluctant our generation is to link love and obedience! We see love and commitment as two separate entities, whether the issue is marriage, friendship, or discipleship. We want to say we love Jesus even when we have no intention of obeying Him. Jesus gives us no such option. Obedience is an indicator of what's in the heart. If we obey Him, it means we love Him. If we don't obey Him, it means we don't really love Him—not as much as our other loves, anyway. Our heart will be wherever our treasure is (Matthew 6:21). If our heart is not invested in His teaching, we won't follow Him, no matter how much we try to convince ourselves that we are His disciples.

Love and commitment are inextricably linked. Our actions and our hearts are bound together. That does not mean that we can't act superficially and hypocritically, as the Pharisees illustrate. A person's actions will sometimes paint a picture that does not originate from his or her internal condition. But a heart that loves Jesus cannot help but be zealous about His teachings; and a heart that does not love Him can only follow His teachings superficially, if at all. Love and obedience go hand in hand.

"Obedience to God is the most infallible evidence of sincere and supreme love to Him."

—Nathanael Emmons

In Deed How is your obedience? Is it sporadic? Then so is your love. Is it half-hearted? Then so is your love. You may not always be full of passionate feelings toward your Savior, but the committed kind of love will follow Him persistently, even when the feelings are not there. Do not fall into the trap of thinking that your love for Him is all that counts and your actions do not. You cannot earn His favor with your obedience, but you cannot really love Him without it. Just as a husband and wife must demonstrate their love for one another, so must a disciple and his master. Jesus has already demonstrated His love. Show Him yours. Obey His teaching.

Enduring Love

"Remain in my love." (John 15:9)

In Word Are you interested in praying a prayer that could revolutionize your life? Try this: Begin each day by asking God a series of questions. "Lord, how can I love You today? What act of worship can I do? What words can I utter that will honor and bless You? What act of service can I do to represent Your love? How would Your Spirit inspire me to pray today?"

If you ask questions like this, and watch for ways God might answer throughout your days, you'll find something happening deep within your soul. You'll find that worship becomes a lifestyle. You'll find that your faith becomes less centered on you and more centered on God. You'll find that the greatest commandment—to love God with all your heart, soul, strength, and mind—becomes your greatest desire. If you think your relationship with God is cold and passionless, you'll find it melting in the warmth of His favor. You'll experience His love in deeper ways than you ever have.

All is vanity but to love God and serve Him."

-Thomas à Kempis

If God created us for worship and commanded us to love Him with all that's in us, it stands to reason that He would answer, with His abundant grace and power, a prayer designed to fulfill that purpose. We spend so much time asking Him to meet our perceived needs that we miss our real need—to know Him in intimacy and to adore Him in worship. Once that need is met, all others find their proper place. But this one is first. When we pray like this, we agree with God on His highest priority for us.

In Deed Try praying this prayer several days in a row. See how God answers it. Make it your personal agenda each day to live for Him in worship and love. Everything else you have ever sought God for will either fade away in irrelevance or be graciously provided by the One who was waiting for you to put first things first. His love is enduring, His fellowship is sweet, and He's really all we need.

Unlimited Potential

"Anyone who has faith in me will do what I have been doing. He will do even greater things than these, because I am going to the Father." (John 14:12)

In Word How we would love to water down this verse! Why? Because we don't live up to it. There are all sorts of reasons we can give: Jesus means that we will do the *kinds* of works He does, compassionate good deeds, but with no miracles; or He means that the church as a whole will accomplish even more of His work throughout history. But neither of these things is really what He says. He implies that when He goes to the Father and sends His Spirit, our potential will be no more limited than that of Jesus. In other words, the sky's the limit.

We who believe that Jesus was fully God and fully man often emphasize the God side of Him more. But the only advantage He had in His humanity over us was His sinlessness, and the Cross has remedied that. Every aspect of His relationship with the Father is available to us. He heard the Father speaking because human beings can hear the Father speaking when their heart is right and their ears are attuned to His voice. He did miracles because human beings can do miracles when empowered by the Holy Spirit as Jesus was empowered. He is unique in His sonship but He confers sonship on us as well. God gave us a picture of what He can do when He clothes Himself in human flesh, and the picture was Jesus. Amazingly, Jesus says that can also be a picture of us.

"Your Christian life is to be a continuous proof that God works impossibilities."
—Andrew Murray

In Deed Do not be satisfied with a powerless faith. It is not consistent with the teachings of Jesus or the New Testament as a whole. Ask Jesus to show you what this verse means, not by informing you but by demonstrating it in you. Make whatever adjustments you must make for this promise to be realized in your life. The work of God is not limited by our concept of weak, human flesh. The potential is amazing. Ask God to let you see it.

The Final Product

"Everyone who is fully trained will be like his teacher."
(Luke 6:40)

In Word What is Jesus like? Forget the Hollywood portrayals—they are only guessing about His expressions, movements, and moods. Go back to the text itself. According to His words and deeds, what is He like? He prefers forgiveness over condemnation; He is merciful to those in all sorts of pain; He hates hypocrisy and loves humility; He welcomes those who are honest about who they are and honest about who He is; He does amazing works and encourages His followers to do the same; and He loves the Word of God. There is more we could say, but that's a good start. And if we call Him teacher, we are committing to a lot: We must be like Him.

Is that frightening or exciting? If you're honest, it's probably some of both. We want to be fully trained, in theory, but if we get a good look at the finished product, we know it's a different sort of life than we first expected. It's the life of Jesus: loved for its simplicity and strength, hated for its penetrating truth and radical departure from social norms. But it is a godly life. We want that. We must. We wouldn't continue in His Word if we didn't.

"The making of a disciple means the creating of a duplicate."

—Juan Carlos Ortiz

In Deed Did you choose to follow Jesus just to become better or to become new? You may have a clear assumption of what a good Christian is. Scrap it. That's not necessarily the model Jesus puts before you. He puts Himself before us and says, "This is what you will be like if you continue with Me and allow Me to fully train you. You will be different and you will be good; you will be both loved and hated; and you will be both blessed and crucified." Do not expect the Teacher to train you toward your own objectives: a comfortable life, exemption from pain, a just-above-average morality. Expect Him to train you for battle and for glory. It's His divine challenge. Are you up for it?

Notes

THANK YOU JESUS
THANK YOU FOR YOUR LOVE.
THANK YOU FOR THE MANY, MANY
BLESSING THAT YOU HAVE GIVEN ME.
BUT MOST OF ALL THANK YOU
FOR DYING ON THE CROSS FOR
MY SINS. THAT I MAY HAVE
EVERLASTING LIFE.

Tom W. Dooley
12-29-22 — 12-29-04

Notes

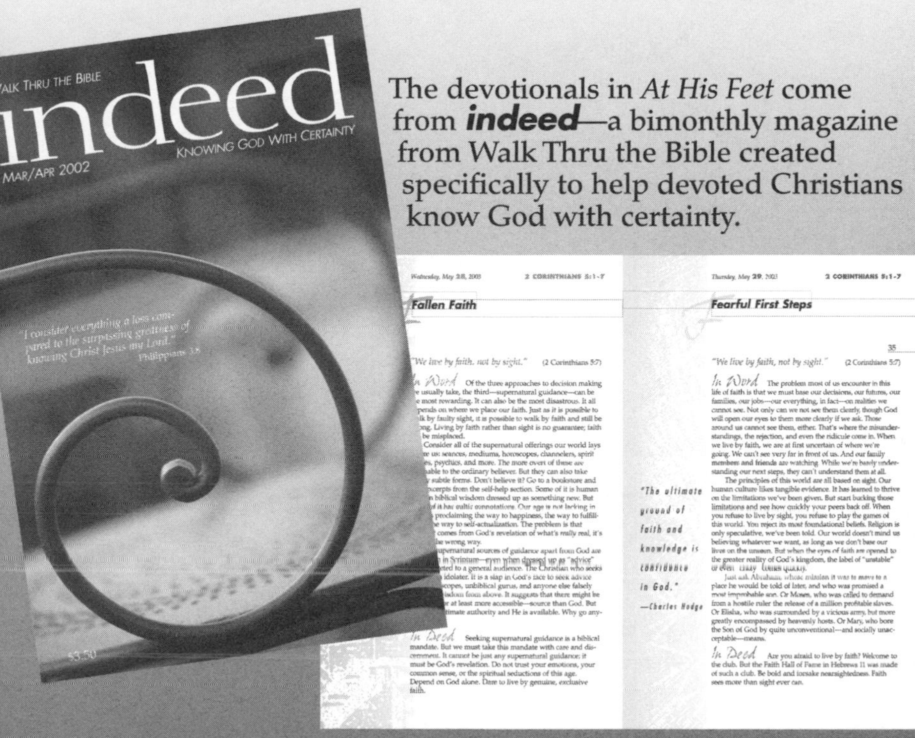

WALK THRU THE BIBLE
indeed
KNOWING GOD WITH CERTAINTY
MAR/APR 2002
"I consider everything a loss compared to the surpassing greatness of knowing Christ Jesus my Lord." Philippians 3:8
$3.50
The devotionals in *At His Feet* come from ***indeed***—a bimonthly magazine from Walk Thru the Bible created specifically to help devoted Christians know God with certainty.
Wednesday, May 28, 2003
2 CORINTHIANS 5:1-7
Fallen Faith
Thursday, May 29, 2003
2 CORINTHIANS 5:1-7
Fearful First Steps
"The ultimate ground of faith and knowledge is confidence in God." —Charles Hodge

Notes

Notes